B

Dictionary
of American
English Usage

C O N T E M P O R A R Y ' S

Basic
Dictionary
of American
English Usage

P. H. Collin
Miriam Lowi
Carol Weiland

Illustrations by
Erasmo Hernandez

CONTEMPORARY
BOOKS

A TRIBUNE EDUCATION COMPANY

CHICAGO • LINCOLNWOOD, ILLINOIS USA

Published by Contemporary Books, a division of NTC/Contemporary Publishing.
© 1986 by NTC Publishing Group, 4255 West Touhy Avenue, Lincolnwood
(Chicago), Illinois 60646-1975, U.S.A.
All rights reserved.

Manufactured in the United States of America.
International Standard Book Number: 0-8092-0848-2
10 9 8 7 6 5 4 3 2 1

This book is also published as *The Beginner's Dictionary of American English Usage*
© 1986 by the National Textbook Company.

About this dictionary

The *Beginner's Dictionary of American English Usage* has been carefully designed with the learner in mind. First, it contains the 4,000 most commonly used words in English. These are the words found in beginning and intermediate English-language textbooks. Secondly, each of the entries has at least one example sentence (in bold type) to show how the word is actually used in everyday speech and writing. Thus, more than a dictionary, this unique reference is a guide to contemporary American English usage.

In addition, this dictionary offers a variety of other features that make it a valuable reference for all students of English. The pronunciation of main entry words is clearly shown in brackets next to the word defined. Parts of speech are identified for all entries. The meaning of each word is explained as briefly and as simply as possible, using only the words contained in this dictionary. And whenever a word has several meanings, they are listed separately, each with its own example sentence.

You will also find many notes that give valuable advice on some of the more difficult aspects of English. (These and other useful language aids are highlighted in shaded boxes.) And throughout the dictionary, you will discover fully labeled drawings that illustrate important topics of everyday English vocabulary: the bathroom, bedroom, parts of the body, clothes, the country, kitchen, living room, office, restaurant, street, and travel. These drawings appear in the alphabetical order of the entry words they illustrate.

The *Beginner's Dictionary of American English Usage* offers students an important key to the everyday vocabulary, grammar, and usage of English. Used in class or by individuals, this book is an ideal reference that will lead its users to a more complete mastery of the English language.

Pronunciation

The way in which words are pronounced can vary widely according to the part of the country and the speaker. The pronunciation shown in the dictionary is that which is most common in the U.S.A.

The following signs are used to show the pronunciation of words in the dictionary. The symbols in the left column represent the pronunciation of the bold face letters in the right column.

Words are also marked with a sign (′) to show where the strong beat should be placed, but you must remember that this is only a guide, and that the pronunciation of a word can change depending on the position of the word in a sentence.

æ	back	əʊ	boat	dʒ	just	r	round
ɑː	farm	ɜ	word	f	fog	s	some
ɒ	top	iː	freeze	g	go	ʃ	short
aɪ	pipe	ɪ	hit	h	hand	t	too
aʊ	how	ɪə	idea	j	yes	tʃ	chop
ɔː	bought	uː	school	k	catch	θ	thing
ɔɪ	toy	ʊ	book	l	last	v	voice
e	fed	ʌ	but	m	mix	w	was
eər	hair	b	back	n	nut	z	zoo
eɪ	take	d	dog	ŋ	sing	ʒ	treasure
ə	afraid	ð	then	p	pick		

Alphabet

These are the letters of the English alphabet, showing how they are pronounced.

Aa	eɪ	**Hh**	eɪtʃ	**Oo**	əʊ	**Vv**	viː
Bb	biː	**Ii**	aɪ	**Pp**	piː	**Ww**	′dʌbəljuː
Cc	siː	**Jj**	dʒeɪ	**Qq**	kjuː	**Xx**	eks
Dd	diː	**Kk**	keɪ	**Rr**	ɑːr	**Yy**	waɪ
Ee	iː	**Ll**	el	**Ss**	es	**Zz**	ziː
Ff	ef	**Mm**	em	**Tt**	tiː		
Gg	dʒiː	**Nn**	en	**Uu**	juː		

Aa

a, an [eɪ, æn *or* ə, ən] *article*
(*a*) not a special one; **I want a glass of water; a big car; he has a good job; an empty house; a useful knife.**
(*b*) for each/in each; **these oranges cost 30¢ a pound; the car was doing 70 miles an hour.**
Note: **an** *is used in front of words beginning with* **a, e, i, o, u** *and with* **h** *if the* **h** *is not pronounced* **(an apple; an hour); a** *is used in front of all the other letters and also* **u** *where* **u** *is pronounced* **ju (a university)**

a·ble [ˈeɪbl] *adjective*
he wasn't able to breathe = he could not breathe; **will you be able to come to the party?** = can you come to the party? **he wasn't able to find the house.**
Note: **able** *is used with* **to** *and a verb*
a·bil·i·ty [əˈbɪlətɪ] *noun*
being able to do something; **I'll do it to the best of my ability** = as well as possible.

a·bout [əˈbaʊt] *adverb & preposition*
(*a*) concerning; **tell me about your vacation; what do you want to speak to me about?** he is worried about his health.
(*b*) more or less; **the room is about ten feet square; the next train leaves at about four o'clock; she's about twenty years old; the town is about ten miles from here.**
(*c*) in several places; **he left his papers lying about on the floor.**
(*d*) **to be about to do something** = to be going to do something; **I was just about to go out when you phoned.**

a·bove [əˈbʌv] *adverb & preposition*
higher than; **the plane flew above the clouds; the temperature was above 40°.**

a·broad [əˈbrɔːd] *adverb*
in another country; to another country; **he lives abroad; they are going abroad on their vacation.**

ab·sence [ˈæbsns] *noun*
not being here/there; **in the absence of Mr. Smith** = when Mr. Smith is not here/there.
ab·sent [ˈæbsnt] *adjective*
not here/not there; **three children are absent because they are sick.**

ac·cept [əkˈsept] *verb*
(*a*) to take (something which someone is giving you); **will you accept this little present?**
(*b*) to agree (to do something); **I invited her to the party and she accepted.**
accepts—accepting—accepted— has accepted

ac·ci·dent [ˈæksədənt] *noun*
(*a*) something which happens by chance; **I met her by accident at the bus stop.**
(*b*) unpleasant thing which happens; **she had an accident and had to go to the hospital; three people were killed in the traffic accident.**
ac·ci·den·tal·ly [æksəˈdentlɪ] *adverb*
by chance; **I found the missing watch accidentally.**

ac·cord·ing to [əˈkɔːrdɪŋ tʊ] *adverb*
as someone says or writes; **according to the newspaper, today is a public holiday; according to the TV, it will be sunny tomorrow.**

ac·count [əˈkaʊnt] *noun*
(*a*) amount of money kept in a bank; **how much money do you have in your account? he put $10 into his account.**
(*b*) **accounts** = record of the money paid and received by a company; **the money is**

shown as a loss in the company accounts.
on account of = because of; the trains are late on account of the fog.

ache [eɪk] 1. *noun*
pain; (*used with other words to show where you have a pain: see* **backache, headache, toothache**)
2. *verb*
to hurt; my tooth aches.
aches—aching—ached—has ached

a·cross [əˈkrɔːs] *adverb & preposition*
(*a*) from one side to the other; he swam across the river; don't run across the road; the river is 50 yards across.
(*b*) on the other side; he lives across the street; their house is across the street from ours = it is just opposite our house.

act [ækt] 1. *noun*
one large part of a play; "Hamlet" has five acts; Act I takes place in a castle.
2. *verb*
(*a*) to take part in a play/film, etc.; she has acted on TV many times; he acted the part of Hamlet in the film.
(*b*) to do something; he had to act quickly to save his sister.
acts—acting—acted—has acted

ac·tion [ˈækʃn] *noun*
thing which has been done; he was sorry for his actions = he was sorry for what he had done.

ac·tive [ˈæktɪv] *adjective*
lively/doing something; although he is over eighty, he is still very active.

ac·tor [ˈæktər] *noun*
man who acts in a play.

ac·tress [ˈæktrəs] *noun*
woman who acts in a play.
plural **actresses**

act up·on, *verb*
to do something as the result of something which has been said; he acted upon your suggestion.

ac·tu·al [ˈæktʃʊəl] *adjective*
real; what are the actual figures for the number of students in high school?

ac·tu·al·ly, *adverb*
really; is he actually going to sell his store?

ad [æd] *see* **advertisement**

add [æd] *verb*
(*a*) to put numbers together; if you add ten and fifteen you get twenty-five.
(*b*) to put in more of something; if your coffee isn't sweet enough, add some more sugar; she added a few words at the end of the letter.
(*c*) to say something more; he added that it was time to go to bed.
adds—adding—added—has added

ad·di·tion [əˈdɪʃn] *noun*
putting numbers together; she is good at addition, but not at multiplication.

ad·di·tion·al, *adjective*
more/extra; the local tax is an additional 8%; the airline runs additional flights at Christmas.

add up, *verb*
to put several numbers together; if you add up all these figures, the answer should be a thousand.
Note: add the numbers up *or* add up the numbers, *but only* add them up

add up to, *verb*
to make a total; the sums of money we have spent add up to over $100.

ad·dress 1. *noun* [ˈædres]
number of a house, name of a street and town where someone lives or where an office is; what is the address of the new bookstore? write all their addresses on a piece of paper; her address is: 1510 York St., Adamsville.
plural **addresses**
2. *verb* [əˈdres]
to write the details of name, where someone is/where a house is, on an envelope; the letter is addressed to your father.
addresses—addressing—addressed—has addressed

ad·jec·tive [ˈædʒɪktɪv] *noun*
word used to describe what a noun is like; in the phrase "a big green door," "big" and "green" are both adjectives.

ad·mire [ədˈmaɪr] *verb*
to look at something with pleasure; to

think that something is good; he was admiring my new car.

admires—admiring—admired—has admired

ad·mi·ra·tion [ædmə'reɪʃn] *noun*
feeling of pleasure in something; I have a great deal of admiration for his work.

ad·mir·ing·ly, *adverb*
with pleasure/showing that you think something is good; she looked admiringly at her son's painting.

ad·mit [əd'mɪt] *verb*
(*a*) to allow (someone) to go in; this ticket admits one person; children are admitted free.
(*b*) to say that something is true; he admitted he was the person who broke the window/he admitted to having broken the window.

admits—admitting—admitted—has admitted

a·dult ['ædʌlt, ə'dʌlt] *noun & adjective*
grown-up (person); fully grown (animal); the price of a ticket for adults is $1; an adult elephant.

ad·van·tage [əd'væntɪdʒ] *noun*
(*a*) something useful which will help you to be successful; it will be an advantage if you can speak Italian.
(*b*) to take advantage of = to use something to help yourself; we took advantage of the fine weather and went on a picnic.

ad·ven·ture [əd'ventʃər] *noun*
new and exciting thing which happens; he told us of his adventures while he was crossing the desert.

ad·verb ['ædvɜrb] *noun*
word which is used to describe a verb or an adjective; in the sentence "he drives quickly," the word "quickly" is an adverb.

ad·ver·tise ['ædvərtaɪz] *verb*
to show that something is for sale/ that you want something; he advertised his car in the newspaper; the company is advertising for new secretaries; jobs are advertised in the local paper.

advertises—advertising—advertised—has advertised

ad·ver·tise·ment [ædvər'taɪzmənt], **ad** [æd] *noun*
notice which shows that something is for sale/that you want something; if you want to sell the carpet, put an ad in the paper; I sold the carpet through an ad in the paper; she answered an advertisement in the paper and got a better job.
Note: **ad** *is used in ordinary speaking, but not usually in writing*

ad·vice [əd'vaɪs] *noun*
suggestion about what should be done; he went to the teacher for advice on how to do his homework; she would not listen to my advice; my advice to you is that you should take a long trip abroad; the doctor's advice was to stay in bed; he took the doctor's advice and went to bed.
no plural: **some advice; a piece of advice**

ad·vise [əd'vaɪz] *verb*
to suggest what should be done; the doctor advised him to stay in bed; she advised me to sell my car; I would advise you to drive slowly.

advises—advising—advised—has advised

ad·vise a·gainst, *verb*
to suggest that something should not be done; I wanted to learn to fly, but she advised against it; the doctor advised against going to bed late.

af·ford [ə'fɔːrd] *verb*
to have enough money to pay for something; I can't afford a new pair of shoes; how can you afford two vacations a year?

affords—affording—afforded—has afforded

a·fraid [ə'freɪd] *adjective*
(*a*) to be afraid (of) = to be frightened (by); I am afraid of snakes; she's afraid of the dark; he's afraid to climb onto the roof.
(*b*) to be afraid = to be sorry to say; I'm afraid we have no seats left; I'm afraid she's sick; do you have a watch?—no, I'm afraid not.
Note: **afraid** *cannot be used in front of a noun:* **she's afraid** *but* **a frightened girl**

af·ter [ˈæftər] 1. *preposition*
(*a*) following/next; if today is Monday, the day after tomorrow is Wednesday; he arrived after me; I must go to bed—it's after midnight; they came in one after the other; after you = please go first.
(*b*) to be after = to be looking for/to be angry with; the police are after him; if you eat all the cake, your mother will be after you; what's he after? = what does he want?
2. *conjunction*
following a time; after the rain came, the grass started to grow; after the driver got in, the bus set off; call me after you get home.
Note: after *is used with many verbs: look after; take after, etc.*

af·ter all, *adverb*
(*a*) in the end/considering everything; he changed his mind and decided to go to the party after all.
(*b*) in any case; I think I'll stay at home—after all, I have no work to do at the office and it's a fine day.

af·ter·noon [æftərˈnuːn] *noun*
part of the day between the morning and the evening; I always have a rest in the afternoon; she doesn't work on Tuesday afternoons; we met at 3 o'clock in the afternoon; I will try to catch the afternoon train; can you come to see me this afternoon or tomorrow afternoon?

af·ter·thought, *noun*
something which you think of later; he added as an afterthought, that he was going downtown.

af·ter·ward, afterwards, *adverb*
later/next; we'll go shopping first, and visit the museum afterward; he was fine before lunch, but felt ill afterward.

a·gain [əˈgen] *adverb*
another time/once more; he sang the song again; you must come to see us again.
once a·gain = another time; once again, the car refused to start.
yet a·gain = once more after many times; he is back in the hospital yet again.

a·gainst [əˈgenst] *preposition*
(*a*) touching; the ladder is leaning against the wall; he hit his head against a low branch.
(*b*) against the rules/against the law = not as the rules say/as the law says; it's against the law to sell beer on Sunday; you can't kick a ball in tennis—it's against the rules; do you have anything against my going out this evening? = do you agree that I can go out? she was against the idea of going to the theater.
(*c*) opposite; it's difficult riding against the wind; swimming against the current makes you tired.

age [eidʒ] 1. *noun*
(*a*) number of years which you have lived; what will his age be on his next birthday? he was sixty years of age; she looks younger than her age; old age = period when you are old.
(*b*) for ages = for a very long time; I've been waiting here for ages.
(*c*) period of history; the Middle Ages = period from about 1000 to 1500; the Space Age = period since men started to explore space.
2. *verb*
to grow old; he has aged since I saw him last year.
ages—aging/ageing—aged—has aged

ag·ed, *adjective*
(*a*) [eidʒd] with a certain age; a boy aged twelve; he died aged, aged 64.
(*b*) [ˈeidʒid] very old; an aged man.

a·gent [ˈeidʒnt] *noun*
person who acts for you, often in another country; he is the agent for Japanese cars; Mr. Smith is our agent in Australia.

a·go [əˈgəʊ] *adverb*
in the past; I saw him five minutes ago; she left home two years ago; it all happened a long time ago.

a·gree [əˈgriː] *verb*
(*a*) to say that you think the same way as someone; I agree with you that we need a new car.

(b) to say yes; **we asked her to come with us and she agreed.**

~~agrees—agreeing—agreed—has agreed~~

a·gree·ment, *noun*
action of agreeing; **he nodded to show his agreement; they are in agreement with our plan = they agree with it.**

a·head [ə'hed] *adverb*
in front; **our team was losing, but now we are ahead; ahead of us was a big old house; he has a lot of work ahead of him; we walked on ahead of the others; run ahead and save some seats for us.**

aid [eɪd] *noun*
help; **he gets aid from his university; they ran to the aid of the drowning boy; in aid of = to help; we are collecting money in aid of poor families;** *see also* **first aid.**

aim [eɪm] *verb*
(a) to point at; **he aimed his gun at the policeman.**
(b) to intend to do something; **we aim to save enough money to go on vacation.**

~~aims—aiming—aimed—has aimed~~

air [eər] *noun*
mixture of gases which you can't see, but which you breathe; **the air felt cold; he kicked the ball up into the air.**
by air = in an airplane; **we are traveling to France by air; I must send this letter by air.**

air·base, *noun*
place where airplanes used in war are based.

air·craft, *noun*
machine which flies in the air; **the pilot got into the aircraft.**

Note: plural is **aircraft: one aircraft, six aircraft**

air·field, *noun*
place where airplanes can land.

air force, *noun*
all the aircraft used in war, with the people who fly them; **he's joining the U.S. Air Force.**

air·line, *noun*
company which runs passenger services by air; **airlines are cutting fares.**

air·mail, *noun*
sending mail by air; **send this letter by airmail.**

air·plane, *noun*
machine which flies in the air; **the pilot flew the airplane through the storm.**

air·port, *noun*
place where aircraft land and take off; **we are due to leave O'Hare Airport at five o'clock; you can take a bus to the airport.**

air·sick, *adjective*
feeling sick because of traveling by air.

a·larm [ə'lɑːrm] *noun*
signal which warns of danger; **when the alarm went off, everyone left the hotel.**

a·larm (clock), *noun*
clock which can wake you up by ringing a bell; **set the alarm for 6 o'clock; he always takes an alarm clock with him when he travels.**

al·co·hol ['ælkəhɔːl] *noun*
liquid which makes you drunk if you drink too much of it.
al·co·hol·ic [ælkə'hɔːlɪk] *adjective*
containing alcohol; **an alcoholic drink.**

a·like [ə'laɪk] *adjective*
almost the same; **the two brothers look alike.**

Note: **alike** *is only used after a verb*

a·live [ə'laɪv] *adjective*
living/not dead; **the fish is still alive, even though it was caught an hour ago; my grandfather was alive when the first airplanes flew.**

Note: **alive** *cannot be used in front of a noun:* **the fish is alive** *but* **a live fish**

all [ɔːl] **1.** *adjective & pronoun*
every; everything/everyone; **all the tomatoes are red; are all the children here? we all like chocolate; let's sing the song all together = everyone at the same time.**
2. *adverb*
completely; **the ground was all white after the snow fell.**

all at once/all of a sud·den = suddenly; **all at once the telephone rang.**

not at all = certainly not; **do you mind waiting for ten minutes?—not at all!**

all by your·self = alone; **he was all by himself; I'm all by myself; she did it all by herself.**

all o·ver = (a) everywhere; **there was sugar all over the cake; she poured water all over the table.**

(b) finished; **when it was all over we went home.**

all right, *adjective*

(a) fine/well; **I was sick yesterday, but I'm all right now.**

(b) **will you answer the telephone for me?—all right** = yes, I will.

all the same, *adverb*

anyway; **I don't like parties, but I'll come to yours all the same.**

all-A·mer·i·can, *adjective*

representing the whole U.S.; **an all-American football player.**

all-im·por·tant, *adjective*

most important; **he kept the all-important ticket in his pocket.**

all-star, *adjective*

with many stars in it; **an all-star show; an all-star baseball team.**

al·low [ə'laʊ] *verb*

to say that someone can do something; **you are not allowed to walk on the grass; he allowed me to see his stamp collection; are we allowed to sit down?**

allows—allowing—allowed—has allowed

al·low·a·ble, *adjective*

which can be allowed.

al·low·ance, *noun*

money given to someone regularly.

al·most ['ɔːlməʊst] *adverb*

nearly; not quite; **he is almost as tall as I am; hurry up, it's almost time for the train to leave.**

a·lone [ə'ləʊn] *adjective*

with no one else; **she was all alone in the house; I want to talk to you alone** = just the two of us together.

a·long [ə'lɔːŋ] 1. *preposition*

by the side of; **there are trees along both sides of the road; he was walking along the bank of the river.**

2. *adverb*

to go along/to come along = to go/to come; **come along with us; he went along to the police station to report the accident.**

a·long·side, *adverb & preposition*

by the side of; **the police car was parked alongside mine.**

a·loud [ə'laʊd] *adverb*

in a voice which can be heard; **he was reading the newspaper aloud; I was just thinking aloud** = just saying what I was thinking.

al·pha·bet ['ælfəbet] *noun*

the 26 letters which are used to write words; **A is the first letter of the alphabet.**

al·pha·bet·i·cal [ælfə'betɪkl] *adjective*

like in the alphabet; **the telephone book has all the names in alphabetical order** = arranged by letters as they come in the alphabet.

al·read·y [ɔːl'redɪ] *adverb*

by this time; **it is already past ten o'clock; has he finished work already?** = so quickly; **I've seen that film already** = I have seen it before.

al·so ['ɔːlsəʊ] *adverb*

as well/at the same time; **he sings and can also play the piano; she came to dinner, and her son also came.**

al·though [ɔːl'ðəʊ] *conjunction*

even if; **although it was snowing, it was not very cold; although he is eighty, he still goes running every morning;** *see also* **though.**

al·ways ['ɔːlwɪz] *adverb*

every time/all the time; **he is always late; it always rains when we want to go for a walk; in some countries it is always hot; she's always in a hurry.**

am [æm] *see* **be**

A.M., a.m. ['eɪ 'em] *adverb*

in the morning; **I have to get up at 6**

A.M. every day; she's going to catch the 10 a.m. flight to Seattle.
Note: **A.M.** *is usually used to show the exact hour and the word* **o'clock** *is left out*

a·maze [ə'meɪz] *verb*
to surprise; it amazes me how he can eat so many pancakes.
amazes—amazing—amazed—has amazed

a·maze·ment, *noun*
surprise; he watched the fire in amazement.

a·maz·ing, *adjective*
surprising; he's an amazing teacher = very good; it's amazing how many people are left-handed.

am·bu·lance ['æmbjələns] *noun*
vehicle for taking sick people to the hospital; the man was taken away in an ambulance.

A·mer·i·ca [ə'merɪkə] *noun*
(*a*) large area of land (North America and South America) between the Atlantic and Pacific Oceans.
(*b*) the United States; they came to America on vacation; they live in America.
A·mer·i·can, 1. *adjective*
referring to the United States; the American President; she drives an American car.
2. *noun*
person who lives in or comes from the United States; Americans enjoy watching football on TV; she is married to an American.

a·mong [ə'mʌŋ] *preposition*
(*a*) in the middle of; the birds built their nests among the leaves; among the people at the party was a man who reads the news on TV.
(*b*) between; the cake was divided among the children.

a·mount [ə'maʊnt] **1.** *noun*
how much there is of something; she drinks a large amount of tea.
2. *verb*
to add up (to); the bill amounted to $100.
amounts—amounting—amounted—has amounted

a·muse [ə'mjuːz] *verb*
to make someone happy; they amused themselves playing football; the teacher amused the children by showing them a movie.
amuses—amusing—amused—has amused

a·muse·ment, *noun*
being happy; he poured a bucket of water over his head to the great amusement of the children.

a·mus·ing, *adjective*
which makes you happy; the TV show was very amusing; I didn't find the book very amusing.

an [æn *or* ən] *see* **a**

and [ænd *or* ən] *conjunction*
(*showing two things are connected in some way*) my mother and father; he likes apples and oranges; he was running and singing at the same time; come and sit down.
Note: **and** *is used to say numbers after 100:* **seven hundred and two (702)**

and so on, *adverb*
in the same way; he talked about gardens, flowers, and so on = and other similar things.

an·ger ['æŋgər] *noun*
being mad; he showed his anger by banging on the table.
no plural

an·gry ['æŋgriː] *adjective*
mad; he's angry with his children because they broke a window; she gets angry if the trains are late; everyone is angry about the gasoline prices.
angry—angrier—angriest

an·gri·ly, *adverb*
in an angry way.

an·i·mal ['ænɪml] *noun*
living and moving thing; dogs and cats are animals, and man is also an animal; we went to see the animals in the zoo.

an·kle ['æŋkl] *noun*
place where your foot is connected to

your leg; **he twisted his ankle** = he hurt it by bending it in an odd direction.

an·nounce [ə'naʊns] *verb*
to tell everyone (something); **the mayor announced the result of the vote; she announced that her son was going to marry the girl next door.**
announces—announcing—
announced—has announced

an·nounce·ment, *noun*
public statement; **I read the announcement in the local paper.**

an·nounc·er, *noun*
person who announces the programs on radio/TV.

an·oth·er [ə'nʌðər] *adjective & pronoun*
(*a*) one more; **would you like another cup of coffee?**
(*b*) a different (one); **she fell down and made her dress dirty, so she had to change into another one;** *see also* **each other, one another.**

an·swer ['ænsər] **1.** *noun*
reply/words spoken or written when someone has spoken to you or asked you a question; **I phoned the office, but there was no answer; have you received an answer to your letter yet?**
2. *verb*
to reply/to speak or write words after someone has spoken to you or asked you a question; **he hasn't answered my letter; when he asked them if they had enjoyed the book, they all answered "no"; to answer the phone** = to speak into it when it rings.
answers—answering—
answered—has answered

an·swer back, *verb*
to answer in a rude way; **if you answer back like that the teacher will be mad at you.**

an·y ['enɪ] **1.** *adjective & pronoun*
(*a*) it doesn't matter which; **wear any hat you like; come any day next week.**
(*b*) some; **do you have any salt? is there any cake left? would you like any more coffee?**

(*c*) **not . . . any** = none; **there aren't any cakes left; give me your money—I don't have any.**
2. *adverb*
not . . . any + *comparative* = not even a little; **I can't sing any louder; the car won't go any faster.**

an·y·bod·y ['enɪbɒdɪ] *see* **anyone.**

an·y·how ['enɪhaʊ] *see* **anyway.**

an·y·one ['enɪwʌn] *pronoun*
(*a*) it doesn't matter who; **anyone can learn to ride a bicycle; anyone could have written that letter.**
(*b*) some person; **can anyone loan me ten dollars? I didn't meet anyone** = I met no one.

an·y·thing ['enɪθɪŋ] *pronoun*
(*a*) it doesn't matter what; **you can take anything you want; our dog will eat anything.**
(*b*) something; **did anything happen during the night? has anything made you sick? do you want anything more to drink? he didn't eat anything** = he ate nothing.

an·y·way ['enɪweɪ], **an·y·how** ['enɪhaʊ] *adverb*
in any case; whatever may happen; **it was raining but I didn't want to go out anyway; the doctor told me to stay in bed, but I'm going to the party anyway.**

an·y·where ['enɪhweər] *adverb*
(*a*) it doesn't matter where; **put the book down anywhere.**
(*b*) somewhere; **is there anywhere where I can put this box? I haven't seen it anywhere.**

a·part [ə'pɑːrt] *adverb*
separate; **the two towns are very far apart; the watch came apart in my hands** = it came to pieces; **they live apart now** = they don't live together any more.
a·part from = except; **they all wore black hats, apart from me.**

a·part·ment [ə'pɑːrtmənt] *noun*
separate group of rooms for one family, usually in a building with other similar groups of rooms; **they live in an apart-**

ment building in downtown Dallas; his apartment is on the fifth floor.

ap·pear [əˈpiːr] *verb*
(a) to start being seen; a ship suddenly appeared in the distance; a man appeared at the door.
(b) to seem; he appears to be ill; it appears to be raining.
appears—appearing—appeared— has appeared

ap·pear·ance [əˈpiːrns] *noun*
how a person or thing looks; you could tell from her appearance that she had been climbing trees; he put in an appearance at the meeting = he came for a short time.

ap·ple [ˈæpl] *noun*
common hard round sweet fruit, growing on a tree; apple pie; don't eat that green apple—it isn't ripe yet.
ap·ple·sauce, *noun*
cooked apples which have been squashed; do you want some more applesauce?
ap·ple tree, *noun*
tree which apples grow on.

ap·ply [əˈplaɪ] *verb*
(a) to ask for a job; she applied for a job as a teacher; he applied to join the police force.
(b) to refer to; this applies to all of you; the rule applies to visitors only.
applies—applying—applied—has applied

ap·pli·ca·tion [æplɪˈkeɪʃn] *noun*
asking for a job (usually in writing); if you are applying for the job, you must fill in an application form.

ap·point [əˈpɔɪnt] *verb*
to give someone a job; he was appointed sales manager.
appoints—appointing— appointed—has appointed

ap·point·ment, *noun*
(a) giving someone a job; on his appointment as manager = when he was appointed manager.
(b) arrangement to see someone at a

particular time; I have an appointment with the doctor/to see the doctor on Tuesday; can I make an appointment to see Dr. Jones? I'm very busy—I have appointments all day.

ap·proach [əˈprəʊtʃ] *verb*
to go/to come nearer; as the cops approached, all the children ran away; the time is approaching when we will have to decide what to do.
approaches—approaching— approached—has approached

A·pril [ˈeɪprəl] *noun*
fourth month of the year; his birthday is in April; she died on April 20, 1922; we went on vacation last April; today is April 5.
Note: April 5: say "April fifth," "April the fifth," or "the fifth of April"

a·pron [ˈeɪprən] *noun*
cloth or plastic cover which you wear in front of your clothes to stop them from getting dirty; put on an apron if you are going to wash the dishes.

are [ɑːr] *see* **be**

ar·e·a [ˈeəriə] *noun*
(a) measurement of the space occupied by something; to measure the area of a room you must multiply the length by the width; the area of the garage is 250 square feet.
(b) district; the houses in this area are very expensive; the police are searching the area around the school; several million people live in the area around Boston.

aren't [ɑːrnt] *see* **be**

ar·gue [ˈɑːrgjuː] *verb*
to discuss something without agreeing/ to fight; she argued with the waiter about the check.
argues—arguing—argued—has argued

ar·gu·ment [ˈɑːrgjʊmənt] *noun*
discussing something without agreeing; they got into an argument about money.

a·rith·me·tic [əˈrɪθmətɪk] *noun*
working with numbers.

arm [ɑːrm] *noun*

(*a*) part of the body which goes from your hand to your shoulder; **his arm hurt after he fell down; she broke her arm skiing; lift your arms up above your head.**

(*b*) part of a chair which you can rest your arms on; **he sat on the arm of my chair.**

(*c*) **arms** = weapons.

arm·chair, *noun*
chair with arms.

armed, *adjective*
(person) who carries weapons; **the soldiers were armed with knives; are the policemen all armed? the armed forces** = the Army, Navy and Air Force.

ar·my [ˈɑːrmɪ] *noun*
all the soldiers of a country; **the Mexican army; he left school and joined the army.**
plural **armies**

a·round [əˈraʊnd] *preposition & adverb*

(*a*) on all sides of; **the water was all around the house; the area around Chicago.**

(*b*) about; **the car cost around $4,000.**

(*c*) in a circle; **the earth turns around the sun.**

(*d*) backwards; **he turned around.**

(*e*) from one person to another; **pass around the plate of cookies.**

(*f*) in various places; **we walked around the town.**

ar·range [əˈreɪndʒ] *verb*

(*a*) to put in order; **she arranged the chairs in rows; the books are arranged in alphabetical order.**

(*b*) to organize; **we arranged to meet at 6 o'clock.**

arranges—arranging—arranged—has arranged

ar·range·ment, *noun*
way in which something is put in order; way in which something is organized; **I don't like the arrangement of the chairs; all the arrangements have been made for the party.**

ar·rest [əˈrest] *verb*
to catch someone and keep him (usually at a police station) because the police believe he has done something wrong;
the policeman arrested the burglar; he was arrested as he was climbing out of the window.

arrests—arresting—arrested— . has arrested

ar·rive [əˈraɪv] *verb*
to reach a place; **the plane arrives in London at 4 o'clock; we arrived at the theater after the film had started; she arrived home tired out.**

arrives—arriving—arrived—has arrived
Note: you **arrive in a town,** *but* **arrive at a place**

ar·riv·al, *noun*

(*a*) reaching a place; **the time of arrival is 4 o'clock.**

(*b*) person who has arrived; **he's a new arrival.**

art [ɑːrt] *noun*
painting/drawing, etc.; **he collects Russian works of art.**

art gal·ler·y, *noun*
building where paintings, etc., are put on show.

ar·ti·cle [ˈɑːrtɪkl] *noun*

(*a*) thing/object; **article of clothing** = piece of clothing.

(*b*) word which shows a noun (*such as* **a** *house,* **the** *tree*).

(*c*) piece of writing in a newspaper; **did you read the article on Germany in yesterday's paper?**

ar·ti·fi·cial [ɑːrtɪˈfɪʃl] *adjective*
which is made by man/which is not the real thing; **an artificial Christmas tree; he has an artificial leg.**

art·ist [ˈɑːrtɪst] *noun*
person who paints/draws, etc.

as [æz *or* əz] *conjunction*

(*a*) because; **as you can't drive, you must go by bus.**

(*b*) at the same time; **as he was opening the door, the telephone rang.**

(*c*) in a certain way; **leave it as it is; you must do as the teacher tells you.**

as for = referring to; **as for you—you must stay here.**

as if = in the same way as; **he walks very slowly, as if he had hurt his leg; she**

looks as if she's going to cry; it looks as if it's going to rain.

as of = from a time; as of tomorrow = starting from tomorrow.

as . . . as = like; he is as tall as me; as green as grass.

as though = as if

as well = also/too; he ate his piece of cake and mine as well; we visited the castle and the old town as well.

as well as = together with; he has a house in the country as well as a house in town; as well as teaching English, he also teaches football.

ash [æ∫] *noun*
gray dust left when something has burned; he dropped cigarette ashes onto the carpet.
no plural: **some ash; a pile of ash; ashes** *means* small pieces of ash

a·shamed [ə'∫eɪmd] *adjective*
sorry because you have done something wrong; he was ashamed of what he had done; don't be ashamed of making mistakes; she was ashamed of her old clothes.

ask [æsk] *verb*
(*a*) to put a question; ask someone to teach you how to swim; he asked the policeman the way to the post office; she went to the station to ask about cheap fares to Montreal.
(*b*) to invite; we asked them in for a cup of coffee; don't ask her to go out with you —she always wants expensive dinners.
asks—asking—asked—has asked

ask for, *verb*
to say that you want something; he asked for more money; someone knocked at the door and asked for my father; he asked for his pencil back = said that he wanted to have the pencil which he had loaned.

a·sleep [ə'sli:p] *adjective*
sleeping; he was asleep and didn't hear the telephone ring; she fell asleep in front of the TV = she began to sleep.
Note: asleep cannot be used in front of a noun: **the cat is asleep** *but a* **sleeping cat**

as·sis·tant [ə'sɪstənt] *noun*
person who helps; my assistant will come to meet you.

as·ton·ish [ə'stɒnɪ∫] *verb*
to surprise; I was astonished to hear that she was married.
astonishes—astonishing—astonished—has astonished

as·ton·ish·ing, *adjective*
which surprises; it's astonishing how many people speak English well; an astonishing number of the students passed their exams.

as·ton·ish·ment, *noun*
great surprise; to his astonishment, she suddenly started to sing.

at [æt *or* ət] *preposition*
(*a*) (*showing time*) at ten o'clock; at night; at noon.
(*b*) (*showing place*) meet me at the corner of the street; at the top of the mountain; she's not at home; he's at work.
(*c*) (*showing speed*) the train was traveling at 50 miles an hour.
at first = in the beginning; at first she walked slowly, and then started to run.
at last = in the end; we drove for miles, and at last reached the mountains.
at once = immediately; I'll do it at once.
at the mo·ment = right now; she's busy at the moment.
at times = sometimes; at times I feel like quitting my job.
Note: **at** *is often used after verbs:* **look at; point at,** *etc.*

ate [eɪt] *see* **eat**

at·tach [ə'tæt∫] *verb*
to fix/to fasten; the seat belt is attached to the floor of the car; the boat was attached with a chain.
attaches—attaching—attached—has attached

at·tack [ə'tæk] 1. *noun*
(*a*) starting to fight; they made an attack on the castle.
(*b*) sudden illness; he had an attack of fever.
2. *verb*
to start to fight; three big men attacked

him and stole his money; the old lady was attacked by robbers.

attacks—attacking—attacked— has attacked

at·tempt [ə'tempt] 1. *noun*
try; he made an attempt to break the record for the high jump.
2. *verb*
to try; she attempted to climb the mountain.

attempts—attempting— attempted—has attempted

at·tend [ə'tend] *verb*
to be present at; will you attend the meeting tomorrow?

attends—attending—attended— has attended

at·tend to, *verb*
to take care of; the doctor is attending to his patients.

at·ten·tion [ə'tenʃn] *noun*
careful thinking; the boy in the back row was not paying attention to what the teacher was saying; attention please!

Au·gust ['ɔːgəst] *noun*
eighth month of the year; my birthday is in August; today is August 15; I start my new job next August.
Note: **August 15:** *say* "August fifteenth," "August the fifteenth" *or* "the fifteenth of August"

aunt [ænt] *noun*
sister of your mother or father; wife of your uncle; here is Aunt Mary.

au·to·mat·ic [ɔːtə'mætɪk] *adjective*
which works by itself, with no one making it work; an automatic door = door which opens as you come to it.
au·to·mat·i·cal·ly [ɔːtə'mætɪklɪ] *adverb*
working by itself; the door opens automatically; when smoke comes into the room, it automatically makes a bell ring.

au·to·mo·bile [ɔːtəmə'biːl] *noun*
car; he works in the automobile industry.

au·tumn ['ɔːtəm] *noun* = **fall**.

av·er·age ['ævrɪdʒ] 1. *noun*
middle figure out of two or more; we scored 10, 12 and 17, so our average is

13; to work out an average you must add all the figures together and then divide by the number of figures which you have added.
2. *adjective*
ordinary/not very good; he gets average grades in school; she is just an average worker.

a·void [ə'vɔɪd] *verb*
to try not to do something; to keep away from something; I want to avoid going out in the rain; leave early to avoid the traffic.

avoids—avoiding—avoided—has avoided

a·wake [ə'weɪk] 1. *verb*
(*a*) to wake someone up; he was awoken by the sound of thunder.
(*b*) to wake up; he awoke when he heard the sound of thunder.

awakes—awaking—awoke—has awoken

2. *adjective*
not asleep; he was still awake at 2 o'clock; the baby is wide awake = very awake.
Note: **awake** *cannot be used in front of a noun*

a·wak·en, *verb*
to wake up; he awakened to the sound of rain.

awakens—awakening—awakened— has awakened

a·way [ə'weɪ] *adverb*
(*a*) not here; far; the nearest town is six miles away; go away! put that knife away.
(*b*) not at home; they went away on vacation; my husband was away on business.
Note: **away** *is used with many verbs:* **go away; keep away.** *etc.*

aw·ful ['ɔːfl] *adjective*
very bad; what an awful smell! he has an awful cold.
aw·ful·ly, *adverb*
very; it is awfully cold outside; I'm awfully hungry.

awk·ward ['ɔːkwərd] *adjective*
(*a*) (person) who has no skill; **he is awkward with a paintbrush.**
(*b*) difficult to reach/to find/to deal with; **that cupboard is in a very awkward place.**

a·woke [ə'wəʊk], **a·wok·en** [ə'wəʊkn] *see* **awake**

ax [æks] *noun*
tool with a sharp metal head for chopping wood; **he chopped the tree down with an ax.**

Bb

ba·by ['beɪbɪ] *noun*
(*a*) very young child; **babies start to walk when they are about 12 months old; I've known Mary since she was a baby; Mrs. Smith had her baby last week** = she gave birth to the baby last week.
(*b*) small animal; **baby elephant.**
plural **babies**
Note: if you do not know the sex of a baby you can refer to it as **it: the baby was sucking its thumb**
ba·by-sit, *verb*
to take care of children when their parents are away from home; **she made $10 baby-sitting for the people next door.**
ba·by-sit·ter, *noun*
person who takes care of children when their parents are away from home.

back [bæk] **1.** *noun*
(*a*) part of the body from your neck down to your waist, which is not in front; **he lay down on his back and looked at the sky; she carried her bag on her back; she hurt his back lifting up the sack; he stood with his back to the wall.**
(*b*) other part or side to the front; **he wrote his name on the back of the photo; she wrote the address on the back of the envelope; he sat in the back of the car and went to sleep; his bedroom is in the back of the house; he put his pants on back to front** = the wrong way around.

2. *adjective*
on the opposite side to the front; **he sat on the back seat of the car; the back tire of my bicycle is flat; she went out the back door.**
3. *adverb*
(*a*) towards the back; **he stepped back; she leaned back against the wall.**
(*b*) (**in**) **back of** = behind; **we play in the field back of Mr. Demster's house.**
(*c*) (*showing how things were before*) **can you pay me back the $10 which you owe me? he went back into the house; she gave me back my book; he only came back home at 10 o'clock.**
4. *verb*
to go back; **she backed away from him** = she went away from him backward.
backs—backing—backed—has backed
Note: **back** *is often used after verbs:* **to give back; to go back; to pay back,** *etc.*

back·ache, *noun*
pain in the back; **Father has had a backache since he tried to move the piano.**
back and forth, *adverb*
from one side to the other; **he walked back and forth in front of the bank entrance.**
back·ground ['bækgraʊnd] *noun*
part (of a picture) which is in the distance; **the picture shows a house with a background of dark trees; her blue dress stands out against the white back-**

ground; can you see the two ships in the background?

back up, *verb*
to make a car go back; can you back up into the garage? he hit the wall as he was backing up.

back·ward, back·wards, *adverb*
from the front towards the back; he stepped backward into the lake; "tab" is "bat" spelled backward.

ba·con [ˈbeɪkn] *noun*
salty meat from a pig; we had bacon and eggs for breakfast; can I have some more bacon please? he has already eaten three pieces of bacon and two eggs.
no plural: **some bacon; a slice of bacon/a piece of bacon**

bad [bæd] *adjective*
(*a*) not good; of poor quality; **too much butter is bad for you; this apple's going bad; she's good at math but bad at English.**
(*b*) not mild; **she's got a bad cold; he had a bad accident in his car.**
(*c*) naughty; **he's a bad boy; those bad children have stolen all my flowers.**
bad—worse—worst

not bad = quite good; this cake isn't bad; what did you think of the film?—not bad!

bad·ly, *adverb*
(*a*) in a bad way; he did badly on his English exam.
(*b*) very much; your hair badly needs cutting.
badly—worse—worst

bag [bæg] *noun*
something made of paper/cloth, etc., in which you can carry things; **a bag of potatoes; he put the apples in a paper bag; she carried her clothes in an old bag; let me take your bags** = your luggage; **shopping bag** = bag for carrying shopping in; **sleeping bag** = comfortable warm bag for sleeping in.

bag·gage [ˈbægɪdʒ] *noun*
cases/bags, etc., which you take with you when you travel containing your clothes; **put all the baggage into the**

back of the car; we have too much baggage—we will have to pay extra.
no plural: **some baggage; a lot of baggage**

bake [beɪk] *verb*
to cook in an oven; **she baked a cake; do you like baked potatoes?**
bakes—baking—baked—has baked

bak·er, *noun*
person who makes bread and cakes.

bak·er·y, *noun*
shop where you can buy bread and cakes; **he bought a loaf of bread at the bakery; the bakery is next door to the bookstore.**

bal·ance [ˈbæləns] 1. *noun*
(*a*) machine which weighs.
(*b*) not falling; **he stood on the top of the fence and kept his balance** = did not fall off.
2. *verb*
to stand on something narrow without falling; **he was balancing on top of the fence; how long can you balance on one foot?**
balances—balancing—balanced—has balanced

bald [bɔːld] *adjective*
with no hair; **his father is bald; he's only 30 but he's already going bald.**
bald—balder—baldest

ball [bɔːl] *noun*
(*a*) round thing for throwing/kicking/for playing games; **tennis ball; he kicked the ball to the center; I threw the ball and he caught it.**
(*b*) game played with a ball, esp. baseball; **they were playing ball when the rain started.**

ball play·er, *noun*
person who plays baseball.

ball-point pen, ball pen, *noun*
pen which writes using a small ball covered with ink.

bal·loon [bəˈluːn] *noun*
large round thing which you blow up with air or gas; **they blew up balloons for the party.**

ba·nan·a [bə'nænə] *noun*

long yellow fruit which grows in hot countries; **he was peeling a banana; the children like to eat bananas; banana split** = dessert made of bananas, whipped cream, ice cream and nuts.

band [bænd] *noun*

(*a*) thin piece of material for tying things together; **the papers were held together with a rubber band.**

(*b*) group of people, esp. people who play music together; **the soldiers marched after the band; the band played music; a dance band.**

Band-Aid, *noun*

small piece of cloth tape to put on a cut; **put a Band-Aid on that cut.**

band·age ['bændɪdʒ] 1. *noun*

piece of cloth which you wrap around a wound; **his head was covered in bandages; put a bandage around your knee.**

2. *verb*

to wrap a piece of cloth around a wound; **she bandaged his leg; his arm is bandaged up.**

bandages—bandaging—bandaged—has bandaged

bang [bæŋ] 1. *noun*

sudden loud noise like that made by a gun; **the gun went bang; there was a bang and the chimney fell down.**

2. *verb*

to make a loud noise; **can't you stop the door from banging? he banged on the table with his hand.**

bangs—banging—banged—has banged

bank [bæŋk] 1. *noun*

(*a*) land along the two sides of a river or at the edge of a lake; **he sat on the bank of the river, trying to catch fish.**

(*b*) place where you can leave your money safely; **how much money do you have in the bank? he put all his money in the bank; she took all her money out of the bank to buy a car.**

2. *verb*

to put money away in a bank; **she banks $50 every week.**

banks—banking—banked—has banked

bank ac·count, *noun*

arrangement which you make with a bank to keep your money safely; **I put all my savings in my bank account; he opened/closed a bank account** = he started/stopped keeping money in a bank.

bank·book, *noun*

book in which notes are kept of money which you put into (or take out of) a bank.

bank on, *verb*

to be sure that something will happen; **don't bank on getting any money from your father; you can bank on the weather being good on Labor Day.**

bar [baːr] *noun*

(*a*) piece of something hard; **a bar of soap; a bar of chocolate.**

(*b*) long piece of wood or metal; **he escaped from the prison by sawing through the bars** = pieces of metal in front of the windows.

(*c*) place/room where you can buy drinks; **a bar in a hotel; after the movie we went to a bar to have a drink.**

bar·ber ['baːrbər] *noun*

person who gives haircuts.

bar·ber·shop, *noun*

shop where you can get a haircut.

bare [beər] *adjective*

(*a*) not covered by clothes; **the children had bare feet; her dress left her arms bare.**

(*b*) with no leaves; **in winter the branches of the trees are bare.**

(*c*) with no furniture; **the bare rooms look cold and frightening.**

bare·ly, *adverb*

almost not/hardly; **we have barely enough money to pay the bill** = we have only just enough money; **he barely had time to sit down before the telephone rang.**

bar·gain ['baːrgɪn] *noun*

something which you buy at a lower price than normal; **a $50 ticket to New York is a bargain; you should buy that fur coat—it's a bargain.**

bark [bɑːrk] 1. *noun*
(*a*) hard outside of a tree trunk.
(*b*) noise made by a dog.
2. *verb*
(*of a dog*) to make a noise; **the dog
barked at the mailman; I can hear a dog
barking.**
**barks—barking—barked—has
barked**

base [beɪs] *noun*
(*a*) bottom part/part which something
stands on; **a glass with a heavy base.**
(*b*) one of the four corners of a baseball
field.
(*c*) **army base** = army headquarters.
base·ball, *noun*
game played between two teams using
a bat and a hard ball; **do you want to
watch the baseball game on TV? he's
playing in the school baseball team.**
based, *adjective*
fixed; with the main part at; **our company is based in Wisconsin.**
base·ment, *noun*
part of a building below the level of the
ground; **our TV room is in the base-
ment.**
ba·sic [ˈbeɪsɪk] *adjective*
very simple/which everything else
comes from; **you should know basic
math if you want to work in a store; a
basic dictionary** = dictionary which
contains the most common words.

bas·ket [ˈbæskɪt] *noun*
container made of thin pieces of
wood, etc.; **throw those papers into the
basket.**
bas·ket·ball, *noun*
game played between two teams where
you have to throw a ball into a high
basket.

bat [bæt] *noun*
type of wooden stick with which you
hit a ball; **he's at bat** = it is his turn to
try to hit the ball.
bat·ter, *noun*
person who is trying to hit a ball.

bath [bæθ] *noun*
(*a*) washing your whole body; **after**
you've been playing football you need a
hot bath; my father has a cold bath every
morning.**
(*b*) the water in a bathtub; **I like to lie
in a hot bath.**
bath·room, *noun*
room in a house, with a bathtub and
usually a toilet; **where's the bathroom?
can I use your bathroom, please? the
bathroom scale must be wrong—I'm
heavier than I was yesterday.**
bath·tub, *noun*
large container for water, in which you
can wash your whole body; **is the bathtub clean? there's a shower and a bathtub
in the bathroom.**

bathe [beɪð] *verb*
(*a*) to take a bath; **I always bathe before
breakfast.**
(*b*) to wash; **Father is bathing the baby.**
(*c*) to wash (a wound); **he bathed his
knee in boiled water.**
bathes—bathing [ˈbeɪðɪŋ]—
bathed [beɪðd]—**has bathed**

bat·ter·y [ˈbætərɪ] *noun*
something which stores electric power
and is used to make something work;
**the car needs a new battery; you ought
to change the batteries in the radio.**
plural **batteries**

bat·tle [ˈbætl] *noun*
fight between armies or navies; **the
French navy was defeated in the battle of
Trafalgar.**

be [biː] 1. *verb*
(*a*) (*showing a state*) the sky is blue; he
is taller than his father; tomatoes are red;
it's cold today; are you hungry?
(*b*) (*showing age/time*) he's sixteen; she's
only two years old; it's nearly six o'clock;
it's time to go to bed; it will soon be
summer.
(*c*) (*showing price*) tomatoes are 30 cents
a pound; sandwiches are 25 cents each.
(*d*) (*showing occupation*) his mother is a
teacher; she wants to be a doctor.
(*e*) (*showing size, height, etc.*) he's six feet
tall; the town is more than two miles away;
the post office is very close to our house.

Bathroom

1. bandages
2. bathtub
3. bath mat
4. bathroom scale
5. comb
6. face cream
7. faucet
8. lipstick
9. mirror
10. plug (on razor)
11. electric razor

12. shower
13. shower curtain
14. sink
15. soap
16. thermometer
17. toilet
18. toothbrush
19. toothpaste
20. towel
21. washcloth

(*f*) (*showing that something exists*) there's a crowd of people waiting for the bus; there are only two chocolates left in the box.

(*g*) (*in the perfect* = go) have you ever been to Florida? she has been to see the film three times; where have you been all day?

2. *making a part of a verb*

(*a*) (*making the present continuous*) don't talk to him when he's reading; I'm waiting for the bus; they are hoping to go on vacation next week.

(*b*) (*making the past continuous*) she was singing in the bathtub; they were walking down the street when it started to rain.

(*c*) (*making the future continuous*) he will be flying to New York tomorrow morning.

(*d*) (*showing the passive*) she was knocked down by a bus; the children were told to go home.

Present: I am, you are, he is, we are, they are

Short forms: I'm, you're, he's, we're, they're

Negative: I'm not; you're not *or* you aren't; he's not *or* he isn't; we're not *or* we aren't; they're not *or* they aren't

Future: I will be/I shall be

Past: I was, you were, he was, we were, they were

Negative: I wasn't, you weren't, he wasn't, we weren't, they weren't

Perfect: I have been, you have been, he/she/it has been, they have been

beach [biːtʃ] *noun*
sandy part by the edge of the sea; we sat on the beach and ate our sandwiches; let's go to the beach this afternoon; some of the beaches are covered with oil.
plural **beaches**

beak [biːk] *noun*
hard part outside a bird's mouth; the chicken picked up the seeds in its beak.

bean [biːn] *noun*

vegetable which produces seeds which you can eat; **green beans; baked beans.**

bear [beər] *noun*
large wild animal covered with fur; **bears like honey; polar bear** = big white bear which lives in the snow near the North Pole.

beard ['biːrd] *noun*
hair growing on a man's chin; **Hank's father has a long white beard.**

beat [biːt] 1. *noun*
regular sound; **the beat of a drum; keep in time with the beat of the music.**
2. *verb*
(*a*) to hit; **he used to beat his wife with a stick.**
(*b*) to win against someone; **our team beat the Rangers 12 to 0; he was easily beaten in the long jump.**
(*c*) to make a regular sound; **his heart was beating fast.**
beats—beating—beat—has beaten

beat up, *verb*
to hit someone hard many times; **the old lady was beaten up by the burglars.**
Note: **they beat the old man up** *or* **they beat up the old man,** *but only* **they beat him up**

beau·ty ['bjuːtı] *noun*
being very nice to look at; **the beauty of the colors of the trees in the fall.**
beau·ty shop, *noun*
place where women go to have their hair/skin/hands, etc., made beautiful.
beau·ti·ful ['bjuːtıfl] *adjective*
very nice (to look at); **the beautiful colors of the leaves in the fall; what beautiful weather! a beautiful Christmas cake.**

be·came [bı'keım] *see* **become**

be·cause [bə'kɒz] *conjunction*
for this reason; **I was late because I missed the bus; he's wet because it's raining; she's fat because she eats too much.**
be·cause of = on account of; due to; **the trains are late because of the fog; we**

don't use the car because of the price of gas.

be·come [bɪˈkʌm] *verb*

to change into something different; he wants to become a dentist; the sky became dark and the wind became stronger; they became friends; she has become rather deaf.

becomes—becoming—became— has become

bed [bed] *noun*

piece of furniture for sleeping on; lie down on the bed if you're tired; she always goes to bed at 9 o'clock; he was sitting in bed drinking a cup of coffee; come on, get out of bed—it's time for breakfast; she's in bed with a cold; have you made your bed? = have you made it neat after having slept in it?

bed·clothes, *plural noun*

sheets and blankets which cover a bed; he woke up when all his bedclothes fell off.

bed·room, *noun*

room where you sleep; my bedroom is painted blue; shut your bedroom door if you want to have quiet.

bed·spread, *noun*

colored cloth which you put over a bed.

bed·time, *noun*

time when you usually go to bed; 9 o'clock is my bedtime; go to bed—it's past your bedtime.

bee [biː] *noun*

small insect which makes honey; the bees were going from flower to flower.

bee·hive, *noun*

box where bees are kept.

beef [biːf] *noun*

meat from cattle; we had roast beef and boiled potatoes for dinner; would you like another slice of beef?

no plural: **some beef; a piece of beef/a slice of beef**

been [bɪn] *see* **be.**

beer [ˈbiːr] *noun*

type of alcohol; can I have a glass of beer? three beers please = three glasses of beer.

Note: **some beer; a glass of beer; plural only used to mean glasses of beer**

be·fore [bɪˈfɔːr] 1. *adverb*

earlier; why didn't you tell me before? I didn't see him on Tuesday, I saw him the day before.

2. *preposition*

earlier than; he got here before me; make sure you arrive before 10:30; G comes before L in the alphabet.

3. *conjunction*

earlier than; before you sit down, can you pass me the salt? think carefully before you answer my question; before coming in, wipe your shoes on the mat.

be·gan [bɪˈɡæn] *see* **begin**

be·gin [bɪˈɡɪn] *verb*

to start; it began to rain; she began to cry; he's beginning to understand; they all began talking at once.

begins—beginning—began—has begun

be·gin·ner, *noun*

person who is beginning; he can't play well, he's only a beginner.

be·gin·ning, *noun*

first part; the beginning of the story is rather dull; hurry up if you want to see the beginning of the movie.

be·have [bɪˈheɪv] *verb*

to do things (usually well); the children behaved (themselves) very well when they stayed with their grandma; after she was ill she began to behave very strangely; if you don't behave, you'll have to stay in your bedroom = if you are naughty.

behaves—behaving—behaved— has behaved

be·hav·ior, *noun*

way of doing things; his behavior was very strange; the police said that the behavior of the young people at the football game was very bad.

no plural

be·hind [bɪˈhaɪnd] 1. *preposition*

at the back of; they hid behind the drapes; my pen has fallen behind the piano; he was second, only three yards behind the winner.

Bedroom

1. bed
2. blanket
3. chest of drawers
4. closet
5. curtain
6. door
7. drawer
8. lamp
9. mattress
10. mirror
11. pajamas
12. photo
13. pillow
14. plant
15. sheet
16. slippers
17. window

2. *adverb*
at the back; **he was second, only three
yards behind; she has left her ticket
behind** = she has forgotten to take her
ticket with her; **he stayed behind to
watch TV** = stayed at home when the
others went out.

be·ing [biːɪŋ] *see* **human**

be·lieve [bɪˈliːv] *verb*
to be sure that something is true, although you can't prove it; **people used
to believe that the earth was flat; I believe
I have seen him before; never believe
what he tells you.**
**believes—believing—believed—
has believed**
be·lief, *noun*
what you believe; **he was jailed for his
religious beliefs.**
be·lieve in, *verb*
to be sure that something exists/that
something is good; **do you believe in
flying saucers? he believes in taking a
cold shower every morning.**

bell [bel] *noun*
metal object, shaped like a cup, which
rings if you hit it or when you shake
it; electric machine which rings if you
push a button; **he rang the door bell;
you ought to have a bell on your bicycle; they rang the church bells at the
beginning of the service.**

bel·ly [ˈbeli] *noun*
stomach/part of the front of the body
lower than the chest; **he hit him in the
belly; he crawled across the yard on
his belly.**
plural: **bellies**
bel·ly·ache, *noun*
pain in the belly from eating too much,
etc.; **he got a bellyache from eating
apples.**

be·long [bɪˈlɒŋ] *verb*
(*a*) to be the property of someone; **this
hat belongs to my sister; who does this
house belong to? the old watch used to
belong to my mother.**

(*b*) to be a member of; **I belong to a
tennis club.**
**belongs—belonging—belonged—
has belonged**
be·long·ings, *plural noun*
things which belong to you; **they lost all
their belongings in the fire.**

be·low [bɪˈləʊ] **1.** *adverb*
lower down; **he looked down from the
hill at the town below.**
2. *preposition*
lower down than something else; **the
temperature was below 60°; can you see
below the surface of the water?**

belt [belt] *noun*
long piece of leather, etc., which goes
around your waist to keep your pants
up or to attach a coat; **she bought a new
belt for her coat; seat belt** = belt in a
car/in a plane which holds you safely in
your seat.

bench [bentʃ] *noun*
(*a*) long seat; **he slept on a bench in the
park.**
(*b*) table where you can work.
plural: **benches**

bend [bend] **1.** *noun*
curved shape; **the road is full of bends;
he drove too fast around the bend; the
pipe has two bends in it.**
2. *verb*
(*a*) to make something curved; to be
curved; **he bent the pipe into the shape of
an S; the road bends and then goes
straight.**
(*b*) to lean towards the ground; **he bent
down to tie up his shoe; she was bending
over the table.**
bends—bending—bent—has bent

be·neath [bɪˈniːθ] **1.** *adverb*
below; **he looked down from the roof at
the people walking beneath.**
2. *preposition*
under; **the ball was stuck beneath the
piano; the ground was soft beneath his
feet.**

bent [bent] *adjective*
curved; **a bent pipe;** *see also* **bend.**

be·side [bɪ'saɪd] *preposition*
at the side of (something); next to; **he sat down beside me; his house is just beside the post office; put the coffee beside the sugar.**

be·sides 1. *preposition*
other than; **he has two other cars besides the red one; besides the football team, the college has a baseball team and a basketball team.**
2. *adverb*
(*a*) as well as; **besides managing the shop, he also teaches in the evening.**
(*b*) in any case; **I don't want to go for a picnic—besides, the car won't start.**

best [best] 1. *adjective*
very good—better than anything else; **this is the best book I've read this year; what is the best way of cleaning a carpet? he put on his best suit to go to the party; she's the best swimmer in the team.**
2. *noun*
thing which is better than anything else; **you must do your best** = do as well as you can; **he did his best—but he still didn't win.**
3. *adverb*
in the best way; **which of the sisters plays the piano best? the motor works best when it's warm; oranges grow best in hot countries.**
best *is the superlative of* **good** *and* **well**

bet·ter ['betər] 1. *adjective*
(*a*) very good (compared to something else); **the weather got better; this book is better than the one I was reading last week; he's better at math than at history; vegetables are better for you than meat** = make you healthier.
(*b*) healthy again; **I had a cold last week, but now I'm better; I hope you're better soon.**
2. *adverb*
(*a*) very well (compared to something else); **she plays the piano better than her sister; these scissors cut cloth better than those ones.**

(*b*) not as ill; **he had a cold but now he's getting better.**
had bet·ter = it would be a good thing if; **you had better hurry up, if you want to catch the train; she'd better go to bed if she has a cold; hadn't you better answer the phone?**
better *is the comparative of* **good** *and* **well**

be·tween [bɪ'twiːn] *preposition*
in the space separating two things; **there's a wall between his office and mine; the airplane was flying between New York and Philadelphia; I'm busy between 10 o'clock and 2:30; can you come to see me between now and next Monday? he can't tell the difference between red and green.**
in be·tween = in the middle; **he had a meeting at 12:00 and another at 2 p.m. but managed to play a game of tennis in between.**

be·yond [bɪ'jɒnd] *preposition*
further than; **I can see your house, but I can't see anything beyond it because of the fog; to find the post office, you have to go about 100 yards beyond the church.**

bi·cy·cle ['baɪsɪkl] *noun*
vehicle with two wheels, which is ridden by one person who makes it go forward by pushing pedals; **he went to school by bicycle; she's going to do the shopping on her bicycle; he can drive but he can't ride a bicycle** = he doesn't know how to ride one.
Note: often called a **bike**

big [bɪg] *adjective*
of a large size; **I don't want a little piece of cake—I want a big one; his father has the biggest car on our street; I'm not afraid of him—I'm bigger than he is.**
big—bigger—biggest

bike [baɪk] *noun*
(*short way of saying*) bicycle; **he came to school by bike; she fell off her bike; she's going to the store on her bike.**

bill [bɪl] *noun*
(*a*) piece of paper showing the amount

of money you have to pay; **the hospital bill comes to more than $1000; I must pay the telephone bill.**
(*b*) hard part outside a bird's mouth; **the hen was pulling at the grass with its bill.**
(*c*) piece of paper money; **a five-dollar bill.**

bill·board, *noun*
large board where advertisements can be shown in the street.

bill·fold, *noun*
special small leather case for keeping money.

bind [baɪnd] *verb*
to tie; to fasten; **the burglars bound his hands and feet with the telephone cord.**
binds—binding—bound [baʊnd]—**has bound**

bird [bɜrd] *noun*
animal with wings and feathers; **the little birds were learning to fly; most birds can fly well, but some can't; the birds were singing in the trees; in the winter we put a table in the yard, and put food on it for the birds.**

birth [bɜrθ] *noun*
being born; **date of birth** = date when you were born; (*of mother*) **to give birth to** = to have (a baby).

birth·day, *noun*
date on which you were born; **my birthday is on June 15; her birthday is next week; he's just had his birthday** = it was only a few days ago; **he'll be 21 on his next birthday; what do you want for your birthday?** = what presents do you want?; **he got a calculator for his birthday; birthday party** = party held for a birthday; **birthday card** = card sent to someone to wish him good luck on his birthday; **birthday cake** = cake made specially for a birthday.
Hap·py Birth·day = greeting to someone on a birthday.

bit [bɪt] *noun*
(*a*) small piece; **he tied up the package with a bit of string; how much cake do you want?—just a bit, please.**
(*b*) **a bit** = a little; **the photo is a**

bit too dark; **let him sleep a bit longer; have you got a piece of wood a little bit bigger than this one? wait a bit, I'm not ready yet.**
(*c*) *see* **bite**
bit by bit = not all at the same time/ little by little; **he painted the house bit by bit.**

bite [baɪt] *verb*
to cut with your teeth; **the dog bit the postman; he bit a piece out of the apple; she was bitten by an insect.**
bites—biting—bit—has bitten

bit·ter [ˈbɪtər] *adjective*
not sweet; **lemons are bitter, but oranges are sweet.**
bitter—more bitter—bitterest

black [blæk] *adjective & noun*
of the darkest color, the opposite to white; **he was wearing a black hat; we have a black and white TV** = one which does not show pictures in color; **why did you paint your front door black? black coffee** = coffee with no milk in it.
black—blacker—blackest

black·ber·ry, *noun*
wild plant with small black fruit; the fruit of this plant; **we went out picking blackberries.**
plural: **blackberries**

black·bird, *noun*
common dark bird.

black·board, *noun*
large board on the wall of a classroom which you can write on with chalk.

blade [bleɪd] *noun*
(*a*) flat piece of metal; **this knife has a very sharp blade; my knife has two blades.**
(*b*) **blade of grass** = one thin leaf of grass.

blank [blæŋk] **1.** *adjective*
(paper) with nothing written on it; **a blank check; write your name in the blank space.**
2. *noun*
empty space which you have to write in;

in the exam, you have to fill in the blanks with the proper words; get a telegram blank from the office.

blan·ket ['blæŋkɪt] 1. *noun*
thick woolen cover which you put over yourself to keep you warm in bed; **he woke up when his blankets fell off.**
2. *verb*
to cover; **the fields were blanketed with snow.**
blankets—blanketing—
blanketed—has blanketed

blast [blæst] 1. *noun*
force of a bomb which goes off; **he was knocked down by the blast.**
2. *verb*
(*a*) to send a rocket; **they blasted a rocket into space.**
(*b*) to blow up; **they blasted a hole in the prison wall.**
blasts—blasting—blasted—has blasted

bled [bled] *see* **bleed**

bleed [bli:d] *verb*
to lose blood; **his knee is bleeding; my nose began to bleed; when she cut her finger it bled.**
bleeds—bleeding—bled—has bled

blew [blu:] *see* **blow**

blind [blaɪnd] *adjective*
not able to see; **a blind man with a white stick; after her illness she became blind.**

block [blɒk] 1. *noun*
(*a*) large piece; **they used blocks of stone to make the wall; a block of wood fell on his foot.**
(*b*) piece of land with streets on all sides; **go for a walk around the block; he lives two blocks down the street.**
2. *verb*
to stop something from moving; **the pipe was blocked by a dead bird; the accident blocked the road for several hours.**
blocks—blocking—blocked—has blocked

blood [blʌd] *noun*
red liquid in your body; **the police followed the spots of blood to find the** wounded man; blood was pouring from the cut in his hand.

blood·stream, *noun*
blood as it runs through your body; **poison had got into his bloodstream.**

blos·som ['blɒsəm] 1. *noun*
blossoms = flowers; **apple blossoms.**
2. *verb*
to produce flowers; **the apple trees are blossoming.**
blossoms—blossoming—
blossomed—has blossomed

blouse [blaʊs] *noun*
shirt; **she wore a skirt and a blouse.**

blow [bləʊ] *verb*
to make air move; **the wind blew hard all day; blow on your soup to make it cool; because she has a cold, she keeps blowing her nose** = she blows through her nose into a handkerchief to get rid of liquid in her nose.
blows—blowing—blew [blu:]—
has blown

blow a·way, *verb*
to (make something) go away by blowing; **the wind blew away the smoke; his hat blew away.**
blow down, *verb*
to (make something) fall down by blowing; **the trees were blown down by the wind; the fence has blown down.**
blow off, *verb*
to (make something) go away by blowing; **the wind blew off her hat; all the leaves were blown off the trees.**
blow out, *verb*
to (make something) go out by blowing; **you must blow out the candles on your birthday cake; the candle has blown out; all my papers blew out of the window.**
blow up, *verb*
(*a*) to make something get bigger by blowing into it; **to blow up a balloon.**
(*b*) to destroy something with a bomb; **the soldiers blew up the bridge.**
Note: **the wind blew the smoke away** *or* **blew away the smoke; they blew the bridge up** *or* **they blew up the bridge,** *etc., but only* **the wind blew it away, they blew it up,** *etc.*

blue [bluː] *adjective & noun*
of a color like the color of the sky in the daytime; **her car is light blue; they live in the house with the dark blue door; she was dressed all in blue;** do you have a cloth of a darker blue than this?
blue—bluer—bluest

blue·ber·ry, *noun*
wild plant; round blue fruit from this plant; **we had blueberry pie with ice cream.**
plural: **blueberries**

blue·bird, *noun*
small bird with a blue back.

board [bɔːrd] *noun*
(*a*) large flat piece of wood, etc.; **write this sentence on the board** = on the blackboard.
(*b*) group of people in charge of something; **Board of Education.**

boat [bəʊt] *noun*
ship; **a sailing boat** = boat which goes with sails; **a fishing boat** = boat used to catch fish at sea; **we took the boat across to France; when is the next boat to New York? they went to Australia by boat.**

bod·y [bɒdɪ] *noun*
(*a*) main part of an animal/of a person (not including the head and arms and legs).
(*b*) all of an animal/of a person; **the dead man's body was found several days later.**
plural **bodies**

boil [bɔɪl] *verb*
(*a*) to heat (water) until it makes steam; (*of water*) to make steam because it is very hot; **the soup's boiling; can you boil some water for me to make the tea? the kettle's boiling** = the water in the kettle is boiling.
(*b*) to cook (vegetables/eggs, etc.) in boiling water; **I had a boiled egg for breakfast; I don't like the smell of boiling cabbage; hard-boiled egg** = egg which has been boiled so long that it is hard.
boils—boiling—boiled—has boiled

boil o·ver, *verb*
to rise up when boiling in a pan and pour over the side; **the milk boiled over and made a mess on the stove.**

bomb [bɒm] **1.** *noun*
large shell which is dropped from an airplane or placed on the ground in order to blow up buildings; **bombs were falling on the town; the enemy dropped bombs on the bridges; his house was destroyed by a bomb.**
2. *verb*
to drop a bomb on something from an airplane; **the enemy tried to bomb the railroad lines; they bombed the hospital.**
bombs—bombing—bombed—has bombed

bone [bəʊn] *noun*
one of the solid pieces which make the skeleton of an animal's body; **he fell over and broke a bone in his ankle; don't try to eat the fish bones.**

book [bʊk] **1.** *noun*
(*a*) printed pages attached together with a cover; **I'm reading a book on gardening; he wrote a book about elephants.**
(*b*) pages attached together; **accounts book; a book of matches** = cardboard matches attached together in a paper cover.
2. *verb*
to reserve a place/a seat/a table in a restaurant/a room in a hotel; **have you booked a table for the party? I want to book a room for Friday night; I'm sorry the play is sold out—all the seats have been booked.**
books—booking—booked—has booked

book·case, *noun*
cupboard with shelves for keeping books.
book·shelf, *noun*
shelf for keeping books.
plural **bookshelves**

book·store, *noun*
store which sells books.
book up, *verb*
to reserve (everything); **the hotel is all booked up** = all the rooms are booked.

Body

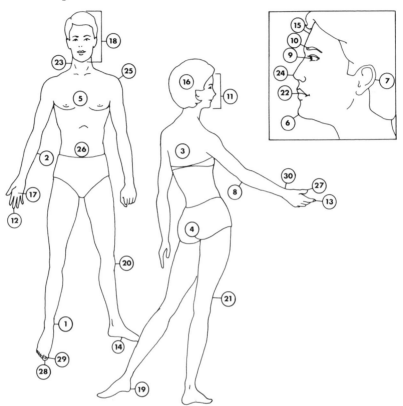

1. ankle
2. arm
3. back
4. buttocks
5. chest
6. chin
7. ear
8. elbow
9. eye
10. eyebrow
11. face
12. finger
13. fingernail
14. foot
15. forehead
16. hair
17. hand
18. head
19. heel
20. knee
21. leg
22. mouth
23. neck
24. nose
25. shoulder
26. stomach
27. thumb
28. toe
29. toenail
30. wrist

boot [buːt] *noun*
strong shoe which goes above your ankle; **she was wearing long black boots; the children wore boots in the rain; work boots** = boots to wear when doing heavy work; **ski boots** = boots to wear when skiing.

bor·der [ˈbɔːrdər] *noun*
line separating two countries; **the border between France and Spain goes along the tops of mountains; border guards** = soldiers guarding the border.

bored [bɔːrd] *adjective*
not interested; **I get bored sitting in the office all day; she's bored—ask her to go to the movies.**
bor·ing, *adjective*
which makes you lose interest/not interesting; **he went to sleep watching a boring film on TV; she thinks golf is so boring.**

born [bɔːrn] *verb*
to be born = to begin to live; **he was born in Germany; she was born in 1962.**
Note: **born** *is usually only used with* **was** *or* **were**

bor·row [ˈbɒrəʊ] *verb*
to take something for a short time by agreement with the owner; **can I borrow your car to go to the store? he borrowed $10 from me, and never paid it back; she borrowed three books from the library.**
borrows—borrowing—borrowed—has borrowed
Note: compare **loan**

boss [bɒs] *noun*
person in charge; **do you like the new boss? I have to ask the boss if I can have a day off.**
plural **bosses**

both [bəʊθ] *adjective & pronoun & conjunction*
two people/two things together; **both my socks have holes in them; you can't eat both of the cakes; both children were sick; hold the handle in both hands; we both like honey; they both fell down on the ice; both the teacher and his wife were**
sick; he ate both his pie and my pie.

both·er [ˈbɒðər] **1.** *noun*
thing which makes you angry or worried; **fixing the car was a big bother.**
2. *verb*
to take trouble to do something; to worry about something; **she didn't bother to send us a bill; don't bother about cleaning the room.**
bothers—bothering—bothered—has bothered

bot·tle [ˈbɒtl] *noun*
glass container for liquids; **wine bottle; beer bottle; he drinks a bottle of orange juice a day; open another bottle of orange juice; you can buy beer in bottles or in cans; he was drinking beer out of the bottle.**
bot·tle cap, *noun*
little cover which goes on the top of a bottle; **he can take bottle caps off with his teeth.**

bot·tom [ˈbɒtəm] *noun*
lowest part; **there was some jam left in the bottom of the jar; the ship sank to the bottom of the sea; turn right at the bottom of the hill; he's at the bottom of his class** = he gets the worst grades.

bought [bɔːt] *see* **buy**

bounce [baʊns] *verb*
to go up and down; to make something go up and down; **he was bouncing up and down on his bed; the ball bounced down the stairs; he bounced the ball against the wall.**
bounces—bouncing—bounced—has bounced

bound [baʊnd] *see* **bind**

bow¹ [bəʊ] *noun*
knot tied so that it looks like a butterfly; **she tied gold bows in her hair; bow tie** = necktie tied in a bow.

bow² [baʊ] **1.** *noun*
bending forward; **he made a bow to the king.**
2. *verb*
to bend forward; **he bowed to the king.**
bows—bowing—bowed—has bowed

bowl [bəʊl] *noun*
wide container with higher sides than a plate; **a bowl of soup; soup bowl** = bowl specially made for soup.

box [bɒks] *noun*
container; **a box of cookies/of matches; put the cakes into a box; she ate two boxes of chocolates.**
plural **boxes**

box·er, *noun*
man who fights another as a sport; **the two boxers went into the ring.**

box·ing, *noun*
sport of fighting, played between two men wearing special gloves.

boy [bɔɪ] *noun*
male child; **they have three children— two boys and a girl; the boys were playing in the field; paper boy** = boy who delivers newspapers to your house.
plural **boys**

brain [breɪn] *noun*
part of the inside of your head which you think with; **use your brain** = think hard; **he has brains** = he's smart.

brake [breɪk] **1.** *noun*
thing which stops a car/a bicycle, etc.; **he put on the brakes; he drove the car with the brake on; you should use your brakes when you go down the hill.**
2. verb
to stop a car/a bicycle by putting on the brakes; **the driver braked as he turned the corner.**
brakes—braking—braked—has braked

branch [bræːntʃ] *noun*
(*a*) part of a tree, growing out of the main trunk; **the children were swinging in the branches of the trees; they jumped from branch to branch.**
(*b*) office of a bank/of a store; **the local branch of the Chase Manhattan Bank; the bank has branches in all large cities; branch manager** = manager in charge of a branch.
plural **branches**

brand [brænd] *noun*
(*a*) mark on cattle to show who owns them.
(*b*) special product made by one company; **he only buys the best brands of coffee.**

brand-new, *adjective*
very new; **she was driving a brand-new Cadillac.**

brave [breɪv] *adjective*
not afraid of danger; **he's a brave man— he saved the little boy from the burning house.**
brave—braver—bravest

brave·ly, *adverb*
in a brave way; **he bravely jumped into the water to save the girl.**

bread [bred] *noun*
food made from flour and water baked in an oven; **go to the bakery and buy a loaf of bread; cut three slices of bread; the children were eating bread and peanut butter** = slices of bread covered with peanut butter.
no plural: **some bread; a loaf of bread; a slice of bread/a piece of bread**

break [breɪk] **1.** *noun*
(*a*) space; interruption; **he spoke for two hours without a break** = without stopping; **the sun came through a break in the clouds.**
(*b*) short rest; **there is a ten-minute break in the middle of the morning; the children drink milk during break; coffee break** = short rest in the middle of work, when you drink coffee; **we'll have a coffee break now.**
2. verb
to make something go to pieces; to go to pieces; **he dropped the cup on the floor and broke it; it fell on the floor and broke; I can't use the elevator because it's broken; she fell off the wall and broke her leg.**
breaks—breaking—broke [brəʊk]—has broken

break down, *verb*
to stop working; **the car broke down and we had to push it.**

break·fast ['brekfəst] *noun*

first meal of the day; **I had a boiled egg for breakfast; she didn't have any breakfast because she was in a hurry; we have breakfast at 7:30 every day.**

break in(to), *verb*
to get into a house by force; **burglars broke in during the night; he was caught breaking into the bookstore.**

break off, *verb*
(*a*) to make something come apart by breaking; **he broke the handle off a cup; the branch was broken off the tree.**
(*b*) to stop suddenly; **he broke off in the middle of his story; they broke off the discussion.**

break out, *verb*
(*a*) to escape; **three prisoners have broken out of jail.**
(*b*) to start to have red spots on your skin; **chocolate makes me break out.**

break up, *verb*
(*a*) to come to pieces; **the ship was breaking up on the rocks.**
(*b*) to stop being together; **the meeting broke up at 3 p.m.**

breath [breθ] *noun*
air which goes into and out of your body when you breathe; **he ran so fast he was out of breath; stop for a moment to get your breath back; she took a deep breath and dived into the water.**

breathe [bri:ð] *verb*
to take air in and out of your body through your nose or mouth; **can fish breathe under water? he breathed in the smoke from the fire, and it made him cough.**
breathes—breathing—breathed—has breathed

brick [brɪk] *noun*
block of earth, baked in an oven, and used to build houses; **a brick house; the wall is built of bricks; he threw a brick through the window.**

bride [braɪd] *noun*
woman who has just got married; **the bride was wearing white.**
bride·groom, *noun*
man who has just got married.

bridge [brɪdʒ] *noun*

thing built across a road/a river, etc., so that traffic can cross from one side to the other; **the road crosses the river by a very long bridge; the river goes under the bridge.**

bright [braɪt] *adjective*
(*a*) which shines; which has a very strong color; **bright sunshine; they have painted their house bright orange.**
(*b*) smart/clever; **he's a bright little boy; both their children are very bright.**
bright—brighter—brightest

bright·ly, *adverb*
in a bright way; **brightly colored flags.**

bring [brɪŋ] *verb*
to carry something to this place; to come with something or someone to this place; **bring me the money; he brought his father with him; he's bringing his friends along to the party.**
brings—bringing—brought [brɔːt] **—has brought**

bring back, *verb*
to carry something back; **bring back my book—I want it; he brought back some presents from his vacation in Mexico.**

bring down, *verb*
to carry something down to here; **can you bring down my coat from the bedroom?**

bring in, *verb*
to carry something or somebody in here; to come with something or somebody in here; **he brought his boots in with him; don't bring your friends in—I've washed the floor.**

bring up, *verb*
(*a*) to take care of and educate a child; **he was brought up by his uncle; I was brought up in California.**
(*b*) to start to talk about; **why did you bring up the subject of money?**
Note: **he brought some presents back** *or* **he brought back some presents; she brought the dog in** *or* **she brought in the dog,** *etc.; but only* **he brought them back, she brought it in,** *etc.*

broad·cast [ˈbrɔːdkæst] *verb*
to send out a program on radio or TV;

the President broadcast to the nation.
**broadcasts—broadcasting—
broadcast—has broadcast**

broke, broken [brəʊk, ˈbrəʊkən] *see*
break

broom [bruːm] *noun*
brush with a long handle for sweeping
the floor.

broth·er [ˈbrʌðər] *noun*
male who has the same mother and
father as another child; **he's my brother;
that girl has three brothers; her brother's
a doctor.**

brought [brɔːt] *see* **bring**

brown [braʊn] *adjective & noun*
of a color like the color of earth or
wood; **he has brown hair and blue eyes;
in the fall the leaves turn brown and fall
off the trees; you're very brown—you
must have been sitting in the sun for a
long time; she was wearing dark brown
shoes.**
brown—browner—brownest

brown·ie, *noun*
small cake made with chocolate and
nuts.

brush [brʌʃ] 1. *noun*
thing with a handle and stiff hairs or
wire which you use for cleaning dust off
the floor/for cleaning your teeth with
toothpaste/for putting paint on a wall,
etc.; **you need a stiff brush to get
all the mud off your shoes; if you paint
with a thin brush you will make fine lines;
he was painting white lines on the road
with a large brush.**
plural **brushes**
2. *verb*
(*a*) to touch gently; **he brushed against
me in the dark.**
(*b*) to clean with a brush; **have you
brushed your shoes? don't forget to brush
your teeth after meals.**
**brushes—brushing—brushed—
has brushed**

brush off, *verb*
to clean something off with a brush; **he
brushed the mud off his pants.**
brush up, *verb*

to make better/to improve; **you must
brush up on your German if you are
going to work in Germany.**

buck·et [ˈbʌkɪt] *noun*
large round container with a handle on
top, used for carrying liquids; **she got a
bucket of water from the river; they
threw buckets of water on the fire.**
buck·et·ful, *noun*
amount you can carry in a bucket; **he
poured a bucketful of milk down the
drain.**

bud [bʌd] *noun*
flower which has not yet opened; **a rose
bud.**
bud·dy, *noun*
friend.
plural **buddies**

bug [bʌg] *noun*
insect; **the bugs were crawling around the
lamp.**

build [bɪld] *verb*
to make something by putting pieces
together/by putting bricks/stones, etc.,
on top of each other; **the house was
built in 1900; we are building a new
church; the government is going to build
a highway across this field; he built the
model plane out of pieces of wood.**
builds—building—built [bɪlt]—**has
built**

build·er, *noun*
person who makes houses/offices, etc.
build·ing, *noun*
thing which has been built (such as a
house/a train station/a factory, etc.);
**the bomb destroyed several buildings; his
office is on the top floor of the building;
they will have to knock several buildings down to build the new highway.**

bulb [bʌlb] *noun*
(*a*) glass ball which produces electric
light; **we must get a new bulb for the light
in the kitchen; I can't use the flashlight—
it hasn't got a bulb.**
(*b*) thick round part of a plant, which
you put in the soil and which grows into
a flower.

bull [bʊl] *noun*

male of cattle; **there are three bulls and ten cows in the field.**
bull·doz·er, *noun*
large tractor which can push earth.

bump [bʌmp] 1. *noun*
(*a*) slight knock against something; **the plane landed with a bump.**
(*b*) slightly raised part; **he has a bump on the back of his head; the car went slowly over the bumps in the road.**
2. *verb*
to knock slightly; **the car bumped into a tree; I bumped into her at the bus stop** = I met her by chance.
bumps—bumping—bumped—has bumped

bump·er, *noun*
metal bar at the front or rear of an automobile.
bump·y, *adjective*
not flat; covered with bumps; **a bumpy road.**
bumpy—bumpier—bumpiest

bunch [bʌntʃ] *noun*
group of flowers tied together; group of grapes/of bananas; **the children picked bunches of flowers; when you go shopping can you buy a bunch of grapes?**
plural **bunches**

bur·glar [ˈbɜrglər] *noun*
person who breaks into a house to steal things; **burglars broke into the house and stole our silver; he woke up to find a burglar in his bedroom.**
bur·gla·ry, *noun*
stealing from a house; **there have been three burglaries on our street.**
plural **burglaries**

bur·ies [ˈbeəriz], **bur·ied** [ˈbeərid] *see* **bury**

burn [bɜrn] *verb*
to destroy by fire; to be on fire; **call the fire department—the school is burning! all our papers were burned in the fire; she burned her hand on the hot pan; look, you've burned the sausages** = cooked them too much, so that they are black.
burns—burning—burned/burnt—has burned/burnt

burn down, *verb*
to burn completely; **he was playing with matches and burned the house down; the school burned down before the firemen arrived.**
burn·er, *noun*
part of a stove which heats a pan.

burst [bɜrst] *verb*
to break; **he blew up the balloon until it burst; she burst all the balloons with a pin; don't eat so much or you'll burst; they burst into the room** = they rushed into the room; **he burst into tears** = he suddenly started to cry; **she burst out laughing** = she suddenly started to laugh.
burst—bursting—burst—has burst

bur·y [ˈbeəri] *verb*
to put something into the ground; to cover; **the dog has buried a bone in the garden; the path was buried under the snow; he died on Monday and was buried on Friday.**
buries—burying—buried—has buried

bus [bʌs] *noun*
motor vehicle for carrying many passengers; **why do you go by bus?—it's cheaper than the train; she takes the bus every morning to go to work; he missed the last bus and had to walk home; London buses are red; a school bus takes the children to school; the number 6 bus goes downtown.**
plural **buses**

bus stop, *noun*
place where you can get on or off a bus; **there was a long line of people waiting at the bus stop.**

bush [buʃ] *noun*
plant which is smaller than a tree; **the children hid in the bushes.**
plural **bushes**

bush·y, *adjective*
(*of hair*) growing close together; **he has bushy eyebrows.**

busi·ness [ˈbiznəs] *noun*
work of buying or selling things; company

which buys or sells things; **he runs a used car business; she's in business selling dresses; they do business with several European countries.**
plural **businesses**

busi·ness·man, *noun*
man who buys or sells things; man who runs a business.
plural **businessmen**

bus·y ['bɪzi:] *adjective*
occupied with doing something; **he was busy washing the car; the shop is very busy today** = there are a lot of customers; **she's busy with her exams; I was too busy to buy you a present; the line's busy** = the telephone is being used.
busy—busier—busiest

but [bʌt] *conjunction*
(*suggesting the opposite*) **he is very tall, but his sister is quite short; I would like to come, but I am not free that evening; but you said you would give me $10!**

butch·er ['bʊtʃər] *noun*
man who sells meat.
butch·er shop, *noun*
store which sells meat; **go to the butcher shop and buy some beef.**

but·ter ['bʌtər] *noun*
solid yellow stuff made from cream; **he was spreading butter on a piece of bread; fry the onions in butter.**
no plural: **some butter; a piece of butter**

but·ter·fly, *noun*
insect with large brightly colored wings.
plural **butterflies**
but·ter·scotch ['bʌtərskɒtʃ] *noun*
candy made of butter and brown sugar.

but·tocks ['bʌtəks] *plural noun*
part of the body which you sit on; **he got a kick in the buttocks.**

but·ton ['bʌtn] 1. *noun*
(*a*) small round object attached to clothes which you use to fasten one part of the clothing to another; **his coat has buttons down the front; do up the buttons on your coat; can you sew this button on?**
(*b*) small round object which you push to ring a bell, etc.; **press the button to**

open the doors of the elevator; press the top button if you want a cup of coffee.
2. *verb*
to attach with buttons; **he buttoned up his coat, because it was cold.**
buttons—buttoning—buttoned— has buttoned
Note: **button your coat up** *or* **button up your coat,** *but only* **button it up**

but·ton·hole, *noun*
hole for putting a button through.

buy [baɪ] *verb*
to get something by paying money; **I bought a book on my way home; he has bought a new car; what have you bought her for Christmas? he bought his wife a fur coat; I've bought myself a new watch; he wants to buy a car for his sister.**
buys—buying—bought [bɔːt]**—has bought**

buy·er, *noun*
person who buys.

by [baɪ] 1. *preposition*
(*a*) near; **the house by the traffic lights; sit down here by the fire.**
(*b*) before; **try to get home by 10 o'clock; you must finish your work by Friday.**
(*c*) (*showing means or method*) **send the letter by airmail; he goes to school by bus; she made the cake by mixing eggs and flour; he caught a cold by standing in the rain.**
(*d*) (*showing the person or thing that did something*) **a play by Shakespeare; now here is some music by the school band; the mailman was bitten by the dog; I was knocked down by a bus.**
(*e*) (all) **by yourself** = alone; **she's all by herself all day; he built his house by himself; you can find the house by yourself.**
(*f*) (*showing amount*) **fares have been increased by 10%; they beat us by 10 points.**
2. *adverb*
past; **he drove by without stopping.**
by and large = generally/mostly; **by and large, fat people are happier than thin ones.**
by heart = from memory/remember-

ing; he could say the whole poem by heart.

by the way (*used to introduce something which does not seem very important*) by the way, did you see the TV program on cats yesterday?

bye (**-bye**) [baɪ('baɪ)] *interjection* (*used when you are leaving someone*) bye!—see you on Thursday!

Cc

cab [kæb] *noun*
car with a driver whom you can pay to take you somewhere; **can you call a cab for me?** there are no buses after ten o'clock so we took a cab to the airport. **cab driv·er, cab·man,** *noun* person who drives a cab.

cab·bage ['kæbɪdʒ] *noun*
green vegetable of which you eat the leaves; **the kitchen smells of boiled cabbage;** he has a row of cabbages in the garden.
Note: as food, **cabbage** *does not have a plural:* **some cabbage; a spoonful of cabbage;** *as plants you can count* **two cabbages,** *etc.*

cab·in ['kæbɪn] *noun*
small wooden house; **he lives in a cabin in the mountains.**

ca·fé [kə'feɪ] *noun*
small restaurant which serves coffee and light meals; **let's meet at the café on the corner of Main Street.**

cage [keɪdʒ] *noun*
box made of thick metal bars or wire, which you keep wild animals or birds in; **the little yellow bird was singing in its cage; the white mouse ran across the cage.**

cake [keɪk] *noun*
food made by baking flour, sugar, eggs, dried fruit, etc., in an oven; **he had a birthday cake with six candles on it; a carrot cake;** would you like some more cake? **have a slice of chocolate cake.**
Note: as food **cake** *does not have a plural:* **some cake; a piece of cake;** *when it means a particular piece of food it can have a plural:* **she baked ten cakes; there are no cakes left in the bakery**

cal·cu·late ['kælkjʊleɪt] *verb*
to find the answer to a sum; **he tried to calculate how much he had spent on gasoline;** can you calculate the distance from Toronto to Ottawa in kilometers? **I calculate that I have spent two hours on the phone to England.**
calculates—calculating— calculated—has calculated

cal·cu·la·tor, *noun*
machine for calculating; **I added up the bill on my pocket calculator.**

cal·en·dar ['kælɪndər] *noun*
piece of paper showing the days and months of a year; **he pinned the calendar onto the wall by his desk;** tear off the next page on the calendar—today is November 1.

calf [kæf] *noun*
baby cow; **a cow and her calf.**
plural **calves** [kævz]

call [kɔːl] 1. *noun*
speaking by telephone; **I want to make a call to Canada;** there were three calls for you while you were out.
2. *verb*
(*a*) to shout to tell someone to come; **call the children—it's time for supper; call me in at 7 o'clock** = tell me to come in at 7; **call a cab** = shout to a cab driver to come.
(*b*) to give someone or something a name; **his son is called Peter; his name is James, but everyone calls him Jim; we call our cat Natasha;** what do you call this thing for spreading glue?
(*c*) to telephone; **if he comes, tell him I'll call him when I'm in the office;** call a

cab—we have to get to the airport; Mr. Smith is out—shall I ask him to call you back? = to phone you.
(*d*) to visit; the police called at the house, but there was no one there; can you call on Aunt Betty tomorrow? he called on me at 10 o'clock.
calls—calling—called—has called
call off, *verb*
to decide not to do something which was planned; he called off his visit to New York.
call up, *verb*
to tell people to join the armed forces; thousands of men were called up at the beginning of the war.

calm [kɑːm] *adjective*
quiet; not rough; not excited; the sea is very calm; a calm evening; stay calm—don't get excited.
calm—calmer—calmest
calm·ly, *adverb*
in a calm way; he calmly walked into the burning house.

calves [kævz] *see* **calf**

came [keɪm] *see* **come**

cam·er·a [ˈkæmrə] *noun*
machine for taking pictures; he took a picture of the church with his new camera; do you have a film in your camera? movie camera = camera for taking movies.

camp [kæmp] 1. *noun*
(*a*) group of tents; the explorers set up their camp by the river.
(*b*) place where you live in the open on summer vacation; the children are going to camp this summer.
2. *verb*
to go on vacation in a tent; we go camping every summer; a camping trip; we camped by the side of the lake.
camps—camping—camped—has camped
camp·site, *noun*
place where you can camp.

can [kæn] 1. *noun*
(*a*) round metal container for keeping

food or drink; he opened a can of beer.
(*b*) container with a separate cover; a garbage can.
2. *verb used with other verbs*
(*a*) *to mean* be able; he can swim, but he can't ride a bicycle; you can't run as fast as I can; can you remember what the cop said?
(*b*) *to mean* be allowed; he says we can go in; the policeman says we can't park here.
(*c*) (*in asking politely*) can we come in? can you shut the door, please?
I can, you can, he can, we can, they can
Negative: **cannot**, *usually* **can't**
Past: **could, could not,** *usually* **couldn't**
Note: **can** *and* **could** *do not have* **to** *and are only used with other verbs*

ca·nal [kəˈnæl] *noun*
river made by men for boats to pass along; the Panama Canal.

can·dle [ˈkændəl] *noun*
stick of white or colored stuff which will burn and give a light; there were six candles on her birthday cake; the power has gone off—can you light a candle?

can·dy [ˈkændɪ] *noun*
small piece of sweet food made with sugar; eating too much candy is bad for your teeth; candy store = store which sells candy; he bought a bag of candies at the candy store.
Note: **candy** *as a food has no plural:* **too much candy/some candy/a piece of candy; candy** *can also mean* **a piece of candy,** *and has a plural:* **he ate three candies**

canned [kænd] *adjective*
in a can; canned fruit; canned beer.

can·not [ˈkænɒt] *see* **can**

can't [kænt] *see* **can**

can·yon [ˈkænjən] *noun*
deep valley with steep sides; we visited the Grand Canyon on our vacation.

cap [kæp] *noun*
(*a*) flat hat with a hard piece sticking

out over your face; **he was wearing an old black cap; a baseball cap.**

(b) top which covers something; **put the cap back on the bottle; a silver pen with a black cap.**

cap·i·tal ['kæpɪtəl] *noun*
(a) main city in a country, where the government is; **Rome is the capital of Italy; what is the capital of the United States?**
(b) large form of a letter of the alphabet; **Rome begins with a capital R; write your name in capitals.**
(c) money which you can use to start a business, or put in a bank to collect interest.
no plural for (c)

cap·tain ['kæptən] *noun*
officer in charge of a ship/of an aircraft; **go to see the captain; Captain Smith.**

car [kɑːr] *noun*
(a) small motor vehicle for carrying people; **he bought a new car; her car was stolen last night.**
(b) one of a group of vehicles which form a train; **dining car** = car where you can eat.
car·port, *noun*
shelter for a car.
car·wash, *noun*
place where cars are washed by a machine.

card [kɑːrd] *noun*
(a) piece of stiff paper with a picture on it which you can send with a message; **he sent me a card from Italy; how much does it cost to send a card to Canada? birthday card** = card which you send to someone to wish them a happy birthday; **Christmas card** = card which you send to someone at Christmas; *see also* **postcard.**
(b) piece of stiff paper with a picture or pattern on it, used to play various games; **a pack/a deck of cards; they were playing cards; do you want a game of cards?**
(c) piece of stiff plastic with numbers and letters printed on it, used to pay with instead of money; **he paid the check with his American Express card.**

card·board, *noun*
thick piece of card; **we put our books into cardboard boxes.**
no plural: **some cardboard; a piece of cardboard**

care ['keər] **1.** *noun*
(a) attention; **take care when you cross the street** = watch out; **he took care to lock the door; to take care of someone** = to look after someone; **he took care of his sister when she was sick.**
(b) (*on a letter*) **Mr. Brown, care of Mrs. Green** = Mr. Brown, at the address of Mrs. Green.
2. *verb*
to worry; to mind; **he doesn't care if his car is dirty; he couldn't care less** = he doesn't worry at all.
cares—caring—cared—has cared
care for, *verb*
(a) to like; **would you care for another piece of cake? I don't care for this music very much.**
(b) to look after; **nurses were caring for the wounded people.**
care·ful, *adjective*
taking care; **he was careful not to make any noise; be careful, that glass is valuable! she is very careful about what she eats.**
care·ful·ly, *adverb*
with great care; **carry the eggs carefully! drive carefully!**
care·less, *adjective*
without care; **he was careless and made mistakes in his homework; she made several careless mistakes.**

car·go ['kɑːrgəʊ] *noun*
goods which are carried (on a ship or airplane); **cargo ship** = ship which does not carry any passengers.
plural **cargoes**

car·pet ['kɑːrpɪt] *noun*
thick wool material for covering the floor, stairs, etc.; **he spilled his coffee on the carpet; we have bought a new carpet for the dining room.**

car·ried ['kærɪd], **car·ries** ['kærɪz] *see* **carry**

car·rot [ˈkærət] *noun*
long orange root vegetable; **boiled carrots; carrot cake; can you go to the supermarket and buy five pounds of carrots?**

car·ry [ˈkærɪ] *verb*
to lift something and move it to another place; **they had to carry the piano up the stairs; the bus was carrying sixty passengers; the box was too heavy to carry.**
carries—carrying—carried—has carried

car·ry on, *verb*
to continue/to go on doing something; **carry on with your work; carry on!** = go ahead!

car·ry out, *verb*
to do (something which has been planned); **they carried out a search for the missing children.**
Note: **we carried the plan out** *or* **we carried out the plan,** *but only* **we carried it out**

car·toon [kɑːrˈtuːn] *noun*
(*a*) funny drawing (usually in a newspaper); **the paper has a cartoon of the President.**
(*b*) movie made of moving drawings; **they were watching a cartoon on TV.**

case [keɪs] *noun*
(*a*) box with a handle, for carrying your things in; **he was packing his case; they bought a case of beer; put the gun in its case.**
(*b*) deciding in a court whether a person is guilty or not; **he is the judge on the murder case.**
in any case = whatever may happen /and yet; **he's late but in any case it doesn't matter.**
in case = because something might happen; **take your coat in case it is cold; I always carry an umbrella in case it rains.**
in that case = if that happens.

cash [kæʃ] 1. *noun*
money either in bills or coins; **he paid for the bicycle in cash; can I pay by check**

as I don't have very much cash on me?
no plural: **some cash; a lot of cash**
2. *verb*
to change a check into money; **he cashed the check at the bank.**
cashes—cashing—cashed—has cashed

cas·sette [kəˈset] *noun*
plastic box with a tape on which music or words can be recorded; **a cassette recorder; he played a cassette of Spanish music.**

cas·tle [ˈkæsəl] *noun*
large building with strong walls which soldiers can defend; **Windsor Castle; the soldiers shut the castle gate.**

cat [kæt] *noun*
furry pet with a long tail; **the cat sat in front of the fire; what a beautiful cat! she gave the cat some fish to eat.**

catch [kætʃ] *verb*
(*a*) to hold something which someone has thrown/which is flying in the air; **see if you can catch the ball; she caught the ball in her left hand.**
(*b*) to stop and hold (an animal); **we caught three fish; he sat by the river all day but didn't catch anything; our cat is good at catching mice.**
(*c*) to get on (a bus/a train, etc.) before it goes; **you will have to run if you want to catch the nine o'clock bus; he caught the last plane to Denver.**
(*d*) to get a disease; **he caught a cold from standing in the rain; she caught mumps.**
(*e*) to find someone doing something wrong; **she caught him stealing apples; the police caught the burglar as he was climbing out the window.**
(*f*) to hear; **I didn't quite catch what you said.**
catches—catching—caught [kɔːt] **—has caught**

catch on, *verb*
to understand.

catch up with, *verb*
to join someone who is moving in front of you; **if you run you will catch up**

with the others; he walked so slowly that we soon caught up with him.

cat·tle [ˈkætəl] *noun*
animals of the cow family; he owns two thousand cattle.
no plural: **many cattle; a few cattle.**

caught [kɔːt] *see* **catch**

cause [kɔːz] 1. *noun*
reason why something happens; what was the cause of the accident?
2. *verb*
to make something happen; the accident was caused by thick fog.
causes—causing—caused—has caused

ceil·ing [ˈsiːlɪŋ] *noun*
top part which covers a room; each room has four walls, a floor and a ceiling; flies can walk on the ceiling; he painted the bathroom ceiling.

cel·lar [ˈselər] *noun*
rooms in a house which are underground; we keep our washer in the cellar.

ce·ment [sɪˈment] *noun*
(a) powder which you mix with sand and water to make concrete; he bought a bag of cement.
(b) strong glue used for making models; you will need some rubber cement to glue the pieces together.
no plural

cent [sent] *noun*
small coin used in the U.S.A. and in many other countries, which is one hundredth of a dollar; this book only costs twenty-five cents (25¢).
cent *is usually written* ¢ *with numbers:* **25¢**

cen·ti·me·ter [ˈsentɪmiːtər] *noun*
measurement of how long something is; one hundredth part of a meter; the table is sixty centimeters (60 cm) wide.
centimeter *is usually written* **cm** *with figures*

cen·ter [ˈsentər] *noun*
(a) middle; a tree was growing in the center of the field; there will be a lot of

traffic in the center of town; this chocolate has orange cream in the center.
(b) large building or group of buildings; **shopping center** = group of several stores together in one place.
(c) (*in sports*) player who is in the middle of the field.

cen·tral, *adjective*
of the center; **central heating** = heating which heats the whole house from one heater.

cen·tu·ry [ˈsentʃərɪ] *noun*
hundred years; **the nineteenth (19th) century** = the period from 1800 to 1899; a 19th-century church.
plural **centuries**

ce·re·al [ˈsiːrɪəl] *noun*
(a) plant whose seeds are used for food, especially to make flour; the farmer grows cereals; a cereal crop.
(b) food made of seeds of corn, etc., which you eat at breakfast; he ate a bowl of cereal; you put milk and sugar on your cereal.

cer·e·mo·ny [ˈseərəməʊnɪ] *noun*
official event; the prize-giving ceremony will be held in the school hall.
plural **ceremonies**

cer·tain [ˈsɜːtən] *adjective*
(a) sure; the police are certain he is the thief; this horse is certain to win the race; he locked the door to make certain that no one could steal his money.
(b) (person/thing) which you don't know or which you are not sure of; a certain Mr. Smith called while you were out; certain plants can make you sick if you eat them.
(c) **a certain amount** = some; the storm did a certain amount of damage; painting the house will take a certain amount of time.

cer·tain·ly, *adverb*
of course; will you come to the party?— certainly I'll come; please tell him to write to me—certainly, sir.

chain [tʃeɪn] 1. *noun*
number of metal rings attached together to make a long line; he wore a gold cross

on a chain around his neck; that dog should be kept on a chain = should be attached with a chain.

2. *verb*

to attach with a chain; **the dog was chained to the gate.**

chains—chaining—chained—has chained

chair [tʃeər] *noun*

piece of furniture which you sit on; **someone has been sitting in my chair; pull up a chair and have some supper; this chair is very hard and not very comfortable.**

chair·man, *noun*

person who is in charge of a meeting; **Mr. Smith was the chairman at the meeting.**

chalk [tʃɔːk] *noun*

soft white rock; piece of material for writing on a blackboard; **the hills are made of chalk; there are chalk hills along the south coast of England; he wrote on the blackboard with colored chalk.**

chalk·board, *noun*

blackboard/large board on the wall of a classroom which you can write on with chalk.

chance [tʃæns] *noun*

(*a*) possibility; **does he have any chance of winning?—yes, I think he has a good chance of winning; is there any chance of getting a cup of coffee? there is no chance of the weather turning cold.**

(*b*) situation which allows you to do something; **I've been waiting for a chance to speak to the manager; he never had the chance to visit Canada.**

(*c*) luck; **it was quite by chance that we were traveling on the same bus.**

Note: **chance of —ing** = possibility, *but* **chance to** = situation allowing you to do something

change [tʃeɪndʒ] 1. *noun*

(*a*) being different; **we usually go on vacation in August, but this year we're going in July for a change; a cup of tea is a change after several cups of coffee; I think it's a change for the better** = I think it has improved things.

(*b*) **small change** = money in coins; **I've only got a $20 bill, I have no small**

change at all; **do you have change for a $10 bill?**

(*c*) money which you get back when you have given more than the correct price; **the book is $3.50, so you get $1.50 change from $5; you've given me too much change.**

no plural for (b) and (c)

2. *verb*

(*a*) to make something different; to become different; **popular music has changed in the last few years; he has changed so much since I saw him last, that I didn't recognize him; I've changed my mind** = I've decided to do something different.

(*b*) to put on different clothes; **he changed into his old clothes before fixing the car; go into my bedroom if you want to change your dress.**

(*c*) to give something in place of something else; **you ought to change your car tires; can you change a $5 bill?** = can you give me small change for it? **to get to New Orleans you will have to change at Birmingham** = to get on to another train or bus.

changes—changing—changed—has changed

char·ac·ter [ˈkærəktər] *noun*

(*a*) part of you which makes you different from other people; all your personal qualities; **she has a pleasant character; he has character** = he is a strong person who acts according to his beliefs.

(*b*) person in a play/book; **at the end of the play all the main characters are dead.**

charge [tʃɑːrdʒ] 1. *noun*

(*a*) money which you have to pay to do something; **there is no charge for service; there is a 10% service charge; we will send the package free of charge** = without asking you to pay.

(*b*) statement by the police which says someone has done something wrong; **he was kept in jail on a charge of trying to kill the President.**

(*c*) **in charge** = giving orders to/being the head of; **he is in charge of the department; who's in charge here? he took** charge of the class while the teacher was out of the room.

2. *verb*

(*a*) to make someone pay; **they charged me $3 for two glasses of orange juice; how much did you charge for fixing the car?**

(*b*) (*of the police*) to say that someone has done something wrong; **he was charged with stealing the silver.**

charges—charging—charged— has charged

chase [tʃeɪs] 1. *noun*

running after something; **the police caught up with the burglar after a 20-minute chase.**

2. *verb*

to run after someone to try to catch him; **the policeman chased the burglar; he was chased by two dogs.**

chases—chasing—chased—has chased

cheap [tʃiːp] *adjective*

(*a*) not costing a lot of money; **this coat is much cheaper than that one; choose the cheapest kind of meat; I bought these books cheap at the sale; how much is the cheapest ticket to the West Coast?**

(*b*) selfish with your money; **he's so cheap, he never leaves tips in restaurants.**

cheap—cheaper—cheapest

cheat [tʃiːt] 1. *noun* (*also* **cheater**)

person who tricks other people.

2. *verb*

to trick someone so that he loses; to break rules; **don't play cards with Paul—he cheats; the teacher caught him cheating in the class; the salesclerk tried to cheat me out of 50¢ by giving me the wrong change.**

cheats—cheating—cheated—has cheated

check [tʃek] 1. *noun*

(*a*) making sure/test to be sure; **the car has to go to the garage for a check; the police made a check on everyone who was in the building.**

(*b*) mark (√) to show that something is correct; **mark the correct answer with**

a check.

(*c*) note asking a bank to pay money from your account to another account; **I wrote my brother a check for $100; can I pay for the gloves by check?**

(*d*) note showing how much money you have to pay in a restaurant; **waiter, can I have the check please?**

(*e*) ticket; **baggage check** = ticket for baggage which you have given to an office to hold for a while.

2. *verb*

(*a*) to make sure; to test; **don't forget to check if the doors are all locked; he checked the times of trains with the travel agent; I asked the man at the garage to check the brakes.**

(*b*) to mark with a check; **check the correct answer.**

checks—checking—checked— has checked

check·book, *noun*

book made of several blank checks attached together.

check·ers, *noun*

game for two people, played on a board with black and white squares, using round pieces to play with; **do you want a game of checkers? don't play checkers with her—she always wins.**

check in(to), *verb*

to arrive and sign in at a hotel; **they checked in at 10 p.m.; he has checked into room 15.**

check out, *verb*

to leave a hotel; **they checked out in the morning; I'm checking out of room 15.**

check·room, *noun*

room in a restaurant where hats and coats are kept.

check up, *verb*

to make sure; **can you check up on the children?** = see if they are all right; **he checked up on the times of flights to Miami.**

check·up, *noun*

test; **I must go to the dentist for a check-up** = to see if there is something wrong with my teeth.

cheek [tʃiːk] *noun*

fat part of your face on each side of

your nose; **a little girl with red cheeks.**

cheer [tʃɪr] *verb*
to shout to show that you like something; **the crowd cheered when the home team won.**
cheers—cheering—cheered—has cheered

cheer up, *verb*
to become happier; to make someone happier; **this cartoon will soon cheer you up; she cheered up after we had been to see her.**

cheer·ful ['tʃiːrfʊl] *adjective*
happy; **he's always cheerful, even when things go wrong; you must try to stay cheerful; they sang a cheerful song as they worked.**

cheer·ful·ly, *adverb*
in a cheerful way; **he cheerfully agreed to make dinner.**

cheer·y, *adjective*
very happy; **the teacher gave a cheery smile.**
cheery—cheerier—cheeriest

cheese [tʃiːz] *noun*
solid food made from milk; **a piece of cheese; at the end of the meal, we'll have crackers and cheese; can I have a pound of cheese, please? cream cheese** = soft cheese; **blue cheese** = cheese with blue pieces in it.
plural **cheeses** *is only used to mean different kinds of cheese or several large round blocks of cheese. Usually no plural:* **some cheese; a piece of cheese**

chess [tʃes] *noun*
game for two people, played on a board with black and white squares; **would you like a game of chess? she plays chess very well; he's no good at chess.**
no plural

chest [tʃest] *noun*
(*a*) large box; **he kept his money in a large chest.**
(*b*) top part of your body where your heart and lungs are; **he hit me in the chest; she has a chest cold** = she has a bad cough.

chest of draw·ers, *noun*
piece of furniture made of several drawers one on top of the other.

chew [tʃuː] *verb*
to crush with your teeth; **he was chewing a piece of meat; you should chew your food slowly.**
chews—chewing—chewed—has chewed

chew·ing gum, *noun*
sweet stuff which you can chew for a long time but do not swallow.
no plural: **some chewing gum/a stick of chewing gum/a piece of chewing gum**

chick [tʃɪk] *noun*
baby hen; **a hen and her chicks.**

chick·en ['tʃɪkən] *noun*
(*a*) young hen; **the chickens were running all around the farm.**
(*b*) meat from a hen; **we had roast chicken for dinner; would you like another slice of chicken? can I have a chicken sandwich?**
no plural for (*b*): **some chicken; a slice of chicken/a piece of chicken**

chief [tʃiːf] **1.** *adjective*
most important; **he's the chief engineer; what is the chief cause of traffic accidents?**
2. *noun*
person in charge, especially the leader of a group of people.

chief·ly, *adverb*
in an important way/mainly.

child [tʃaɪld] *noun*
young boy or girl; **when I was a child TV didn't exist; here is a picture of him as a child; all the children were playing in the field; when do the children get out of school? how many children do they have?** = how many sons or daughters?
plural **children** ['tʃɪldrən]

child·hood, *noun*
time when you were a child; **he had a happy childhood in the country; she spent her childhood in Canada.**

chim·ney ['tʃɪmnɪ] *noun*
tall tube for taking away the smoke

from a fire; **all the smoke went up the chimney.**

plural **chimneys**

chin [tʃɪn] *noun*
bottom part of your face, below your mouth; **she hit him on the chin; he rested his chin on his hand while he was thinking.**

chi·na [ˈtʃaɪnə] *noun*
hard white material for making cups/plates, etc.; **a china teacup; put all the china away in the cupboard** = put away all the cups/saucers/plates, etc.

no plural: **some china; a piece of china** = a cup/a saucer, etc.

chip [tʃɪp] 1. *noun*
(*a*) little piece of wood/stone, etc.; **chips of stone flew in all directions.**
(*b*) **(potato) chips** = thin slices of potato fried until they are crisp.
2. *verb*
to take off in little pieces; **he chipped the old paint off the door.**

chips—chipping—chipped—has chipped

chip in, *verb*
to pay your part of something; **everyone chipped in to buy the boss a present.**

chip·munk [ˈtʃɪpmʌŋk] *noun*
small animal like a big mouse.

chipped, *adjective*
with a little piece broken off; **a chipped cup; this plate is chipped.**

choc·o·late [ˈtʃɒklət] *noun*
(*a*) sweet food made from seeds of a tree; **can I have a piece of chocolate? his mother made a chocolate cake; a bar of chocolate costs 40¢; milk chocolate** = light brown sweet chocolate.
(*b*) a single candy made from chocolate; **a box of chocolates; John ate six chocolates, and then felt sick.**
(*c*) drink made from chocolate powder; **I always have a cup of hot chocolate before I go to bed.**
(*d*) brown color, like chocolate; **we have a chocolate-colored carpet in the dining room.**

no plural for (a), (c) or (d)

choice [tʃɔɪs] *noun*

choosing/something which you choose; **the shop has a wonderful choice of shoes** = very many types of shoes for you to choose from; **I don't like her choice of music; have you made your choice yet? choice meat** = very good meat.

choose [tʃuːz] *verb*
to decide to take something/to buy something/to do something; **have you chosen what you want to eat? in the end, they chose to go to Mexico on vacation; there are too many dishes to choose from—I can't decide which one to choose; don't take too long choosing a book to read on vacation.**

chooses—choosing—chose [tʃəʊz]**—has chosen** [tʃəʊzən]

chop [tʃɒp] 1. *noun*
piece of meat on a curved bone from a pig or sheep; **we had lamb chops and potatoes; a pork chop.**
2. *verb*
to cut something into pieces with an ax/a knife; **he's in the yard chopping up wood for the fire; chop the onions into little pieces; they chopped down the tree** = made it fall down by cutting it with an ax.

chops—chopping—chopped—has chopped

chose [tʃəʊz], **cho·sen** [ˈtʃəʊzən] *see* **choose**

Chris·tian [ˈkrɪstʃən] *noun & adjective*
(person) who believes in Jesus Christ; **Christian name** = a person's first name; **I know his name is Smith, but what's his Christian name?**

Christ·mas [ˈkrɪsməs] *noun*
Christian holiday on December 25, the birthday of Jesus Christ; **Christmas Day** = December 25; **Christmas tree** = tree which is brought into the house at Christmas; **what did you get for Christmas?** = what presents did you get? **have you opened your Christmas presents yet? Christmas card** = special card sent to friends at Christmas.

church [tʃɜrtʃ] *noun*
building where Christians pray to God;

we go to church on Sundays; this is St. Mary's Church.

plural **churches**

ci·gar [sɪ'gɑːr] *noun*
thick brown roll of tobacco which you can light and smoke; **he was smoking a long cigar.**

cig·a·rette ['sɪgəret] *noun*
chopped tobacco rolled up in paper which you can light and smoke; **how many cigarettes does he smoke a day? she went into the store to buy some cigarettes.**

cir·cle ['sɜrkəl] *noun*
round shape; ring; **draw a circle in the middle of the piece of paper; the children sat in a circle.**

cit·y ['sɪtɪ] *noun*
large town; **which is the largest city in the United States? traffic is a big problem in large cities.**

plural **cities**

cit·i·zen ['sɪtɪzən] *noun*
person who lives in a town or country; **the citizens of New York are called New Yorkers; she's an American citizen.**

cit·y hall, *noun*
building where the city is governed.

claim [kleɪm] *verb*
(*a*) to ask for something as a right; **he claimed the prize.**
(*b*) to say that you own something; **we found a watch in the street, but no one has come to claim it.**
(*c*) to say something is true (but without being able to prove it); **he claimed he was a relative of mine; she claims that the police attacked her.**

claims—claiming—claimed—has claimed

clap [klæp] *verb*
to hit your hands together several times to show that you are pleased; **when the play finished everyone started clapping; the children all clapped when the principal said they would have a day's vacation.**

claps—clapping—clapped—has clapped

class [klæs] *noun*
(*a*) group of people (usually children) who study together; **the French class; there are thirty children in Gary's class; we attend an evening class to learn German** = lessons in German given in the evening; **she was in the class of 1976** = she finished her studies in 1976.
(*b*) people of the same general group; **working class** = people who mainly work with their hands; **middle class** = people who have studied for their jobs, such as doctors/teachers, etc.
(*c*) level at which something is judged; **first class** = very good; **second class** = not very good.
(*d*) type of seats or service in a plane/on a train; **he always travels first class; first class passengers; the second class fare is much less than the first class.**

plural **classes**

class·mate, *noun*
person who is or was in the same class as someone; **they were classmates at school; she invited her classmates to the party.**

class·room, *noun*
room in a school where children are taught; **when the teacher came into the classroom all the children stood up.**

clean [kliːn] **1.** *adjective*
not dirty; **do you have a clean handkerchief? these plates aren't clean; you won't get any food if your hands aren't clean.**

clean—cleaner—cleanest

2. *verb*
to make clean, by taking away dirt; **did you clean your room today? don't forget to clean your shoes; she was cleaning the bathroom when the telephone rang.**

cleans—cleaning—cleaned—has cleaned

clean·er, *noun*
person or thing which cleans; **the cleaner's** = store where clothes are cleaned; **I'm taking my suit to the cleaner's.**

clean out, *verb*
to make very clean; **you must clean out your room; she was cleaning out the kitchen cupboards.**

cleans·er ['klenzər] *noun*
powder for cleaning.

clean up, *verb*
to make everything neat (after a party, etc.).

clear ['klɪr] 1. *adjective*
(*a*) with nothing in the way; **the road is clear now; do you have a clear view of the TV picture? a clear blue sky.**
(*b*) easily understood; **he made it clear that he wanted us to leave; the words on the medicine bottle are not very clear.**
(*c*) which is not covered and which you can easily see through; **clear glass.**
clear—clearer—clearest

2. *verb*
to take something away which is blocking; **they cleared the streets of snow/they cleared the snow from the streets; he's clearing a blocked pipe in the kitchen; to clear the table** = to take away dirty knives/forks/plates, etc., after a meal.
clears—clearing—cleared—has cleared

clear a·way, *verb*
to remove something completely; **can you help to clear away the snow from the path?**
clear·ly, *adverb*
plainly/obviously; **he clearly did not like her dress; he didn't speak very clearly, so nobody understood what he said.**
clear out, *verb*
(*a*) to go away; **clear out! I don't want you here.**
(*b*) to empty completely; **can you clear out the drawers in your bedroom?**
clear up, *verb*
(*a*) to clean completely; **we had to clear up the mess after the party.**
(*b*) to solve a problem; **the police finally cleared up the mystery.**
(*c*) to get better; **I hope the weather clears up because tomorrow is our baseball game.**
Note: **clear that mess up** *or* **clear up that mess,** *but only* **clear it up**

clev·er ['klevər] *adjective*
smart/able to learn quickly; **she's very clever at business; he's the cleverest person in the family.**
clever—cleverer—cleverest

cli·mate ['klaɪmət] *noun*
general condition of the weather; **the climate here is very hot and dry.**

climb [klaɪm] *verb*
to go up; **he climbed up a tree; the children climbed over the wall; she climbed through the window and down the wall by a rope; the car climbed the steep hill with some difficulty; when you have climbed Everest, there is nothing higher to climb; he goes climbing every weekend** = he climbs mountains.
climbs—climbing—climbed—has climbed

clin·ic ['klɪnɪk] *noun*
small building where doctors and nurses care for patients; **she went to the school health clinic for a blood test.**

clock [klɒk] *noun*
machine which shows the time; **the school clock is always right; your clock is five minutes slow; the clock has stopped—it needs winding up;** *see also* **o'clock.**
clock·wise, *adverb*
in the direction the hands of a clock move; **turn the key clockwise to open the door.**

close¹ [kləʊs] *adjective & adverb*
very near/just next to something; **our house is close to the post office; stay close to me if you don't want to get lost; go further away—you're too close.**
close—closer—closest

close² [kləʊz] *verb*
(*a*) to shut; **please close the window; would you mind closing the door? the stores are closed on Sundays; he closed his book and turned on the TV.**
(*b*) to end (a business); **the store closed last week; they are going to close the factory.**
closes—closing—closed—has closed

clos·et ['klɒzət] *noun*
very small room where you can hang your clothes; **hang your coat in the closet.**

Clothes

1. belt
2. boot
3. button
4. cap
5. collar
6. dress
7. glove
8. handkerchief
9. hat
10. heel
11. helmet
12. jacket
13. jeans/pants
14. pocket
15. purse
16. raincoat
17. sandal
18. shirt
19. shoe
20. shorts
21. skirt
22. sleeve
23. sock
24. suit
25. sweater
26. tie
27. wallet
28. zipper

cloth [klɔ:θ] *noun*
material made of cotton, wool, etc.;
wipe the floor with a wet cloth.
Note: as material **cloth** *does not have
a plural:* **some cloth; a piece of
cloth;** *when it means a piece of
material* **cloth** *can have a plural:*
three cloths.

clothes [kləʊz] *plural noun*
things which you wear to cover your
body and keep you warm; he doesn't have
any clothes on; the policeman took off
his clothes and jumped into the river;
you ought to put some clean clothes on;
they haven't had any new clothes for
years.
clothes·line, *noun*
long rope for hanging wet clothes on to
dry.
clothes·pin, *noun*
small wood or plastic pin to attach
clothes to a line.
cloth·ing, *noun*
clothes.
no plural: **some clothing; a piece
of clothing**

cloud [klaʊd] *noun*
light white or gray mass floating in the
air; I think it is going to rain—look at
those clouds; the airplane flew above the
clouds; clouds of smoke poured out of the
house.
cloud·y, *adjective*
where the sky is covered with clouds; a
dull, cloudy day; the weather turned
cloudy; when it's cloudy, it isn't easy to
take good pictures.
cloudy—cloudier—cloudiest

club [klʌb] *noun*
(a) group of people who have the same
interest; place where these people meet;
a church club; I'm joining a health club;
our town has one of the best stamp clubs
in the country.
(b) large stick.
club·house, *noun*
place where a club meets.

Co. *see* **company**

coach [kəʊtʃ] 1. *noun*
(a) car for passengers on a train;

a train with eight coaches.
(b) person who trains people to play a
sport; tennis coach; he's a football coach.
plural **coaches**
2. *verb*
to train people to play a sport; he's
coaching the college tennis team.
**coaches—coaching—coached—
has coached**

coal [kəʊl] *noun*
black mineral which you can burn to
make heat; the power station burns coal.
no plural: **some coal; a lot of coal**

coast [kəʊst] *noun*
part of the land by the sea; after ten
days, they saw the coast of Africa in the
distance; the south coast is the warmest
part of the country.

coat [kəʊt] *noun*
(a) thing which you wear on top of other
clothes to keep yourself warm; you'll
need to put on a coat—it has just started
to snow; she was wearing a fur coat.
(b) fur on an animal; our cat has a
beautiful soft coat.
(c) a coat of paint = paint covering
something; we gave the door two coats
of paint = we painted the door twice.

co·coa ['kəʊkəʊ] *noun*
chocolate powder used to make a drink;
drink made from this powder; I always
have a cup of cocoa in the evening; put a
spoonful of cocoa into each cup.
no plural: **some cocoa; a spoonful
of cocoa; a cup of cocoa**

cof·fee ['kɔ:fi] *noun*
(a) drink made from ground seeds of a
plant; would you like a cup of coffee?
this coffee is too bitter; black coffee =
coffee with no cream in it.
(b) cup of coffee; three coffees and two
teas, please.
(c) brown color, like coffee; we have a
coffee-colored carpet in the living room.
no plural except when it means **a cup
of coffee**

cof·fee break, *noun*
short rest from work; we work from 8
to 12:30, with a coffee break at 10; we

went to talk to the manager during the coffee break.

cof·fee pot, *noun*
special pot for making coffee in.

cof·fee ta·ble, *noun*
low table for putting cups/glasses, etc. on.

coin [kɔɪn] *noun*
piece of metal money; he gave me my change in 10¢ and 5¢ coins; this telephone takes 10¢ coins; I've dropped a coin inside the piano.

cold [kəʊld] 1. *adjective*
not warm; not hot; you'll have to wash with cold water; the weather is colder than last week; they say it will be even colder tomorrow; it's so cold—I think it's going to snow; if you're cold, come and sit in the kitchen; my hands are cold, but my toes are warm; start eating, or your soup will get cold.

cold—colder—coldest

2. *noun*
illness, when you sneeze and cough; he caught a cold by standing in the rain; she has a cold, so she can't go out; mother is in bed with a cold; don't come near me—I've got a cold.

col·lar ['kɒlər] *noun*
(a) part of a coat/shirt, etc., which goes around your neck; my shirt collar's too tight; she turned up her coat collar because of the wind.
(b) piece of leather which goes around an animal's neck; our dog has his name written on his collar.

col·lect [kə'lekt] 1. *verb*
(a) to bring together various things; he collects stamps.
(b) to ask people to give money; I'm collecting for the children's home.

collects—collecting—collected— has collected

2. *adverb & adjective*
to call collect/to make a collect call = to ask the person you are calling to pay for the call; he called me collect from Los Angeles.

col·lec·tion [kə'lekʃən] *noun*
group of things which have been

brought together; he showed me his collection of gold coins; have you seen his stamp collection?

col·lege ['kɒlɪdʒ] *noun*
place where people study after they have left high school; I'm going to college next fall; my brother is on the college football team/my brother plays football for the college.

col·or ['kʌlər] *noun*
red/blue/yellow, etc., which allows you to tell the difference between two things which are exactly the same in shape and size; what color is your hat?—it's a pale blue color; I don't like the color of her dress; all the pictures in the book are in color; his socks are the same color as his shirt; color TV/color film = TV/film in all colors, and not just black and white.

col·or-blind, *adjective*
not able to tell the difference between certain colors; he's color-blind.

col·ored, *adjective*
in color; a colored postcard; a book with colored pictures.

col·or·ful, *adjective*
with many colors; a colorful painting.

comb [kəʊm] 1. *noun*
thing with many long teeth for making your hair look neat.
2. *verb*
to make your hair neat, using a comb; she was combing her hair; have you combed your hair?

combs—combing—combed—has combed

come [kʌm] *verb*
(a) to move toward here; come and see me again soon; he came to see me yesterday; they came to school by car; hide behind the door, there's someone coming; come up to my room for a cup of coffee; the teacher told him to come in.
(b) to happen; what comes after B in the alphabet? T comes before U; what comes next in the program?

comes—coming—came [keɪm]— **has come**

come a·cross, *verb*
to find by chance; I came across

this book in a little store.

come a·long, *verb*
to go with someone; come along with us = walk with us; come along, or you'll miss the bus! = hurry up.

come back, *verb*
to return; he left the house to go to work, but came back for his newspaper; come back here, I want to talk to you.

come down with, *verb*
to become sick; we all came down with colds; the baby has come down with measles.

come off, *verb*
to fall off; to stop being attached; the button has come off my shirt; the handle came off in my hand; the gum won't come off the chair.

come on, *verb*
(*a*) to hurry; come on, or we'll be late.
(*b*) to arrive; there's a storm coming on; I think I have a cold coming on.

come out, *verb*
(*a*) to move outside; he came out of the house.
(*b*) to appear for sale; the magazine comes out on Fridays.

come to, *verb*
to add up to; the check comes to more than $10.

come up, *verb*
(*a*) to come closer; his vacation is coming up soon.
(*b*) to be mentioned (in conversation); his name came up in the discussion.

come up with, *verb*
to mention; she came up with a good idea.

com·fort ['kʌmfərt] *verb*
to make someone feel better/less sad; the nurses were comforting the sick.
comforts—comforting—comforted—has comforted

com·fort·a·ble ['kʌmfərtəbəl] *adjective*
soft; (chair) which is soft to sit on; what a comfortable bed! the seats in the theater aren't very comfortable; make yourself comfortable = choose a soft chair, etc.

com·mand [kə'mænd] *noun*

(*a*) order; the soldiers were given the command to stop fighting.
(*b*) **in command** = in charge of (soldiers); who is in command here?

com·mand·er, *noun*
person who is in command of soldiers; General MacArthur was a famous army commander.

com·mit·tee [kə'mɪtɪ] *noun*
official group of people who decide/organize; the tennis club committee organizes the matches; he's on a committee of the art club; would you like to join the committee? there's a committee meeting at ten o'clock.

com·mon ['kɒmən] *adjective*
(*a*) ordinary/happening very frequently; accidents are quite common on this part of the highway; that's a common mistake.
(*b*) **in common** = belonging to more than one person; we have two things in common—we are all American and we all have red hair.
common—commoner—commonest

com·mon sense, *noun*
good sense; it's common sense to lock your car at night.

com·pa·ny ['kʌmpənɪ] *noun*
(*a*) business firm; the company is doing well; John Smith and Company.
(*b*) being together with other people; I always enjoy his company = enjoy being with him; will you keep me company? = will you stay with me so that I am not lonely?
plural companies *but no plural for* (*b*)
Note: Company *is written* Co. *in names of companies:* John Smith & Co.

com·pare [kəm'peər] *verb*
to look at two things to see how they are different; try on the two pairs of shoes to compare them; you can't compare canned fruit to/with fresh fruit; compared with/to his father, he is not very tall.
compares—comparing—compared—has compared

com·par·a·tive [kəm'pærətɪv] *noun*
form of an adjective or adverb which
compares; "fatter" is the comparative of
"fat"; "faster" is the comparative of
"fast."

com·par·i·son, *noun*
way of comparing; you can't make a
comparison between the two men.

com·pe·ti·tion [kɒmpə'tɪʃən] *noun*
test where several people try to win a
prize; a chess competition; she entered a
competition to win a vacation on the
West Coast.

com·plete [kəm'pliːt] **1.** *adjective*
whole/with all parts; I have a complete
set of the new stamps; he has read the
complete works of Shakespeare.
2. *verb*
to finish; he completed the whole job in
two days.
completes—completing—
completed—has completed

com·plete·ly, *adverb*
totally/all; the house was completely
destroyed; I completely forgot about her
birthday.

com·put·er [kʌm'pjuːtər] *noun*
machine which holds information and
which can solve problems; the list of
addresses is on the computer; the pay-
checks are sent out by the computer; the
police computer has a list of all car numbers and owners.

con·cern [kən'sɜrn] **1.** *noun*
(*a*) business; a large industrial concern.
(*b*) being worried about something;
concern for poor people; his health is
giving cause for concern.
2. *verb*
to deal with; to be connected with; it
doesn't concern you = it has nothing to
do with you; as far as food is concerned
= referring to food; as far as I'm concerned = as for me.
concerns—concerning—
concerned—has concerned

con·cerned, *adjective*
worried; I really am concerned about
your health.

con·cern·ing, *preposition*
about; I want to talk to you concerning
your son's behavior.

con·crete ['kɒnkriːt] *noun*
hard material like stone, made by mixing
cement, sand and water together; a concrete sidewalk; they made a path out of
concrete.
no plural

con·di·tion [kən'dɪʃən] *noun*
(*a*) state; the old car is in very good condition; he is sick, and his condition is getting worse; living conditions are very bad.
(*b*) term/something which has to be
agreed before something else is done;
I will come on condition that you pay me
= only if you pay me; I don't agree with
some of the conditions in the deal.

con·duct 1. *noun* ['kɒndʌkt]
way of behaving; the teacher sent him
out of the classroom because his conduct
was so bad; she got a prize for good conduct.
no plural
2. *verb* [kən'dʌkt]
to be in charge of (an orchestra).
conducts—conducting—
conducted—has conducted

con·duc·tor [kən'dʌktər] *noun*
(*a*) man who is in charge of an orchestra.
(*b*) man who is in charge of a train.

con·fuse [kən'fjuːz] *verb*
to make someone think wrongly; to
make things difficult for someone to
understand; if you all ask questions at the
same time, you will only confuse the
teacher; the program was confusing—I
couldn't understand it at all.
confuses—confusing—
confused—has confused

con·grat·u·late [kən'grætʃʊleɪt] *verb*
to give someone good wishes/to praise
someone for having done something; we
want to congratulate you on winning the
prize.
congratulates—congratulating—
congratulated—
has congratulated

con·grat·u·la·tions [kəngrætʃʊ'-leɪʃənz] *plural noun*
good wishes to someone on having done something; **congratulations on your success!/on your 21st birthday!**

Con·gress ['kɒŋgris] *noun*
group of people who are elected to make laws in the U.S.; **Congress has voted to increase spending; he has been elected to Congress.**
Note: **Congress** *is usually used without* **the**

Con·gress·man, **Con·gress·wom·an,** *noun*
man/woman who is a member of Congress.

con·junc·tion [kən'dʒʌŋkʃən]
word (like **and** or **but**) which joins two parts of a sentence.

con·nect [kə'nekt] *verb*
to join; **the stove is connected to the gas pipe; have you connected the electric wires to the power supply?**
connects—connecting—connected—has connected

con·nec·tion [kə'nekʃən] *noun*
something which joins; **what is the connection between the dead man and the murderer? is there any connection between the bombs and the election?**
in con·nec·tion with = concerning/referring to; **I want to speak to you in connection with your letter.**

con·science ['kɒnʃəns] *noun*
feeling which tells you if you have done something wrong; **he has a guilty conscience** = he knows he has done something wrong.

con·scious ['kɒnʃəs] *adjective*
knowing what is happening around you; **he became conscious of two red eyes looking at him in the dark; it was two days after the accident before she became conscious.**

con·sid·er [kən'sɪdər] *verb*
to think about something; **he is considering going on vacation to Europe; have you considered complaining to the manager?**
considers—considering—considered—has considered

con·sid·er·a·ble, *adjective*
quite large; **he lost a considerable amount of money; she has put a considerable amount of effort into her business.**
con·sid·er·a·bly, *adverb*
quite a lot; **he's considerably thinner than he was last year.**

con·sist of [kən'sɪstəv] *verb*
to be made of; **our English class consists of twenty girls and two boys; he had a snack consisting of an apple and a glass of milk.**
consists—consisting—consisted—has consisted

con·tain [kən'teɪn] *verb*
to hold; **this bottle contains two pints of milk; he had a box containing a knife, a piece of thread and some buttons.**
contains—containing—contained—has contained
con·tain·er, *noun*
thing (such as a box/a bottle) which holds something; **do you have a container for this soft cheese? the container cracked, and all the contents spilled out onto the road.**

con·tents ['kɒntents] *plural noun*
(*a*) things which are held in a container; **he turned the box upside down and the contents fell out onto the floor; the police were examining the contents of her suitcases.**
(*b*) what is written in a book/letter, etc.; **she wouldn't tell me the contents of the letter.**

con·test ['kɒntest] *noun*
game in which several people try to win a prize; **she took third place in the spelling contest; he entered a contest to win a trip to Spain.**

con·tin·ue [kən'tɪnjuː] *verb*
to go on doing something/to do something which you were doing before; **the talks continued for three days; the snow continued to fall for 24 hours; they continued their conversation; they continued eating as if nothing had happened.**
continues—continuing—continued—has continued

con·tin·u·al, *adjective*
which goes on all the time without stopping; which happens again and again; there were continual interruptions.

con·tin·u·ous, *adjective*
put together without breaks or stops; a continuous performance = film show where there are no breaks between the films.

con·trol [kən'trəʊl] 1. *noun*
power/keeping in order; he has no control over his children; the fireman brought the fire under control = stopped it from spreading; the fire got out of control = spread quickly.
2. *verb*
to keep in order; the police were controlling the traffic; we can't control the sales of foreign cars; the government controls the price of bread.
controls—controlling—controlled—has controlled

con·trol tow·er, *noun*
tall building at an airport where the radio station is.

con·ven·ient [kən'viːnjənt] *adjective*
being near; being easy; it is so convenient to have your own washer; is 8:00 a convenient time for you?

cook [kʊk] 1. *noun*
person who fixes food; she's a very good cook = she makes very good food.
2. *verb*
(a) to fix food; you should learn how to cook—it's quite easy; I'm cooking breakfast; how do you cook cabbage?
(b) (of food) to be got ready; supper is cooking in the oven; how long does this meat take to cook? the chicken isn't cooked enough.
cooks—cooking—cooked—has cooked

cook·book, *noun*
book which tells you how to cook food.

cook·ie, *noun*
small hard sweet cake; she has eaten a pack of chocolate cookies.

cook·out, *noun*
party where food is cooked and eaten outdoors.

cool [kuːl] 1. *adjective*
not very warm/quite cold; the weather has suddenly become cooler; keep this bottle in a cool place; what I want is a tall, cool drink.
cool—cooler—coolest
2. *verb*
to become cool; put the milk in the refrigerator to cool.
cools—cooling—cooled—has cooled

cool down, *verb*
to become cool; has your soup cooled down enough? we sat in the shade of a tree to cool down.

cool off, *verb*
to become cool; we cooled off by going for a swim; wait until your soup has cooled off a little.

cop [kɒp] *noun*
policeman; the burglars were caught by the cops.

cop·y ['kɒpɪ] 1. *noun*
(a) thing which is made to look like something else; this isn't a real picture by Picasso, it's only a copy; to type a letter and make two copies.
(b) a book/a newspaper; have you got a copy of Shakespeare's plays? I've lost my copy of "The New York Times."
plural copies
2. *verb*
to make something which looks like something else; she copied the letter; he copies his father's way of walking; if you are caught copying answers from your neighbor you will be punished.
copies—copying—copied—has copied

cord [kɔːrd] *noun*
electric wire; he tripped over the cord leading to the TV; the burglars cut the telephone cord.

cork [kɔːrk] 1. *noun*
(a) very light material from the bark of a tree; the floor was covered with cork.
(b) round piece of this material, used to close a wine bottle; he pulled the cork

out of the bottle; the cork won't go back into the bottle.

2. *verb*

to cork a bottle = to put a cork into a bottle.

corks—corking—corked—has corked

cork·screw, *noun*

tool like a twisted nail with a handle, used to pull corks out of bottles.

corn [kɔːrn] *noun*

type of cereal crop with big seeds; **the farmers grow thousands of tons of corn.**

no plural: **some corn, a field of corn**

corn·field, *noun*

a field with corn growing in it.

corn·flakes, *plural noun*

breakfast cereals made from corn.

corn·meal, *noun*

yellow flour made from corn.

cor·ner [ˈkɔːrnər] *noun*

place where two walls, sides or streets join; **the store is on the corner of the street; put the chair in the far corner of the room; the police car went around the corner at top speed; she was waiting at the street corner; he turned the corner** = went around the corner.

cor·rect [kəˈrekt] **1.** *adjective*

right; **what is the correct time? you have to give correct answers to all the questions if you want to win a prize; your answer isn't correct—try again.**

2. *verb*

to show the mistakes in something; to change something from wrong to right; **the teacher is correcting our homework; you must try to correct your spelling; the car keeps turning to the left—can you correct this fault?**

corrects—correcting—corrected—has corrected

cor·rec·tion [kəˈrekʃən] *noun*

showing the mistake in something; making something correct.

cor·rect·ly, *adverb*

in a correct way; **he answered all the questions correctly and won the prize.**

cost [kɒst] **1.** *noun*

amount which you have to pay for something; **what is the cost of a ticket for the movies? the cost of living** = amount which you pay for food, heating, etc.

2. *verb*

to have a price; **apples cost 50¢ a pound; gasoline seems to cost more all the time; this table cost $50; what does it cost?** = how much is it?

costs—costing—cost—has cost

cot·ton [ˈkɒtən] *noun*

soft white material from a plant growing in warm climates; **a cotton shirt; this suit is made of cotton.**

no plural: **some cotton; a piece of cotton**

cough [kɔːf] **1.** *noun*

noise made when you send air out of your lungs suddenly because your throat hurts; **he gave a little cough to get the waiter's attention; I have a bad cough** = my throat hurts and this makes me cough frequently.

2. *verb*

to send air out of your lungs suddenly because your throat hurts; **the smoke made me cough; he has a cold and keeps on coughing and sneezing.**

coughs—coughing—coughed—has coughed

could [kʊd] *verb used with other verbs*

(*a*) *to mean* was able/were able/would be able; **he fell down and couldn't get up; you could still catch the train if you ran fast.**

(*b*) *to mean* was allowed/were allowed; **the policeman said we could cross the street.**

(*c*) (*in asking politely*) **could you pass me the sugar, please? could you shut the door?**

Negative: **could not,** *usually* **couldn't** *Note:* **could** *is the past of* **can; could** *does not have* **to** *and is only used with other verbs*

coun·cil [ˈkaʊnsəl] *noun*

group of people elected to run something; **city council** = elected committee which runs a city.

The Country

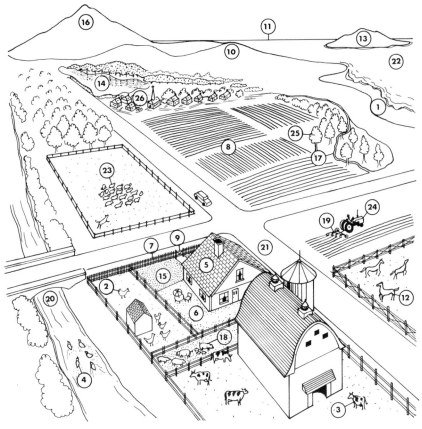

1. beach
2. chicken
3. cow
4. duck
5. farmhouse
6. farmyard
7. fence
8. field
9. gate
10. hill
11. horizon
12. horse
13. island
14. lake
15. lawn
16. mountain
17. path
18. pig
19. plow
20. river
21. road
22. sea
23. sheep
24. tractor
25. tree
26. village

count [kaʊnt] *verb*

(*a*) to say numbers in order; **the little girl can count up to ten; count to three, and then start running.**

(*b*) to add up to a total; **can you count how many books we have? he counted up the figures on the bill.**

(*c*) to include; **there were thirty people, if you count the children; we have four television sets, not counting the one which doesn't work.**

counts—counting—counted—has counted

count on, *verb*

to expect; **can I count on you to help? don't count on having nice weather for your picnic.**

coun·try [ˈkʌntrɪ] *noun*

(*a*) area of land which is separate and which governs itself; **Mexico is a country to the south of the United States; the countries in the United Nations.**

(*b*) area which is not the city; **he has a house in the country/a country house.**

plural **countries,** *but no plural for (b)*

coun·try·side, *noun*

large area away from cities; **the New England countryside.**

no plural

cou·ple [ˈkʌpəl] *noun*

two things/two people; **it will only take a couple of minutes; there are a couple of questions I want to ask; he ate a couple of sandwiches; the book only costs a couple of dollars** = about $2; **a married couple** = two people who are married.

course [kɔːrs] *noun*

(*a*) passing of time; **in the course of the last few years** = during the last few years.

(*b*) group of lessons; **I'm taking a course in mathematics; she's taking a painting course; he teaches a course in French at the college.**

(*c*) dish of food for part of a meal; **the first course is soup, and then you can have chicken or beef; we had a three-course dinner.**

of course = naturally; **he is rich, so of course he has a big car; are you coming**

with us?—**of course! do you want to lose all your money?—of course not!**

court [kɔːrt] *noun*

(*a*) place where a judge decides if someone is guilty or not; **he appeared in court, charged with stealing the TV set.**

(*b*) place where a game of tennis is played.

court·room, *noun*

room where a judge decides if someone is guilty or not; **the crowd filled the courtroom; the courtroom was quiet when the judge began to speak.**

cous·in [ˈkʌzən] *noun*

son or daughter of your uncle or aunt; **he went to stay with his cousin; I got a letter from Cousin Charles.**

cov·er [ˈkʌvər] 1. *noun*

(*a*) thing put over something to keep it clean, etc.; **keep a cover over your type-writer when you are not using it; book with a hard cover** = book with stiff cardboard back and front.

(*b*) **to take cover** = to hide/to shelter; **when people began to shoot, the police-man took cover behind a wall.**

2. *verb*

to put something over something to keep it clean, etc.; **you should cover the floor with newspapers before you start painting the ceiling; she covered her face with her hands.**

covers—covering—covered—has covered

cov·er up, *verb*

to cover completely; **he covered up the mark on the wall with white paint.**

cow [kaʊ] *noun*

(*a*) large female animal, kept to produce milk and used for meat; **a field of cows; the farmer was milking a cow.**

(*b*) female of some animals; **a cow elephant.**

Note: the meat from a **cow** *is* **beef**

cow·boy, *noun*

man who takes care of cattle.

crack [kræk] 1. *noun*

thin break; **there's a crack in this glass;**

we looked through a crack in the fence
= through a long thin hole.
2. *verb*
(*a*) to make a thin break in something;
to split; **the stone cracked the window;
she cracked a bone in her leg; he
dropped the cup and it cracked.**
(*b*) **to crack a joke** = to tell a joke.
**cracks—cracking—cracked—has
cracked**

crack·er, *noun*
small hard cake, often salty, but not
sweet; **he had crackers with his soup.**

crane [kreɪn] *noun*
tall machine for lifting heavy objects;
**they lifted the parts of the factory roof
with a crane.**

crash [kræʃ] 1. *noun*
(*a*) accident where cars/planes, etc. are
damaged; **he was killed in an automobile
crash; none of the passengers was hurt in
the crash; crash helmet** = hard hat worn
by motorcyclists, etc.
(*b*) loud noise; **the chair fell over with a
crash; there was a crash, and the plates
lay on the floor in pieces.**
plural **crashes**

2. *verb*
(*a*) (*of vehicles*) to hit something and be
damaged; **the car crashed into the wall;
the plane crashed** = it hit the ground.
(*b*) to make a loud noise; **the tree came
crashing down; the pile of plates crashed
onto the floor.**
**crashes—crashing—crashed—has
crashed**

3. *adjective*
rapid; **he took a crash course in German** = a course to learn German very
quickly.

crawl [krɔːl] *verb*
(*a*) to go forward on your hands and
knees; **he crawled through the hole in the
fence; the baby is learning to crawl.**
(*b*) to go very slowly; **the traffic was
crawling over the bridge.**
**crawls—crawling—crawled—has
crawled**

cra·zy [ˈkreɪzɪ] *adjective*
very stupid; mad; **what a crazy thing to**

do! **that loud music is driving me crazy;
she is crazy about skiing** = she loves
skiing.
crazy—crazier—craziest

cream [kriːm] *noun*
(*a*) rich part of milk full of fat which
rises to the top; **I like fruit with cream;
will you take cream in your coffee?**
(*b*) soft paste; **face cream** = paste for
putting on your face to make the skin
soft.

crew [kruː] *noun*
group of people who work on a boat/
airplane, etc.; **the plane had twenty passengers and a crew of six; when the ship
began to sink, the crew jumped into the
water.**

cried [kraɪd], **cries** [kraɪz] *see* **cry**

crime [kraɪm] *noun*
action which is against the law; **it is a
crime to steal someone's money; the
police are trying to reduce crime in the
city** = reduce the number of crimes.
crim·i·nal [ˈkrɪmɪnəl] *noun*
person who has done a crime; **the
policeman arrested a group of criminals.**

crisp [krɪsp] *adjective*
dry; making a cracking noise when
broken; **the snow is crisp; the crackers
aren't crisp—they must have got wet.**
crisp—crisper—crispest

crop [krɒp] *noun*
vegetables/plants, etc., grown for food;
**we have a good crop of tomatoes this year;
the corn crop will be small; root crops** =
vegetables like carrots, where you eat the
root and not the leaves.

cross [krɒs] 1. *adjective*
angry; **mother is cross with you for
drawing on the kitchen wall; don't be
cross—he didn't do it on purpose.**
2. *noun*
shape made of a line standing straight
up with another going across it, used as
a sign of the Christian church; **there is a
cross on the top of the church; the Red
Cross** = international organization
which provides medical help.
plural **crosses**

3. *verb*
to go across; don't cross the road without looking to see if there is any traffic coming; he crossed the river in a small boat; the railroad crosses the road about two miles from here; she sat down and crossed her legs = put one leg over the other.

crosses—crossing—crossed—has crossed

cross·ing, *noun*
(*a*) action of going across water; how long is the crossing from England to France? we had a rough crossing = the sea was rough.
(*b*) place where you go across a street; place where two steets cross; you must cross the street at the crossing; cars have to take care at the railroad crossing.

cross off, cross out, *verb*
to put a line through something which has been written, to show that it should not be there; he was sick, so we crossed his name off the list; I can't read her letter—she has crossed out so many words.

cross·roads, *noun*
place where two roads cross.

cross·walk, *noun*
place where you go across a street; only cross the street at the crosswalk.

cross·word puz·zle, *noun*
puzzle where small squares have to be filled with letters to spell words; I can't do the crossword puzzle in today's paper; I finished the crossword puzzle in 25 minutes.

crowd [kraʊd] **1.** *noun*
large number of people; there were crowds of people trying to do their Christmas shopping; a crowd of children rushed into the museum.
2. *verb*
to come together in a crowd; people crowded into the stores to do their Christmas shopping; the train was crowded = was full of people.

crowds—crowding—crowded—has crowded

cru·el [ˈkruːəl] *adjective*
which likes to cause pain; it is cruel to hit your dog with a stick.

cry [kraɪ] **1.** *noun*
shout; no one heard his cries for help.
plural **cries**
2. *verb*
to have tears coming out of your eyes; she cried when her mother took away her toys; onions make me cry; why is the baby crying? she cries every time she sees this movie.

cries—crying—cried—has cried

cup [kʌp] *noun*
(*a*) small bowl with a handle for drinking tea or coffee, etc.; he was drinking milk out of a cup.
(*b*) drink contained in a cup; would you like a cup of tea? she drank two cups of coffee.
(*c*) silver jar given as a prize for winning a sports competition; he has won three cups in sailing.

cup·ful [ˈkʌpfʊl] *noun*
amount which a cup can hold; add two cupfuls of sugar.

cup·board [ˈkʌbərd] *noun*
piece of furniture with shelves and doors; put the flour in the cupboard; the plates are on the top shelf in the kitchen cupboard; the cupboard doors are painted white.

cure [kjʊr] **1.** *noun*
way of making an illness better; there is no cure for an ordinary cold.
2. *verb*
to make better; he was completely cured; can you cure bad eyesight? this disease can't be cured.

cures—curing—cured—has cured

curl [kɜrl] **1.** *noun*
piece of hair which twists into a small ring.
2. *verb*
to twist into small rings; her hair curls; the smoke curled up from the fire.

curls—curling—curled—has curled

curl up, *verb*
to roll up into a ball; **the cat was curled up in front of the fire; the little girl was curled up in the armchair.**
curl·y, *adjective*
twisting into small rings; **she has long, curly hair.**
curly—curlier—curliest

cur·rent [ˈkʌrənt] **1.** *noun*
water/electricity which flows; **the current in the river is strong; the boat was carried away by the current; the electric current is too weak to make the machine work.**
2. *adjective*
referring to the present time; **current events** = things which are happening at the present time.
cur·rent·ly, *adverb*
at the present time.

cur·tain [ˈkɜrtən] *noun*
(*a*) long piece of cloth hanging in front of a window, etc.; **can you open the curtains? draw the curtains—it is getting cold** = close the curtains.
(*b*) long piece of cloth hanging in front of the stage in a theater; **the curtain goes up at 8:30** = the performance begins at 8:30.

curve [kɜrv] **1.** *noun*
line which bends around; road which bends around; **be careful when you drive around this curve; the car takes the curves very well** = is easy to drive around curves; **the cloth has a pattern of curves and straight lines.**
2. *verb*
to make a round shape; to bend around; **the road curves around the hill.**
curves—curving—curved—has curved

curved, *adjective*
with a shape which is not straight or flat; **a curved line; a curved window in a car.**

cush·ion [ˈkʊʃən] *noun*
bag filled with feathers or soft material, used for sitting on; **the sofa has three cushions; the chair with a red cushion.**

cus·tom·er [ˈkʌstəmər] *noun*
person who buys things in a store; person who is eating in a restaurant; **will you serve this customer, please? we had no customers, so we closed the store early.**

cus·toms [ˈkʌstəmz] *plural noun*
tax on goods coming into a country; government department which charges tax on goods coming into a country; **will I have to pay customs on this jewelry? when you come into the country, you have to pass through customs; the customs officer asked me to open my suitcase.**

cut [kʌt] **1.** *noun*
(*a*) piece which has been taken off, using a knife.
(*b*) place where something has been cut; **I had a bad cut on my leg; put a bandage on your cut.**
2. *verb*
(*a*) to make an opening, using a knife/scissors, etc.; to remove a piece of something, using a knife/scissors, etc.; **he cut the meat with his knife; she cut her finger on the broken glass; when are you going to get your hair cut? cut the cake into six pieces; he cut himself shaving.**
(*b*) to reduce the number of something; **accidents have been cut by 10%.**
cuts—cutting—cut—has cut
cut down, *verb*
(*a*) to make a tree fall down by using an ax/a saw, etc.; **he cut the tree down/he cut down the tree.**
(*b*) to reduce; **he's trying to cut down the number of cigarettes he smokes; the police hope that speed limits will cut down the number of accidents.**
cut off, *verb*
(*a*) to take away part of something by using a knife, etc.; **he cut off a piece of cake; she cut off a little piece of string.**
(*b*) to keep someone separate; **she was cut off from her friends by a crowd of schoolchildren.**
cut out, *verb*
(*a*) to remove a small piece from a large

piece; she cut out the picture from the newspaper; he cut the picture out with a pair of scissors.

(*b*) to stop; he's trying to cut out smoking; she's decided to cut out sweets; cut it out = stop it!

cut up, *verb*

to make into small pieces; cut the meat up into little pieces.

Note: he cut the tree down *or* he cut down the tree; she cut out the picture *or* she cut the picture out, *etc.*, but *only* he cut it down, she cut it out, *etc.*

cute [kjuːt] *adjective*

nice-looking; what a cute dog! a cute picture of the baby.

cute—cuter—cutest

Dd

dad [dæd], **dad·dy** ['dædɪ] *noun*

child's name for father; come over here, Dad, and look at my book; my dad has bought a new car.

Note: spelled **Dad** *or* **Daddy** *when used to speak to your father, but* **dad** *and* **daddy** *when used to talk about a father*

dai·ly ['deɪlɪ] **1.** *adjective*

happening or appearing every day; a daily newspaper; you should do daily exercises to keep in shape.

2. *adverb*

every day; take the medicine twice daily.

3. *noun*

newspaper which comes out every day; all the dailies had the story about the President.

plural **dailies**

dam·age ['dæmɪdʒ] **1.** *noun*

harm done to things; the storm caused a lot of damage; flood damage = damage caused by a flood.

no plural **some damage; a lot of damage**

2. *verb*

to harm something; the car was badly damaged in the accident; if it rains hard the crops will be damaged.

damages—damaging—damaged—has damaged

damp [dæmp] *adjective*

a little wet; don't sit on the grass—it's damp; the damp climate makes me cough.

damp—damper—dampest

dance [dæns] **1.** *noun*

way of moving in time to music; dance band = group of people who play music for people to dance.

2. *verb*

to move in time to music; he was dancing with my sister; the crowds were dancing in the streets; I'm taking dancing lessons.

dances—dancing—danced—has danced

dan·ger ['deɪndʒər] *noun*

possibility of harm or death; in dry weather there's a danger of forest fires; he's in danger of losing his job = he may easily lose his job; she's out of danger = not likely to die.

dan·ger·ous, *adjective*

which can cause harm or death; don't touch the electric wires—they're dangerous; it's dangerous to walk on the railroad track.

dare [deər] *verb*

(*a*) to be brave enough to do something dangerous or naughty; I would never dare (to) jump from that wall; he doesn't dare go out of the house; how dare you tell me what to do! I dare say he's ill = perhaps he is ill.

(b) to say that someone is not brave enough to do something; **I dared him to steal some candy from the store.**

dares—daring—dared—has dared

dark [dɑːrk] 1. *adjective*

(a) with very little light; **during the storm the sky turned dark; switch the lights on—it's getting too dark to read; in the winter it gets dark early; the sky got darker and darker as night came on.**

(b) not a light color; **his shirt is dark green.**

(c) with black or brown hair; **he's dark, but his sister is fair; he has dark hair.**

dark—darker—darkest

2. *noun*

lack of light; **she is afraid of the dark; cats can see in the dark; we're completely in the dark** = we don't understand.

no plural

dark·ness, *noun*

being dark; **the house was in complete darkness** = there were no lights on in the house.

no plural

date [deɪt] *noun*

(a) number of a day or year, name of a month (when something happened); **what's the date today? what are the dates of the Second World War? do you remember the date of your last letter?**

(b) time agreed for a meeting, usually between a boy and girl; **let's make it a date, shall we? I asked her out for a date; she has a date tonight.**

up-to-date = very modern/using very recent information; **the new phone book is completely up-to-date; keep me up-to-date on what has been happening** = tell me all the latest information about what has been happening.

out-of-date = not modern; **this old book is out-of-date** = the information in it is not recent.

daugh·ter [ˈdɔːtər] *noun*

girl child of a parent; **they have two sons and one daughter; have you met my daughter, Mary?**

day [deɪ] *noun*

(a) period of 24 hours; **there are 365 days in the year; July has 31 days; Christmas Day is December 25; what day is it today?** = is it Monday, Tuesday, etc.? **I saw him the day before yesterday; we will meet the day after tomorrow; he phones me every other day** = once every two days; **I saw him the other day** = I saw him very recently.

(b) period from morning until night, when it is light; **he works all day in the office, and then goes to German classes in the evening; it will take me two days to finish this work.**

a day = every day; **he eats a loaf of bread a day.**

all day = the whole day; **he has been working hard all day.**

day off = day when you do not work; **I have a day off every month; tomorrow is my day off.**

day·light, *noun*

light during the day; **the robbers attacked the bank in full daylight.**

day·time, *noun*

period of light between morning and night; **he works at night, and sleeps during the daytime.**

dead [ded] *adjective*

(a) not alive; **my grandparents are both dead; dead fish were floating in the lake; the wind blew piles of dead leaves into the road.**

(b) complete; **dead silence; the car came to a dead stop.**

dead·ly, *adjective*

likely to kill; **these snakes are deadly so stay away from them.**

deadly—deadlier—deadliest

deaf [def] *adjective*

not able to hear; **you have to shout when you speak to Mr. Jones because he's deaf.**

deaf—deafer—deafest

deal [diːl] 1. *noun*

(a) business agreement; **we made a deal with a German company to buy steel.**

(b) **a good deal of/a great deal of** = a lot; **he made a great deal of money; we wasted a good deal of time.**

2. *verb*
(*a*) to hand out cards in a game; **he dealt me three cards.**
(*b*) **to deal with** = to organize things; to have to do with; **don't worry about the passports—I will deal with them; the government is trying to deal with the problem of crime; I don't like dealing with difficult people.**
(*c*) **to deal in** = to do business in; **he deals in old cars.**
deals—dealing—dealt [delt]**—has dealt**

deal·er, *noun*
person who buys and sells; **he's a dealer in gold coins.**

dear [dɪr] *adjective*
(*a*) well-liked; **a very dear friend; I met dear old Mrs. Jones.**
(*b*) (*at the beginning of a letter*) **Dear Mr. Smith; Dear John; Dear Sir.**
(*c*) **oh dear!** = what a nuisance!/how surprising!
dear—dearer—dearest

death [deθ] *noun*
dying; end of life; **his sudden death surprised his friends; he met his death in a car crash** = he died in a crash.

De·cem·ber [dɪ'sembər] *noun*
twelfth and last month of the year; **her birthday is in December; she was born on December 20; we went on vacation last December; today is December 6.**
Note: **December 6:** *say* "December sixth," "the sixth of December" *or* "December the sixth"

de·cide [dɪ'saɪd] *verb*
to make up your mind to do something; **have you decided where to go for your vacation? they decided to stay at home; he decided not to go away.**
decides—deciding—decided—has decided

de·ci·sion [dɪ'sɪʒən] *noun*
making up your mind to do something; **they have been talking for hours, but still haven't reached a decision.**

deck [dek] *noun*
(*a*) flat floor in a ship; **the restaurant is**

on the third deck; there are seats on the top deck.
(*b*) group of cards put together; **he took out a deck of cards.**

de·clare [dɪ'kleər] *verb*
to tell a customs official that you have goods which you may have to pay tax on; **do you have anything to declare? I declared three bottles of wine.**
declares—declaring—declared—has declared

deep [di:p] *adjective*
(*a*) which goes a long way down; **be careful—the water is very deep here; this is the deepest mine in Pennsylvania; the water is only five feet deep.**
(*b*) dark; **the carpet is a deep chocolate color.**
deep—deeper—deepest

de·feat [dɪ'fi:t] **1.** *noun*
loss of a battle/of a vote; **many people were surprised by the governor's defeat in the election; the defeat of the British army at Yorktown.**
2. *verb*
to beat someone in a battle/a vote; **the President's plan was defeated in Congress; Napoleon defeated the German army.**
defeats—defeating—defeated—has defeated

de·fend [dɪ'fend] *verb*
to protect someone/something from an attack; **the town was defended by a large army.**
defends—defending—defended—has defended

de·fense, *noun*
protection against an attack; **defense of a country against an enemy.**

de·gree [dɪ'gri:] *noun*
(*a*) (*in science*) part of a series of measurements; **a circle has 360°** (*say* "three hundred and sixty degrees"); **the temperature is only 20°** (*say* "twenty degrees").
(*b*) **he has a degree in English** = he completed a course of study in English at a college or university.
Note: with figures **degree** *is written* °

de·lay [dɪ'leɪ] 1. *noun*
time when something/someone is late;
the meeting started after twenty minutes'
delay/after a delay of twenty minutes; I
am sorry for the delay in answering your
letter.
2. *verb*
to make something/someone late; the
train was delayed by snow; the fog has
delayed all planes.
**delays—delaying—delayed—
has delayed**

de·li·cious [də'lɪʃəs] *adjective*
tasting or smelling very good; she bakes
the most delicious cakes I've ever had.

de·light [dɪ'laɪt] 1. *noun*
enjoyment; pleasure; he takes delight in
being rude to people = he enjoys it; our
cat's greatest delight is sleeping in front
of the fire.
2. *verb*
to delight in = to enjoy; he delights in
being rude to his friends.
**delights—delighting—
delighted—has delighted**
de·light·ed, *adjective*
very pleased; I'd be delighted to come to
your party; she was delighted with her
present.
de·light·ful, *adjective*
very pleasant; what delightful weather!
they gave a delightful party.

de·liv·er [dɪ'lɪvər] *verb*
to bring something to someone; the
mailman delivers the mail to our house;
can you deliver this package for me? the
store will deliver the new table tomorrow.
**delivers—delivering—delivered—
has delivered**

de·mand [dɪ'mænd] 1. *noun*
asking for something; this book is in great
demand = everyone is asking for it.
2. *verb*
to ask for something and expect to get
it; she demanded to see the manager; he
is demanding his money back.
**demands—demanding—
demanded—has demanded**

den·tist ['dentɪst] *noun*
doctor who takes care of your teeth; I
must go to the dentist—I've got a toothache; she had to wait for an hour at the
dentist's; I hate going to see the dentist.

de·part·ment [dɪ'pɑːrtmənt] *noun*
part of a large organization/of a large
store; if you want cheese, you must go to
the food department; he is manager of
the sales department; State Department
= part of the U.S. government which
deals with other countries.

de·pend on [dɪ'pend ɒn] *verb*
(*a*) to be sure that something will happen/
that someone will do something; he
depends on his wife to take care of
the house; we're depending on you
to pay for the food.
(*b*) to happen because of something;
whether or not we go on a picnic depends
on the weather; depending on her test
results, she will go to college or start
work in an office.
**depends—depending—
depended—has depended**
de·pend·a·ble, *noun*
which you can depend on; it is a very
dependable car.

depth [depθ] *noun*
measurement of how deep something is;
what is the depth of the pool? the river is
at least 12 feet in depth.
no plural

de·scribe [dɪ'skraɪb] *verb*
to say or write what something/
someone is like; can you describe the
man who stole the money? she described
how her car suddenly hit a tree; the police
asked her to describe what happened.
**describes—describing—
described—has described**
de·scrip·tion [dɪ'skrɪpʃən] *noun*
saying or writing what something/some-
one is like; her description of the accident.

des·ert ['dezərt] *noun*
place which is very dry and covered
with sand; the Sahara Desert; he lived
for three years on a desert island.

de·sign [dɪ'zaɪn] 1. *noun*
drawing of something before it is built or made; **he showed us the designs for his new house; this is the latest in aircraft design.**
2. *verb*
to draw something to show how it should be made; **she designed her coat herself; he is designing all the furniture for his house.**
designs—designing—designed— has designed

desk [desk] *noun*
table for writing (sometimes with drawers); **put the papers away in your desk; he was sitting at his desk when the telephone rang.**

des·sert [dɪ'zɜrt] *noun*
sweet food which you eat at the end of a meal; **what's for dessert? we'll have ice cream for dessert.**

de·stroy [dɪ'strɔɪ] *verb*
to knock something completely to pieces; **the house was destroyed by fire; she destroyed all his letters.**
destroys—destroying— destroyed—has destroyed

de·tail [dɪ'teɪl] *noun*
small part of a description; **he went into a lot of detail when describing the accident; he told us how to get to her house, but left out the most important detail— the name of the street.**

de·tec·tive [dɪ'tektɪv] *noun*
person who tries to find out how crimes take place.

de·vel·op [dɪ'veləp] *verb*
(*a*) to grow or make grow; to use for a better purpose; **the town is going to develop the land near the railroad station; computers are a rapidly developing industry.**
(*b*) to start to get; **she developed a cold; he developed a liking for chocolate.**
(*c*) to make a film ready to print photos from it.
develops—developing— developed—has developed

de·vel·op·ment, *noun*
(*a*) thing which develops; being developed.
(*b*) area where new houses are built.

di·al ['daɪəl] 1. *noun*
round face on a clock/telephone, etc.; **the pilot looked at the dials in front of him; the dial of the clock is lit up at night.**
2. *verb*
to make a telephone number by turning the dial: **you dial 514 for Montreal; he dialed the number of the police station.**
dials—dialing—dialed—has dialed

dic·tion·ar·y ['dɪkʃənerɪ] *noun*
book which lists words in alphabetical order and gives their meanings or gives the same words in another language: **a French dictionary; if you don't understand the word, look it up in a dictionary.**
plural **dictionaries**

did [dɪd], **didn't** [dɪdnt] *see* **do**

die [daɪ] *verb*
(*a*) to stop living; **his father died last year; she died in a car crash; if you take a fish out of water it will die.**
(*b*) **dying for** = very eager to have; **I'm dying for a cup of coffee** = I would like a cup of coffee very much.
dies—dying—died—has died
die a·way, *verb*
to get fainter; **the sound of the car died away.**
die down, *verb*
to get less; **the fire began to die down.**

dif·fer·ence ['dɪfrəns] *noun*
way in which two things are not the same; **can you tell the difference between red and green? you can use water or oil—it doesn't make any difference** = the result is the same.
dif·fer·ent, *adjective*
not the same; **living in the country is different from living in the city; I went to six different stores, but couldn't find what I wanted; he looks different—I think he has had his hair cut.**

dif·fi·cult ['dɪfɪkəlt] *adjective*
hard to do; not easy; **the examination**

was very difficult—half the students failed; it is difficult to find somewhere to park on Saturday mornings.

dif·fi·cul·ty, *noun*
problem/thing which is not easy; **the difficulty is how to start the car; she has difficulty in getting up in the morning.**
plural **difficulties**

dig [dɪg] *verb*
to make a hole in the ground; **he was digging in his garden; the prisoner dug a hole under the prison wall; we dug up an old coin** = found it while digging.
digs—digging—dug—has dug

dime [daɪm] *noun*
ten-cent coin; **do you have a dime?—I want to make a phone call.**

din·ing room [ˈdaɪnɪŋ rʊm] *noun*
room in a house where you usually eat; **we were sitting in the dining room having supper; come into the dining room—dinner is ready; he was doing his homework on the dining room table.**

din·ner [ˈdɪnər] *noun*
main meal (either eaten after noon or in the evening); **we were having dinner in the dining room when the telephone rang; we always have dinner at 7:30; would you like to come to dinner next week? eat up your dinner; hurry up, it's almost time for dinner; what's for dinner?**
Note: if you call the afternoon meal **dinner,** *then you call the evening meal* **supper;** *if you call the evening meal* **dinner,** *then you call the afternoon meal* **lunch**

din·ner·time, *noun*
time when you usually have dinner.

di·rect [dɪˈrekt *or* daɪˈrekt] **1.** *adjective & adverb*
straight; **the plane flies direct to Chicago, a direct flight to Chicago** = flight with no stops or where you do not have to change planes.
2. *verb*
to tell someone where to go; **the policeman was directing the traffic; can you

direct me to the Post Office?** = can you tell me how to get to the Post Office?
directs—directing—directed—has directed

di·rec·tion [dɪˈrekʃn *or* daɪˈrekʃn] *noun*
(*a*) way in which you are going; **turn around—you are going in the wrong direction; the station is in the other direction; leaves were blowing in all directions** = everywhere.
(*b*) **directions** = telling how to do something; **the policeman gave us directions for getting to the station; I can't use this, as there are no directions on how to switch it on.**

di·rect·ly, *adverb*
immediately/at once; **he came home directly; she called the police directly.**

dirt [dɜrt] *noun*
material which is not clean, like mud, dust, earth, etc.; **don't sit in the dirt—you'll get your clothes dirty.**

dirt·y, *adjective*
not clean; **if you lie on the ground you will get your clothes dirty; we must wash all these dirty plates; you can't have any dinner if your hands are dirty.**
dirty—dirtier—dirtiest

dis·ap·pear [dɪsəˈpɪr] *verb*
not to be seen any more; **the thieves disappeared when they heard the police coming; the sun disappeared behind the clouds.**
disappears—disappearing—disappeared—has disappeared

dis·cov·er [dɪˈskʌvər] *verb*
to find something, especially something new; **who discovered America? scientists are trying to discover a cure for this disease; he discovered a hole in the floor under his bed.**
discovers—discovering—discovered—has discovered

dis·cov·er·y, *noun*
(*a*) action of discovering something; **the discovery of a cure for colds; the discovery of America.**
(*b*) thing which you have discovered; **he told me about his latest discoveries.**
plural **discoveries**

dis·cuss [dɪ'skʌs] *verb*
to talk about a problem/a subject; **they started discussing politics; we were discussing how to get to Anaheim; they discussed the best way of going to Europe.**
discusses—discussing—discussed—has discussed

dis·cus·sion [dɪ'skʌʃən] *noun*
general talk about a problem; **the discussion went on for hours, but no decision was made.**

dis·ease [dɪ'ziːz] *noun*
serious illness (of people/animals/plants, etc.); **he caught a disease while in Africa; she is suffering from a very serious disease.**

dish [dɪʃ] *noun*
(*a*) large plate for serving food; **a vegetable dish.**
(*b*) **dishes** = plates/cups, etc.; **can I wash all these dirty dishes?**
(*c*) (plate of) food; **you ought to have a meat dish to start with.**
plural dishes

dish·cloth, dish·rag *noun*
cloth for washing dishes.
dish tow·el, *noun*
cloth used to dry dishes.
dish·wash·er, *noun*
machine for washing dishes; **put all the dirty plates in the dishwasher.**
dish·wa·ter, *noun*
dirty water, which has been used for washing dishes.

dis·tance ['dɪstəns] *noun*
space between one thing and another; **what is the distance between the police station and the post office? can you see that white house in the distance?** = far away; **long-distance race** = very long race.

dis·trict ['dɪstrɪkt] *noun*
area; **he lives in a country district; the southern districts of the city.**

dive [daɪv] *verb*
to go down head first; **he dived into the water; she dived off the rocks into the sea.**
dives—diving—dived/dove—has dived

di·vide [dɪ'vaɪd] *verb*
(*a*) to cut into parts; **he divided the cake up between the children** = he gave them each a piece.
(*b*) to see how many of one number there are in another; **can you divide 27 by 9? 27 divided by 9 gives 3.**
divides—dividing—divided—has divided

di·vi·sion [dɪ'vɪʒən] *noun*
cutting into parts; seeing how many of one number there are in another; **I am good at multiplication but not at division.**

diz·zy ['dɪzɪ] *adjective*
feeling that everything is turning around you; **he felt dizzy and had to sit down; if the car goes too fast it makes me dizzy.**
dizzy—dizzier—dizziest

do [duː] *verb*
(*a*) (*used with other verbs to make questions*) does it matter? did he laugh? do your parents live in England? do you smoke? did she go with them?
(*b*) (*used with other verbs to make the negative*) it doesn't matter; he didn't laugh; my parents don't live in England; I don't smoke; she didn't go with them.
(*c*) (*used to make a verb stronger*) please do sit down; he does like ice cream!
(*d*) (*used instead of another verb with so and* neither) I don't smoke—neither do I; he likes chocolate—so does she = she likes chocolate too.
(*e*) (*used in short answers instead of another verb*) does it matter?—yes, it does; do you live here?—yes, I do; did he laugh?—no, he didn't; do your parents live in England?—yes, they do.
(*f*) (*used instead of another verb at the end of a question or statement*) you live here, don't you? it doesn't look very nice, does it? it rains a lot, doesn't it!
(*g*) (*used instead of another verb*) I don't eat as much as she does; she arrived before we did; he speaks English better than I do.
(*h*) (*telling someone not to do something*) don't play in the road! don't put that chair there! don't go away!
(*i*) (*with nouns ending in* -ing) she's doing the cleaning; he always does the cooking.

(*j*) (*used in certain expressions*) **how do you do? he's doing very well in his new job; he's a difficult person to do business with; that will do** = that's enough; **that won't do at all** = that's not what is needed; **the car was doing 100 miles an hour** = was traveling at 100 miles an hour; **what do you do for a living?** = what is your job?

(*k*) (*with things*) **go and do your room** = clean your room; **I must do my hair** = arrange my hair; **he's doing the dishes** = he's washing them; **have you done your homework? what have you been doing?** *see also* **make do with.**

I do/**you do**/**he, she, it does** [dʌz]/ **they do**
doing—did [dɪd]—**has done** [dʌn]
Negative: **do not,** *usually* **don't** [dəʊnt]; **does not,** *usually* **doesn't** [dʌznt]; **did not,** *usually* **didn't** [dɪdnt]

do a·way with, *verb*
to get rid of something; **the government did away with taxes on food.**

do up, *verb*
to fasten; **do up your buttons; can you do up the zipper at the back of my dress?**
Note: **do your buttons up** *or* **do up your buttons** *but only* **do them up**

do with, *verb*
(*a*) to concern; **it has nothing to do with me; it has something to do with my new book.**
(*b*) **what have you done with my hat?** = where did you put my hat?

do with·out, *verb*
to be able to manage without something; **can't you do without a car? we had to do without coffee; plants can't do without water.**

dock [dɒk] **1.** *noun*
place near a town where ships tie up to load and unload; **dry dock** = dock which can be emptied of water for ships to be repaired; **the ship is in dock.**
2. *verb*
to come into dock; **we will be docking in twenty minutes.**
docks—docking—docked—has docked

doc·tor [ˈdɒktər] *noun*
person who examines people when they are sick to find out what is wrong with them; **I have an appointment with Dr. Jones; if you have a pain in your chest, you ought to see a doctor.**
doctor *is shortened to* **Dr.** *with names*

does [dʌz], **doesn't** [dʌznt] *see* **do**

dog [dɔːg] *noun*
animal kept as a pet, which barks, and waves its tail when it is pleased; **our dog bit the mailman; I must take the dog out for a walk.**

dol·lar [ˈdɒlər] *noun*
money used in the U.S.A. and in many other countries; **this book costs four dollars ($4); he gave me a $10 bill.**
dollar *is written* **$** *with numbers:* **$20, $525,** *etc.*
Note: with the word **bill, dollar** *is singular:* **five dollars,** *but* **a five-dollar bill**

done [dʌn] *see* **do**

don·key [ˈdɒŋkɪ] *noun*
gray farm animal, like a small horse, but with long ears.

don't [dəʊnt] *see* **do**

door [dɔːr] *noun*
piece of wood/metal, etc., which closes an entrance; **our house has a blue door; shut the oven door; he opened the door with his key; the back door leads out into the yard, and the front door on to the sidewalk; someone is knocking at the door; they live two doors away** = two houses away; *see also* **next door.**
door·bell, *noun*
bell near a door, which shows that someone wants you to open the door.
door·man, *noun*
man who stands near a door in a hotel, etc., and opens it for you.
door·step, *noun*
step which is the base of a doorway.
door·way, *noun*
space filled by a door; **he stood in the doorway and wouldn't let anyone go in.**

dot [dɒt] *noun*
round spot; her dress is blue with white dots.

dou·ble [ˈdʌbəl] 1. *adjective*
(a) with two similar parts; **double figures** = numbers from 10 to 99.
(b) twice as big/ twice as much/twice as many; I am double your age = I am twice as old as you; **double bed** = bed for two people.
2. *verb*
to multiply by two; think of a number, and then double it.
doubles—doubling—doubled—has doubled

doubt [daʊt] *verb*
not to be sure of something; I doubt if he will come = I don't think he will come.
doubts—doubting—doubted—has doubted
doubt·ful, *adjective*
not certain; I am doubtful if he will ever come.

dove [dəʊv] *see* **dive**

down [daʊn] 1. *preposition*
(a) toward the bottom; he went down the stairs; she fell down the ladder; they ran down the hill.
(b) at the bottom; he is not down here; it was cool down below.
(c) away from where the person is speaking; I'm just going down the street to buy something.
2. *adverb*
(a) toward the bottom; put your case down on the floor; he sat down on the sofa; she lay down on the carpet.
(b) on paper; did you write down the phone number? I'll just take down your address.
(c) toward the south; I'm going down to Alabama tomorrow (from New York).
3. *adjective*
at the bottom; the sun is down.
Note: **down** *is often used with verbs:* **to go down; to break down; to fall down,** *etc.*

down·hill, *adverb*
toward the bottom of a hill; the road went downhill for three miles.

down·stairs, *adverb & noun*
(on or to) the ground floor of a house; he lives downstairs; the downstairs of the house is larger than the upstairs; the dining room is downstairs; come downstairs at once! did you leave your watch downstairs?

down·town, *adverb and adjective*
to or in the business center of a city; I have to go downtown on business; the downtown stores are busy at this time of year; there are several theaters downtown.

down·ward, down·wards, *adverb*
toward the bottom; he put the card face downwards on the table.

doz·en [ˈdʌzən] *noun*
(a) twelve; two dozen eggs = 24 eggs; a dozen bottles of beer.
(b) **dozens** = lots; I've been there dozens of times.
Note: after numbers **dozen** *does not take an* -s: **two dozen, ten dozen,** *etc.*

drag [dræg] *verb*
to pull something heavy along; he dragged the sack into the corner; he was dragging a table behind him.
drags—dragging—dragged—has dragged

drain [dreɪn] 1. *noun*
pipe for carrying dirty water from a house; there is a smell—the drains must be blocked.
2. *verb*
to remove liquid which is not needed; the water will slowly drain away; the land needs draining.
drains—draining—drained—has drained
drain·pipe, *noun*
pipe which takes water down to the drains.

drank [dræŋk] *see* **drink**

drapes [dreɪps] *plural noun*
long pieces of cloth hanging in front of a window.

draw [drɔː] 1. *noun*
result of a game where there is no winner; **the game ended in a draw, 2–2.** 2. *verb*
(*a*) to make a picture with a pen or pencil; **he drew a picture of the church; what is he doing?—he is drawing the church.**
(*b*) to pull; **can you draw the curtains—it is getting dark.**
(*c*) not to have a winner in a game; **the teams drew 1–1.**
draws—drawing—drew—has drawn

draw·er, *noun*
part of a desk or cupboard like an open box which slides in or out; **my desk has three drawers; chest of drawers** = piece of furniture with several drawers for clothes.

draw·ing, *noun*
picture done with a pen or pencil; **here is a drawing of the church.**

draw up, *verb*
to prepare and write down; **he drew up a plan to build three new schools; we've drawn up a list of people to invite to the party.**

dream [driːm] 1. *noun*
things which you think you see happening while you are asleep; **I had a bad dream about spiders.**
2. *verb*
to think you see something happening while you are asleep; **I dreamt I was swimming; I wouldn't dream of wearing green shoes** = I would never even think of it.
dreams—dreaming—dreamed/ dreamt [dremt]**—has dreamed/ dreamt**

dress [dres] 1. *noun*
(*a*) piece of woman's/girl's clothing, covering the body from the neck down to the knees or below; **she was wearing a green dress.**
(*b*) special clothes; **he was wearing evening dress** = black suit, with a black or white necktie.
plural **dresses** *for (*a*); no plural for (*b*)*

2. *verb*
to put on clothes; **he (got) dressed, and then had breakfast; she was dressed in white.**
dresses—dressing—dressed—has dressed

dress·er, *noun*
chest of drawers with a mirror attached.

dress·ing, *noun*
sauce which you put on salads; **what dressing do you want on your salad?**

drew [druː] *see* **draw**

dried [draɪd], **drier** [ˈdraɪr], **dries** [draɪz], **driest** [ˈdraɪəst] *see* **dry**

drill [drɪl] 1. *noun*
machine for making holes in wood/ metal, etc.; **he made a hole in the wall with his electric drill.**
2. *verb*
to make a hole; **he drilled a hole in the wall; they are drilling for oil.**
drills—drilling—drilled—has drilled

drink [drɪŋk] 1. *noun*
(*a*) liquid which you swallow; **have a drink of water; I always have a hot drink before I go to bed; would you like a drink?** = are you thirsty? **soft drinks** = drinks (like orange pop) with no alcohol.
(*b*) alcoholic drink; **would you like a drink? I'll order the drinks.**
2. *verb*
(*a*) to swallow liquid; **he drank two cups of coffee; someone has drunk my beer! what would you like to drink?**
(*b*) to drink alcoholic drinks; **he never drinks/he doesn't drink.**
drinks—drinking—drank—has drunk

drink up, *verb*
to drink all of something; **drink up your milk.**
Note: **drink your milk up** *or* **drink up your milk** *but only* **drink it up**

drive [draɪv] 1. *noun*
car journey; **let's go for a drive; I don't like long drives.**

2. *verb*

(*a*) to make a car/truck, etc., travel in a certain direction; **I can swim, but I can't drive; he's taking driving lessons; he was driving a tractor; can I drive you to the station?** = can I take you to the station in my car? **in England, cars drive on the left-hand side of the road.**

(*b*) to make; **the noise is driving her crazy.**

drives—driving—drove [drəʊv]**— has driven**

driv·er, *noun*

person who drives a car/a bus, etc.; **he's a bus driver; the driver of the car was hurt in the accident.**

drive·way, *noun*

small private road which leads to a house or a garage.

driv·ing test, *noun*

test to see if you can drive a car; **he has just passed his driving test; she is taking her driving test tomorrow.**

drop [drɒp] **1.** *noun*

(*a*) small amount of liquid which falls; **a drop of water fell on my head; drops of rain splashed into the river; would you like a drop of wine?**

(*b*) distance which you might fall; **there is a drop of twenty feet from the window to the ground.**

2. *verb*

to fall; to let something fall; **he dropped the cup and broke it; prices are dropping.**

drops—dropping—dropped—has dropped

drop in, *verb*

to visit; **he dropped in to have a cup of tea; drop in for coffee if you're nearby.**

drop off, *verb*

(*a*) to begin to sleep; **she dropped off in front of the TV.**

(*b*) **I'll drop you off at the library** = I'll take you to the library by car.

drove [drəʊv] *see* **drive**

drown [draʊn] *verb*

to die or to be killed by being unable to breathe under water; **he fell into the sea and (was) drowned; the drowning man shouted for help; six people drowned when the boat sank.**

drowns—drowning—drowned— has drowned

drug [drʌg] **1.** *noun*

(*a*) medicine; **the doctors are trying to cure him with a new drug.**

(*b*) something which it becomes a habit to take; **he takes drugs.**

2. *verb*

to give a drug to someone, so that he falls asleep; **the burglars must have drugged the dog.**

drugs—drugging—drugged—has drugged

drug·store, *noun*

store where you can buy medicines, soap, food, etc.

drum [drʌm] *noun*

large round musical instrument covered with a tight skin, and which you play by hitting it with a stick; **he plays the drums in a band.**

drum·mer, *noun*

person who plays a drum.

drunk [drʌŋk] *adjective*

ill because of drinking too much alcohol; *see also* **drink.**

dry [draɪ] **1.** *adjective*

not wet; **don't sit on that chair—the paint isn't dry yet; it hasn't rained for weeks so the earth is very dry.**

dry—drier—driest

2. *verb*

to stop being wet; to wipe something until it is dry; **the clothes are drying in the sun; can you dry the dishes for me?**

dries—drying—dried—has dried

dry out, *verb*

to dry completely; **hang up your coat until it dries out.**

Note: **dry your coat out** *or* **dry out your coat** *but only* **dry it out**

duck [dʌk] **1.** *noun*

farm bird, also a wild bird, which lives near water and can swim; meat from this bird used as food; **we're going to** feed the ducks; we're having roast duck for dinner.

Note: as a food duck *does not have a plural:* some duck; a slice of duck

2. *verb*

to lower your head quickly to avoid hitting or being hit by something; **he ducked as the stone went past his head; tall people have to duck as they go through that door.**

ducks—ducking—ducked—has ducked

due [djuː] 1. *adjective*

(*a*) expected; **the train is due to arrive at 10:00.**

(*b*) which ought to be paid; **the rent is due next week.**

(*c*) **due to** = caused by; **the cracks in the wall are due to the cold; the plane is late due to fog.**

2. *adverb*

straight (in a direction); **the boat sailed due west.**

dug [dʌg] *see* **dig**

dull [dʌl] *adjective*

(*a*) not exciting: **he went to sleep watching a dull film on TV; life here is very dull—nothing ever happens.**

(*b*) not bright; **dull weather; the car is painted dull gray.**

dull—duller—dullest

dumb [dʌm] *adjective*

(*a*) not able to speak; **she's deaf and dumb.**

(*b*) stupid; **that's a dumb way to open a bottle; what a dumb idea!**

dump [dʌmp] 1. *noun*

dirty place; place where you put garbage; **take that old TV to the dump.**

2. *verb*

to put something in a pile on the ground; **he dumped the bag of apples in the middle of the floor.**

dumps—dumping—dumped—has dumped

dur·ing [ˈdjʊrɪŋ] *preposition*

for the time something lasts/while somethings lasts; **he went to sleep during the TV show; during the war we never had any butter.**

dust [dʌst] 1. *noun*

dirt like powder; **the table is covered with dust; wipe the dust off your shoes.**

no plural

2. *verb*

to wipe dust off something; **have you dusted the dining room table?**

dusts—dusting—dusted—has dusted

dust·pan, *noun*

small container for picking up dust which has been pushed into a pile with a broom.

dust·y, *adjective*

covered with dust; **the top of the car is dusty; we walked for miles along a dusty road.**

dusty—dustier—dustiest

du·ty [ˈdjuːtɪ] *noun*

(*a*) tax which has to be paid; **you have to pay duty if you want to bring cigarettes into the country.**

(*b*) something which has to be done (especially in a certain job); **what are your duties as manager of the sales department?**

plural **duties**

dy·ing [ˈdaɪɪŋ] *see* **die**.

Ee

each [iːtʃ] 1. *adjective referring to single things or people separately*

every; **each house has a number; he was**

holding a knife in each hand; **each one of us has a bicycle.**

2. *pronoun*

(*a*) every person; **they have two cars each/each of them has two cars; she gave them each a cake/she gave them a cake each.**

(*b*) every thing; **each of the houses has three bedrooms/the houses have three bedrooms each.**

each oth·er = both of two people/of two things; **they were talking to each other; we always send each other Christmas cards; the cups fit into each other.**

ea·ger ['iːgər] *adjective*
wanting to do something/very interested; **he is eager to play on the college team; she was eager to start work as soon as possible.**

ear ['ɪr] *noun*
(*a*) part of the head which is used for hearing; **donkeys have long ears; have you washed your neck and ears? he's up to his ears in work** = he has a lot of work to do.

(*b*) sense of music; **he has a good ear for music; she can play the piano by ear** = without reading printed notes.

ear·ache ['iːreɪk] *noun*
pain in your ear.

ear·drum, *noun*
tight skin inside your ear which allows you to hear sounds.

ear·ring, *noun*
ring or jewel which you wear attached to your ear.

ear·ly ['ɜrlɪ] **1.** *adverb*
(*a*) before the proper time; **the train arrived five minutes early; we must get up early tomorrow as we have a lot of work to do; can you come earlier next time?**
(*b*) at the beginning of a period of time; **we went out early in the afternoon; early in the year.**
2. *adjective*
which happens at the beginning of a period of time; **early vegetables** = vegetables which are ready to eat in the spring; **I caught an early train; these flowers open in early summer; we hope to meet you at an early date** = quite soon.
early—earlier—earliest

earn [ɜrn] *verb*
to get money by working; **he earns $50 a week; how much does a cabdriver earn?**
earns—earning—earned—has earned

earn·ings, *plural noun*
money which you earn; **he gave all his earnings to his wife.**

earth [ɜrθ] *noun*
(*a*) the planet on which we live; **the earth goes around the sun; the spaceship came back to earth.**
(*b*) soil; **plant your seeds in fine earth.**
on earth (*phrase used to make questions stronger*) **why on earth did you do that? who on earth is going to read this book? how on earth did he find all that money?**

eas·i·er ['iːzɪər], **eas·i·est** ['iːzɪəst], **eas·i·ly** ['iːzɪlɪ] *see* **easy**

east [iːst] **1.** *noun*
direction of where the sun rises; **the sun rises in the east and sets in the west; the city is to the east of the mountains; the East** = parts of the U.S. near the Atlantic Ocean; **the Far East/the Middle East/the Near East** = countries to the east of India/to the east of Egypt and west of Pakistan/to the east of the Mediterranean.
2. *adjective*
referring to the east; **the east coast; there was an east wind blowing** = a wind from the east.
3. *adverb*
towards the east; **the ship is sailing east; go due east for ten miles.**

east·ern, *adjective*
of the east; **Poland is in eastern Europe; the capital is in the eastern part of the country.**

east·ward, *adverb*
towards the east; **we drove eastward for ten hours.**

East·er ['iːstər] *noun*
Christian holiday in the spring, the time of Christ's death and return to life; **Easter egg** = colored egg eaten at

Easter; we have two days off at Easter;
are you going away for the Easter vacation? we went to Canada last Easter.

eas·y ['iːzɪ] *adjective*
not difficult; **the test is too easy—
everyone passed; it's easy to understand
why he passed the test; the house is
within easy reach of the station** = is
quite close to the station.
easy—easier—easiest

eas·i·ly, *adverb*
without difficulty; **I could do the test
easily; she is easily the tallest in the class**
= much taller than all the others.

eat [iːt] *verb*
to chew and swallow food; **can I have
something to eat? I haven't eaten anything since breakfast; he ate all the
cookies; who has eaten my chocolates?**
eats—eating—ate [eɪt]**—has eaten**
['iːtən]

eat a·way, *verb*
to destroy bit by bit; **the rocks have been
eaten away by the sea.**

eat up, *verb*
to finish eating/to eat everything; **eat up
your meat!**
Note: **eat up your meat** *or* **eat your
meat up,** *but only* **eat it up**

edge [edʒ] *noun*
(*a*) side of a flat object; **don't put your
cup so close to the edge of the table; he
lay down on the flat roof of the building
and looked over the edge; she stood the
coin on its edge.**
(*b*) side of a blade that you cut with;
the knife has a very sharp edge.
(*c*) line separating two quite different
things; **he stood at the edge of the water;
the house is built on the edge of the wood.**

ed·u·cate ['edjuːkeɪt] *verb*
to teach someone; **he was educated in
Scotland** = he went to school in Scotland.
**educates—educating—
educated—has educated**

ed·u·ca·tion [edjuː'keɪʃən] *noun*
teaching; **adult education** = teaching of
adults; **she has had a college education**
= she studied at college.

ef·fect [ɪ'fekt] *noun*
result; **he poured water on the fire but it
had no effect; this rule comes into effect
on January 1** = starts working.

ef·fec·tive, *adjective*
which has the right effect; **his way of
making the children keep quiet is very
effective.**

ef·fort ['efərt] *noun*
using your mind or the muscles of your
body; **he made an effort to paint the
whole house** = he tried to paint the
house; **it took a lot of effort to carry the
food to the top of the mountain; if he
made an effort he would pass his exams**
= if he tried hard.

egg [eg] *noun*
(*a*) round object with a hard shell,
produced by a female bird, which contains a baby bird; **the birds have laid
three eggs in their nest.**
(*b*) egg of a hen, used as food; **I had a
boiled egg for breakfast; can I have
bacon and eggs? this cake is made with
three eggs.**

egg·shell, *noun*
hard outside shell of an egg.

eight [eɪt] number 8
she ate eight sandwiches; he's eight
(years old); come to see us at eight
(o'clock).

eight·een, number 18
there are eighteen children in the class;
she's eighteen (years old).

eight·eenth, 18th, *adjective & noun*
May eighteenth (May 18); the eighteenth
name on the list; it's her eighteenth
birthday tomorrow.

eighth, 8th, *adjective & noun*
May eighth (May 8); an eighth of the
time; Henry the Eighth (Henry VIII); her
eighth birthday is next Tuesday.
Note: with dates **eighth** *is usually
written* **8: May 8, 1979; October 8,
1880;** *with names of kings and
queens* **eighth** *is usually written* **VIII:
King Henry VIII**

eight·i·eth, 80th, *adjective & noun*
an eightieth of the money; tomorrow is
grandfather's eightieth birthday.

eight·y, number 80
you need more than eighty bricks to build a wall; he's eighty (years old); she's in her eighties = she is between 80 and 89 years old.
Note: **eighty-one** (81), **eighty-two** (82) *but* **eighty-first** (81st), **eighty-second** (82nd), *etc.*

ei·ther [ˈiːðər] 1. *adjective & pronoun*
(*a*) one or the other; I don't believe either of them; you can use either car—it doesn't matter which.
(*b*) each of two; they sat on either side of him = one on each side.
2. *conjunction*
(*showing choice*) either you come to see us or we'll go to see you; he's either sick or he doesn't want to come.
3. *adverb*
(*with a negative, making a statement stronger*) he isn't French, and he isn't Canadian either; you don't want to go, and I don't want to either; it wasn't on the TV news, and it wasn't on the radio either.

el·bow [ˈelbəʊ] *noun*
place where your arm bends in the middle; don't put your elbows on the table; he pushed me with his elbow.

e·lect [ɪˈlekt] *verb*
to choose by voting; he was elected President.
elects—electing—elected—has elected

e·lec·tion [ɪˈlekʃən] *noun*
act of choosing by voting; he was elected to the Senate in the last election; presidential election = election to choose a president.

e·lec·tric·i·ty [ɪlekˈtrɪsəti] *noun*
current used to make light/heat/power; the motor is run by electricity; the house is in the country and doesn't have any electricity.
no plural

e·lec·tric [ɪˈlektrɪk] *adjective*
worked by electricity; used for carrying electricity; electric light; an electric saw; don't touch that electric cord.
e·lec·tri·cal, *adjective*
referring to electricity; he is studying electrical engineering; they are fixing an electrical fault.
e·lec·tri·cian [ɪlekˈtrɪʃən] *noun*
person who repairs electric wires/puts in electric machines, etc.

el·e·phant [ˈelɪfənt] *noun*
very large animal, living in Africa or India, with large ears, and a long trunk; you can go for a ride on an elephant.

el·e·va·tor [ˈeləveɪtər] *noun*
machine which takes people from one floor to another in a tall building; he took the elevator to the sixth floor; push the button to get the elevator.

e·lev·en [ɪˈlevn] number 11
you can't eat eleven candy bars all by yourself! he's eleven (years old); come and see me at eleven (o'clock).
e·lev·enth, 11th, *adjective & noun*
May eleventh (May 11); he came eleventh in the race; it's his eleventh birthday tomorrow.

else [els] 1. *adjective*
(*after pronouns*) other; anyone else = any other person; anything else = any other thing; somebody else = some other person; is there anyone else who hasn't got a ticket? did you see anyone else? is there anything else you would like to eat? I couldn't go to the game, so someone else took my ticket; who else was there? there was nowhere else to put it; can we go somewhere else?
2. *adverb*
or else = or if not; come in or else stay outside; you must have a ticket, or else you won't be able to get in.
else·where, *adverb*
somewhere else; if you can't find it here, I would look elsewhere.

em·ploy [ɪmˈplɔɪ] *verb*
(*a*) to pay someone for regular work; the factory employs a staff of two hundred; she is employed as a secretary.
(*b*) to use; don't employ too much force.
employs—employing—employed—has employed

em·ploy·ee [emplɔɪ'iː] *noun*
person who is paid for doing work; **the firm has two hundred employees.**

em·ploy·er [ɪm'plɔɪər] *noun*
person who gives work to people and pays them for it.

em·ploy·ment, *noun*
regular paid work.

emp·ty ['emtɪ] 1. *adjective*
with nothing inside; **the bottle is empty; find an empty bottle and fill it with water; the refrigerator is empty—we must buy some more food.**

empty—emptier—emptiest

2. *verb*
to take everything out; **he emptied the water out of the bottle; she emptied the box onto the table.**

empties—emptying—emptied— has emptied

end [end] 1. *noun*
last part of something; **tie the ends of the piece of string together; go to the end of the road and turn left; we missed the end of the TV film, because we had to go to dinner; wait until the end of the month.**
in the end = finally/at last; **in the end the police let him go home.**
on end = with no breaks; **he worked for hours on end.**
2. *verb*
to finish; to come to an end; **the movie ends with the wedding of the boy and girl; the game should end about four o'clock; the game ended in a draw.**

ends—ending—ended—has ended

end·ing, *noun*
way a story/a movie, etc., finishes; **the book has a happy ending.**

end·less, *adjective*
with no end; **we had endless discussions about where to go on vacation.**

end up, *verb*
to finish; **we all ended up at my girl friend's house; he ended up getting arrested by the police.**

en·e·my ['enəmɪ] *noun*
person who you fight in a war; person who you don't like; **the enemy aircraft**
dropped bombs on our city.

plural **enemies**

en·gine ['endʒɪn] *noun*
(a) machine which drives something; **my car has a small engine and can't go very fast.**
(b) motor vehicle which pulls a train; **the train is pulled by an electric engine.**

en·gi·neer [endʒɪ'nɪər] *noun*
(a) person who drives a train.
(b) person who designs or takes care of engines or other machinery; **he works as a telephone engineer.**

en·gi·neer·ing, *noun*
study of machinery.

no plural

Eng·land ['ɪŋglənd] *noun*
country which is the largest part of Great Britain; **they went to live in England; why do you want to go to England for your vacation? England is north of France.**

Eng·lish ['ɪŋglɪʃ] 1. *adjective*
referring to England; **do you like English cheese? English weather can be very good; is she English or American?**
2. *noun*
(a) **the English** = people who live in or come from England; **the English like sports.**
(b) language spoken in the USA, Britain, Australia and many other countries; **he speaks English very well; what is the English for "burro"?**

Eng·lish·man,   **Eng·lish·wom·an**, *noun*
man or woman from England.

plural **Englishmen, Englishwomen**

en·joy [ɪn'dʒɔɪ] *verb*
to take pleasure in something; **I enjoy going to the movies; did you enjoy the film on TV last night? we didn't enjoy the game at all; to enjoy yourself** = to have a good time; **the children are making a lot of noise—they must be enjoying themselves; did she enjoy herself at the party?**

enjoys—enjoying—enjoyed—has enjoyed

en·joy·a·ble, *adjective*

which people enjoy; **we had an enjoyable day by the sea.**
en·joy·ment, *noun*
pleasure.

e·nough [ɪ'nʌf] **1.** *adjective*
as much as is needed; **do you have enough money to pay the bill? there isn't enough light to take a picture.**
2. *pronoun*
as much of something as is needed; **have you had enough to eat?**
3. *adverb*
as much as is needed; **you are not walking quickly enough; your hands aren't clean enough; this knife isn't sharp enough; he doesn't work hard enough.**

en·quire [ɪŋ'kwaɪr], **en·qui·ry** [ɪŋ'kwaɪrɪ] *see* **inquire, inquiry**

en·ter ['entər] *verb*
to go in; **he entered the room; the burglars entered the house through a bedroom window.**
enters—entering—entered—has entered
en·trance, *noun*
(*a*) way in; **this is the main entrance = the main door.**
(*b*) going in; **entrance—10¢ = it costs 10¢ to go in.**

en·ve·lope ['envələʊp] *noun*
flat paper cover which you put a letter into before sending it; **don't forget to lick the envelope and put a stamp on it.**

e·qual ['iːkwəl] **1.** *adjective*
exactly the same in amount/size, etc., as something else; **weigh three equal amounts of sugar; the two pieces of string are not equal in length.**
2. *verb*
(*a*) to be exactly the same in number/amount; **two and four equals six (2 + 4 = 6); two from ten equals eight (10 − 2 = 8).**
(*b*) to be as good/clever/fast, etc., as someone else; **he equaled the world record; there's no one to equal him at tennis.**
equals—equaling—equaled—has equaled
Note: **equals** *is written* **=** *when used in sums:* **6 + 4 = 10**

e·quip·ment [ɪ'kwɪpmənt] *noun*
things which you need to do something; **office equipment; he brought his camping equipment with him; the soldiers carried their equipment on their backs.**
no plural: **some equipment; a piece of equipment**

e·rase [ɪ'reɪs] *verb*
to rub out something written; **erase those pencil marks at the top of the page.**
erases—erasing—erased—has erased
e·ras·er, *noun*
piece of rubber which you use to rub out writing; **do you have a pencil with an eraser?**

es·cape [ɪ'skeɪp] **1.** *verb*
to get away; **he escaped from jail by climbing over a wall.**
escapes—escaped—escaping—has escaped
2. *noun*
getting away from jail/from a dangerous situation; **we had a narrow escape when the train hit our car = we were almost killed.**

es·pe·cial·ly [ɪ'speʃəlɪ] *adverb*
in particular; **he especially likes chocolates; you mustn't go out without a coat, especially when it's raining.**

etc. [et'setərə]
and so on; **vegetables, such as carrots, potatoes, etc.**

Eu·rope ['jʊərəp] *noun*
group of countries to the west of Asia and north of Africa; **Germany and Holland are countries in Europe; many Americans go to Europe on vacation.**
Eu·ro·pe·an [jʊərə'piːən] *adjective*
of Europe; **the European countries; he collects European stamps.**

e·ven ['iːvn] **1.** *adjective*
(*a*) **even numbers = numbers which can be divided by 2; on the left side of the street, all the houses have even numbers.**
(*b*) with equal scores; **at the end of the game, the two teams were even.**

(*c*) regular; **blood flows around the body at an even rate.**
2. *adverb*
(*showing surprise or making an expression stronger*) **even the smartest students can make silly mistakes; even the biggest apples were rotten** = not only the small ones, but also the large ones; **he even tried to swim across the lake** = he did many strange things, and in particular tried to swim across the lake; **that movie was bad, but this one is even worse.**
e·ven if = it doesn't matter if; **he never wears a coat, even if it's snowing.**
e·ven so = but still; **it rained all day, but even so we had our picnic.**
e·ven though = although; **he didn't wear a coat, even though it was snowing.**
e·ven up, *verb*
to make equal; **I paid $10 and you paid $12, so I will give you a dollar to even things up.**

eve·ning ['iːvnɪŋ] *noun*
late part of the day, when it is getting dark; **this evening** = today in the evening; **I'll meet you this evening after work; I saw him yesterday evening; the accident took place at nine o'clock in the evening; we arrived in New York in the morning, having left London the evening before; on Sunday evening we stayed in to watch television; we always watch television on Sunday evenings.**

e·vent [ɪ'vent] *noun*
(*a*) thing which happens; **strange events took place in the church at night.**
(*b*) sports competition; **track-and-field events** = jumping, running and throwing competitions.

ev·er ['evər] *adverb*
(*a*) at any time; **nothing ever happens; did you ever meet Mr. Smith? have you ever been to Canada? I hardly ever see her** = almost never; **he sang louder than ever** = louder than he had sung before.
(*b*) always; **ever since** = from that time on; *see also* **however, whatever, whenever, wherever, whoever.**

eve·ry ['evrɪ] *adjective*
each; **every day; every evening; we have a party every Christmas; every time we go on a picnic it rains; I bought six apples and every one of them was rotten; every other day** = on one day, not on the next, but on the day after that (e.g. on Monday, Wednesday, Friday, etc.); **every two hours** = with a period of 2 hours in between; **have your car checked every 5,000 miles** = when it has traveled 5,000, 10,000, etc. miles; **every now and then** = from time to time.

eve·ry·bod·y, eve·ry·one, *pronoun*
all people; **everybody/everyone is going to the party; I sent Christmas cards to everybody/everyone at work; everybody/everyone has to show their tickets; everybody is here, aren't they?**

Note: **everybody** *and* **everyone** *are singular, but can be followed by* **they/their/themselves,** *etc. The verb stays singular, except when followed by a question:* **is everyone enjoying themselves?** *but* **not everyone works here do they?**

eve·ry·thing, *pronoun*
all things; **have you brought everything with you? everything was dark in the house; the burglars stole everything that was valuable.**

eve·ry·where, *adverb*
in all places; **there were papers everywhere; I have looked everywhere for the key and I can't find it.**

eve·ry which way, *adverb*
in all directions; **the crowd ran every which way.**

ex·act [ɪg'zækt] *adjective*
very correct; **this is an exact copy; what is the exact time?**
ex·act·ly, *adverb*
very correctly; **the time is exactly 6:24; he looks exactly like his brother** = completely.

ex·am [ɪg'zæm] *see* **examination**

ex·am·ine [ɪg'zæmɪn] *verb*
to look at something/someone carefully to see if everything is correct; to see if someone knows something; **the doctor examined the sick man's heart; the boxes**

were examined by the customs officials.

**examines—examining—
examined—has examined**

ex·am·i·na·tion [ɪgzæmɪˈneɪʃn],
ex·am [ɪgˈzæm] *noun*
looking at something to see if everything is correct or at someone to see if he knows something; **there is a written examination in French; he passed his English exam; she was sad when she failed her music exams.**

ex·am·ple [ɪgˈzæmpəl] *noun*
something chosen to show something; **this is a good example of German poetry; for example** = to name one thing out of many; **he likes to keep in shape—for example, he goes running every morning; to set an example** = to show people how to behave, by doing things yourself; **he sets everyone a good example by getting up early; she sets a bad example to everyone else in the office.**

ex·cel·lent [ˈeksələnt] *adjective*
very good; **we had an excellent meal.**

ex·cept [ɪkˈsept] *preposition & conjunction*
other than; not including; **you can eat anything except fish; he doesn't do anything except sit and watch television; the party was very good, except that there wasn't enough to eat.**

ex·cit·ed [ɪkˈsaɪtɪd] *adjective*
very lively and happy because you hope something will happen; **the children were excited at the thought of going on vacation; don't get too excited—you may not win the prize.**

ex·cite·ment, *noun*
being excited; **what's all the excitement about? the children are in a state of excitement before Christmas.**
no plural

ex·cit·ing, *adjective*
which makes you excited; **an exciting movie; the news about your job is really exciting.**

ex·er·cise [ˈeksərsaɪz] *noun*
(*a*) use of your muscles as a way of keeping fit; **regular exercise is good for your**

heart; you ought to do five minutes' exercise every morning; he doesn't get enough exercise—that's why he's too fat.
(*b*) work done as practice; **have you done all your piano exercises?**

ex·hib·it [ɪgˈzɪbɪt] *noun*
showing; **they went to see a special exhibit at the art museum.**

ex·ist [ɪgˈzɪst] *verb*
to live/to be; **can fish exist out of water? don't be silly—such a thing doesn't exist.**

**exists—existing—existed—has
existed**

ex·it [ˈegzɪt] 1. *noun*
way out (of a building, etc.); **use the exit at the back of the room; passengers must go in by the front door—the back door is the exit.**
2. *verb*
to go out; **exit Mr. Smith** = Mr. Smith goes out.
Note: the form is the same for all parts of the verb.

ex·pect [ɪkˈspekt] *verb*
to think/to hope that something is going to happen or is true; **I expect it will rain; I expect she is tired after a day at the office; he expects his wife to do all the work for him; do you think it's going to snow?—yes, I expect so.**

**expects—expecting—expected—
has expected**

ex·pen·sive [ɪkˈspensɪv] *adjective*
which costs a lot of money; **he was wearing an expensive watch; I'll buy two watches—they're not very expensive; this hotel is more expensive than I expected.**

ex·pe·ri·ence [ɪkˈspɪrɪəns] *noun*
something which happens to you; **my first camping trip was an exciting experience.**

ex·per·i·ment [ɪkˈsperɪmənt] *noun*
scientific test; **he did some experiments to show that water boils at a temperature of 212°.**

ex·plain [ɪkˈspleɪn] *verb*
to give reasons for something; to make something clear; **can you explain why it**

is colder in winter than in summer? she tried to explain what had happened, but the cop didn't listen; he explained that the car hadn't stopped at the red light.
explains—explaining—explained—has explained

ex·pla·na·tion [eksplə'neɪʃən] *noun*
reason for something; **the police asked him for an explanation of his strange behavior; there is no explanation for this sudden cold weather.**

ex·plore [ik'splɔːr] *verb*
to travel and discover unknown places; **they explored the forest of West Africa; they sent rockets to explore space.**
explores—exploring—explored—has explored
ex·plor·er, *noun*
person who explores; **explorers have discovered a new river.**

ex·press [ik'spres] 1. *verb*
(*a*) to say what you think or feel; **she expresses herself very well.**
(*b*) to send by fast train or plane; **they expressed the package to the West Coast.**
expresses—expressing—expressed—has expressed
2. *noun & adjective*
way of sending goods by fast train or plane; **send that package express; is this an express bus?**
ex·press·way, *noun*
highway where you can drive fast.

ex·pres·sion [ik'spreʃən] *noun*
(*a*) word or group of words; **"for ages" is an expression meaning "for a long time."**

(*b*) look on your face which shows what you think; **she had a sad expression; his expression showed that he was angry.**

ex·tra ['ekstrə] *adjective & adverb*
more than usual; **the first-class ticket will cost you an extra $10/will cost you $10 extra; you should find some extra strong string/some extra thick paper.**

ex·treme·ly [ik'striːmli] *adverb*
very much; **he is extremely small; this watch is extremely expensive.**

eye [aɪ] 1. *noun*
part of your head which you see with; **she has blue eyes; shut your eyes while we all hide; I've got something in my eye; to keep an eye on something** = to watch something carefully/to look after something, so that it doesn't get harmed or stolen; **can you keep an eye on the house while we are on vacation?**
2. *verb*
to watch closely; **the cat is eyeing the fish.**
eyes—eyeing—eyed—has eyed
eye·brow, *noun*
small line of hair above your eye; **he raised his eyebrows** = he looked surprised.
eye·lash, *noun*
hair which grows on the edge of an eyelid.
plural **eyelashes**
eye·lid, *noun*
piece of skin which covers the eye.
eye·sight, *noun*
being able to see; **he has very good eyesight.**
no plural

Ff

face [feɪs] 1. *noun*
(*a*) front part of your head, where your eyes, nose and mouth are; **don't forget to**

wash your face and hands; **face to face** = looking toward each other; **they came face to face with an elephant; he** tried to keep a straight face = he tried not to laugh; he was making funny faces and the children laughed.

(b) front part of something; a clock face; he put the picture face downwards on the table.

2. verb

to have your face toward; please face the camera; the house faces east.

faces—facing—faced—has faced

face up to, verb

to agree that a problem exists and try to deal with it; he faced up to the fact that he wasn't good enough for the race; you must try to face up to the problem.

fact [fækt] noun

something which is real and true; it is a fact that he did well on the test; tell me all the facts so that I can decide what to do. **in fact** = actually/really; he said he was going to the office when in fact he went to the movies.

fac·to·ry ['fæktəri] noun

building where things are made; a shoe factory; he works in a car factory; he runs a factory which makes furniture.

plural factories

fail [feɪl] verb

not to be successful in doing something/ not to do something which you are trying to do; the car failed to stop at the red light; she has failed her music exams again; he failed his driving test three times.

fails—failing—failed—has failed

fail·ure ['feɪljər] noun

not a success; he tried to make a machine to change coal into oil, but it was a failure.

faint [feɪnt] 1. verb

to fall down and not know what is happening/to stop being conscious; she fainted when she saw the blood; it was so hot standing in the sun that he fainted.

faints—fainting—fainted—has fainted

2. adjective

not very clear/difficult to see or hear; we could hear a faint noise behind the door; there's a faint smell of paint.

faint—fainter—faintest

fair [feər] adjective

(a) light colored (hair); she has fair hair; he's dark, but his sister is fair.

(b) not very good; her work was only fair.

(c) right/correct; it isn't fair to eat all the cake yourself; that's not fair—you must let everyone play with the ball; the teacher was very fair when she marked our tests.

(d) bright (weather); the weatherman says it will be fair tomorrow.

fair—fairer—fairest

fair·ly, adverb

quite; I'm fairly certain I have met him before; he has been working here a fairly short time.

Note the order of words he's a fairly good student but he's quite a good student

fall [fɔːl] 1. noun

(a) dropping (of something); there has been a heavy fall of snow; falls = waterfall.

(b) losing balance; she had a fall and hurt her back.

(c) season of the year between summer and winter; the leaves turn red in the fall; I started work last fall; we are moving to Florida next fall.

2. verb

(a) to drop down; he fell down the stairs; she fell off the wall; did he fall into the water or did someone push him? don't put the bottle on the cushion—it will fall over.

(b) to become less; the price of gasoline has fallen.

falls—falling—fell—has fallen

fall a·sleep, verb

to go to sleep; he fell asleep in front of the TV.

fall off, verb

to get smaller; the number of jobs has fallen off this summer.

fall through, verb

not to take place as planned; the trip to London fell through.

false [fɔːls] adjective

not true; please tell me if the following statement is true or false.

fam·i·ly [ˈfæməlɪ] *noun*
group of people who are related to each other, especially mother, father and children; **John is the youngest in our family; the Jones family have gone on vacation to Spain; they have a very big family—five sons and three daughters.**
plural **families,** *but* **family** *can be used as a plural*

fa·mous [ˈfeɪməs] *adjective*
well-known; **he's a famous singer; that restaurant is famous for its desserts.**

far [fɑːr] *adverb & adjective*
(*a*) a long way away; **the post office is not far from here; how far is it from New York to Miami?**
(*b*) much; **it is far cheaper to go by bus than to take a cab; the food in this restaurant is far better than at home.**
by far = very much; **it is by far the cheapest way to travel; this car uses the least amount of gasoline by far.**
so far = up till now; **so far the weather has been beautiful; have you enjoyed your vacation so far?**
far—farther/further—farthest/furthest

fare [feər] *noun*
money which you pay for a journey; **bus fares have increased again; what is the fare from Washington to Montreal?**
round trip fare = price for a journey to a place and back again.

farm [fɑːrm] *noun*
land used for growing crops and keeping animals; **he went to work on the farm during the vacation; we spent six weeks on a farm; you can buy eggs and vegetables at the farm.**
farm·er, *noun*
man who works on or owns a farm.
farm·house, *noun*
house where the farmer and his family live.
farm·ing, *noun*
working on a farm/keeping animals, etc.
farm·yard, *noun*
place around a farmhouse where tractors are kept/where cows are milked, etc.

fast [fæst] *adjective & adverb*
(*a*) quick; quickly; **this is a fast train to the city—it doesn't stop anywhere; if you walk fast you can catch up with the children in front; my watch is fast** = is showing a time which is later than the correct time; **my watch is five minutes fast** = is showing a time five minutes later than the correct time (e.g. 7:15 instead of 7:10).
(*b*) **fast asleep** = sleeping so that it is difficult to wake up.
fast—faster—fastest

fas·ten [ˈfæsən] *verb*
to fix tightly; **fasten your seat belt when you drive a car; the dress is fastened with a zipper down the back.**
fastens—fastening—fastened—has fastened

fat [fæt] **1.** *adjective*
big and round; **you ought to eat less—you're getting too fat; that fat man has a very thin wife; he's the fattest boy in the class.**
fat—fatter—fattest
2. *noun*
part of meat which is white; solid white oil used for cooking; **if you don't like the fat, cut it off; fry the eggs in some fat.**

fa·ther [ˈfɑːðər] *noun*
man who has a son or daughter; **ask your father if you can borrow his car; Jane is coming to dinner with her father and mother.**

fau·cet [ˈfɔːsət] *noun*
pipe with a handle which allows water to come out when you turn it; **turn the faucet off—the tub is full.**

fault [fɔːlt] *noun*
making a mistake; not being correct; **whose fault is it that we haven't any food? it's all your fault—if you hadn't stayed in bed all morning we would be at the seaside by now; the engineer is trying to repair an electrical fault.**

fa·vor·ite [ˈfeɪvərɪt] *adjective & noun*
(thing/person) which you like best; **what is your favorite ice cream? which**

film star is your favorite? this is my favorite TV program.

fear [fır] *noun*
being afraid; he has a fear of flying.

feath·er ['feðǝr] *noun*
soft thing which grows on a bird's body; a duck with green feathers on its head.

Feb·ru·ar·y ['februǝrı] *noun*
second month of the year; his birthday is in February; she died on February 6; we are moving to a new house next February; today is February 7.
Note: **February 7:** *say* "February seventh", "February the seventh" *or* "the seventh of February"

fed [fed] *see* **feed**
fed up ['fed'ʌp] *adjective*
sad/unhappy because you have had enough of something; I'm fed up with listening to all this talk; she's fed up with school.

feed [fi:d] *verb*
to give food (to someone/an animal); it's time to feed the cows; how can you feed the family when you don't have any money? cows feed on grass.
feeds—feeding—fed [fed]**—has fed**

feel [fi:l] *verb*
(*a*) to touch (usually with your fingers); feel how soft the cushion is; when the lights went out we had to feel our way to the door.
(*b*) to give off a certain quality when touched; the knife felt cold; the floor feels hard.
(*c*) to have an experience; I felt the table move; did you feel the elevator go down suddenly? I feel cold/warm/happy/hungry, etc.; when she saw the film she felt sad; are you feeling better?
(*d*) to believe/to think; to have an opinion; he feels it would be wrong to leave the children alone in the house; the police felt that the accident was the fault of the driver of the car.
feels—feeling—felt [felt]**—has felt**
feel bad, *verb*
to be sorry; I feel bad about you losing your job.

feel·ing, *noun*
experience of your senses/something which you feel; I had a feeling that someone was watching me; you hurt his feelings = you make him unhappy.
feel like, *verb*
I felt like going for a swim = I suddenly wanted to go for a swim; do you feel like a cup of coffee? = would you like a cup of coffee?

feet [fi:t] *see* **foot**

fell [fel] *see* **fall**

felt [felt] *see* **feel**

fe·male ['fi:meıl] *adjective & noun*
(animal/plant) of the same sex as a woman or girl; a female cat.

fence [fens] *noun*
wooden or wire wall used to keep people or animals inside or out of a place; you need a strong wire fence around the chickens; the sheep pushed through the hole in the fence; he was leaning on the garden fence.

fen·der ['fendǝr] *noun*
metal piece at the front or rear of a car; the back fender was damaged in the accident.

fer·ry ['ferı] *noun*
boat which carries goods or people across water; we will take the ferry across the lake to Cleveland; a car ferry = boat which carries cars and trucks.
plural **ferries**

fe·ver ['fi:vǝr] *noun*
sickness when the temperature of your body is very high; you must stay in bed until the fever has gone.

few [fju:] *adjective & noun*
(*a*) not many; he has few friends; we go to fewer parties than last year.
(*b*) a few = some; take a few pictures and we will choose which one is best; I'll be ready in a few minutes.
few—fewer—fewest

field [fi:ld] *noun*
(*a*) piece of ground on a farm, often with a fence around it; the cows are all in the field; a field of grass.

(*b*) piece of ground for playing a game; the crowd is going to the football **field.**

fif·teen [fif'tiːn] *number* 15
he's fifteen (years old); come and see me in fifteen minutes.

fif·teenth, 15th, *adjective & noun*
May fifteenth (May 15); that's the fifteenth phone call I've had this morning; it's his fifteenth birthday next week.

fifth [fifθ] **5th,** *adjective & noun*
June fifth (June 5); Henry the Fifth (Henry V); a fifth = 20%; he spends a fifth of his time writing letters; it's her fifth birthday tomorrow.
Note: with dates **fifth** *is usually written* **5:** **June 5, 1935; December 5, 1981;** *with names of kings and queens* **fifth** *is usually written* **V: King Henry V**

fif·ty [fiftɪ] *number* 50
I've made fifty jars of jam; he's fifty (years old); she's in her fifties = she is between 50 and 59 years old.
Note: **fifty-one** (51), **fifty-two** (52), *but* **fifty-first** (51st), **fifty-second** (52nd), *etc.*

fif·ti·eth, 50th, *adjective & noun*
a fiftieth = 2%; she came fiftieth in the race; it's his fiftieth birthday on Monday.

fight [fait] *verb*
to try to beat someone using force; the boys are fighting in the street; the police are fighting to reduce traffic accidents; doctors are fighting against disease; the two dogs were fighting over a bone.
fights—fighting—fought [fɔːt]—**has fought**

fig·ure ['figjər] 1. *noun*
written number; write two hundred and twenty-three in figures; double figures = between 10 and 99; his salary is in five figures = he earns more than $10,000.
2. *verb*
(*a*) to think; I figured it was time to go home.
(*b*) to figure something out = to try to understand; I can't figure it out; that figures = that makes sense.
figures—figuring—figured—has figured

fill [fil] *verb*
(*a*) to make something full; he filled the box with books; she was filling the bottle with water.
(*b*) to fill a tooth = to put metal into a hole in a tooth to stop it from going bad.
fills—filling—filled—has filled

fill in, *verb*
to write in the blank spaces; fill in your name and address; fill in the missing words.

fill·ing, *noun*
(*a*) metal put into a hole in your tooth by a dentist; I had to have two fillings when I went to the dentist's.
(*b*) food which goes inside some other food; cake with a chocolate filling.

fill·ing sta·tion, *noun*
place where you can buy gasoline; stop at the next filling station to ask the way.

fill up, *verb*
to make something completely full; he filled up the bottle and put the top back on; fill her up = please fill the car with gasoline.
Note: **fill the glass up** *or* **fill up the glass** *but only* **fill it up**

film [film] 1. *noun*
(*a*) moving pictures shown in a theater, taken with a movie camera; have you seen this Charlie Chaplin film? we watched the film on TV.
(*b*) roll of material which you put into a camera which is used for taking photos or movies; I must buy a film before I go on vacation; do you want a color film or a black and white one?
2. *verb*
to make a movie of something; the TV cameras filmed the President's speech.
films—filming—filmed—has filmed

fi·nal ['fainəl] *adjective*
which comes at the end; he dies in the final minutes of the movie; what was the final score in the football game?

fi·nal·ly ['fainəlɪ] *adverb*
in the end; the car wouldn't start, there were no buses, so finally we had to walk; we waited for half an hour, and he finally arrived at 8:30.

find [faɪnd] *verb*

(*a*) to discover something (either by chance or by looking for it) which was hidden or lost; to discover something which was not known before; **I found a $10 bill in the street; did she find the book she was looking for? scientists have found that cold water helps a headache; doctors are still trying to find a cure for colds.**

(*b*) to feel/to have an opinion; **I found this film very interesting; he finds his work too easy.**

finds—finding—found [faʊnd]—**has found**

find out, *verb*

to discover (a fact); **the police are trying to find out why she went to Pittsburgh; I'm going to the library to find out about how to take care of a dog.**

find time, *verb*

to make enough time to do something; **although he was very busy, he found time to phone his wife.**

fine [faɪn] 1. *adjective*

(*a*) well/good; **I was sick yesterday, but I'm feeling fine today; how are things?—fine! it's a fine day for a picnic.**

(*b*) very thin/very small; **sharpen your pencil to a very fine point; I can't read this book—the print is too fine.**

fine—finer—finest

2. *noun*

money which you have to pay for doing something wrong; **I had to pay a $100 fine for driving too fast.**

3. *verb*

to make someone pay money for having done something wrong; **he was fined $100 for driving too fast.**

fines—fining—fined—has fined

fin·ger ['fɪŋgər] *noun*

one of the five parts at the end of your hand, but usually not including your thumb; part of a glove into which a finger goes; **she wears a ring on her little finger; he touched the switch with his finger; to keep your fingers crossed** = to hope that something will happen as you want it to happen.

fin·ger·nail, *noun*

thin hard part covering the end of a finger; **she painted her fingernails red.**

fin·ger·print, *noun*

mark left by a finger when you touch something; **the police found fingerprints near the broken window.**

fin·ger·tip, *noun*

the end of a finger; **she touched the leaf with her fingertip.**

fin·ish ['fɪnɪʃ] 1. *noun*

the end; **the crowd waited to see the finish of the race.**

plural **finishes**

2. *verb*

to do something completely; to come to an end; **I've finished my homework; tell me when you've finished reading the book; we can't watch TV until we've finished the dishes; the movie finished at 10:30.**

finishes—finishing—finished—has finished

fin·ish off, *verb*

to do something completely; **have you finished off your work?**

fin·ish up, *verb*

to eat something completely; **you must finish up your potatoes** = eat them all.

Note: **he finished his work off** *or* **he finished off his work, finish up your meat** *or* **finish your meat up,** *etc., but only* **finish it off, finish it up,** *etc.*

fin·ish with, *verb*

to finish using something; **have you finished with the newspaper? can I borrow the can opener when you've finished with it?**

fire ['faɪr] 1. *noun*

(*a*) something which is burning/which heats; **we sat in front of a log fire; we made a fire in the yard to burn the dead leaves.**

(*b*) burning buildings; **the firemen raced to the fire.**

to catch fire = to start to burn because of something else which is burning; **the house caught fire; take that carpet away—it might catch fire.**

to set fire to = to make something start burning; **his cigarette set fire to the chair.**

on fire = burning; **call the fire department—the house is on fire.**

2. verb

to shoot a gun; **the police fired at the car; we could hear the guns firing in the distance.**

fires—firing—fired—has fired

fire de·part·ment, *noun*

group of people in a city, who try to put out fires.

fire en·gine, *noun*

large vehicle, with ladders and pumps, which is used to put out fires.

fire·fly, *noun*

bug which glows when it is dark.

plural **fireflies**

fire·house, *noun*

place where firemen are based.

fire·man, *noun*

man who tries to put out fires; **the firemen were fighting the fire on the west side of the town.**

plural **firemen**

fire·place, *noun*

place in a room where you can light a fire with coal or wood to heat the room.

fire·proof, *adjective*

which cannot burn or be burned by fire; **a fireproof dish.**

fire sta·tion, *noun*

place where firemen are based.

fire·wood, *noun*

wood which is ready to be used to make a fire; **bring some more firewood in; they chopped the table up for firewood.**

no plural: **some firewood; a pile of firewood**

firm [fɜrm] *1. noun*

business company; **he works for a law firm in New York; it is the biggest engineering firm in the country.**

2. adjective

solid/strong; **make sure that chair is firm before you sit on it.**

firm—firmer—firmest

firm·ly, *adverb*

in a strong way; **she told them firmly to keep quiet.**

first [fɜrst] **1. 1st** *adjective & noun*

referring to one; **my birthday is on August first (August 1); King Charles the First (Charles I); it's the baby's first birthday on Tuesday; the post office is the first building on the left.**

Note: with dates **first** *is usually written* **1: August 1, 1980; December 1, 1669;** *with names of kings and queens* **first** *is usually written* **I: King Charles I**

2. adverb

(*a*) at the beginning/before doing anything else; **he came first in the race; do your homework first, and then we can go out.**

(*b*) for the first time: **when did you first go to Germany?**

at first = at the beginning; **he didn't like his job at first but later got used to it; at first I didn't want to go to the party, but then I changed my mind.**

first aid, *noun*

helping people who are hurt; **the police gave the driver first aid; he carries a first aid kit in his car.**

first class, *noun & adverb*
first-class, *adjective*

most expensive seats in a train or plane; most expensive and fastest way of sending a letter; **a first-class ticket to Miami; he always travels first class; send that letter first class—I want it to arrive quickly; first class is always very comfortable.**

first·ly, *adverb*

to begin with; **firstly I don't want to go to school and secondly I'm too sick to go to school.**

fish [fɪʃ] *1. noun*

animal which lives in water and which you can usually eat; **look at all those fish in the lake; I caught six little fish; we're having fried fish for dinner.**

plural is usually **fish: some fish; three fish**

2. verb

to try to catch fish; **we go fishing in the river every Sunday; don't fish in that lake.**

fishes—fishing—fished—has fished

fish·ing, *noun*
sport where you try to catch fish; **he doesn't like fishing.**

fit [fɪt] **1.** *adjective*
in good condition for something; **he isn't fit enough to work** = he is still too sick to work; **you'll have to get fit before the football game; he's not fit to be a teacher.**
fit—fitter—fittest

2. *verb*
(*a*) to be the right size/shape; **he has grown so tall that his pants don't fit him any more; these shoes don't fit me— they're too tight.**
(*b*) to put in place; **I want to fit a new bathtub in the bathroom.**
fits—fitting—fitted—has fitted

fit in, fit into, *verb*
to arrange something so that it goes into the space allowed for it; **I don't think I can fit in any vacation this year as I have too much work; how can you fit everything into that little box?**

five [faɪv] number 5
she drank five cups of coffee; he's five (years old); come for dinner at five (o'clock).

fix [fiks] *verb*
(*a*) to fasten/to attach; **he fixed the cup- board to the wall; she fixed a notice to the post with a thumbtack.**
(*b*) to repair; **can you fix the car engine for me?**
(*c*) to arrange; **the meeting has been fixed for next week.**
(*d*) to get food ready; **she's fixing some drinks; can you fix me some breakfast?**
fixes—fixing—fixed—has fixed

flag [flæg] *noun*
piece of cloth with a pattern on it which is attached to a pole, to show a country/a club, etc.; **each ship carries the flag of its country; a ship flying the U.S. flag; for the Fourth of July, we hung a flag in our window.**
flag·pole, *noun*
pole which you attach a flag to.

flame [fleɪm] *noun*
bright light coming from something which is burning; **the flame of a candle;**

the house was in flames = was burning; **the car burst into flames** = suddenly started to burn.

flash [flæʃ] **1.** *noun*
sudden light; **a flash of lightning; if you want to take a picture in the dark, you should use a flash; a news flash** = short piece of important news.
plural **flashes**

2. *verb*
(*a*) to shine (a light) very quickly; **the light flashed twice; a police car has a blue flashing light; he flashed a light in my eyes.**
(*b*) to go very quickly; **the car flashed past the traffic lights; several motor- cycles flashed by.**
flashes—flashing—flashed—has flashed
flash bulb, *noun*
special bulb which gives a quick light so that you can take a picture.
flash·light, *noun*
electric light which you can carry in your hand; **the policeman shone his flash- light into the room; I can't see anything in the dark—do you have a flashlight?**

flat [flæt] **1.** *adjective & adverb*
level; **a flat road; spread the paper out flat on the table; the soldiers lay flat on the ground; a flat tire** = tire which has lost all the air in it.
2. *noun*
tire which has no air in it; **his bicycle had a flat and so he had to walk home.**

flew [fluː] *see* **fly**

flies [flaɪz] *see* **fly**

flight [flaɪt] *noun*
(*a*) journey through the air; **the flight to New York leaves in 15 minutes; there are six flights a day to Chicago; when does the New York flight leave? how long is the flight from Washington to Atlanta? the flight lasts about 3 hours.**
(*b*) **flight of stairs** = set of stairs which go up straight; **turn left at the top of the first flight of stairs.**

float [floʊt] *verb*
to lie on top of a liquid/not to sink;

leaves were floating on the lake; he put his model boat into the water and it floated.

floats—floating—floated—has floated

flood [flʌd] 1. *noun*
large amount of water over land which is usually dry; **after the rainstorm there were floods in the valley.**
2. *verb*
to cover with a large amount of water; **the fields were flooded; the washing machine flooded the floor.**

floods—flooding—flooded—has flooded

floor [flɔːr] *noun*
(*a*) part of a room on which you walk; **put that box down on the floor; she lay on the floor and looked up at the ceiling.**
(*b*) all the rooms on one level in a building; **the shop is on the first floor** = the floor which is level with the street; **his office is on the second floor; he walked up the stairs to the top floor.**

flour ['flaʊər] *noun*
seeds of cereal ground to powder, used for making bread and cakes, etc.; **mix flour and butter together in a bowl.**
no plural

flow [fləʊ] *verb*
to go past like a liquid; **the water flowed down the pipe; the traffic was flowing around the square; the river flows into the sea.**

flows—flowing—flowed—has flowed

flow·er ['flaʊər] 1. *noun*
part of a plant which usually has a bright color, which attracts bees, and which then forms fruit; **she picked a bunch of flowers; the apple trees are in flower** = they are covered with flowers.
2. *verb*
to produce flowers; **the apple trees flowered early this year; this plant only flowers once every ten years.**

flowers—flowering—flowered—has flowered

flow·er·pot, *noun*
container for a plant.

flown [fləʊn] *see* **fly**

flunk [flʌŋk] *verb*
to fail (a test); **she flunked her driving test; he flunked math.**

flunks—flunking—flunked—has flunked

fly [flaɪ] 1. *noun*
small insect with two wings, often living in houses; **try to kill that fly; flies can walk on the ceiling.**
plural **flies**
2. *verb*
(*a*) to move through the air; to make (a plane) move through the air; **he is flying his own plane; the birds flew away; I'm flying to Hong Kong next week; to go from New York to Los Angeles you have to fly over sixteen different states; he has flown across the Atlantic twice.**
(*b*) to put up (a flag); **the ship was flying the U.S. flag.**

flies—flying—flew—has flown

fog [fɔːg] *noun*
thick cloud near the ground which it is difficult to see through; **the planes couldn't take off because of fog; the fog is so thick that you must drive slowly.**
fog·gy, *adjective*
covered in fog; **foggy weather; he walked around the foggy streets; don't drive fast when it's foggy.**

foggy—foggier—foggiest

fold [fəʊld] *verb*
to bend something so that part of it is on top of the rest; **he folded the letter and put it in an envelope; he folded up the newspaper; to fold your arms** = to rest one arm on the other across your chest.

folds—folding—folded—has folded

fol·low ['fɒləʊ] *verb*
(*a*) to come after or behind; **follow me and I will show you the way; C follows B in the alphabet; the police followed the man across the town.**

(*b*) to be the result of something; **if he wrote the letter, it follows that he must have known the news.**
follows—following—followed—has followed

fol·low·ing, *adjective*
which comes after; **look at the following pages; the following day** = the next day.

fond of ['fɒnd 'əv] *adjective*
having a liking for; **I'm fond of food; she's fond of dancing** = she likes dancing; **he's very fond of cheese; I'm not very fond of loud music.**
fond—fonder—fondest

food [fuːd] *noun*
things which you eat; **this restaurant is famous for its food; do you like Chinese food? we went on a picnic but forgot to bring the food; this food tastes funny.**
food *is usually used in the singular*

foot [fʊt] *noun*
(*a*) end part of your leg on which you stand; **he has big feet; you stepped on my foot; on foot** = walking; **we went to the stores on foot; don't wait for the bus—it's quicker to go on foot.**
(*b*) bottom part/end; **she was sitting on the foot of my bed; he sat at the foot of the stairs; the house is at the foot of the hill; the page number is at the foot of the page.**
(*c*) measurement of how long something is (= 12 inches); **the table is three feet wide; he is almost six feet tall; she is five foot six inches tall (5′ 6″;** *say* "**she's five foot six**").
plural **feet**
Note: when used with **inches foot** *has no plural:* **five foot six (inches tall)** *but* **six feet tall**
Note: with numbers **foot** *is often written* ′: **a 6′ ladder; he is 5′ 6″ (five foot six);** *see also* **inch**

foot·ball, *noun*
(*a*) ball used for kicking; **he was kicking a football around in the yard; throw me that football.**
(*b*) game played by two teams with a

ball which can be kicked; **a football game; they were playing football in the field; come and have a game of football; do you always watch the football games on TV?**

foot·ball field, foot·ball ground, *noun*
place where football is played.

foot·path, *noun*
path for people to walk on, but not to ride on.

foot·step, *noun*
sound made by a foot touching the ground; **we heard quiet footsteps outside the room.**

for [fɔːr] *preposition*
(*a*) (*showing how something is used*) **this box is for old papers; what's that key for? what did she say that for?** = why did she say that?
(*b*) (*showing why something is given*) **what did your parents give you for Christmas? what shall we buy John for his birthday?**
(*c*) (*showing person who gets something*) **the mailman has brought a package for you; this present is for your mother.**
(*d*) (*showing how long something happens*) **he has gone to Germany for a week; I have been waiting for hours.**
(*e*) (*showing direction*) **is this the train for Boston?**
as for = as far as something is concerned; **as for me, I'm going to bed.**
for ex·am·ple/for in·stance = to show one thing among many; **large animals, for example elephants, are expensive to feed.**
Note: **for example** *is often written* **e.g.**
for good = for always; **he left the house for good.**
for keeps = for always; **he gave her the ring for keeps.**

for·bid [fər'bɪd] *verb*
to tell someone not to do something; **smoking is forbidden in the theater; the committee has forbidden any discussion**

of the plan; the rules of baseball forbid the batter to touch the ball.
forbids—forbidding—forbade [fər'bæd]—has forbidden

force [fɔːrs] 1. *noun*
(a) strength; the tree was blown down by the force of the wind.
(b) group of people in uniform; the police force = all the police; the armed forces = the army, navy, and air force.
2. *verb*
to make someone do something; they forced him to lie on the floor; she was forced to do whatever they wanted.
forces—forcing—forced—has forced

fore·head ['fɔːrɪd] *noun*
part of your face above your eyes.

for·eign ['fɔːrɪn] *adjective*
not belonging to your own country; he speaks several foreign languages.
for·eign·er, *noun*
person who comes from another country.

for·est ['fɔːrɪst] *noun*
large area covered with trees; many wild animals live in the forests of South America.

for·ev·er [fə'revər] *adverb*
always; I will love you forever; he's forever watching TV.

for·gave [fər'geɪv] *see* **forgive**

for·get [fər'get] *verb*
not to remember; he forgot to put on his pants; he has forgotten how to ride a bike; I forgot all about my appointment with the dentist; don't forget to lock the door.
forgets—forgetting—forgot [fər'gɒt]—forgotten [fər'gɒtn]

for·give [fər'gɪv] *verb*
to stop being angry with someone who has done something bad; she forgave him when he said he was sorry; please forgive me for being so late.
forgives—forgiving—forgave [fər'geɪv]—has forgiven

for·got [fər'gɒt], **for·got·ten [fər'gɒtn],** *see* **forget**

fork [fɔːrk] *noun*
tool with a handle at one end and several sharp points at the other, used for picking things up especially when eating; you can't eat soup with a knife and fork; use your fork to eat your meat—don't use your fingers; each person had a knife, fork and spoon.

form [fɔːrm] 1. *noun*
(a) shape; she has a ring in the form of a letter A.
(b) paper with blank spaces which you have to write in; you have to fill in a form when you want to pay your taxes.
(c) state/condition; our team was in good form and won easily; he's in good form today = he is very amusing/is doing things well.
2. *verb*
to make; to be; the children formed a circle around the teacher; meat forms the most expensive part of what we eat.
forms—forming—formed—has formed

for·mer ['fɔːrmər] *adjective*
at an earlier time; he's a former army officer = he used to be an officer in the past.
for·mer·ly, *adverb*
at an earlier time; this house was formerly a railroad station; she was formerly the principal of the local school.

for·tu·nate ['fɔːrtʃənət] *adjective*
lucky; how fortunate that you happened to be there!
fortunately, *adverb*
luckily.

for·ty ['fɔːrtɪ] number 40
he's forty (years old); she has forty pairs of shoes; he's in his forties = he is between 40 and 49 years old.
Note: **forty-one** (41), **forty-two** (42), *but* **forty-first** (41st), **forty-second** (42nd), *etc.*

for·ti·eth, 40th, *adjective & noun*
she came fortieth in the race; it's my fortieth birthday tomorrow.

for·ward ['fɔ:rwərd] 1. *adverb* (*also* **forwards**)
toward the front; **he ran forwards to shake my hand; the police asked the crowd to move forward;** *see also* **backward.**
2. *noun*
player in football and other games who plays in the front row.
3. *verb*
to send something on; **he forwarded the letter to his lawyer.**
fowards—forwarding—forwarded—has forwarded

fought [fɔ:t] *see* **fight**

found [faʊnd] *see* **find**

four [fɔ:r] number 4
she's four (years old); come and see me at four (o'clock); a square has four corners.
four·teen, number 14
I have fourteen books to read for my English test; she's fourteen (years old).
four·teenth, 14th, *adjective & noun*
she came fourteenth in her race; July fourteenth (July 14); it was his fourteenth birthday yesterday.
fourth, 4th, *adjective & noun*
they live in the fourth house from the corner; August fourth (August 4); Charles the Fourth (Charles IV); it's her fourth birthday tomorrow; a fourth = 25%.
Note: instead of "a fourth" you usually say "a quarter."
Note: with dates **fourth** *is usually written* 4: June 4, 1979; August 4, 1981; *with names of kings and queens* **fourth** *is usually written* IV: King Charles IV

frame [freɪm] *noun*
main part of a building/ship/bicycle, etc., which holds it together; **the bicycle has a very light frame; I've broken the frame of my glasses; picture frame =** wooden edge around a picture.

free [fri:] *adjective*
(*a*) not busy/not occupied; **are you free tonight? there is a table free in the corner of the restaurant.**
(*b*) not costing any money; **if you cut off the top of the cereal box you can get a free book; I didn't pay anything for my ticket—I got it free! children are admitted free, but adults have to pay $1.**
(*c*) able to do what you want/not forced to do anything; **he's free to do what he wants; it's a free country.**
free—freer—freest

free·way, *noun*
highway where you can drive fast.

freeze [fri:z] *verb*
(*a*) to be so cold that water turns to ice; **it is freezing outside; they say it will freeze tomorrow; I'm freezing =** I'm very cold.
(*b*) to make something very cold; to become very cold; **I'll cook some frozen peas to eat with the fish; we freeze a lot of vegetables from our farm; the river has frozen over =** is covered with ice.
freezes—freezing—froze [frəʊz]**—has frozen** ['frəʊzn]

freez·er, *noun*
powerful refrigerator which keeps food frozen.
freeze up, *verb*
to freeze completely; **all the pipes in the house froze up.**

fre·quent ['fri:kwənt] *adjective*
which happens or comes often; **there are frequent trains to Washington; she is a frequent visitor.**
fre·quent·ly, *adverb*
happening often; **it frequently rains in the western part of the country.**

fresh [freʃ] *adjective*
(*a*) not used/not dirty; **I'll get some fresh towels; fresh air =** open air; **they came out of the mine into the fresh air.**
(*b*) recently made; **fresh bread.**
(*c*) not canned or frozen; **fresh fish; fresh fruit salad; fresh vegetables are expensive in winter.**
(*d*) **fresh water =** water which is not salt (i.e. in a river or lake).
fresh—fresher—freshest

Fri·day ['fraɪdɪ] *noun*
day between Thursday and Saturday,
the sixth day of the week; **he came to see
me last Friday; we always go to the
movies on Fridays; I'll see you next
Friday; today is Friday, June 20.**

fried [fraɪd] *see* **fry**

friend [frend] *noun*
person whom you know well and like;
**Henry is my best friend; she's going on
vacation with some friends from college; to make friends with someone** =
to get to know and like someone; **these
are the people we made friends with on
our vacation.**
friend·ly, *adjective*
kind/helpful; **don't be afraid of the
dog—he's very friendly; we're on friendly
terms with the people who live next door**
= we are friends.
friendly—friendlier—friendliest

fries [fraɪz] *see* **fry**

fright·en ['fraɪtən] *verb*
to make someone afraid; **the noise
frightened me; a frightening movie about
insects which eat people.**
**frightens—frightening—
frightened—has frightened**

fright·ened, *adjective*
afraid; **I'm frightened by spiders; don't
leave me alone—I'm frightened in the
dark.**

frog [frɔ:g] *noun*
small animal with no tail, which lives in
water or on land and can jump; **a little
green frog jumped into the river.**
frog·man, *noun*
man who wears a special suit and
works under water.
plural **frogmen**

from [frɒm *or* frəm] *preposition*
(*a*) out of; **take two from three, and you
have one left; he comes from Mexico.**
(*b*) (*showing where something starts or
started*) **the bee moved from flower to
flower; I'll be at home from 9 o'clock in
the morning; she works from Monday to
Friday; it is two miles from here to the
post office; here's a letter from Peter.**

(*c*) (*showing difference*) **I can't tell butter
from margarine; your job is very different
from mine.**
(*d*) (*showing cause*) **he died from his disease; she suffers from headaches.**

front [frʌnt] *noun*
part of something which faces forwards;
**the front of the house faces south; there
is a picture of the Golden Gate Bridge
on the front of the book; he spilled soup
down the front of his shirt; there was a
picture of him on the front page of the
newspaper.**
in front of = on the front side of
something; **he was standing in front of
the bus when it suddenly started; there
are two people in front of me in the line;
park your car in front of the house.**

frost [frɔ:st] *noun*
freezing weather when the temperature
is below the freezing point of water;
there was a frost last night.
frost·ing, *noun*
sweet paste which is put on top of a
cake.
frost·y, *adjective*
very cold; **frosty weather.**
frosty—frostier—frostiest

froze [frəʊz], **fro·zen** ['frəʊzn] *see*
freeze

frown [fraʊn] **1.** *noun*
look on your face when you pull down
your eyebrows to show you are angry.
2. *verb*
to show you are angry by pulling down
your eyebrows; **the teacher frowned
when he saw my work.**
**frowns—frowning—frowned—
has frowned**

fruit [fru:t] *noun*
part of a plant which contains the seeds,
and which is often eaten; **can you buy
me some fruit at the market? his yard
is full of fruit trees; we ought to eat all
the fruit quickly or it will go bad; fruit
salad** = pieces of fruit chopped up and
mixed together.
no plural: **some fruit/a lot of fruit**

fry [fraɪ] *verb*
to cook in hot oil or fat; fried eggs; do you want your eggs fried or boiled? he was frying onions in the kitchen.
fries [fraɪz]—**frying**—**fried** [fraɪd]—**has fried**

French fries = long thin pieces of potato fried in deep oil.
fry·ing pan, *noun*
wide pan with low sides and a long handle, used for frying.

fudge [fʌdʒ] *noun*
type of chocolate candy; a fudge cake; ice cream with fudge sauce.
no plural

fu·el [ˈfjuːəl] *noun*
something which you burn to give heat, to drive a car, etc.; scientists are trying to find new types of fuel; the plane had to land in the field because it ran out of fuel.
no plural

full [fʊl] *adjective*
(*a*) with as much inside as possible; is the bottle full? the bag is full of apples; the bus was so full we couldn't get on; I'm full = I have eaten so much that I can't eat any more.
(*b*) complete; you must write down the full details of your job; children over 12 must pay full fare = the same fare as an adult; full moon = when the moon is round.
full—fuller—fullest

fun [fʌn] *noun*
amusement; we had some fun on the beach = we enjoyed ourselves; to make fun of someone = to laugh at someone; for fun = as a joke; she poured water down his neck for fun.
no plural
fun·ny, *adjective*
(*a*) which makes you laugh; we saw a

funny program on TV; she wore a funny hat; let me tell you a funny story about my brother.
(*b*) strange/odd; he was behaving in a funny way; there's a funny smell in the kitchen.
funny—funnier—funniest

fur [fɜr] *noun*
thick hair on an animal; our cat has soft white fur; the lady was wearing a fur coat.
no plural
fur·ry, *adjective*
covered with fur; a little furry animal.
furry—furrier—furriest

fur·ni·ture [ˈfɜrnɪtʃər] *noun*
tables/chairs/beds/cupboards, etc.; someone has stolen all our furniture; you should move the furniture out of the room before you paint the ceiling.
no plural: **some furniture; a lot of furniture; a piece of furniture**

fur·ther [ˈfɜrðər] *adverb & adjective*
(*a*) at a greater distance away; can you move further back? they went further away; the post office is further away than the police station; Los Angeles is further from Miami than it is from Seattle.
(*b*) more; we want further information; can you give me further details of when the accident took place?
fur·thest, *adverb & adjective*
at the greatest distance; he lives furthest from the office; the furthest distance I have traveled by train is 800 miles.

fu·ture [ˈfjuːtʃər] *noun*
(*a*) time which has not yet happened; in the future, I will try to eat less; I'll be more careful in the future = next time this happens.
(*b*) (*also* future tense) part of a verb which shows that something will happen; "he will go" and "he is going to go" are forms of the future of "to go."

Gg

gal·lon ['gælən] *noun*
measurement of liquids which equals four quarts; **the car does twenty miles to the gallon** = each gallon of gas is enough to drive twenty miles; **the bucket can hold two gallons.**

game [geɪm] *noun*
(*a*) sport which you play, and which you can win because of your skill, strength or luck; **would you like to play a game of tennis? he's not very good at games; our team won all its games this year.**
(*b*) single round which is part of a tennis match; **he's winning, six games to three.**

gang [gæŋ] *noun*
group of people who go around or work together; **there's a gang of kids in the schoolyard.**
gang·ster, *noun*
member of a gang of criminals.

ga·rage [gə'rɑːʒ] *noun*
(*a*) small building where you can keep a car; **put the car in the garage; he drove the car out of the garage; don't forget to lock the garage door.**
(*b*) business where cars, etc., are repaired; **where's the nearest garage?— my car has broken down; I can't drive you to the station—my car is in the garage.**

gar·bage ['gɑːrbɪdʒ] *noun*
things which are not needed and which have been thrown away; **put all that garbage in the trash can; there was garbage all over the street after the football game.**
no plural: **some garbage; a bag of garbage**

gar·bage can, *noun*

special container in which you put garbage.

gar·den ['gɑːrdən] *noun*
(*a*) ground used for growing vegetables, flowers, etc.; **he grows tomatoes in his garden; a vegetable garden; your mother's working in the garden.**
(*b*) **public gardens** = place where there are flowers and grass and where people can go to walk around and enjoy themselves.
gar·den·er, *noun*
person who takes care of a garden.
gar·den·ing, *noun*
taking care of a garden; **he likes gardening; she does some gardening every Saturday.**

gas [gæs] *noun*
(*a*) something which, like air, has no shape and cannot usually be seen; often produced from coal or found underground, and used to cook or heat; **a gas stove; we heat our house by gas.**
(*b*) gasoline/liquid used to drive a motor; **my Ford doesn't use much gas; can you see a gas station somewhere—I need to buy some gas; gas prices are going up all the time.**
plural **gases** *is only used to mean different types of gas*

gas sta·tion, *noun*
place where you can buy gasoline; **we ran out of gasoline and there was no gas station for miles.**

gas·o·line ['gæsəliːn] *noun*
liquid used to drive a motor; **how many miles does your car do to a gallon of gasoline?**
no plural

gate [geɪt] *noun*
(*a*) outside door which is in an open

wall or fence; **if you leave the gate open, the sheep will get out of the field; close the gate; there is a white gate which opens into the yard.**
(*b*) door which leads to an airplane at an airport; **go to gate 25 for flight AB193.**
gate·way, *noun*
place where a gate is fixed; **he stood in the gateway and wouldn't let us go through.**

gath·er [ˈgæðər] *verb*
(*a*) to bring together/to collect; **she was gathering peas; the speaker gathered up his papers; the children gathered around the Christmas tree.**
(*b*) to understand; **I gather you're leaving for Africa tomorrow; she gathered that you would come to the party.**
(*c*) **to gather speed** = to go faster; **he tried to jump off the truck as it was gathering speed.**
gathers—gathering—gathered— has gathered

gave [geɪv] *see* **give**

gen·er·al [ˈdʒenərəl] 1. *adjective*
not particular; which concerns everything or everybody; **there was a general feeling of excitement; a general election** = election where all the voters in a country can vote or where many offices are voted on; **in general** = normally; **in general, the winters are wet and cold.**
2. *noun*
important officer in the army; **General Robinson.**
gen·er·al·ly, *adverb*
normally; **we generally spend our vacation in Florida.**

gen·tle [ˈdʒentl] *adjective*
soft; kind; **the doctor has gentle hands; you must be gentle when you are holding a little baby.**
gentle—gentler—gentlest

gen·tle·man, *noun*
(*a*) (*polite way of referring to men*) **well, gentlemen, you may sit down.**
(*b*) polite man; **he's a real gentleman.**
gen·tle·man·ly, *adjective*
polite; **he spoke in a gentlemanly way.**

gent·ly, *adverb*
softly and kindly; **the doctor gently examined the baby.**

ge·og·ra·phy [dʒiːˈɒgrəfiː] *noun*
study of the earth/weather/countries, etc.; **geography is my best subject; he got the best grades in geography; I lost my geography book.**
no plural

get [get] *verb*
(*a*) to receive; **I got a letter this morning; he will get $10 for cutting the grass; she gets more money than I do.**
(*b*) to arrive; **we got home late; when will you get to Baltimore?**
(*c*) to become; **he's getting old; she got fat from eating too much; the light got brighter and brighter; this towel is getting dirty.**
(*d*) to make something happen; to pay someone to do something; to talk someone into doing something; **I must get my shoes fixed; can you get my car filled up at the gas station? I'll try and get him to bring his car.**
(*e*) **to have got to** = must; **you have got to come** = you must come.
(*f*) to catch (a disease); **I think I'm getting a cold; she got measles.**
(*g*) *used with adjectives or past of verbs to mean* to do; **I got my work finished in time; she's getting the dinner ready.**
gets—getting—got [gɒt]—**has got/gotten**

get a·cross, *verb*
(*a*) to go across; **they got across the river by boat.**
(*b*) to make someone understand; **we managed to get the message across, although no one understood English; I'm trying to get across to him that he has to work harder.**

get a·long, *verb*
(*a*) to manage/to work; **we seem to get along fine without any electricity.**
(*b*) to be friendly with; **my neighbor and I don't get along very well; he gets along with his boss.**

get a·round, *verb*

(a) to move about; since she had the accident she gets around with difficulty; the news soon got around that he was married.

(b) to find time to do something; hopefully I will get around to painting the kitchen next month.

get a·way, *verb*
to escape; the thieves got away in a stolen car.

get a·way with, *verb*
to do something wrong without being punished; he always gets away with not doing his homework.

get back, *verb*
(a) to return; we got back home very late; when did you get back from your vacation?

(b) to get something again which you had before; he got his book back; I want to get my coat back.

get by, *verb*
(a) to pass; the truck is so wide no one can get by.

(b) to manage to live; I can't get by on $100 a week.

get down, *verb*
(a) to go down; she got down off the ladder.

(b) to bring down; can you get that box down for me?

get down to, *verb*
to start working hard; he will have to get down to work if he wants to pass his final exams.

get dressed, *verb*
to put your clothes on; he got dressed quickly because he didn't want to be late for work; she was getting dressed when the phone rang.

get in, *verb*
to go inside (a car, etc.); hurry up and get in—the train is waiting to leave; she got in and sat down; the burglars got in through the kitchen window.

get in·to, *verb*
to go inside (a car, etc.); he got into the car and sat down; I was getting into bed when the phone rang; the burglars got into the house through the kitchen window.
Note: **get into** *is always followed by a noun*

get off, *verb*
to come down from; he got off his bicycle; you'll have to get off the bus at the next stop.

get on, *verb*
(a) to go into (a bus, etc.); we got on the bus in front of the post office; she got on her bike and rode away.

(b) to become old; Mr. Jones is getting on.

get on with, *verb*
(a) to continue to do some work; I have to get on with my homework.

(b) to be friendly with someone; he gets on very well with everyone; I didn't get on with the boss.

get out, *verb*
(a) to take out; get your books out of the box; he was getting his car out of the garage.

(b) to go outside; she was getting out of her car; the truck stopped and the driver got out; the burglars got out through the front door.

get o·ver, *verb*
to become better after an illness or upsetting event; he got over his cold; she never got over her mother's death.

get through, *verb*
(a) to go through; the sheep got through the hole in the fence.

(b) to finish; she got through all her homework.

get through with, *verb*
to finish; when you get through with the gardening, perhaps you could paint the fence.

get up, *verb*
to stand up; to get out of bed; he got up from his chair and walked out of the room; what time did you get up? I was getting up when the phone rang.

girl [gɜrl] *noun*
female child; she's only a little girl; they have three children—two boys and a girl; he met a girl at the bus stop; my sister goes to a girls' school.

give [gɪv] *verb*
(a) to pass something to someone; give me another apple; she gave him a kiss; you ought to give that book to the teacher.

(*b*) to pass a present to someone; **I gave him a watch for his birthday.**

gives—giving—gave [geɪv]**—has given**

give back, *verb*
to hand something back to someone; **give me back my watch/give me my watch back; he gave back everything he had stolen.**
Note: **give the watch back** *or* **give back the watch** *but only* **give it back**

give in, *verb*
to agree with something even if you did not want to before; **we asked him every day if we could go to the movies, and in the end he gave in** = he said we could go.

give out, *verb*
to come to an end; **the battery gave out so I can't use my radio.**

giv·er, *noun*
person who gives.

give up, *verb*
to stop doing something; **he gave up smoking; I give up!** = I will never guess the answer, please tell me.

glad [glæd] *adjective*
pleased; **I'm glad to see you; we're glad you came; she was glad to sit down.**

glance [glæns] **1.** *noun*
quick look; **he took only a glance at the picture.**
2. *verb*
to look quickly; **she glanced around the room; the teacher glanced at his book.**
glances—glancing—glanced—has glanced

glass [glæs] *noun*
(*a*) material which you can see through, used to make windows; **the doors are made of glass; a glass roof.**
no plural: **some glass; a piece of glass**
(*b*) thing to drink out of, usually made of glass; **put the glasses on the table; he broke a glass as he was washing the dishes; give him some more milk, his glass is empty.**
(*c*) contents of a glass; **he drinks a glass of**

milk every evening; **two glasses of wine.**
plural **glasses** *for* (*b*) *and* (*c*)

glas·ses, *plural noun*
pieces of glass which you wear in front of your eyes to help you see better; **she was wearing dark glasses; he has glasses with gold frames; can you see my glasses anywhere?**

glove [glʌv] *noun*
piece of clothing which you wear on your hand; **the doctor was wearing rubber gloves; I've bought a new pair of gloves; put your gloves on if you are going to play in the snow.**

glow [gləʊ] **1.** *noun*
bright warm light; **the glow of the fire.**
2. *verb*
to shine with a warm light; **the fire glowed in the dark.**
glows—glowing—glowed—has glowed

glue [gluː] **1.** *noun*
material which sticks things together; **you can fix the broken cup with glue; he put some glue on the teacher's chair.**
no plural: **some glue; a tube of glue**
2. *verb*
to stick things together with glue; **he glued the handle onto the cup; she glued the pieces together.**
glues—gluing—glued—has glued

go [gəʊ] *verb*
(*a*) to move from one place to another; **he has gone to New York; she went from Boston to Montreal; they all went across the street; he went down the stairs; the car went up the hill; do you go to school by bus? she has gone shopping; we all went for a walk.**
(*b*) to work; **my watch won't go; the plans are going smoothly; I'm trying to get my motorcycle to go.**
(*c*) to leave; **it's time for us to go.**
(*d*) to fit; **this box won't go into the back of the car; this book goes on the top shelf.**
(*e*) to become; **she went pale; cows go mad when they see red; his hair is**

going gray; the old lady is going deaf.

goes—going—went [went]—**has gone** [gɒn]

to be go·ing to, *verb*
to be just about to do something; to intend to do something; **that tree is going to fall down; are you going to sing? it's going to be sunny tomorrow; I am going to read the newspaper.**

go a·way, *verb*
to leave; **they went away and we never saw them again.**

go back, *verb*
to return; **he went back home; let's all go back to the bus stop.**

go on, *verb*
(*a*) to continue; **go on, don't stop; he went on singing; go on with your work.**
(*b*) to happen; **what has been going on here?**

go out, *verb*
(*a*) to move outside; **she went out of the house.**
(*b*) to stop shining/to stop burning; **the fire has gone out; the lights went out and we were left in the dark.**

go with·out, *verb*
not to have something which you usually have; **he got up late and had to go without breakfast; we don't have enough money so we'll have to go without a vacation this year.**

goal [gɔʊl] *noun*
(*a*) place (in a game), such as two posts, where you have to kick the ball to score a point.
(*b*) point scored by kicking the ball between the posts; **he scored a goal; our team scored six goals.**

goal·ie, goal·keep·er, *noun*
player in some games who stands in front of the goal to stop the ball from going in.

God [gɒd] *noun*
person who made the world and to whom people pray.

gold [gɔʊld] *noun*
(*a*) valuable yellow-colored metal; **a gold chain; she has a gold ring on her left hand; that ring isn't made of gold; gold is worth more than silver.**

(*b*) dark yellow color; **a gold carpet.**
no plural: **some gold; a piece of gold**

gold·en, *adjective*
colored like gold; **her golden hair; golden wedding** = day when you have been married for fifty years.

gold·fish, *noun*
small orange fish which is kept as a pet; **he has two goldfish in a glass bowl.**
no plural: **one goldfish; three goldfish**

golf [gɒlf] *noun*
game where you have to hit a small white ball into a hole in the ground; **he plays golf every Saturday; how about a game of golf?**
no plural

good [gʊd] *adjective*
(*a*) not bad; **we had a good meal; did you have a good time at the party?**
(*b*) clever; **he's good at making things out of wood; she's good with her hands.**
(*c*) well-behaved; **be a good girl and I'll give you some candy.**
(*d*) **a good deal of/a good many** = a lot of; **he made a good deal of money; a good many people know her.**

for good = for ever; **he left the city for good.**

no good = useless/which doesn't work; **this radio's no good.**

good—better ['betər]—**best** [best]

good-bye, *noun & interjection used when leaving someone*
say good-bye to Aunt Anne; Good-bye! we'll see you again next week.

good-look·ing, *adjective*
attractive/pleasant to look at; **she's a good-looking girl; he's very good-looking.**

good morn·ing/af·ter·noon/ eve·ning, *interjections used when meeting or leaving someone in the morning/afternoon/evening*
good morning, Mrs. Smith; he said good afternoon to Aunt Jane.

good night, *interjection used when leaving someone late in the evening* **good night! sleep well!**

goods, *plural noun*
things, especially things for sale; **the goods will be on sale tomorrow; the store sells goods from various countries.**

got [gɒt], **got·ten** [gɒtən] *see* **get**

gov·ern [ˈgʌvərn] *verb*
to rule (a country); **the country is governed by a group of army officers.**
governs—governing—governed—has governed

gov·ern·ment [ˈgʌvərmənt] *noun*
group of people who rule a country; **the President is head of the government; local government; government employees are asking for more money.**

gov·er·nor, *noun*
person who is in charge of a state; **the governor of California.**
Note: **governor** *can be used with a name:* **Governor Smith.**

grab [græb] *verb*
to take hold of something suddenly; **she grabbed my hand; the police chief grabbed his gun.**
grabs—grabbing—grabbed—has grabbed

grade [greɪd] *noun*
(*a*) mark which you get on a test; **he got good grades in math; if you want to get to college you must get good grades.**
(*b*) group of children who study together in school; **he's in the sixth grade; most kids in grade 10 are 15 years old.**

grad·u·al·ly [ˈgrædʒʊəlɪ] *adverb*
little by little; **he gradually got better after his operation; the snow gradually melted.**

grain [greɪn] *noun*
seed from a cereal plant; **the farmer plants grain.**
no plural

gram [græm] *noun*
measure of weight; **a thousand grams make one kilogram; there are 500 g.** (*say* five hundred grams) **of sugar in this box.**
Note: when used with numbers **gram** *is usually written* **g**

grand [grænd] *adjective*
(*a*) looking large and important; **a grand entrance; grand piano** = large horizontal piano.
(*b*) very good; **that's a grand idea; it's a grand day for a picnic.**
grand—grander—grandest

grand·child, *noun*
child of a son or daughter; **old Mr. and Mrs. Smith have one son and three grandchildren.**
plural **grandchildren**

grand·daugh·ter, *noun*
daughter of a son or daughter; **old Mr. and Mrs. Smith have only girls in their family—they have a daughter and three granddaughters.**

grand·fa·ther, *noun*
father of a mother or father; **both my father's father and my mother's father are still alive, so I have two grandfathers; grandfather clock** = tall clock which stands on the floor.
Note: often called **granddad** *or* **grandpa**

grand·moth·er, *noun*
mother of a mother or father; **both my grandmothers are still alive.**
Note: often called **grandma**

grand·par·ents, *plural noun*
parents of a mother or father; **my wife's grandparents are staying with us.**

grand·son, *noun*
son of a son or daughter; **old Mr. and Mrs. Smith have three grandsons.**

grape [greɪp] *noun*
fruit of a climbing plant, which can be eaten or used for making wine; **have another grape; what a beautiful bunch of grapes!**

grape·fruit [ˈgreɪpfruːt] *noun*
large round yellow fruit, of the same family as oranges and lemons; **we had grapefruit for breakfast.**
no plural: **one grapefruit, two grapefruit**

grass [græs] *noun*
low green plant, which is eaten by cows and sheep in fields, or used to make

lawns; the grass is getting too long; keep off the grass! we'll sit on the grass and have our lunch.
no plural

grass·hop·per, *noun*
small green insect which leaps.

grass·y, *adjective*
covered with grass; a grassy slope.

grave [greɪv] *noun*
place where a dead person is buried; his grave is covered with flowers.

grave·yard, *noun*
area (often near a church) where dead people are buried.

gra·vy ['greɪvɪ] *noun*
sauce which you pour over meat; would you like some more gravy?
no plural: some gravy; a spoonful of gravy

gray [greɪ] *adjective & noun*
of a color like a mixture of black and white; his hair is quite gray; look at the gray clouds—it's going to rain; he's wearing dark gray pants.
gray—grayer—grayest

gray-head·ed, *adjective*
with gray hair; a gray-headed man.

grease [griːs] 1. *noun*
thick oil used to put on machines to make them work smoothly; have you put any grease on your back wheel?
2. *verb*
to put grease on a machine; he was greasing the engine.
greases—greasing—greased—has greased

greas·y, *adjective*
(*a*) covered with grease; don't wipe your greasy hands on your shirt.
(*b*) full of oil; greasy foods are not good for your skin.
greasy—greasier—greasiest

great [greɪt] *adjective*
(*a*) large; she's eating a great big sandwich; a great deal of = a lot of; there's a great deal of work to do.
(*b*) important/famous; New York is a great city; Picasso was a great artist.

(*c*) very good; we had a great time on our vacation; did you see that movie?—it was great!
great—greater—greatest

great·ly, *adverb*
very much; we greatly enjoyed the party.

greed·y ['griːdɪ] *adjective*
always wanting to eat a lot of food; don't be greedy—leave some cake for the others.
greedy—greedier—greediest

green [griːn] *adjective & noun*
(*a*) of a color like the color of leaves; her coat is bright green; I have painted the door dark green; he was dressed all in green; do you have any paint of a lighter green than this? you can go ahead—the traffic signals are green.
(*b*) not ripe; don't eat that green banana!
green—greener—greenest

greens, *plural noun*
green vegetables; we had greens with our meat.

greet [griːt] *verb*
to welcome someone whom you are meeting; he greeted his mother as she got off the bus.
greets—greeting—greeted—has greeted

greet·ings, *plural noun*
good wishes; to send someone birthday greetings.

grew [gruː] *see* **grow**

grey [greɪ] *adjective & noun*
see **gray.**

grin [grɪn] 1. *noun*
big smile; he had a big grin on his face when he left the room.
2. *verb*
to smile; she grinned at the teacher; what are you grinning at?
grins—grinning—grinned—has grinned

grind [graɪnd] *verb*
to make into very small pieces; the butcher ground the meat to make ham-

burgers; **ground beef** = beef which has been made into very small pieces.

grinds—grinding—ground— has ground

gro·cer [ˈgrəʊsər] *noun*
person who sells sugar/butter/cans of food, etc.

gro·cer·y, *noun*
(*a*) **grocery store** = store where you can buy sugar/butter/cans of food, etc.; **go to the grocery store and get me a couple of cans of applesauce.**
(*b*) **groceries** = things which you buy at a grocery store; **my bag is full of groceries.**

plural **groceries**

ground [graʊnd] *noun*
(*a*) soil/earth; **the tree must be planted in wet ground.**
(*b*) surface of the earth; **the house was burned to the ground; it has been so dry that the ground is hard; let's sit on the ground to have our lunch; he lay down on the ground and went to sleep.**
(*c*) place set aside for a special purpose; **picnic ground.**
(*d*) *see also* **grind**

ground floor, *noun*
floor (in a store, apartment building, etc.) which is level with the street; **the clothing department is on the ground floor; he lives in a ground floor apartment.**

grounds, *plural noun*
(*a*) land around a big house; **they walked around the grounds of the hospital.**
(*b*) reasons; **what grounds do you have for saying that he should get more money?**

group [gruːp] 1. *noun*
(*a*) several people/animals/things which are all close together; **a group of policemen waited at the corner of the street; let's meet by that group of trees over there.**
(*b*) way of putting similar things together; **blood group** = type of blood; **age group** = all people of a certain age.
(*c*) small number of people who play music together.

2. *verb*
to gather together; **the children are grouped together according to their ages; the cows were grouped under the trees.**

groups—grouping—grouped— has grouped

grow [grəʊ] *verb*
(*a*) to become larger (as a plant); **these trees grow very tall; cabbages grow well in our garden.**
(*b*) to make plants grow; **we are growing tomatoes; farmers grow grass to feed their cows.**
(*c*) to become taller/bigger; **your son has grown since I last saw him; the population is growing very fast.**
(*d*) to become; **it's growing colder at night now; he grew richer all the time.**

grows—growing—grew [gruː]— **has grown**

grown-up, *noun*
adult; **there are three grown-ups and ten children.**

grow up, *verb*
to become an adult; **what do you want to do when you grow up?**

growth, *noun*
increase in size; **the growth of the population since 1960.**

no plural

guard [gɑːrd] 1. *noun*
(*a*) person who protects someone or something; **armed guards were at the door of the bank.**
(*b*) protection against attack; **he is on guard** = is watching out in case someone might attack; **to be caught off guard** = to be caught by surprise.

2. *verb*
to protect; to take care of; **the soldiers were guarding the airbase.**

guards—guarding—guarded—has guarded

guess [ges] 1. *verb*
(*a*) to try to imagine or think of something; **guess who is coming to see us; can you guess what we are having for dinner? he guessed right** = he got the right answer.

(b) to think; to suppose; **I guess the snow will melt soon; I guess it's my turn to do the dishes.**
guesses—guessing—guessed— has guessed

2. *noun*
opinion which you reach without having any information; **do you know who is coming to see us?—I'll give you three guesses; I don't know if the answer is right—I only took a guess.**
plural **guesses**

guest [gest] *noun*
person who comes to see someone and has a meal or stays the night; visitor; **all the guests in the hotel had to leave because of the fire.**

guide [gaɪd] 1. *noun*
person/book which shows you how to do something/where to go; **I'll act as your guide to Chicago; read this guide to growing vegetables.**
2. *verb*
to show someone around a town/building/museum, etc.; **he guided the visitors around the town.**
guides—guiding—guided—has guided
guide·book, *noun*
book which tells you where to go; **a guidebook to Washington.**
guide dog, *noun*
dog which shows a blind person where to go.

guilt·y [ˈgɪltɪ] *adjective*
having done something wrong; **the judge decided he was guilty of murder.**
guilty—guiltier—guiltiest

gui·tar [gɪˈtɑːr] *noun*
musical instrument with several strings, which you play by pulling the strings with your fingers; **he likes to play the guitar; Spanish guitar music.**

gum [gʌm] *noun*
(a) sweet stuff which you chew for a long time but do not swallow; **he hit me on the back and made me swallow my piece of gum.**
(b) type of glue.
(c) **gums** = part of your mouth which is around your teeth.
no plural for (a) and (b): **some gum; a piece of gum**

gun [gʌn] 1. *noun*
weapon which you shoot with; **the policeman pulled out his gun; she took his gun and shot him dead.**
2. *verb*
to gun someone down = to shoot someone so that he falls down; **the police gunned down the leader of the gang; the soldiers tried to gun down the enemy helicopter.**
guns—gunning—gunned— has gunned

guy [gaɪ] *noun*
man; **she met this guy at the party.**

gym [dʒɪm] *noun*
large room where you can do exercises, play games, etc.; **we are going to watch a basketball game in the school gym.**

Hh

hab·it ['hæbɪt] *noun*
regular way of doing things; **he got
into the habit of swimming every day
before breakfast; she has gotten out of
the habit of doing exercise; by force of
habit** = because you do it regularly; **I
wake up at 6 o'clock by force of habit.**

had [hæd], **hadn't** ['hædənt] *see* **have**

hair [heər] *noun*
(*a*) long thread growing on your head/
on the body of an animal; **the dog left
hairs all over the armchair; there's a hair
in my soup; my mother has a few gray
hairs.**
plural **hairs**
(*b*) mass of hairs growing on your head;
**she's got long black hair; you ought to
wash your hair; his hair is too long; he is
going to have his hair cut.**
no plural
hair·cut, *noun*
cutting of hair on your head; **you need
a haircut.**
hair·dress·er, *noun*
person who cuts/washes, etc., your hair;
**you must go to the hairdresser's before
the party; I met her at the hairdresser's.**
hair·pin, *noun*
pin for keeping your hair in place; **hair-
pin curve** = very sharp curve in a road.
hair·y, *adjective*
covered with hair; **a hairy dog; he has
hairy arms.**
hairy—hairier—hairiest

half [hæf] **1.** *noun*
one of two equal parts; **he cut the apple
in half; half the apple fell on the floor;
our team scored twice in the first half**
= in the first part of the game; **half of
six is three.**
plural **halves** [hævz]

2. *adjective*
divided into two parts; **half an apple;
two and a half hours; I only want half a
cup of coffee** = not a full cup.
3. *adverb*
not completely; **the work is only half
finished; this book is half as big/half
as thick as that one** = it is only 50%
of the size; **but this book is half as big
again** = it is 150% of the size of that
one.
half past = 30 minutes after an hour;
come and see me at half past six
(6:30).
half dol·lar, *noun*
50-cent coin.
half·way, *adverb*
in the middle; **halfway across the street;
halfway up the mountain; I'm halfway
through this book.**

hall [hɔːl] *noun*
(*a*) (*also* **hallway**) small room when you
go into a house, where you can leave
your coat, etc.; **don't stand in the hall,
come into the dining room; I've left my
umbrella in the hall.**
(*b*) (*also* **hallway**) room which joins two
rooms together; **they had trouble moving
the piano through the hallway.**
(*c*) large room for meetings; **we all
ate in the church hall; concert hall** =
large building where concerts are given;
city hall = building where the city
council meets and where the city is
governed.

ham [hæm] *noun*
salted meat from the leg of a pig,
usually eaten cold; **he had a ham salad;
can I have two ham sandwiches, please?
would you like another slice of ham?**
no plural: **some ham; a slice of
ham**

ham·burg·er ['hæmbɜrgər] *noun*
ground beef shaped like a cake, cooked and eaten in a sandwich.

ham·mer ['hæmər] *noun*
heavy metal tool for knocking nails into wood, etc.; **he hit his thumb with the hammer.**

hand [hænd] 1. *noun*
(*a*) part of the body at the end of each arm, which you use for holding things; **he had a cup in each hand; to shake hands** = to greet someone by holding their right hand; **he shook hands with me; can you lend a hand?** = can you help? **give me a hand with the dishes** = help me; **the store has changed hands** = it has a new owner; **they walked along hand in hand** = holding each other by the hand.
(*b*) one of the two pieces on a clock which turn around and point to the figures; **the hour hand/the minute hand.**
(*c*) cards held by a player in a game of cards.
by hand = using your hands and tools, but not large machines; **he made the table by hand.**
on the other hand = however; **it is quite cold outside, but on the other hand it has stopped snowing.**
2. *verb*
to pass; **can you hand me that book? he handed me all his money.**
~~hands—handing—handed—has handed~~

hand·bag, *noun*
small bag which women carry to hold their money/pens/handkerchiefs, etc.

hand·ful, *noun*
amount you can hold in your hand; **he gave me a handful of dollar bills; only a handful of people came** = very few.

hand·ker·chief ['hæŋkərtʃıf] *noun*
piece of cloth for wiping your nose; **he blew his nose with his handkerchief; do you have a handkerchief?—my glasses are dirty.**

hand·made, *adjective*
made by hand without using a machine; **a handmade table; a box of handmade chocolates.**

hand o·ver, *verb*
to pass something to someone; **hand over all your money; she handed over the keys to her apartment.**

hand·shake, *noun*
greeting, where two people shake hands.

hand·work, *noun*
work done by hand and not by machine.
no plural

han·dle ['hændəl] 1. *noun*
part of an object which you hold in your hand to pick it up/to open it, etc.; **he turned the door handle; she broke the handle off the cup; the handle of my suitcase is broken.**
2. *verb*
(*a*) to touch with your hands; **please don't handle the fruit.**
(*b*) to manage; **do you think she can handle all the work in the department?**
~~handles—handling—handled—has handled~~

han·dle·bars, *plural noun*
bar on the front of a bicycle or motorcycle which steers the front wheel; **hold on to the handlebars.**

hand·some ['hænsəm] *adjective*
good-looking/very pleasant to look at; **a handsome young man.**
Note: usually used of men, but not women or children

hand·writ·ing ['hændraıtıŋ] *noun*
writing done by hand; **his handwriting is very difficult to read;** *see also* **writing.**
no plural

hand·y ['hændı] *adjective*
(*a*) useful; in a convenient place; **having a set of tools at home would be quite handy; keep the salt handy when you are cooking; the shopping center is handy; these scissors will come in handy** = will be useful.
(*b*) (person) who can make things; **he's handy with a paintbrush; she's handy at fixing things around the house.**
~~handy—handier—handiest~~

hang [hæŋ] *verb*
to attach (something) above the ground (to a nail or to a hook, etc.); to be attached above the ground (to a nail, a hook, etc.); **hang your coat on the hook; I like that picture hanging over the bed; she hung the photograph over her bed; he's hanging the lights on the Christmas tree.**
hangs—hanging—hung [ˈhʌŋ]—**has hung**

hang·er, *noun*
object for hanging a piece of clothing; **put your coat on a hanger.**

hang on, *verb*
to wait; **hang on a minute.**

hang up, *verb*
to end a telephone call; **he hung up after saying good-bye.**

hap·pen [ˈhæpən] *verb*
(*a*) to take place; **the accident happened at the corner of the street; how did it happen? something has happened to make the train late; she's late—something must have happened; what happened to his brother?** = what is his brother doing now?
(*b*) to be (by chance); **I happened to be there when the fire started; the house happened to be empty; we happened to meet him at the restaurant; do you happen to have a street plan of New York?**
happens—happening—happened—has happened

hap·py [ˈhæpɪ] *adjective*
very pleased; **I'm happy to say we're going to get a vacation; we're so happy to hear that you are better; she's not very happy at her job; are you happy with the plans for the new school? Happy Birthday/Happy New Year** = greetings said to someone on their birthday/at New Year's; **many Happy Returns** = greetings said to someone on their birthday.
happy—happier—happiest

hap·pi·ly, *adverb*
in a happy way; **the children played happily for hours.**

hap·pi·ness, *noun*
being happy.
no plural

har·bor [ˈhɑːrbər] *noun*
place where ships are tied; **the sailboats are all in the harbor; the ships tried to reach the harbor in the storm.**

hard [hɑːrd] 1. *adjective*
(*a*) not soft; **this bed is too hard; the cake is so hard I can't bite into it.**
(*b*) difficult; **today's crossword puzzle is too hard—I can't finish it; if the test is too hard, nobody will pass; he's hard of hearing** = he is rather deaf.
(*c*) **a hard winter** = very cold winter; **hard times** = times when life is not easy.
hard—harder—hardest

2. *adverb*
with a lot of effort; **hit the nail hard with the hammer; it's snowing hard; if we all work hard, we'll earn a lot of money.**

hard·ly, *adverb*
almost not; **I hardly know her; it hardly ever rains in the desert** = almost never; **hardly anyone came to the meeting** = almost no one.

harm [hɑːrm] 1. *noun*
damage (esp. to a person); **walking to work every day won't do you any harm; I hope my guitar won't come to any harm if I leave it on the chair; there's no harm in calling him** = it might possibly be useful to call him.
no plural

2. *verb*
to damage/to hurt; **the dog won't harm you; walking to work every day won't harm you.**
harms—harming—harmed—has harmed

harm·ful, *adjective*
which causes damage; **bright light can be harmful to your eyes.**

harm·less, *adjective*
which causes no damage; **the dog is old—he's quite harmless.**

har·vest [ˈhɑːrvəst] *noun*
picking of a ripe crop; **the apple harvest has begun; the harvest starts in September.**

har·vest·er, *noun*
person or machine which picks a ripe
crop.

has [hæz], **hasn't** ['hæzənt] *see* **have**

hat [hæt] *noun*
piece of clothing which you wear on
your head; **take your hat off when you
go into a church; she put on her new hat;
keep it under your hat!** = keep it a
secret.

hate [heit] *verb*
not to like at all; **I hate cold eggs; she
hates getting up in the morning.**
hates—hating—hated—has hated

have [hæv] *verb*
(a) (*sometimes* **to have got**) to own;
**he has a lot of money; she has a new
green car; do you have enough to eat? he
has very big muscles.**
(b) to take/to eat, etc.; **have you had
breakfast yet? I'll have sugar in my
coffee; I'm going to have a drink; we had
a long talk.**
(c) to get someone to do something
and pay them for it; **he is having his
house painted; you should have your hair
cut.**
(d) (*used to form the past of verbs*) **he
has eaten his breakfast; have you finished
your work? she hadn't seen him for two
days; if they had asked me I would have
said yes.**
Present: **I/you have; he/she/it has;
we/you/they have**
having—had—has had
Negative: **I haven't, etc.; he hasn't,
etc.**
Note the short forms (*only used to
form the past of verbs and with* **got**):
**I've; you've; he's; she's; it's;
we've; they've; he's, she's, it's** *are
used in spoken English, but not
usually in writing.*

have got, *verb*
(a) to own; **she's got a lot of money; he's
got very big muscles.**
(b) (*used to mean* must) **you've got to do
what the doctor says; have you got to go
so soon?**

have to, *verb used with other verbs to*
mean must; **you have to do what the
policeman says; you have to drive on the
right; I had to walk to work because I
missed the bus; do you have to go so
soon?**

have to do with, *verb*
to concern; **that has nothing to do with
you.**

he [hi:] *pronoun referring to a man or boy,
and some male animals*
**he's my father; he and I went there to-
gether; I'm mad at John—he has eaten
all the chocolates; don't be frightened of
the dog—he won't hurt you; he'll be
here soon.**
Note: when it is the object, **he**
becomes **him: he hit the ball/the
ball hit him;** *when it follows the verb*
be, **he** *usually becomes* **him; who's
that?—it's him, the man who stole
my bike!**

head [hed] 1. *noun*
(a) top part of the body, which contains
the eyes/nose/mouth/brain, etc.; **can you
stand on your head? he hit his head on the
low branch; she rolled head over heels
down the hill** = rolled over and over like
a ball; **he shook his head** = he moved his
head from side to side to mean "no"; **she
tried to do the sum in her head** = using
her brain, and not writing it down.
(b) first place/top part; **he stood at the
head of the line; whose name is at the
head of the list?**
(c) most important person; **he's the head
of the sales department; head teacher.**
(d) top side of a coin, usually with a
picture of the head of a president or
king on it; **let's play heads or tails** =
let's throw a coin in the air to see which
side comes down on top; **heads you win**
= if the coin falls with the top side up,
then you will win.
2. *verb*
(a) to be the first/to lead; **his name heads
the list.**
(b) to go towards; **they are heading/
headed north; he headed for the
manager's office.**
**heads—heading—headed—has
headed**

head·ache [ˈhedeɪk] *noun*
pain in your head; **I must lie down—I have a headache; she can't come with us because she has a headache.**

head·lights, *plural noun*
main white lights on the front of a car.

head·line, *noun*
words in capital letters at the top of a newspaper article; **did you see the headlines about the President? the newspaper headline says TAXES TO BE RAISED.**

head·quar·ters, *plural noun*
main office of the police/of a business company, etc.; **the police took him to headquarters.**

health [helθ] *noun*
being well/not being ill; **he's in good health; health insurance** = insurance to pay for the doctors/hospital, etc., if you become sick.
no plural

health·y, *adjective*
(*a*) likely to make you well; **being a farmer is a healthy job; this city is the healthiest place in California.**
(*b*) full of good health; **although 95 years old, my grandfather still is very healthy.**
healthy—healthier—healthiest

hear [hɪr] *verb*
(*a*) to catch sounds with your ears; **can you hear footsteps? I can't hear what you're saying because of the noise of the airplane; I heard her shut the front door; we heard him singing in the shower.**
(*b*) to get information; **I hear you're going to Mexico on vacation; have you heard that the President has died? where did you hear that?—I heard it on the radio.**
hears—hearing—heard [hɜrd]**—has heard**

heart [hɑːrt] *noun*
(*a*) part of the body which beats regularly as it pumps blood around the body; **the doctor listened to his heart; he has heart trouble.**
(*b*) center/middle; **he lives in the heart of the forest; she has a house in the heart of the city.**

(*c*) **he learned the whole book by heart** = so that he could repeat it from memory; **don't take it to heart** = don't be too sad about it; **his heart isn't in it** = he has lost interest in it; **my heart sank when I heard the news** = I suddenly became sad.

heart at·tack, *noun*
bad illness when your heart suddenly stops working for a short time.

heart·y, *adjective*
strong/big; **she ate a hearty breakfast.**

heat [hiːt] **1.** *noun*
(*a*) being hot; **the heat of the sun made the paint melt.**
(*b*) one part of a sports event; **there are three heats before the main competition; dead heat** = race where two runners finish at the same time.
2. *verb*
to make hot; **heat up the soup while I set the table; a heated swimming pool** = pool where the water is kept warm.
heats—heating—heated—has heated

heat·er, *noun*
machine for heating; **water heater** = machine for heating water in a house; **electric heater** = heating machine which runs on electricity.

heat·ing, *noun*
way of warming a house; **the heating has been switched off; central heating** = heating of a whole house from one heater.

heav·y [ˈhevɪ] *adjective*
(*a*) which weighs a lot; **this box is so heavy I can hardly lift it.**
(*b*) strong; in large amounts; **don't go to bed after you've had a heavy meal; there has been a heavy snowfall during the night; there was heavy traffic in the center of town.**
heavy—heavier—heaviest

heel [hiːl] *noun*
(*a*) back part of your foot; part of a sock into which the back part of your foot fits; **you have a hole in the heel of your stocking.**

(*b*) block under the back part of a shoe;
she wore shoes with very high heels.

height [haɪt] *noun*
measurement of how tall/how high
something is; **the height of the ceiling is
10 feet; what is the height of that mountain?**

held [held] *see* **hold**

hel·i·cop·ter [ˈhelɪkɒptər] *noun*
type of aircraft which is lifted off the
ground by a large set of rapidly turning
blades on its roof.

he'll [hiːl] *see* **he**

hel·lo [həˈləʊ] *interjection showing a
greeting*
hello, James, where have you been? say
hello to her from me; he shouted hello
from the other side of the street.

hel·met [ˈhelmɪt] *noun*
hard hat which you wear to protect
your head; **if you ride a motorcycle you
ought to wear a helmet.**

help [help] **1.** *noun*
(*a*) something which makes it easier for
you to do something; **he cleaned the car
with the help of a big brush; do you need
any help?**
(*b*) making someone safe; **she was calling for help.**
2. *verb*
(*a*) to make it easier for someone to do
something; **can you help me with my
homework? I got a friend to help put the
piano into the bedroom; he helped the old
lady across the street.**
(*b*) (*with* **cannot**) not to be able to stop
doing something; **he couldn't help
laughing; he can't help it if he's deaf.**
(*c*) **help yourself** = to serve yourself
with food, etc.; **he helped himself to some
dessert; if you want anything to eat just
help yourself.**
3. help! *interjection which you shout when
you are in difficulty;* **help, help, call a
doctor! help, the brakes aren't working.**
**helps—helping—helped—has
helped**

help·er, *noun*
person who helps.
help·ful, *adjective*
which helps; **he gave us a very helpful
map of the state.**
help·ing, *noun*
amount of food for one person; **can I
have a second helping of ice cream?**
help·less, *adjective*
not able to do anything.

hen [hen] *noun*
female bird, especially a chicken which
you keep on a farm; **the hen has laid an
egg.**

her [hɜr] **1.** *object pronoun referring to a
female person, a female animal and
sometimes to machines and countries*
**have you seen her? tell her to go away;
that's her in the white dress; there's a
letter for her.**
2. *adjective referring to a female, a ship
or a country*
**she had lost all her money; have you seen
her brother? the cat won't eat her food;
Germany is helping her industries to sell
more goods abroad.**
hers, *pronoun*
belonging to her; **this book is hers, not
mine; she introduced me to a friend of
hers** = to one of her friends.
her·self, *pronoun referring to a female
subject*
**the cat was washing herself; she is all by
herself** = all alone; **she did it all by herself** = with no one to help her; **she wrote
to me herself; did your mother enjoy herself?**

here [hɪr] *adverb*
in this place; to this place; **I put the book
down here next to my cup; we have been
living here in Baltimore for twenty years;
can you come here, please? they brought
the money here; here's the newspaper;
here comes Frank; here you are** = take
this.
Note: when **here** *comes at the beginning of a sentence the following
subject comes after the verb if the subject is a noun and not a pronoun:*
here comes the bus/here it comes

he's [hi:z] *see* **he is, he has**

hes·i·tate ['hezɪteɪt] *verb*
not to be able to decide; to stop for a moment while you decide what to do; **I'm hesitating about what to do next; he hesitated for a few seconds, then went into the store.**
hesitates—hesitating—hesitated—has hesitated
hes·i·ta·tion, *noun*
act of hesitating; **after a few minutes' hesitation he went into the store.**

hi [haɪ] *interjection showing a greeting*
hi John, did you have a good day?

hide [haɪd] *verb*
(*a*) to put something where no one can see or find it; **he hid the gold coins under the bed; someone has hidden the key to the desk drawer.**
(*b*) to put yourself where no one can see or find you; **he's hiding from the police; they hid behind the door.**
hides—hiding—hid [hɪd]**—has hidden** ['hɪdən]

high [haɪ] 1. *adjective*
(*a*) tall; **the office building is 60 stories high; which is the highest mountain in the world? the living room has a high ceiling.**
(*b*) (*referring to numbers*) big; **the car runs well at high speeds; gas prices seem to be higher every year; glass will melt at very high temperatures.**
Note: **high** *is used with figures:* **the mountain is 7000 feet high**
2. *adverb*
above; up in the air; **the balloon flew high up into the sky; airplanes fly high to avoid storms; the bird flew higher and higher.**
high—higher—highest
high·ly, *adverb*
he thinks highly of her = he admires her very much.
high school, *noun*
school for children in grades 9 to 12; **the high school football team; he goes to Central High School.**
high·way, *noun*
main road in the country; **the truck is**

traveling north along the highway.

hill [hɪl] *noun*
piece of high land, but lower than a mountain; **his house is on top of a hill; if you climb up the hill, you will get a good view.**
hill·y, *adjective*
(country) with many hills.
hilly—hillier—hilliest

him [hɪm] *object pronoun referring to a man, boy or some male animals*
have you seen him lately? tell him to come in; there is a letter for him; that's him over there.
him·self, *pronoun referring to a male subject*
he's all by himself = all alone; **he did it all by himself** = with no one to help him; **he wrote to me himself; the doctor is ill himself; did your father enjoy himself?**

hire ['haɪr] *verb*
to give someone a job; **the bank hired him as a manager; the store will hire new people only next year.**
hires—hiring—hired—has hired

his [hɪz] 1. *adjective referring to a man, boy or animal*
belonging to him; **he has lost all his money; have you met his mother? our dog wants his food.**
2. *pronoun*
belonging to him; **this book is his, not mine; he introduced me to a friend of his called Anne.**

his·to·ry ['hɪstərɪ] *noun*
study of what happened in the past; **he is writing a history of the First World War; she's reading a history book; I got top grades in History.**
no plural

hit [hɪt] *verb*
to knock; to go against something hard using a lot of force; **the car hit the pole and knocked it down; she was hitting her husband with a bottle; he hit the ball**

so hard, that we can't find it; I hit my head on the door.

hits—hitting—hit—has hit

hob·by ['hɒbɪ] *noun*
thing which you do to amuse yourself when you are not working; his hobby is collecting stamps; do you have any hobbies?
plural **hobbies**

hog [hɒg] *noun*
large pig; the farmer keeps hogs.

hold [həʊld] *verb*
(*a*) to have, especially in your hand; he was holding a gun in his right hand; she held the knife between her teeth; hold on—the ship is moving fast.
(*b*) to contain; this bottle holds two quarts; will the car hold six people? the box isn't big enough to hold all the potatoes.
(*c*) to arrange for something to happen; we held the meeting at City Hall; we are holding the flower show next week.
(*d*) to control; can you hold your breath under water = stop breathing.

holds—holding—held [held]**—has held**

hold·er, *noun*
thing which holds; he put the pen back into its holder.

hold on, *verb*
(*a*) to hold something tightly; hold on to the handle; hold on, we're turning.
(*b*) to wait; hold on a moment; you want to speak to Mr. Smith—hold on, I'll find him for you.

hold out, *verb*
to stay/to last; will the good weather hold out until next week?

hold up, *verb*
(*a*) to lift; he held up his hand; the tent is held up by four poles.
(*b*) to make late; we were held up in a traffic jam; the train was held up by the snow.
(*c*) to attack and rob; three men held up the bank.

Note: **the accident held the traffic up** *or* **held up the traffic** *but only* **the accident held us up**

holdup, *noun*
(*a*) delay; the accident caused holdups downtown.
(*b*) armed attack; two people were hurt in the bank holdup.

hole [həʊl] *noun*
opening/space in something; the boys looked through the hole in the fence; I have a hole in my sock; the rabbit ran down its hole; you must try to pull the piece of thread through the hole in the needle.

hol·i·day ['hɒlɪdeɪ] *noun*
day when you do not have to work or be at school; May 30 is a public holiday; she's coming home for the holidays = at Christmas.

home [həʊm] 1. *noun*
(*a*) place where you live; house/apartment which you live in; are you going to be at home tomorrow? our home is the house on the corner of the street; she's staying at home instead of going to work; when do you leave home in the morning? make yourself at home! = act as if you were in your own home.
(*b*) house where people are cared for; a nursing home; a children's home = a house where children with no parents are cared for.
(*c*) **at home** = on the local sports field; our team is playing at home next Saturday.
2. *adverb*
towards the place where you usually live; I'm going home; I usually get home at 7 o'clock = reach the house where I live; I'll take it home with me; she can take the bus home = she can go home by bus.
Note: used without a preposition: **he went home; she's coming home, etc.**

home·less, *adjective*
with nowhere to live; thousands of people were made homeless by the storm.

home·ly, *adjective*
not pretty; she's a homely girl.

home·made, *adjective*
made at home, and not bought; **a jar of homemade jam.**

home run, *noun*
run made by the batter in baseball when he touches all the bases.

home·sick, *adjective*
feeling sad because you are away from home.

home·ward, *adverb & adjective*
going toward home; **the homeward journey; they were traveling homeward when the car ran out of gas.**

home·work, *noun*
work which children take home from school to do in the evening; **have you done your math homework? I don't have any homework, so I can watch TV.**
no plural

hon·est ['ɒnɪst] *adjective*
who tells the truth; who doesn't cheat.

hon·ey ['hʌnɪ] *noun*
sweet stuff produced by bees; **put some honey on your bread.**
no plural

hood [hʊd] *noun*
(*a*) cover over the motor in a car; **he lifted up the hood to see what was wrong with the motor.**
(*b*) covering for your head, often attached to a coat; **does your coat have a hood?**

hook [hʊk] 1. *noun*
bent piece of metal used for holding or pulling; **hang your coat on the hook behind the door; he caught a fish on his hook.**
2. *verb*
to attach something with a hook; to catch (a fish) with a hook; **he hooked his umbrella over the back of the chair; she hooked a huge fish.**
hooks—hooking—hooked—has hooked

hook·y, *noun*
to play hooky = to avoid going to school.

hop [hɒp] 1. *noun*
little jump standing on one foot.

2. *verb*
to jump on one foot or move around in little jumps; **he hopped up and down; the birds were hopping around on the grass.**
hops—hopping—hopped—has hopped

hope [həʊp] *verb*
to expect something to happen; to want something to happen; **we hope to be back home at 6 o'clock; I had hoped to be there, but in the end I couldn't go; I hope our team wins; she hoped she would soon be able to drive a car; I hope so** = I want it to happen; **I hope not** = I don't want it to happen; **will you come to the party?—yes, I hope so; is it going to rain tomorrow?—I hope not!**
hopes—hoping—hoped—has hoped

hope·ful·ly, *adverb*
which we hope will happen; **hopefully, it will stop raining soon.**

ho·ri·zon [hə'raɪzən] *noun*
line where the earth seems to meet the sky; **can you see that ship on the horizon?**
hor·i·zon·tal [hɒrɪ'zɒntəl] *adjective*
which is lying flat; **a horizontal line.**

horn [hɔːrn] *noun*
(*a*) hard part growing on the head of an animal (such as cow); **the cow tried to push him with its horns.**
(*b*) musical instrument; part of a car which makes a loud noise to warn people; **he plays the horn in an orchestra; blow your horn when you come to the corner.**

hor·ri·ble ['hɒrəbəl] *adjective*
terrible/bad; **I had a horrible dream last night; the dinner I had in the restaurant was horrible; what horrible weather!**

horse [hɔːrs] *noun*
large animal used for riding or pulling; **she rides her horse every morning; some farmers still use horses to plow the fields.**
on horse·back = riding on a horse; **there were six policemen on horseback.**

horse·man, *noun*
man riding a horse.
plural **horsemen**

horse·shoe, *noun*
piece of metal nailed to the foot of a
horse.

hose [həʊz] *noun*
long rubber or plastic tube; **he was
watering his garden with a hose; the firemen used their hoses to put out the fire.**

hos·pi·tal ['hɒspɪtəl] *noun*
place where sick or hurt people are
cared for; **she's so sick, she has been
taken to the hospital; he's been in the
hospital for several days; the children's
hospital is at the end of our street.**

hot [hɒt] *adjective*
very warm; with a high temperature;
**my bath water is too hot; what hot
weather we're having! it's usually hot
in August; if you're hot, take your coat
off.**
hot—hotter—hottest

hot dog, *noun*
food made of a hot sausage eaten in a
roll of bread.

ho·tel [həʊ'tel] *noun*
place where you can buy a meal and
rent a room for the night; **all the rooms
in the hotel are booked; which is the best
hotel in the city? we're staying at the
Grand Hotel; aren't there any hotels near
the sea? ask the hotel manager if he has
found your keys.**

hour ['aʊər] *noun*
period of time lasting sixty minutes;
**there are 24 hours in the day; he is paid
by the hour** = he is paid for each hour
he works; **the hours of work are from 9
to 5; when is your lunch hour?** = when
do you stop work for lunch? **I'll be
ready in a quarter of an hour/in half an
hour** = in 15 minutes/in 30 minutes; **the
car was traveling at over 100 miles an
hour.**
hour·ly, *adjective*
happening every hour; **there's an hourly
news program.**

house 1. [haʊs] *noun*
building which someone lives in; **he has
an apartment in the city and a house in
the country; all the houses on our street
look the same; his house has six bedrooms.**
Note: plural **houses** ['haʊzɪz]
2. [haʊz] *verb*
to give someone a place to live; **the state
government housed the homeless people
in the high school.**
house·hold, *noun & adjective*
(referring to) people living together in a
house; **she is the head of the household;
household goods department** = part of a
big store which sells things for the
house.
house·work, *noun*
cleaning of a house or apartment; **I have
some housework to do.**
no plural: **some housework; a lot
of housework**

how [haʊ] *adverb*
(*a*) (*showing or asking the way in which
something is done*)   how do you make
chocolate cookies? how can you get to
the post office from here? tell me how
fish breathe.
(*b*) (*showing or asking in what amount*)
**how big is your car? how long is the flight
to Seattle? how often do you have a
vacation? he showed how strong he was.**
(*c*) (*showing surprise*) **how tall you have
grown! how blue the sky is! how she cried
when she hit her thumb with the hammer!**
how are you?/how do you do?
showing greeting
**how do you do, Mrs. Jones; hello,
Charles, how are you? the teacher asked
me how I was.**
how·ev·er, *adverb*
(*a*) in whatever amount; **however hard
he tried, he couldn't swim; I must buy
that old clock, however expensive it is.**
(*b*) but; even so; **I never go out on
Saturdays, however, this Saturday I'm
going to a picnic.**
how much, *adverb*
(*a*) what is the price? **how much is that
carpet? how much did you pay for your
house?**

(b) what amount? **how much sugar do you want in your coffee?**

hug [hʌg] 1. *noun*
putting your arms around someone; **she gave her uncle a hug.**
2. *verb*
to put your arms around someone; **he hugged his mother.**
hugs—hugging—hugged— has hugged

huge [hju:dʒ] *adjective*
very large; **a huge dog came running to meet us; I've just gotten a huge telephone bill.**

hu·man [ˈhjuːmən] 1. *adjective*
referring to any man, woman or child; **a human being** = a person.
2. *noun*
person; **most animals are afraid of humans.**

hu·mor [ˈhjuːmər] *noun*
ability to be funny or to see something as funny; **he has no sense of humor** = he doesn't think anything is funny.

hun·dred [ˈhʌndrəd] number 100
he's over a hundred (years old); the house was built several hundred years ago; hundreds of people caught the disease = very many people.
Note: in numbers **hundred** *does not change and is followed by* **and** *when reading:* **491** = four hundred and ninety-one; **102** = a hundred and two
Note: **a hundred and one** (101), **three hundred and six** (306), *etc., but* **hundred and first** (101st), **three hundred and sixth** (306th), *etc.*

hun·dredth, 100th *adjective & noun*
the clock is correct to one hundredth of a second (100th of a second); tomorrow is grandfather's hundredth birthday.

hung [hʌŋ] *see* **hang**

hun·gry [ˈhʌŋgrɪ] *adjective*
wanting to eat; **I'm hungry; are you hungry? you must be hungry after that long walk; I'm not very hungry—I had a** big breakfast; hurry up with the dinner—we're getting hungry.
hungry—hungrier—hungriest

hunt [hʌnt] *verb*
(a) to look for someone or something; **the police are hunting for the gang who held up the bank; I've been hunting in all the stores, but I can't find any shoes that fit me.**
(b) to chase wild animals to kill them; **the cat went out hunting mice; the farmer's sons are hunting rats.**
hunts—hunting—hunted—has hunted

hunt·er, *noun*
person who hunts.

hur·ry [ˈhɜrɪ] 1. *noun*
rush; **he's always in a hurry** = always rushing around; **get out of the way—we're in a hurry! what's the hurry?** = why are you going so fast?
no plural
2. *verb*
to go or do something fast; to make someone go faster; **she hurried along the street; you'll have to hurry if you want to catch the train; don't hurry—we have plenty of time; don't hurry me, I'm going as fast as I can.**
hurries—hurrying—hurried—has hurried

hur·ried, *adjective*
done quickly; **we had a hurried meal.**

hurt [hɜrt] *verb*
to have pain; to give pain; **he hurt his hand; she fell down and hurt herself; are you hurt? is he badly hurt? my foot hurts; he was slightly hurt in the crash; two players were hurt in the football game.**
hurts—hurting—hurt—has hurt

hus·band [ˈhʌzbənd] *noun*
man to whom a woman is married; **he's my secretary's husband; I know Mrs. Jones, but I have never met her husband.**

hut [hʌt] *noun*
small house, usually made of wood.

Ii

I [aɪ] *pronoun used by the speaker when talking about himself or herself.*

he said: "I can do it," and he did it; he and I are great friends; the manager said I could have a vacation; I told you I was going to be late.

Note: when it is the object, **I** *becomes* **me: I gave it to him/he gave it to me: I hit him/he hit me;** *when it follows the verb* **be, I** *usually becomes* **me: who is it?—it's me!**

ice [aɪs] *noun*

frozen water; **when the lake freezes, ice covers the surface; don't try to walk on the ice, it isn't thick enough yet; do you want some more ice in your drink? my hands are like ice** = are very cold.

no plural: **some ice; a block of ice**

ice·box, *noun*

refrigerator/machine in the kitchen which keeps food cold; **put the milk in the icebox.**

ice cream, *noun*

frozen dessert made of cream, water and fruit juice; **chocolate ice cream; what kind of ice cream do you want—lemon or coffee?**

ice skates, *plural noun*

boots with special blades for sliding on ice; **she was putting on her ice skates.**

ice-skat·ing, *noun*

sliding on ice wearing skates; **we are going ice-skating tomorrow.**

i·ci·cle ['aɪsɪkəl] *noun*

long piece of ice hanging from a roof, etc., made by water dripping in cold weather.

i·cy, *adjective*

covered with ice; **be careful, the sidewalks are icy.**

icy—icier—iciest

i·de·a [aɪ'dɪə] *noun*

something which you think of/plan which you make in your mind; **I have an idea—let's all go swimming; what a good idea! I get the idea that he doesn't want to go to college** = I think that he doesn't want to go; **where's your brother?—I have no idea** = I don't know; **I had no idea it was so late** = I didn't know it was so late.

i·de·al [aɪ'dɪəl] *adjective*

very suitable/perfect; **this is an ideal place for a picnic; a small car is ideal for shopping downtown.**

if [ɪf] *conjunction*

(*a*) (*showing what might happen*) **if it rains, you'll get wet; if I'm free, I'll come to the party; if you had told me you were sick, I would have come to see you; if I won $1000, I would take a long vacation.**

(*b*) (*asking questions*) **do you know if the train is going to be late? I wonder if he has ever been to Russia?**

(*c*) when; **if she goes out, she always wears a coat; if he was late, he always used to telephone.**

ill [ɪl] *adjective*

not well/sick; **eating green bananas will make you ill; if you feel ill, you ought to see a doctor; he's not as ill as he was last week.**

ill—worse—worst

ill·ness, *noun*

not being well; **his illness makes him very tired; a lot of children stay home from school because of illness.**

plural **illnesses**

I'll [aɪl] *see* **I shall, I will**

I'm [aɪm] *see* **I am**

im·ag·ine [ɪ'mædʒɪn] *verb*

to see or hear something in your mind; **imagine yourself sitting on the beach in** the sun; you can't imagine how difficult it is to get away from the office; I thought I heard someone shout, but I must have imagined it because there is no one there.

imagines—imagining— imagined—has imagined

im·ag·i·na·tion [ɪmædʒɪˈneɪʃən] *noun*
being able to see things in your mind; in his imagination he saw himself sitting on a beach in the sun.

im·me·di·ate [ɪˈmiːdɪət] *adjective*
which happens now/without waiting; this letter needs an immediate reply.
im·me·di·ate·ly, *adverb*
just after; he became ill immediately after he came back from vacation; you can start working immediately; if the house catches fire, you must call the fire department immediately.

im·por·tant [ɪmˈpɔːrtənt] *adjective*
serious/which matters a lot; is it important for you to get to Washington tomorrow? I must go to New York, because I have an important meeting; he has an important job in the government.
im·por·tance, *noun*
being serious/having a serious effect; the importance of the automobile industry.

im·pos·si·ble [ɪmˈpɒsɪbəl] *adjective*
which cannot be done; it's impossible to get tickets for the concert; it was impossible to get the car out of the garage because of the snow; driving to my downtown office is impossible because of the traffic.

im·prove [ɪmˈpruːv] *verb*
to get better; to make better; he has improved the look of his house by painting it white; his grades were very bad, but they are improving now; I scored two—can you improve on that? = can you do better than that?

improves—improving— improved—has improved

im·prove·ment, *noun*
getting better; there is no improvement in his work.

in [ɪn] *preposition & adverb*
(*a*) (*showing place*) they live in Japan; in

Russia it can be very cold during the winter; he's in the bathroom; she's in bed; why are you sitting outside in the snow? is your mother in? = is she at home?
(*b*) (*showing time*) in the fall the leaves fall off the trees; in the evening we sit and watch TV; he was born in 1963; I will be back home in January; she should be here in half an hour; he finished the crossword puzzle in 20 minutes.
(*c*) (*showing state*) she was dressed in white; he ran outside in his pajamas; she's in a hurry; the dictionary is in alphabetical order; he was in trouble with his boss for always coming late.

in for, *adverb*
I think we're in for some rain = I think we are going to get some rain; he's in for a big surprise = he's going to get a big surprise.

in on, *adverb*
is he in on the secret? = does he know the secret?

inch [ɪntʃ] *noun*
measurement of how long something is; the table is 18 inches (18″) across; she is 5 foot 6 inches tall (5′6″) (*say* "she's five foot six").

plural **inches**
Note: with numbers **inch** *is often written* ″: **7½″** = seven and a half inches

in·clude [ɪnˈkluːd] *verb*
to count something/someone with others; did you include your mother in the list of people you have asked to the party? there were ten of us, if you include the children; I will be on vacation up to and including next Tuesday; everyone had a good time, including the grown-ups.

includes—including—included— has included

in·come [ˈɪnkʌm] *noun*
money which you receive (usually for work); his income changes from year to year; she has a very low income.

in·crease 1. *noun* [ˈɪnkriːs]
getting larger or higher; an increase in the price of gasoline; he asked for a salary increase = he asked to have more money.

2. *verb* [ɪnˈkriːs]
to get larger or higher; **gas prices have increased twice this year; his salary was increased by ten percent.**
increases—increasing— increased—has increased

in·de·pen·dent [ɪndɪˈpendənt] *adjective*
free/not controlled by someone else; **she's a very independent girl; the country became independent on January 1; an independent** = person who does not belong to any political party.

in·doors [ɪnˈdɔːrz] *adverb*
inside a building; **you ought to stay indoors until your cold is better; they were playing tennis, but when it started to rain they went indoors.**
in·door [ˈɪndɔːr] *adjective*
which is inside a building; **the room is full of indoor plants; there's an indoor swimming pool in town, so we can swim even in winter.**

in·dus·try [ˈɪndəstrɪ] *noun*
making goods in factories; **the automobile industry; heavy industry** = factories which make large products (like cars/aircraft, etc.); **light industry** = factories which make small things (like watches/toys, etc.).
plural **industries**
in·dus·tri·al [ɪnˈdʌstrɪəl] *adjective*
referring to industry; **an industrial area** = an area where there are many factories.

in·flu·ence [ˈɪnfluːəns] 1. *noun*
being able to have an effect on someone/something; **the moon has an influence on animal behavior; the principal has no influence over the teachers in the school** = he cannot make them do what he wants.
2. *verb*
to have an effect on someone/something; **the government has tried to influence the voters; I liked the movie—I wasn't influenced by what the papers said about it.**
influences—influencing— influenced—has influenced

in·form [ɪnˈfɔːrm] *verb*
to tell someone; **have you informed the police that your car has been stolen? I must inform you that you will be arrested.**
informs—informing—informed —has informed

in·for·ma·tion [ɪnfərˈmeɪʃən] *noun*
facts about something; **do you have any information about trips to Europe? the police will give no information about how the accident happened; could you send me some more information about the job? you haven't given me enough information about your stolen car; that's a very useful piece/ bit of information**
no plural: **some information; a piece of information**

ink [ɪŋk] *noun*
colored liquid which is used for writing; **he wrote his name in red ink; my pen is dry—do you have any blue ink? she dropped a bottle of ink on the floor.**

in·quire [ɪnˈkwaɪr] *verb*
to ask questions; **have you inquired at the police station about your lost car? she inquired about the weather in Spain.**
inquires—inquiring—inquired— has inquired
Note: can be spelled **enquire**

in·quir·y, *noun*
question; **she is making inquiries about her cat which is missing; he wrote in answer to my inquiry about trips to Europe.**
plural **inquiries**
Note: can be spelled **enquiry**

in·sect [ˈɪnsekt] *noun*
small animal with six legs and a body in three parts; **flies and butterflies are insects but spiders are not; lots of insects were flying around the lamp.**

in·side [ɪnˈsaɪd] 1. *adverb*
in; indoors; **come inside—it's starting to rain; the weather was so bad that we just stayed inside and watched TV; the house is dark inside.**
2. *preposition*
in; **there is nothing inside the box; he was sitting inside his car listening to the**

radio; I know his house from the outside, but I've never been inside it.

3. *noun*

part which is in something; **I know his house from the outside, but what is the inside like? the inside of this cake is quite hard; he put his pajamas on inside out =** with the inside part facing out; **he knows Chicago inside out =** very well.

in·stant ['ınstənt] **1.** *noun*

moment; **come here this instant! =** at once; **he stopped running for an instant, and then started again.**

2. *adjective*

instant coffee = coffee powder to which you add hot water to make coffee quickly.

in·stant·ly, *adverb*

immediately; **all the passengers were killed instantly in the crash.**

in·stead (of) [ın'stedəv] *adverb*

in place of; **he'll go instead of me; instead of talking to the police, he just ran away; instead of playing ball, why don't you help me wash the car? would you like an orange instead of that apple? if she can't go, can I go instead? =** in her place; **we don't have tea—would you like some coffee instead?**

in·stru·ment ['ınstrəmənt] *noun*

(*a*) piece of equipment; tool; **the doctor had a box of instruments; I can't test your car—I haven't brought the right instruments.**

(*b*) **musical instrument =** thing with which you make music; **wind instruments =** ones which you blow to make a musical note; **string instruments =** ones with strings which make different notes when you pull them.

in·sure [ın'ʃʊr] *verb*

to arrange with a company that they will pay you money if something is lost or damaged; **is your car insured? I insured my luggage for $200.**
insures—insuring—insured—has insured

in·sur·ance, *noun*

agreement with a company that they

will pay you money if something is lost or damaged; **she has insurance against fire; life insurance =** insurance against someone dying; **auto insurance =** insurance against damage to your car.

in·tend [ın'tend] *verb*

to plan to do something; **they intend to go to Spain on vacation; she's intending to study English at college.**
intends—intending—intended—has intended

in·ter·est ['ıntrəst] **1.** *noun*

(*a*) special attention; **he takes a lot of interest in his students; she has no interest in plants; why doesn't he take more interest in what his sister is doing?**

(*b*) something which attracts you particularly; **her main interest is politics; do you have any special interests apart from your work?**

(*c*) money which is paid to someone who lends money; **if you put your money in the bank you'll get 10% interest on it; this type of bank account pays 10% interest; what interest do I have to pay if I borrow $1000?**

2. *verb*

to attract someone's attention; **he's especially interested in politics; nothing seems to interest her very much; the movie didn't interest me at all.**
interests—interesting—interested—has interested

in·ter·est·ing, *adjective*

which attracts your attention; **there's an interesting article on fishing in the newspaper; I didn't find the TV program interesting at all; what's so interesting about old churches?—I think they're dull.**

in·ter·fere [ıntər'fır] *verb*

to get in the way/to do something when no one wants you to do it; **don't interfere with their plans for the party; she doesn't like people who interfere in in her business affairs.**
interferes—interfering—interfered—has interfered

in·ter·jec·tion [ɪntərˈdʒekʃən] *noun*
word used to show that you are excited, hurt, angry, etc.; "oh!" and "help!" are interjections.

in·ter·na·tion·al [ɪntərˈnæʃənl] *adjective*
between different countries; **an international agreement; I have to make an international phone call.**

in·ter·rupt [ɪntəˈrʌpt] *verb*
to do something (such as to start to speak) when someone else is speaking and so keep them from continuing; **I was just starting to tell my story, when I was interrupted by the telephone; he couldn't finish his speech because he was being interrupted all the time; I'm sorry to interrupt, but your wife wants to speak to you on the phone.**
interrupts—interrupting—interrupted—has interrupted

in·ter·rup·tion, *noun*
act of interrupting; **he couldn't finish his work because of all the interruptions.**

in·to [ˈɪntʊ] *preposition*
(*a*) (*showing movement toward the inside*) he went into the house; she fell into the swimming pool; put the knives back into their box; you can't get 150 people into that bus; when he came into the room we were all talking about him; are you driving into the center of town?
(*b*) against; **the car ran into a tree.**
(*c*) (*showing a change*) it turned into a butterfly; when does water turn into steam? you ought to change into some clean clothes for the party; she burst into tears = suddenly started crying.
(*d*) (*showing you are dividing*) cut the cake into six pieces; four into three won't go = you can't divide three by four.

in·tro·duce [ɪntrəˈdjuːs] *verb*
to make two people know each other, when they have never met before; **I will introduce you to my sister; can I introduce my new assistant?**
introduces—introducing—introduced—has introduced

in·vent [ɪnˈvent] *verb*
(*a*) to make something which has never been made before; **he invented a new type of motor; who invented the telephone? he invents new machines.**
(*b*) to make up, using your imagination; **he invented the whole story.**
invents—inventing—invented—has invented

in·ven·tion, *noun*
thing which someone has invented; **we have seen his latest invention—a machine for putting fruit into jars.**

in·ven·tor, *noun*
person who invents; **who was the inventor of the telephone?**

in·vite [ɪnˈvaɪt] *verb*
to ask someone to do something (especially to come to a party, etc.); **how many people have you invited to your party? we invited them to come in; don't invite him—he's too rude; he has been invited to speak at the meeting.**
invites—inviting—invited—has invited

in·vi·ta·tion [ɪnvɪˈteɪʃən] *noun*
letter or card sent to someone asking them to do something; **they sent me an invitation to their party; he has received an invitation to speak at the meeting.**

i·ron [ˈaɪərn] 1. *noun*
(*a*) common gray metal; **the building has an iron roof; this hammer is made of iron.**
no plural: **some iron; sheets of iron/pieces of iron**
(*b*) metal instrument used to make cloth smooth after washing; **she has two irons—but only one of them works; if the iron is too hot it will make a brown mark on my shirt.**
2. *verb*
to make cloth smooth, using an iron; **he was ironing his shirt when the telephone rang; that shirt doesn't look as if it has been ironed.**
irons—ironing—ironed—has ironed

i·ron·ing, *noun*
clothes which have been washed and are

ready to be ironed; **she was doing the ironing.**

is [ız] *see* **be**

is·land [ˈaılənd] *noun*
piece of land with water all around it; **he lives on a little island in the middle of the river; Australia is really a very large island.**

isn't [ˈɪzənt] *see* **be**

it [ɪt] *subject or object pronoun referring to a thing or an animal*
(a) (*used to show something which has just been mentioned*) **he picked up an apple and then dropped it on the ground; I put my hat down somewhere, and now I can't find it; where's my book?—it's on the chair; the dog is hungry—give it something to eat.**
(b) (*referring to no particular thing*) **it's** raining; it's a long way from here to the post office; is it Tuesday today? it's very difficult to get a ticket at this time of year; what time is it?—it's 6 o'clock; it's silly to walk when we've got a car.
Note: **it's = it is** *or* **it has**

its [ɪts] *adjective*
belonging to it; **I can't use my bicycle— one of its tires is flat; that company pays its employees very badly.**
Note: written **its** *not* **it's**

it·self [ɪtˈself] *pronoun referring to a thing or an animal*
the house stands all by itself = all alone; the horse seems to have hurt itself; the car started to move all by itself; the cat is washing itself; the wires are all right, so there must be something wrong with the TV itself.

I've [aıv] *see* **I have**

Jj

jack [dʒæk] **1.** *noun*
tool used for lifting a heavy weight, such as a car; **always keep the jack in the trunk.**
2. *verb*
to jack up = to lift a heavy weight with a jack; they jacked the car up to change the tires.
jacks—jacking—jacked—has jacked

jack·pot, *noun*
to hit the jackpot = to win the big prize in a game.

jack·et [ˈdʒækɪt] *noun*
short coat; **he took his jacket off because it was hot; he was wearing gray pants and a blue jacket.**

jail [dʒeɪl] *noun*
prison/place where people are kept when they have been found guilty of a crime; **he was sent to jail for four years; she spent six months in jail; six prisoners escaped from the jail.**
Note: often used without **the**

jam [dʒæm] **1.** *noun*
(a) sweet food made by boiling fruit and sugar; **have some jam on your bread; she made jam out of all the fruit; open another jar of jam—this one is empty.**
(b) difficult situation; **can we get ourselves out of this jam?**
(c) **traffic jam = too much traffic on the road, so that vehicles can't move; the accident caused a big traffic jam.**
no plural for (a): **some jam; a jar of jam**

2. *verb*
(a) to block; **the streets downtown are always jammed around dinnertime.**

(b) to stop working properly; **my type-writer has jammed.**
jams—jamming—jammed—has jammed

Jan·u·ar·y [ˈdʒænjʊərɪ] *noun*
first month of the year; **her birthday is in January; he was born on January 26; we never go on vacation in January; he went to Canada last January; today is January 6.**
Note: **January 6** *say* "January sixth," "January the sixth" *or* "the sixth of January"

jar [dʒɑːr] *noun*
usually glass container for keeping food in; **a jar of honey; put those nuts into that glass jar.**

jaw [dʒɔː] *noun*
bones in your face which move up and down and make your mouth open and shut; **your teeth are fixed in your jaw; he fell down and broke his jaw.**

jeal·ous [ˈdʒeləs] *adjective*
feeling angry because someone has something which you would like to have; **I'm jealous of him because he gets more money than I do; don't be jealous—he works harder than you do; we're all jealous of the long vacations he takes.**

jeans [dʒiːnz] *plural noun*
pants made of a type of strong cloth, usually blue; **she was wearing jeans and a red sweater; I bought a new pair of jeans/some new jeans.**
Note: say **a pair of jeans** *if you want to show that there is only one*

jel·ly [ˈdʒelɪ] *noun*
sweet food made by boiling fruit juice and sugar; **he put grape jelly on his bread.**

jet [dʒet] *noun*
type of plane, which is pushed forward by gases from the motors; **the plane was attacked by two enemy jets.**

jew·el [ˈdʒuːəl] *noun*
valuable stone; **she had jewels in her hair.**
jew·el·ry, *noun*

jewels which are worn; **a burglar stole all her jewelry.**
no plural

job [dʒɒb] *noun*
(a) piece of work; **you've done a good job of fixing that table** = you've done it well; **I have a couple of jobs for you to do; do you have any little jobs you want done in the house?**
(b) regular work which you get paid for; **he has a job in an automobile factory; it's difficult for him to find a job because he can't drive; she has applied for a job as a teacher; he lost his job when the factory closed.**
(c) difficulty; **it was a job to find your house.**

join [dʒɔɪn] *verb*
(a) to put things together; to come together; **the two roads join about three miles further on; you must join the two wires together.**
(b) to become a member of a group/a club, etc.; to do something with someone; **we are going to the theater tomorrow—why don't you join us? will you join me for a cup of coffee? his daughter is going to join the police department; he joined the army.**
joins—joining—joined—has joined

joke [dʒəʊk] 1. *noun*
something said to make people laugh; **he was cracking jokes all the time; she made jokes about his hat.**
2. *verb*
to say something to make people laugh; **they laughed and joked at the party all evening; you're joking** = you're not serious.
jokes—joking—joked—has joked

jour·ney [ˈdʒɜrnɪ] *noun*
traveling a long distance; **he went on a journey across Russia.**

joy [dʒɔɪ] *noun*
very great happiness; **she jumped for joy** = because she was so happy.
joy ride *noun*
wild ride (esp. in a car that does not

belong to you); **after the party they all went on a joy ride in her father's car.**

judge [dʒʌdʒ] 1. *noun*
person who makes decisions, especially in law; **the judge ordered him to pay a $50 fine; she's the judge in the flower show; he's one of the judges in the Olympics.**
2. *verb*
(*a*) to decide which is the best; **she's judging the flowers in the flower show.**
(*b*) to calculate; **I'm no good at judging distances.**
judges—judging—judged—has judged

jug [dʒʌg] *noun*
large pot with a handle, used for keeping liquids in and pouring them; **milk jug; a jug of wine.**

juice [dʒuːs] *noun*
liquid inside fruit/vegetables, etc.; **a glass of orange juice; a can of tomato juice.**
juic·y, *adjective*
with a lot of juice in it; **a juicy orange.**
juicy—juicier—juiciest

Ju·ly [dʒʊˈlaɪ] *noun*
seventh month of the year; **he was born in July; she died last July; we are going to Spain next July; today is July 25.**
Note: **July 25:** *say* "July twenty-fifth," "July the twenty-fifth" *or* "the twenty-fifth of July"

jump [dʒʌmp] 1. *noun*
sudden movement off the ground; **long jump/high jump** = sports where you see who can jump furthest or highest.
2. *verb*
to go into the air off the ground; **he jumped over the wall; can you jump across this stream? she jumped down from the chair** = she was standing on the chair and then came down to the floor suddenly; **when they fired the gun, it made me jump** = move suddenly because I was surprised or frightened.
to jump the gun = to go first,

before you are supposed to; to do something too early.
to jump a traffic light = to go forward before it is green.
jumps—jumping—jumped—has jumped

June [dʒuːn] *noun*
sixth month of the year; **he was born in June; her birthday is on June 15; last June we went to Idaho; today is June 7.**
Note: **June 7:** *say* "June seventh," "June the seventh" *or* "the seventh of June"

junk [dʒʌŋk] *noun*
things which are old and useless; **he threw away a lot of junk when he cleaned out the garage.**
no plural: **some junk; a lot of junk**

just [dʒʌst] *adverb*
(*a*) exactly; **it's just by the door; don't come in just yet—we're not ready; just how many of the children can read? she's just sixteen—her birthday was yesterday; what time is it?—it's just six o'clock.**
(*b*) (*showing something which happened very recently or will happen very soon*) **I had just got into the bathtub when the phone rang; I'm just going to the supermarket; I was just going to call her, when she called me; they've just arrived from New York; he's just leaving for the office.**
(*c*) only; **I've been there just once; wait just a minute!**
just a·bout = nearly; more or less; **I've just about finished my homework.**
just a·bout to = will very soon; **he's just about to leave; we were just about to go to bed when the phone rang.**
just as = (*a*) at the same time; **just as I got into the bathtub the phone rang.**
(*b*) in exactly the same way; **this book is just as good as the film; it is just as cold inside the house as it is outside.**
just now = (*a*) at the present time; **we're very busy just now.**
(*b*) a short time ago; **I saw him just now in the bank.**

Kk

keep [ki:p] *verb*

(*a*) to have for a very long time or forever; **can I keep the book I borrowed from you? I don't want that paper any more—you can keep it; he has kept my watch and won't give it back.**

(*b*) to continue to do something; **this watch will keep going even under water; he had to keep running so that the police wouldn't catch him; keep quiet or they'll hear you; she just kept talking.**

(*c*) to make someone stay in a state; **what kept you?** = why are you late? **he kept us waiting for twenty minutes; this coat will keep you warm.**

(*d*) **to keep an eye on** = to watch carefully; **he's keeping an eye on the store while I'm away.**

keeps—keeping—kept [kept]—**has kept**

keep off, *verb*

to stay away from; **keep off the grass!**

keep on, *verb*

to continue to do something; **my watch keeps on stopping; the traffic kept on moving although the snow was very deep.**

keep up, *verb*

to continue at the same level; **you're doing very well—keep it up!** = keep doing the same; **he finds it difficult to keep up in his French class.**

keep up with, *verb*

to go at the same speed; **he couldn't keep up with a car on his bicycle; wages can't keep up with the cost of food; she walked so fast that I had difficulty keeping up with her.**

ket·tle [′ketəl] *noun*

metal container which you use for boiling water; **the tea kettle's boiling—please turn off the gas.**

key [ki:] 1. *noun*

(*a*) piece of metal used to open a lock; **I can't get into the house—I've lost the key to the front door; where did you put your car keys?**

(*b*) part of a piano/a typewriter, etc., which you push down with your fingers.

(*c*) answer to a problem/explanation; **is there a key to explain what these signs mean?**

2. *adjective*

most important; **he has the key position in the company; oil is a key industry.**

key·hole, *noun*

hole in a lock, into which you put a key; **he looked through the keyhole into the room.**

kick [kɪk] 1. *noun*

hitting with your foot; **he gave the ball a kick.**

2. *verb*

to hit something with your foot; **he kicked the ball into the goal.**

kicks—kicking—kicked—has kicked

kid [kɪd] 1. *noun*

young child; **all the kids play in the street; we're taking the kids to Disneyland.**

2. *verb*

to make someone believe something which is not true; **he kidded the teacher that he'd been sick; don't get worried, he's only kidding.**

kids—kidding—kidded—has kidded

kill [kɪl] *verb*

to make something or someone die; **the dry weather has killed all my**

plants; the car hit the dog and killed it; he was killed in a plane crash.
kills—killing—killed—has killed

kil·ler, noun
person who kills; the police are looking for two killers.

kil·o·gram [ˈkɪləgræm], **kil·o** [ˈkiːləʊ] noun
measurement of weight; two kilos of sugar; he weighs 62 kilos (62 kg).
Note: when used with numbers, **kilos** is usually written **kg**

kil·o·me·ter [kɪˈlɒmɪtər] noun
measurement of distance equal to 1000 meters; it is about twenty kilometers (20 km) from here to the railroad station; the speed limit is 80 kilometers per hour (80 kmh).
Note: when used with numbers **kilometers** *is usually written* **km: 26 km;** *note also* **kilometers per hour** *is usually written* **kmh: eighty kilometers per hour** = 80 kmh

kind [kaɪnd] 1. noun
type: a butterfly is a kind of insect; how many kinds of apples do you carry in your store? we were talking about all kinds of things = about several subjects.
2. adjective
friendly; helpful; thinking about other people; it's very kind of you to lend me your car; how kind of him to ask you to the party; you always should be kind to animals; she's the kindest person I know.
kind—kinder—kindest

kind-heart·ed, adjective
kind and good; he's too kind-hearted—he never gets mad at the children.
kind·ly, adverb
please; kindly shut the door when you go out.

king [kɪŋ] noun
man who rules a country; King John; the King and Queen came to visit the city.
Note: **king** *is spelled with a capital when used with a name or when referring to a particular person*

king-size, adjective
very large; a king-size bed.

kiss [kɪs] 1. noun
touching someone with your lips to show love; she gave her mother a kiss.
plural **kisses**
2. verb
to touch someone with your lips to show that you love or like them; they kissed each other good-bye; he kissed his daughter and went away.
kiss—kissing—kissed—has kissed

kit [kɪt] noun
box of tools or equipment; the nurse was carrying her first aid kit.

kitch·en [ˈkɪtʃən] noun
room where you cook food/wash dishes, etc.; don't come into the kitchen with your dirty shoes on; he put the bread down on the kitchen table; the ice cream is in the refrigerator in the kitchen.

knee [niː] noun
place where your leg bends in the middle; he was on his knees looking for something under the bed; the baby can go quite fast on his hands and knees; the little girl sat on her grandfather's knee.

kneel [niːl] verb
to be or to go on your knees; he kneeled down to look under the car; she was kneeling by the bed.
kneels—kneeling—kneeled/ knelt [nelt]**—has kneeled/knelt**

knew [njuː] see **know**

knife [naɪf] noun
tool with a sharp metal blade fixed in a handle; to set the table, you put down a knife, fork and spoon for each person; cut up your meat with your knife; bread knife = special large knife for cutting bread.
plural **knives** [naɪvz]

knit [nɪt] verb
to make something out of yarn, using two long needles; she's knitting a pair of socks; he was wearing a red knitted hat; my mother knit/knitted this scarf for me.
knits—knitting—knit/knitted— has knit/knitted

Kitchen

1. can opener
2. coffepot
3. cup
4. cupboard
5. dish towel
6. dishwasher
7. electric light
8. electric plug
9. faucet
10. frying pan
11. glass
12. handle
13. kettle
14. kitchen scale
15. lid
16. matchbox
17. oven
18. pan or saucepan
19. plate
20. refrigerator
21. saucer
22. shelf
23. sink
24. steam
25. stove
26. teapot
27. toaster

knock [nɒk] 1. *noun*

(*a*) sound made by hitting something; **there was a knock at the door.**

(*b*) the hitting of something; **he got a knock on the head.**

2. *verb*

to hit something; **he knocked on the door before going in; you need a hammer to knock that nail in.**

knocks—knocking—knocked— has knocked

knock down, *verb*

to make something fall down by hitting it hard; **they are going to knock down the old church to build a new one; he was knocked down by another man.**

Note: **they knocked the church down** *or* **they knocked down the church** *but only* **they knocked it down**

knock·er, *noun*

metal ring on a door which you can use to knock with.

knock off, *verb*

(*a*) to make something fall off by hitting it; **the cat knocked the milk bottle off the table.**

(*b*) to stop work; **the workmen all knocked off at 4:30.**

knock out, *verb*

to hit someone so hard that he is no longer conscious; **he was knocked out by a blow on the head.**

knot [nɒt] *noun*

place where two pieces of string are tied together; **he tied a knot at the end of the piece of string; tie the two ropes together in a knot.**

know [nəʊ] *verb*

(*a*) to be informed about something; **do you know how to get to Montreal from here? I didn't know she was married; he knew he would have to spend a lot of money; do you know the German for "one—two—three"? he doesn't know where she has gone; I didn't know when he was going to come.**

(*b*) to have met someone/to have been to a place often; **I know your brother— we were at school together; I used to know a man called Johnson; I know California very well.**

knows—knowing—knew [njuː]— **has known**

knowl·edge [ˈnɒlɪdʒ] *noun*

what is known; **he has no knowledge of what is happening; he has a good knowledge of French.**

Ll

La·bor Day [ˈleɪbərdeɪ] *noun*

public holiday (usu. the first Monday in September).

lad·der [ˈlædər] *noun*

thing made of a row of bars which you use to climb up or down; **he climbed up a ladder to look at the roof; you have to go down a ladder to get into the hole in the ground.**

la·dy [ˈleɪdiː] *noun*

(*polite way of referring to a woman*) **there's a lady waiting to see you; a lady doctor.**

plural **ladies**

la·dy·bug, *noun*

small red bug with black spots.

laid [leɪd] *see* **lay**

lain [leɪn] *see* **lie**

lake [leɪk] *noun*

large piece of water with land all around it; **they went out in a boat on the lake; he swam across the lake.**

lamb [læm] *noun*

(*a*) baby sheep; **we saw hundreds of lambs in the fields.**

(*b*) meat from a young sheep; **we had**

roast lamb for dinner.
Note: no plural when it means meat:
some lamb; a slice of lamb

lamp [læmp] *noun*
thing which makes light; **a desk lamp; a
floor lamp.**
lamp·light, *noun*
light from a lamp.
lamp·shade, *noun*
cover over a lamp.

land [lænd] 1. *noun*
(*a*) solid soil; **I am glad to be on land
again after ten days at sea.**
(*b*) country; **people of many lands.**
(*c*) part of a country; area of ground;
**he owns land in Ohio; I have bought a
piece of land to build a house on.**
2. *verb*
(*a*) to come to earth; **the plane landed at
the airport; we will be landing at London
Airport in 15 minutes.**
(*b*) to finish up/to end up (in a place);
he tried to steal a car and landed in jail.
**lands—landing—landed—has
landed**
land·ing, *noun*
(*a*) action of coming to earth; **the plane
made a good landing.**
(*b*) flat space at the top of a flight of
stairs; **go up the stairs and wait for me
on the landing.**

lan·guage ['læŋgwɪdʒ] *noun*
way of speaking/writing used by people
of a country or area; **Swedish is a very
difficult language; English is a language
which is used everywhere; I don't enjoy
vacationing in a country where I don't
speak or understand the language;
Chinese is the language spoken by most
people in the world.**

large [lɑːrdʒ] *adjective*
very big; **he was carrying one large suitcase and two small ones; I want a large
cup of coffee, please; how large is your
office?**
large—larger—largest
large·ly, *adverb*
mainly/mostly; **the country is largely
forest.**

last [læst] 1. *adjective*
(*a*) which comes at the end; **they live in
the last house on the right; you must pay
me by the last day of the month; December 31 is the last day of the year.**
(*b*) most recent; **last Monday** = the
Monday before today; **last week** = the
week before this one; **I saw her last
Thursday; where did you go on vacation
last year? last month it rained almost
every day; she has been sick for the last
ten days.**
(*c*) **before last** = the one before the most
recent; **the Monday before last** = two
Mondays ago; **the week before last** =
two weeks ago.
2. *noun*
thing/person coming at the end; **she was
the last to arrive; that's the last of the
apples** = we have finished the apples.
3. *adverb*
(*a*) at the end; **he came last in the race.**
(*b*) most recently; **when did you see her
last? she was not looking well when I saw
her last.**
4. *verb*
to stay/to go on; **the good weather won't
last; vacations never seem to last very
long; the storm lasted all night.**
**lasts—lasting—lasted—has
lasted**
at last/at long last = in the end/
finally/after a long delay; **I walked for
hours, and got home at last at 6 o'clock;
at long last the train arrived.**
last·ing, *adjective*
going on for a long time; **she had a lasting love of nature.**
last·ly, *adverb*
finally; **lastly I want to thank my friends
for their help.**

late [leɪt] 1. *adjective*
(*a*) after the usual time; after the
expected time; **the train is ten minutes
late; it's too late to go to the store; if
you don't hurry you'll be late.**
(*b*) at the end of a period of time; **we
had lunch in the late afternoon; they went
to the late show at the theater.**
(*c*) towards the end of the day; **it's
late—I'm going to bed.**

(d) **latest** = most recent; **the radio gives the latest news at 10:00; have you read his latest book?**

late—later—last/latest

2. *adverb*

(a) after the usual time; **the train arrived late; last night we went to bed late; she got up late this morning.**

(b) at a time after the present; after a time which has been mentioned; **he came a month later; can I see you later this afternoon? see you later!** = good-bye/I hope to see you again later today.

late—later—last

late·ly, *adverb*

recently; **have you seen her lately? he's been very busy lately.**

laugh [læf] 1. *noun*

sound you make when you are amused; **she's got a loud laugh; he said it with a laugh; he did it for laughs** = as a joke.

2. *verb*

to make a sound to show you are amused; **they all laughed at his jokes; when he fell off his bicycle everyone laughed; don't laugh at him because he's so fat; you mustn't laugh at her hat.**

laughs—laughing—laughed—has laughed

laun·dry [ˈlɔːndriː] *noun*

(a) place where clothes, etc., are washed; **you'd better send your shirts to the laundry.**

(b) clothes, etc., which need to be washed or which have been washed; **she piled up the laundry on the table.**

plural **laundries, but no plural for (b)**

law [lɔː] *noun*

set of rules which govern a country; **you must always obey the law; driving at night without lights is against the law; Congress has passed a law forbidding the use of dangerous drugs.**

law·yer [ˈlɔːjər] *noun*

person who knows about laws and can advise you about them; **if you are arrested, you must try to speak to your lawyer.**

lawn [lɔːn] *noun*

area in a yard/garden covered with short grass; **let's have our drinks outside on the lawn; the lawn needs cutting; the city hall has a large lawn in front of it; she has bought some new lawn chairs.**

lay [leɪ] *verb*

(a) to put something down; **he laid the book down on the table; they are laying a new carpet in the dining room; the hen has laid an egg.**

(b) **to lay the table** = to put knives/forks/spoons, etc., on the table ready for a meal; **the table is laid for four people.**

(c) *see also* **lie.**

lays—laying—laid—has laid

lay a·way, *verb*

to save (money); **he has $20,000 laid away in the bank.**

lay off, *verb*

(a) to put out of work for a time; **he was laid off for three months.**

(b) **lay off!** = stop it!

lay out, *verb*

to put out; to spread out; **the map was laid out on the table; the presents are laid out under the Christmas tree.**

la·zy [ˈleɪziː] *adjective*

not wanting to do any work; **he's too lazy to earn a lot of money; she's the laziest girl in the school.**

lazy—lazier—laziest

lb., *see* **pound**

lead¹ [led] *noun*

(a) very heavy soft metal; **you should tie a piece of lead to your fishing line to make it sink.**

(b) part in the middle of a pencil which you write with; **the lead's broken—I must sharpen the pencil.**

no plural for (a)

lead² [liːd] 1. *noun*

(a) first place (in a race); **he went into the lead; who's in the lead?**

(b) string or thin piece of leather to hold a dog; **dogs must be kept on a lead.**

2. *verb*

(a) to be in first place; **our team was leading at half time; he is leading by two meters.**

(b) to go in front to show the way; **she**

led us to our seats; the path leads to the top of the hill.

(c) to be in charge of/to be the main person; **he is leading a group of businessmen on a tour of Japanese factories.**

(d) to lead to = to be the cause of; **the discussion led to a big argument.**

leads—leading—led [led]**—has led**

lead·er, *noun*

person who leads; **he is the leader of the group.**

lead up to, *verb*

to be the cause of; to take place just before; **the events leading up to the war; the discussions led up to an agreement.**

leaf [liːf] *noun*

flat green part of a plant; **in the winter the leaves fall off the trees and grow again in the spring; insects have eaten the leaves of the cabbages.**

plural **leaves** [liːvz]; *see also* **leave**

leak [liːk] **1.** *noun*

hole through which liquid can get out; **there is a leak in the pipe.**

2. *verb*

to flow out; **water is leaking from the pipe; the tire is leaking air.**

leaks—leaking—leaked— has leaked

leak·y, *adjective*

having holes where liquid can get out; **a leaky faucet.**

leaky—leakier—leakiest

lean [liːn] *verb*

to keep standing by resting against something; to bend over; **lean the ladder against the wall; he leaned his elbows on the table; the ladder is leaning up against the wall; don't lean over the edge of the roof; he was leaning out of the window.**

leans—leaning—leaned— has leaned

leap [liːp] *verb*

to jump; **the guests leapt out of the windows of the burning hotel; don't try to leap over that wall.**

leaps—leaping—leaped/ leapt [lept]**—has leaped/ leapt**

learn [lɜrn] *verb*

(a) to find out about something/how to do something; **she's learning to swim; we learn English at school; have you learned how to drive yet?**

(b) to hear (news); **I learnt that they were leaving; when did you learn that she was getting married?**

learns—learning—learned/ learnt [lɜrnt]**—has learned/learnt**

learn·er, *noun*

person who is learning.

least [liːst] *adverb, adjective & noun*

smallest; less than anything; **that's the least of my problems; it's the thing I worry about least of all; it doesn't matter in the least** = it doesn't matter at all.

at least = at any rate; **even if the job is boring, at least you have enough money to live on.**

leath·er [ˈleðər] *noun*

skin of animals used to make shoes, etc.; **a leather belt; her jacket is made of leather.**

no plural

leave [liːv] *verb*

(a) to go away; **he left the house; the train leaves at 10:00.**

(b) to forget (to do something); to let something stay; **she left her toothbrush at home; someone has left the light on; did you leave the door locked?**

(c) not to take; **leave a piece of cake for your brother.**

(d) **left** *or* **left over** = remaining; **after paying for the meal and the theater tickets, I still have $10 left over; if you eat three apples there will be only two left; there is nobody left in the office.**

leaves—leaving—left [left]**—has left**

leave a·lone, *verb*

not to worry someone; **leave her alone, she wants to sleep; the dog won't leave the cat alone.**

leave be·hind, *verb*

to forget to take; not to take; **he left his keys behind in the store; we had to leave the dog behind when we went on vacation.**

leave for, *verb*

to go away from one place toward

another; when does the train leave for Chicago?

leave off, *verb*

(*a*) to stop; where did you leave off in telling the story?

(*b*) to forget to put on; she left the address off the envelope; the waiter left the drinks off the bill.

(*c*) to keep off; he left the phone off the hook because he didn't want to speak to anyone.

leave out, *verb*

to forget to put in; not to include; he left out the most important detail when he reported the accident to the police; we left him out of the team because he has a cold.

Note: don't leave your sister out *or* don't leave out your sister *but only* don't leave her out

led [led] *see* **lead²**

left [left] *adverb, adjective & noun*

referring to the side of the body which usually has the weaker hand; he can't catch with his left hand; in England, cars drive on the left; his house is on the left side of the street; go down the street and turn left at the traffic light; keep going left if you want to get to the beach; *see also* **leave.**

left-hand, *adjective*

on the left side; look in the left-hand drawer; they live on the left-hand side of the street.

left-hand·ed, *adjective*

using the left hand more often than the right for writing; he's left-handed.

left·o·ver, *noun & adjective*

food which has not been eaten; what shall we do with these leftover potatoes? she hates to have leftovers for dinner.

leg [leg] *noun*

(*a*) part of the body with which a person or animal walks; one of the parts of a chair, etc., which touch the floor; he's standing on one leg; the table has four legs; some dogs can stand on their back legs; she fell off the ladder and broke her leg; he's pulling your leg = he's making you believe something which is untrue/ he's joking.

(*b*) leg of an animal used for food; a leg of lamb; would you like a chicken leg?

lem·on ['lemən] *noun*

(*a*) bitter yellow fruit; put some lemon juice on your fish; do you want a piece of lemon in your drink?

(*b*) pale yellow color; lemon curtains.

lem·on·ade [lemə'neɪd] *noun*

drink made from lemons; can I have a glass of lemonade?

lend [lend] *verb*

to loan/to give something to someone for a certain period of time; can you lend me your dictionary? can you lend me $5 till Monday? I lent her my bike and now she won't give it back; to lend a hand = to help; can you lend a hand with the cooking?

lends—lending—lent [lent]**—has lent**

Note: compare **borrow**

length [leŋkθ] *noun*

measurement of how long something is; the garden is 25 meters in length; he swam a length of the pool = he swam from one end to the other.

lent [lent] *see* **lend**

less [les] **1.** *adjective & noun*

smaller (amount/size, etc.); you ought to eat less bread; the bill comes to less than $20; he finished his work in less than an hour.

2. *preposition*

without/taking a number away; ten less six equals four; the price is $70 less 10%.

3. *adverb*

not as much; she's trying to eat less; the second book is less well-known than the first; I want a suitcase which is less heavy than this one.

les·son ['lesn] *noun*

period of time in school, etc., when you are taught something; he went to sleep during the math lesson; he's taking/ having driving lessons; she gives English lessons at home in the evenings.

let [let] *verb*

(*a*) to allow someone to do something; let me wash the car; will he let us go home early today? can you let me have two pounds of sugar? they let her borrow their car; let them come in—it's raining hard; can you let me know as soon as possible? = can you tell me.

(b) to rent/to allow someone to borrow a house for a time and pay for it; I'm letting my house to an English family for the summer.

(c) (showing a suggestion) let's all go to the movies; let's not start yet.

lets—letting—let—has let

let down, verb

(a) to allow something to go down; they let down the bucket on a rope.

(b) to allow the air to go out of a tire, etc.; he let down my back tire.

(c) not to help someone who was expecting you to help; to fail someone; I asked him to speak at the meeting but he let me down; she let me down by not coming to my party.

(d) to stop trying; our team let down at the end of the game.

let go, verb

to stop holding on to something; don't let go of the handle; he held on to the branch, and then had to let go of it.

let in, verb

to allow to come in; don't let the dog in if he's wet; these shoes are no good—they let in water/they let the water in.

let your·self in for, verb

to allow something to happen to you; he didn't realize what he was letting himself in for when he said he would paint the house = didn't realize what a big job it was.

let off, verb

not to punish someone/not to give someone work; he was arrested for stealing, but the judge let him off with a fine; the teacher let us off early today = let us leave school early.

let on, verb

to tell; don't let on that I was there.

let out, verb

to allow to go out; they let the sheep out of the field; don't let the dog out when the mailman is coming; he let the air out of my back tire.

let up, verb

to stop/to become less; the rain didn't let up all day; he's working too hard—he ought to let up a bit.

Note: don't let the dog in or don't let in the dog; he let the bucket down or he let down the bucket, etc., but only don't let it in, he let it down, etc.

let·ter ['letər] noun

(a) message in writing sent from one person to another; the mailman has brought two letters for you; I must write a letter to my mother to tell her how we all are; I've gotten a letter from the manager of the bank; can you mail this letter for me?

(b) sign used in writing: A is the first letter of the alphabet; can you think of a word with eight letters beginning with A and ending with T?

let·ter box, noun

hole in a front door through which the mailman delivers letters; the package is too thick to go into the letter box.

plural letter boxes

let·tuce ['letɪs] noun

green vegetable with large leaves used to make salads; a hamburger with lettuce and tomato.

lev·el ['levəl] 1. adjective

(a) horizontal/not sloping; this table isn't level, put a piece of wood under the leg.

(b) at the same height as something; can you hang this picture level with the other one? the water is level with the top of the glass.

2. noun

height; the room is on the same level as the yard; the town is 900 feet above sea level; the government wants to reduce the level of public spending.

3. verb

to make something flat; they are leveling the ground before they start building; the road goes up and down, and then levels out for a few miles.

levels—leveling—leveled—has leveled

li·brar·y ['laɪbreriː] *noun*
place where books are kept which can then be borrowed; collection of books/ records, etc.; **he has a big library of records; don't forget to take your books back to the library; this book isn't mine—it's a library book.**
plural **libraries**
li·brar·i·an [laɪ'breriən] *noun*
person who works in a library.

lick [lɪk] *verb*
to make your tongue move over something; **she was licking an ice cream; the cat licked up the spilled milk; he forgot to lick the envelope.**
licks—licking—licked—has licked

lid [lɪd] *noun*
top which covers a container; **put the lid back on the peanut butter jar; I've lost the lid of the saucepan.**

lie [laɪ] **1.** *noun*
something which is not true; **he has been telling lies about his brother.**
2. *verb*
to say something which is not true; **he was lying when he said he hadn't touched the money; he lied to the police about the accident.**
lies—lying—lied—has lied
3. *verb*
to be in a flat position; **the dog was lying in front of the fire; the snow lay six inches deep on the ground; there were leaves lying all over the sidewalk; we lay in the sun all afternoon.**
lies—lying—lay [leɪ]**—has lain**
lie down, *verb*
to put yourself in a flat position; **she lay down on the floor; just as I was lying down the telephone rang.**

life [laɪf] *noun*
time when you are alive; being alive; **he spent his whole life working on the farm; a miner has a hard life; life insurance =** insurance against death; **she saved my life =** saved me from dying; **there's no sign of life in the house =** it looks as though there is no one in it.

life·belt, life jack·et, *noun*
large ring or jacket which helps you to float in water.
life·boat, *noun*
special boat used to rescue people at sea; **the lifeboat rescued the crew of the sinking ship.**
life·guard, *noun*
person who rescues people who are in difficulties when swimming.

lift [lɪft] **1.** *noun*
ride offered to someone; **can I give you a lift to the station in my car?**
2. *verb*
to raise to a higher position; to pick something up; **this case is so heavy, I can't lift it off the floor; he hurt his back while lifting a heavy box.**
lifts—lifting—lifted—has lifted

light [laɪt] **1.** *adjective*
(*a*) not heavy; **a light meal; I can carry this case easily—it's quite light; she was only wearing a light coat; he's not healthy, and so can only do light work.**
(*b*) pale; fair; **a light blue shirt; our house has a light green door; she has light hair.**
(*c*) bright so that you can see well; **the kitchen is lighter than our dining room; at six o'clock in the morning it was just getting light.**
(*d*) not serious; **light music; light reading.**
light—lighter—lightest
2. *noun*
(*a*) thing which shines and helps you to see; **you can't read by the light of the moon; the light of the sun makes plants green; there's not enough light in here to take a picture.**
(*b*) object (usually a glass bulb) which gives out light; **turn on the lights—it's getting dark; the car was traveling with no lights; I could see the red lights of the car in front of me; I'm going to put a light on the wall so that I can read in bed.**
(*c*) **can you give me a light? =** do you have a match or lighter to light my cigarette?
3. *verb*
to make something start to burn; **can**

you light the burner under the kettle? I
can't get the fire to light; light a match—
we can't see in the dark.

lights—lighting—lit [lɪt]—has lit

light·er, *noun*
small machine for lighting cigarettes;
**can I borrow your lighter? mine has
broken.**

light·house, *noun*
tall building near the sea which shines a
bright light at night to warn ships that
rocks are near.

light·ing, *noun*
way of giving light; **the lighting is very
bad in the dining room—we can't see
what we are eating.**

lights, *plural noun*
red, green and yellow lights for making
traffic stop and start; **turn right at the
lights; he crossed the street when the light
was red.**

light·ning [ˈlaɪtnɪŋ] *noun*
flash of electricity in the sky, followed
by the noise of thunder; **during the
storm, lightning struck the city hall
clock; a flash of lightning lit the sky.**

no plural: **some lightning; a flash
of lightning**

light·ning bug, *noun*
flying insect which glows.

like [laɪk] **1.** *preposition*
(*a*) nearly the same as/similar to; **he's
like his father; the picture doesn't
look like her at all; what was the weather
like on your vacation? he swims like a
fish; it tastes like jam; it sounds like
Beethoven; it feels like rain** = as if it is
going to rain.
(*b*) wanting to; **I feel like eating.**
(*c*) as for example; **fruit like apples and
oranges.**
2. *verb*
(*a*) to be pleased with; to enjoy; **do you
like butter? he doesn't like fish; I like
my new teacher; do you like driving? I
like to sit and read quietly in the evening.**
(*b*) to want; **I'd like you to meet my
father; we'd like to go to Mexico; take
as much sugar as you like.**

likes—liking—liked—has liked

like·ly, *adjective*
which you expect to happen; **it's likely
to rain** = it'll probably rain; **he's not
likely to win** = he will probably not
win.

likely—likelier—likeliest

lik·ing, *noun*
being fond of; **he has a liking for sweets;
I've taken a liking to her** = I've started
to like her.

lim·it [ˈlɪmɪt] **1.** *noun*
furthest point/place past which you
cannot go; **there is a speed limit of 30
miles per hour in the city; there is no age
limit for joining the club** = people of all
ages can join.
2. *verb*
to set a limit to something; **the club is
limited to 200 members** = only 200
people may belong to it; **parking is
limited to 30 minutes** = you can only
park for 30 minutes.

**limits—limiting—limited—has
limited**

line [laɪn] **1.** *noun*
(*a*) long thin mark; **he drew a straight
line with his pencil; she has lines on her
forehead; you must not park on the
yellow lines; I want some notepaper
without any lines; the ball went over the
line.**
(*b*) long wire/string; **fishing line;
telephone line; speak more clearly—
the line's bad; we had a crossed line** =
two telephone conversations were
mixed together; **he's on the line now** =
he is on the phone waiting to speak to
you.
(*c*) row (of cars/people/words, etc.); **we
stood in line for half an hour waiting to
get into the theater; the line of cars
stretched for three miles from the accident; she only typed two lines and made
six mistakes; start at the top line on page
6; can you read that line again?**
(*d*) **railroad line** = metal rails on which
trains run; company which runs a railroad; **the town has just one railroad line.**
2. *verb*
(*a*) to make a line; **the soldiers lined the**

streets = stood in line along the sidewalks; **lined paper** = paper with lines printed on it.

(b) to put a lining inside a piece of clothing; **she was wearing a dress lined with silk; do you have any fur-lined boots?**

lines—lining—lined—has lined

line up, *verb*
to stand in a line; **if you want tickets, line up over here.**

lin·ing, *noun*
material put on the inside of a piece of clothing; **a dress with a silk lining.**

li·on ['laɪən] *noun*
large animal of the cat family; **they saw a lion at the zoo.**

lip [lɪp] *noun*
one of two parts around the edge of your mouth; **he licked his lips when he thought of dinner; she fell down and cut her lip.**

lip·stick, *noun*
stick of red color which you put on your lips; **she put her lipstick on.**

liq·uid ['lɪkwɪd] *adjective & noun*
something (like water) which is not solid and is not a gas; **heat the butter until it is quite liquid; he's sick and needs to drink a lot of liquids.**

liq·uor ['lɪkər] *noun*
alcohol/liquid which makes you drunk if you drink too much of it.

list [lɪst] **1.** *noun*
number of things written down one after the other; **there is a list of names in alphabetical order; we couldn't remember what to buy because we forgot the shopping list; he's on the danger list** = he is very seriously ill.
2. *verb*
to write in the form of a list; **the streets are listed at the back of the book; all the restaurants are listed in the yellow pages.**

lists—listing—listed—has listed

lis·ten ['lɪsn] *verb*
to pay attention to something which

you hear; **be quiet—I'm listening to the news; if you listened to what I tell you, you wouldn't make so many mistakes; will you listen for the telephone while I'm outside?** = will you wait to see if it rings?

listens—listening—listened—has listened

lis·ten·er, *noun*
person who listens.

lit [lɪt] *see* **light**

li·ter ['li:tər] *noun*
measurement of liquids; **can you buy a liter of wine? this bucket contains two liters.**

lit·tle ['lɪtl] **1.** *adjective*
(a) small/not big; **they have two children—a boy and a little girl** = a young girl; **he has a ring on his little finger; she stood on my little toe.**
(b) not much; **she eats very little bread; the car uses very little gasoline.**

little—less—least
Note: **little** *is used with nouns which you cannot count:* **very little money,** *but* **very few boys**

2. *noun*
a little = a small amount; **give me a little of that soup; would you like some more coffee?—just a little, please.**
3. *adverb*
not much; **it was little more than fifteen minutes ago; I see her very little these days.**
lit·tle by lit·tle = not all at the same time; **little by little, he got better.**

live 1. *adjective* [laɪv]
(a) living/not dead; **a real live movie star** = an actual movie star.
(b) not recorded; **a live TV program.**
(c) carrying electricity; **don't walk on the live rail; watch out—that's a live wire.**
2. *verb* [lɪv]
(a) to have your home in a place; **we live in Atlanta; they used to live in Texas; do you like living in the city better than in the country? they live in a house by the river; where do your parents live? they live at 1510 West Harbor Street.**
(b) to be alive; **George Washington lived**

in the 18th century; he is sick, and the doctor doesn't expect him to live much longer.

lives—living—lived—has lived

live·ly ['laɪvlɪ] *adjective*
active; my grandfather is very lively; we had a very lively party with dozens of guests.

live on, *verb*
to use something to stay alive; he lives on eggs and bread; you can't live on $10 a week; he doesn't earn enough to live on.

liv·ing room, *noun*
room in a house which the family spend most time in; we sat in the living room and watched TV; the living room door is shut; they were eating in the living room.

load [ləʊd] 1. *noun*
things which are carried in a vehicle; a truck with a load of potatoes; the airplane had a load of supplies; loads of = a lot of; he has loads of money.
2. *verb*
to put things into a vehicle; we're loading the truck with bags of coal; the ship's loading in the harbor; the airplane was loaded with supplies for the soldiers.

loads—loading—loaded—has loaded

loaf [ləʊf] *noun*
large piece of bread baked separately; can you buy me one white loaf and one wheat? have you eaten that whole loaf of bread? the baker took the loaves out of the oven.

plural **loaves** [ləʊvz]

loan [ləʊn] 1. *noun*
something (esp. money) which is lent to someone; the manager of the bank refused to give me a loan; he has no money, so he can't pay back his loans.
2. *verb*
to lend/to give something to someone for a certain period of time; can you loan me $5 till Monday? I loaned her my bike and now she won't give it back.

loans—loaning—loaned—has loaned

lo·cal ['ləʊkl] *adjective*
referring to the place/area near where you live; we do all our shopping in the local stores; local government = organization of cities and areas in the country.

lo·ca·ted ['ləʊkeɪtɪd] *adjective*
in a particular place; the church is located down by the harbor.

lock [lɒk] 1. *noun*
thing which closes a door/a box, etc., so that you can only open it with a key; you left the key in the lock, so anyone could have opened the door; the lock is very stiff—I can't turn the key.
2. *verb*
to close a door/a box, etc., so that it has to be opened with a key; the door's locked—can you climb in through a window? did you remember to lock the car? my father locks all the doors each night before he goes to bed.

locks—locking—locked—has locked

lock in/lock out, *verb*
to make someone stay inside/outside because a door is locked; my mother went shopping and locked my father out; he came back late and found he was locked out; I've left the keys inside and locked myself out; I think we've been locked in.

lock up, *verb*
(*a*) to close a building by locking the doors; don't forget to lock up before you go home; he was locking up the store when a customer called.
(*b*) to keep a person/a thing inside by locking a door; I'll lock up these jewels in the safe/I'll lock these jewels up in the safe; the police locked him up in prison for the night.

Note: he locked the jewels up *or* he locked up the jewels *but only* he locked them up

log [lɔ:g] *noun*
long piece of tree trunk; she stepped onto a log which lay across the stream.

Living Room

1. armchair
2. bookcase
3. bookshelf
4. carpet
5. ceiling
6. chair
7. clock
8. cushion
9. fire
10. fireplace
11. floor
12. lamp
13. (loud)speaker
14. picture
15. radio
16. record
17. record player
18. rocker *or* rocking chair
19. rug
20. sofa
21. telephone
22. television

lone·ly [ˈləʊnlɪ] *adjective*
sad because you are alone; **come and
stay with me—it's lonely being in this big
house all by myself; she was so lonely on
vacation that she came back early.**
lonely—lonelier—loneliest

lone·li·ness, *noun*
being lonely.

long [lɒŋ] **1.** *adjective*
not short; which measures a lot; **a long
piece of string; what a long movie—it
lasted for more than three hours; we've
been waiting for a long time; do you get
a long vacation? how long is it before
your vacation begins? the table is three
feet long; is the Amazon the longest river
in the world? your hair is getting long—
it needs cutting.**
long—longer—longest
Note: used with figures: **the road is
six miles long; a piece of string
three inches long**

2. *adverb*
for a long time; **have you been waiting
long? I couldn't wait any longer; she died
long ago.**
long—longer—longest
as long as/so long as = provided
that; **it's nice to go on a picnic as long as
it doesn't rain.**
before long = soon; **she'll be back
before long.**
3. *verb*
to want something very much; **I'm
longing for warm weather; they long to
be back home.**
**longs—longing—longed—has
longed**

look [lʊk] **1.** *noun*
(*a*) seeing something with your eyes;
**take a look at this picture; they had a
quick look around the town.**
(*b*) the way someone/something seems
to be; **he has a foreign look about him.**
(*c*) **good looks** = beautiful appearance.
2. *verb*
(*a*) to turn your eyes towards something; **look at this picture; we spent all
evening looking at slides; can you look in
the oven and see if the meat is cooked?**

**she looked out the window and saw the
mailman; he was looking under the bed.**
(*b*) to be seen to be; to seem; **he looks
sick; she looks at least eighty** = she
seems to be at least 80 years old; **that
cake looks good; what does she look
like? he looks like his father; it looks as
if it may rain/it looks like rain** = it
seems that it will rain.
**looks—looking—looked—has
looked**

look af·ter, *verb*
to take care of; **the nurses looked after
their patients; who's looking after your
cat when you're away?**
look a·round, *verb*
(*a*) to turn to see what is behind you;
**when he heard footsteps in the street he
quickly looked around.**
(*b*) to go around looking at something;
**did you look around the museum? do you
want to buy something?—no, I'm just
looking around.**
look for, *verb*
to try to find; **he looked everywhere for
his missing watch; the police are looking
for the prisoner who has escaped; he's
looking for a new secretary; I'll look for
you at the party.**
look for·ward to, *verb*
to think happily about something which
is going to happen; **I'm looking forward
to my vacation; he isn't looking forward
to the test; I'm looking forward to seeing
her again.**
look in on, *verb*
to pay a short visit; **I'll look in on her on
my way home.**
look out, *verb*
to be careful; **look out! the sidewalk is
covered with ice.**
look out for, *verb*
to be careful about; **look out for snakes
in the desert.**
look o·ver, *verb*
to check/to examine; **before handing in
your test, look it over carefully.**
Note: **look the test over** *or* **look
over the test** *but only* **look it over**
look up, *verb*
(*a*) to aim your eyes upwards; **he looked**

up and saw a bird on the roof; if you look up the chimney you can see the sky. (b) to try to find some information in a book; I'll look him up in the telephone book to try to find his address; look up the word in the dictionary if you don't know what it means.

Note: **look the words up** *or* **look up the words** *but only* **look them up**

loop [luːp] *noun*
circle formed when part of a thread or rope is crossed over another part.

loose [luːs] *adjective*
not fixed/not attached; not tight; part of the engine is loose; tie the rope in a loose knot; the knot came loose and the boat floated away.
loose—looser—loosest

loose·ly, *adverb*
not tightly; the boat was only loosely tied to the tree.

loos·en, *verb*
to make loose; loosen the rope; she loosened the knot.
loosens—loosening—loosened—has loosened

lose [luːz] *verb*
(a) to put something somewhere and not to know where it is; I can't find my watch—I think I lost it on the bus; don't lose your ticket or you'll have to buy another one.
(b) not to have something any longer; she has lost weight since last summer = has got thinner; my watch loses 10 minutes every day = is 10 minutes slower; don't lose any time in mailing the letter = mail it as soon as you can; has he lost his way? = doesn't he know where he is? he lost his temper = he became angry.
(c) not to win; we lost the game 10–0; did you win?—no, we lost!
loses—losing—lost [lɔːst]**—has lost**

los·er, *noun*
person who does not win.

lost, *adjective*
not knowing where you are; we went for a walk in the woods and got lost; she

looks like she's lost; the lost child cried loudly.

loss [lɔːs] *noun*
(a) not having something any more; weight loss; with no loss of time = without any delay.
(b) amount of money which you don't have any more; he took a loss of $100; we sold the car at a loss.
(c) not winning; the loss of a battle; our team had several losses this summer.
plural **losses**

lot [lɒt] *noun*
(a) **a lot of/lots of** = a large number of/ a large amount of; we have lots of time; what a lot of apples! I've seen him quite a lot recently; I'm feeling a lot better now; lots of people go to Florida on vacation; a lot of people were waiting for the bus.
(b) piece of land; I have bought a lot by a lake; parking lot = place where cars can be parked.

lo·tion [ˈləʊʃən] *noun*
liquid used to soften the skin; she rubbed lotion into her hands.

loud [laʊd] *adjective & adverb*
making a sound which you can hear easily; don't talk too loud—your father is asleep; a loud noise made him jump.
loud—louder—loudest

loud·ness [ˈlaʊdnəs] *noun*
being easily heard; the loudness of the music made him cover his ears.
no plural

loud·speak·er, *noun*
instrument from which sounds come, especially part of a radio/a record player, etc.

love [lʌv] **1.** *noun*
great liking for someone/something; give my love to your parents; her great love is music; to fall in love with someone = to start to like them very much.
2. *verb*
to like something/someone a great deal; to be very fond of; he loves his children; the children love their teacher; we love

going to the sea; he just loves ice cream; I'd love to come with you, but I have too much work to do.

loves—loving—loved—has loved

love·ly, *adjective*
very pleasant; delightful; a lovely warm day; she was wearing a lovely blue hat.

lovely—lovelier—loveliest

lov·er, *noun*
person who has a great liking for someone or something; a lover of music.

low [ləʊ] *adjective & adverb*
near the bottom/toward the bottom; not high; he hit his head on the low ceiling; this store has the lowest prices in town; the town is set among low hills; the engine works best at low speeds; that airplane is flying too low—it'll hit the trees; the temperature is too low for oranges to grow here; he spoke in a low voice because the baby was sleeping.

low—lower—lowest

low·er [ˈləʊər] *verb*
to make something go down; to reduce; we lowered a bucket into the water; the stores are lowering their prices to draw customers.

lowers—lowering—lowered—has lowered

luck [lʌk] *noun*
something, usually good, which happens to you by chance; good luck with your exams! = I hope you do well in your exams; he always has bad luck with cars = there is always something wrong with them; I wear this ring for good luck = because I hope it will bring me luck; just my luck to have homework to do when everyone else is swimming.

no plural

luck·y, *adjective*
having good things which happen; which brings luck; he is lucky not to have been sent to prison; 13 is my lucky number.

lucky—luckier—luckiest

luck·i·ly, *adverb*
by luck; it started to rain, but luckily I had taken my umbrella.

lug·gage [ˈlʌɡɪdʒ] *noun*
cases/bags, etc., which you take with you when you travel, containing your clothes, etc.; put all the luggage into the back of the car; we have too much luggage—we will have to pay extra; I can't carry all that luggage—can someone help me?

no plural: **some luggage; a piece of luggage**

lum·ber [ˈlʌmbər] *noun*
wood which has been cut in pieces, ready to be used; we loaded the lumber onto the roof of the car.

no plural: **some lumber**

lump [lʌmp] *noun*
mass of something which often has no particular shape; he drew a picture with a lump of coal; how many lumps of sugar do you take in your coffee?

lump·y, *adjective*
with hard lumps in it; I can't sleep on a lumpy mattress.

lumpy—lumpier—lumpiest

lunch [lʌntʃ] *noun*
meal eaten in the middle of the day; hurry up—lunch is ready; will it soon be time for lunch? we always have lunch at one o'clock; we are having hamburgers for lunch; I'm not hungry so I don't want a big lunch.

plural **lunches;** *see also note at* **dinner**

lunch·room, *noun*
place where you can eat lunch.

lunch·time, *noun*
time when you usually have lunch; it's half past twelve—almost lunchtime.

lung [lʌŋ] *noun*
one of two parts of the body which pull air in when you breathe; the doctor listened to his chest to see if his lungs were all right.

lying [ˈlaɪŋ] *see* **lie**

Mm

ma [mɑ:] *noun*
child's name for mother; **Ma, can I have a cookie please?**

ma·chine [məˈʃiːn] *noun*
thing which works with a motor; **washing machine; sewing machine; the factory has put in a new machine for making electric light bulbs.**
ma·chin·er·y, *noun*
machines; **the factory has put in a lot of new machinery.**
no plural: **some machinery; a piece of machinery**

mad [mæd] *adjective*
(*a*) crazy; **you're mad to go out in the snow without a coat; he had a mad idea to walk right across Canada.**
(*b*) very angry; **your father will be mad at you if you don't stop that singing.**
(*c*) very interested; **she's mad about movie stars; he's mad about old cars.**
mad—madder—maddest

made [meɪd] *see* **make**

mag·a·zine [mægəˈziːn] *noun*
paper which comes out regularly, (every week or month) usually with many pictures in it; **the gardening magazine comes out on Tuesdays; do you have this week's TV magazine? she prefers reading magazines to newspapers.**

mag·ic [ˈmædʒɪk] *noun*
power or action that cannot be explained; **he did magic tricks; the dirt disappeared like magic.**
no plural

mail [meɪl] 1. *noun*
(*a*) service of sending letters, etc., from one place to another; **you should send the letter by air mail; if the present is valuable, don't send it through the mail; he received a gift in the mail.**
(*b*) letters which have been delivered to you; **has the mail come yet? he opened his mail before he had his breakfast.**
2. *verb*
to send by mail; **I mailed a birthday card to my friend in New York.**
mails—mailing—mailed—has mailed
mail·box, *noun*
(*a*) box in the street where you can mail letters; **can you put these letters in the mailbox for me?**
(*b*) hole in a front door/box near the door into which the mailman delivers letters; **the package was too thick to go into the mailbox.**
plural **mailboxes**
mail·man, *noun*
person who delivers letters to houses; **the mailman only brought me bills this morning.**
plural **mailmen**

main [meɪn] 1. *adjective*
most important; **the main thing is to work well; our main office is in New York; there is always a lot of traffic on main roads; August is the main month for vacations.**
2. *noun*
large pipe for delivering water/gas, etc.; **a water main burst in High Street.**
main·ly, *adverb*
largely/mostly; **we have mainly women working in our office; people mainly go on vacation in August.**

make [meɪk] 1. *noun*
showing where or by which company something is made; **an Italian make of car; what make is your new record-player?**
2. *verb*
(*a*) to produce/to build; **he made a table**

out of pieces of lumber; this cup is made of plastic; he is making a cake.

(*b*) to get ready; **do you want me to make breakfast? have you made your bed?** = arranged it after having slept in it.

(*c*) to add up to; **two and three make five.**

(*d*) to earn (money); **he made $10 from selling old newspapers.**

(*e*) to cause someone to feel something; **the smell of cooking makes me hungry; the movement of the boat made him sick; will the present make him happier? he made himself comfortable in the armchair.**

(*f*) to force someone/something to do something; **I made him clean his shoes; the teacher made him stay after school; the rain will make the grass grow; can't you make the car go any faster?**

makes—making—made [meɪd]—**has made**

make do with, *verb*
to use something, because there is nothing better; **I lost my toothpaste, so I had to make do with soap; the bakery had run out of whole wheat bread, so we had to make do with white; all the plates were dirty, so we made do with paper ones.**

make for, *verb*
to go towards; **he is making for Calgary; when he saw her he made straight for the door.**

make of, *verb*
to think about; **what do you make of the news? I don't know what to make of it** = I can't understand it.

make off with, *verb*
to go away with something/to steal something; **the burglar made off with the jewelry.**

make out, *verb*
(*a*) to see clearly; to understand; **I can't make out the details in the picture because the light is bad; she couldn't make out why he didn't want to come.**

(*b*) to say something which is probably not true; **is English weather really as bad as it is made out to be? stop trying**

to make out that you're the best singer in the world.

(*c*) to write (a name on a check); **he made out the check to Mr. Smith.**
Note: **can you make the writing out?** *or* **can you make out the writing?** *but only* **can you make it out?**

mak·er, *noun*
person or company that produces something; **if the watch doesn't work, we'll send it back to the maker.**

make up, *verb*
(*a*) to invent (a story); **he told the police he had seen a man steal a car but in fact he made the whole story up.**

(*b*) **to make up your mind** = to decide; **I can't make up my mind what to do; his mind is made up** = he has decided what to do.
Note: **he made the story up** *or* **he made up the story** *but only* **he made it up**

make·up, *noun*
things like colored creams, lipstick, etc., which you put on your face to make it more beautiful.
no plural

male [meɪl] *adjective & noun*
of the same sex as a man; **a male spider; the male is taller than the female.**

ma·ma ['mɑːmɑː] *noun*
child's name for mother; **can I go outside, Mama?**

man [mæn] *noun*
(*a*) male human being; **my father is a very tall man; ask that old man if he wants some coffee.**

(*b*) human being; **men have only existed on earth for a short time compared to fish.**

(*c*) person; **the man in the street** = average, ordinary person; **the man in the street isn't interested in politics.**
plural **men** [men]

man·age ['mænɪdʒ] *verb*
(*a*) to control; to be in charge of; **she manages our Chicago office; we want to appoint someone to manage our sales department.**

(*b*) to be able to do something/to succeed in doing something; **did you manage to call your mother? he managed to get the lid off; can she manage all by herself? how are we going to manage without her?**
manages—managing—managed—has managed

man·ag·er, *noun*
person in charge of a department in a store/in a business; **the sales manager; the manager of the sports department.**

man·ner ['mænər] *noun*
(*a*) way of doing something; **he was behaving in a strange manner.**
(*b*) **manners** = polite way of behaving; **he has very good table manners** = he behaves well when he's eating; **it's bad manners to put your knife in your mouth.**

man·y ['menı] *adjective & pronoun*
a large number (of); **many retired people live by the seaside; many of us knew him when he was at school; so many people wanted tickets that they sold out quickly; how many apples do you have? he ate twice as many slices of bread as you did; a good many** = a large number; **a good many people thought the movie was no good.**
many—more [mɔːr]**—most** [məʊst]
Note: **many** *is used with nouns which you can count:* **not many apples** *but* **not much bread**

map [mæp] *noun*
drawing which shows a town/a country as if seen from the air; **here's a big map of Germany; do you have a street map of Washington? can you show me the mountains on the map? we soon got lost because we'd forgotten to take a map.**

March [mɑːtʃ] *noun*
third month of the year; **his birthday is in March; today is March 6; last March we went to California.**
Note: **March 6:** *say* "March sixth," "March the sixth" *or* "the sixth of March"

march [mɑːtʃ] *verb*
to walk in step; **the soldiers marched up**

the street; **quick march!** = order given to soldiers to walk quickly.
marches—marching—marched—has marched

mar·ga·rine ['mɑːrdʒərin] *noun*
vegetable fat which looks like butter and is used instead of butter; **spread some margarine on your bread.**
no plural: **some margarine**

mark [mɑːrk] **1.** *noun*
(*a*) spot/small area of a different color; **he has ink marks on his shirt; your cup has made a mark on the table; there's a red mark where you hit your head; on your mark!** = get ready at your places (*order given to runners at the beginning of a race*).
(*b*) grade/number of points given to a student; **he got top marks in French** = he was best in his class; **did you get a good mark on your math test? when are your marks going to improve?**
2. *verb*
(*a*) to make a mark; **the table has been marked by coffee cups; the can is marked "dangerous"** = it has the word "dangerous" written on it.
(*b*) to correct and give points to work; **the teacher is marking our homework; have the math tests been marked yet?**
marks—marking—marked—has marked

mark·er, *noun*
thing used for making marks; **use a black marker to make the sign.**

mar·ket ['mɑːrkıt] *noun*
place where fruit and vegetables, etc., are sold from small tables, often in the open air; **we bought some vegetables and fish at the market; market day is Saturday.**

mar·ry ['mærı] *verb*
to make two people husband and wife; to become the husband or wife of someone; **he married the girl next door; they were married in church; how long have you been married? she's married to a soldier; they got married last Saturday.**
marries—marrying—married—has married

mar·riage ['mærɪdʒ] *noun*
(*a*) event of marrying; **the marriage will take place at two o'clock; the marriage ceremony was lovely.**
(*b*) being husband and wife; **he is not interested in marriage** = he doesn't want to marry.

mask [mæsk] **1.** *noun*
cover for the face; **they all wore masks to the Halloween party.**
2. *verb*
to cover up; **this cream is supposed to mask wrinkles.**
masks—masking—masked—has masked

mass [mæs] *noun*
large number; **there's a mass of dead leaves on the lawn; masses of people went to the show; have some more meat—there's masses of it left; a mass meeting** = meeting where a large number of people come together; **the masses** = the common people.
plural **masses**

mat [mæt] *noun*
(*a*) small rug; **wipe your shoes on the mat; bath mat** = small rug which you stand on when you get out of the bathtub; **door mat** = thick stiff rug to wipe your shoes on in front of a door.
(*b*) small piece of cloth/wood, etc., which you put under a plate on a table; **put place mats out for everyone.**

match [mætʃ] **1.** *noun*
(*a*) game between two teams, etc.; **are you going to watch the boxing match? I won the last two tennis matches I played.**
(*b*) small piece of wood or cardboard with a tip which catches fire when you rub it against a rough surface; **a box of matches; he struck a match and lit his cigarette; the matches are wet—they won't light.**
plural **matches**
2. *verb*
to go well with; **the skirt matches the blouse in color.**
matches—matching—matched—has matched

match·box, *noun*
small box containing matches.
plural **matchboxes**

ma·te·ri·al [mə'tɪrɪəl] *noun*
(*a*) something which can be used to make something; **building materials** = bricks, wood, etc.; **raw materials** = materials like iron or oil which have not been made into anything.
(*b*) cloth; **I bought some cotton material to make a skirt.**

math·e·mat·ics [mæθə'mætɪks], **math** [mæθ] *noun*
study of numbers and measurements; **the math teacher; I found the math exam very difficult; my sister is no good at math; math is my best subject.**
Note: the verb is in the singular: **mathematics is an important subject**

mat·ter ['mætər] **1.** *noun*
problem; **what's the matter? there's something the matter with the engine** = there is something which does not work properly; **it's a matter for the police** = something which the police should know about; **as a matter of fact** = really; **as a matter of course** = in the usual way.
2. *verb*
to be important; **it doesn't matter if you're late; it matters a lot to him; does it matter where we sit?**
matters—mattering—mattered—has mattered

mat·tress ['mætrəs] *noun*
thick soft part of a bed which you lie on; **this mattress has lumps in it.**
plural **mattresses**

May [meɪ] *noun*
fifth month of the year; **she was born in May; today is May 15; last May we moved to Kentucky; are you going away next May?**
Note: **May 15**: *say* "May fifteenth," "May the fifteenth" *or* "the fifteenth of May"

may [meɪ] *verb used with other verbs*
(*a*) *to mean* it is possible; **if he doesn't hurry he may miss the train; take your**

umbrella, it may rain; he may be waiting outside; you may have left your gloves on the train; it may not rain after all; she may not have heard.

(b) to mean it is allowed; mother says you may come in; you may sit down if you want to; may I ask you a question? may we have dinner early today?

I may, you may, he may, we may, they may
Past: [(a) *only*] **might, might not,** *usually* **mightn't**
Note: **may** *and* **might** *do not have* **to** *and are always used with other verbs*

may·be, *adverb*
perhaps: maybe it will be nice tomorrow.

may·or ['meɪər] *noun*
person who is in charge of a town or city; he was elected mayor of Cleveland.

me [miː] *object pronoun used by the person who is speaking, to talk about himself*
give it to me; can you hear me? he is taller than me; who is it?—it's me!

mead·ow ['medəʊ] *noun*
large field of grass; the cows were in the meadow.

meal [miːl] *noun*
(a) eating food at the table at a particular time; we have three meals a day—breakfast, lunch and dinner; you should only have a light meal in the evening; when they had eaten their evening meal they went for a walk.
(b) rough grain; the animals were fed meal.

meal·time, *noun*
time when you usually eat.

mean [miːn] **1.** *adjective*
(a) bad/not kind; he played a mean trick on his sister; that was a mean thing to say.
(b) not wanting to give; don't be mean—lend me your ball; he's very mean with his money.
mean—meaner—meanest
2. *verb*
(a) to refer to/to talk about; did he mean

Uncle Richard when he was talking about fat men? what do you mean?
(b) to show; a red light means that you have to stop; "Tisch" in German means "table"; what does that sign mean?—I know what it means, it means that you can't park here on Saturdays.
(c) to intend/to plan to do something; we meant to be there by nine o'clock; he means to leave shortly; this medicine is meant to be used only for coughs = ought to be used only for coughs.
means—meaning—meant [ment]—**has meant**

mean·ing, *noun*
what a word means; if you want to find the meaning of this word, look it up in the dictionary.

means, *noun*
(a) way of doing something; is there any means of getting to Miami tonight? a motorbike is a cheap means of traveling.
by all means = of course; by all means call the office if you want to.
by means of = using; he got to the roof by means of a ladder.
by no means = not at all; he's by no means rich.
(b) money; it is beyond my means = it is too expensive for me to buy it.
mean·while, *adverb*
during this time; he hid in an empty house—meanwhile, the police were coming nearer.

mea·sles ['miːzlz] *plural noun*
children's disease which makes red spots on your skin; she's in bed with measles; have you had measles? he has measles; they caught measles from their friends at school.

meas·ure ['meʒər] **1.** *noun*
thing used to calculate the size of something; a meter is a measure of length; tape measure = long tape with centimeters/inches, etc., marked on it.
2. *verb*
to find out the size of something; to be a certain size; the room measures 20 feet by 16 feet; a thermometer measures temperature; how much do you measure

around the waist? she measured the room before buying the carpet.

measures—measuring— measured—has measured

meas·ure·ment, *noun*
size/length, etc., of something which you have measured; **what are the measurements of the tent? do you know your waist measurement? he had to take the measurements of the room to calculate how much paint he needed.**

meat [mi:t] *noun*
part of an animal which you eat; **can I have some more meat? would you like another slice of meat? this meat is very well-cooked.**
no plural: **some meat; a piece of meat/a slice of meat**

med·i·cine ['medəsɪn] *noun*
(*a*) something which you eat or drink to make you well; **take some cough medicine if your cough is bad; you should take the medicine three times a day.**
(*b*) study of diseases and how to cure them; **he is studying medicine because he wants to be a doctor.**
no plural for (b)

med·i·cal ['medɪkl] *adjective*
referring to the study of diseases; **a medical student; medical help was provided by the Red Cross.**

me·di·um   ['mi:dɪəm]   *noun,*
me·di·um-sized, *adjective*
average/not big or small; **he takes a medium in shirts; she has a medium-sized kitchen.**

meet [mi:t] *verb*
(*a*) to come together (with someone); **I'll meet you at the bus stop; they met at Central Station; let's arrange to meet somewhere before we go to the theater; I'm meeting her at the post office at six o'clock.**
(*b*) to get to know someone; to be introduced to someone; **I think I have met him before; I have never met your mother—come and meet her, then.**
meets—meeting—met—has met

meet·ing, *noun*
coming together of a group of people; **there will be a meeting of the stamp club next Thursday; there were only six people at the meeting.**

melt [melt] *verb*
to change from solid to liquid because of heating; **the butter has melted in the sun; you must melt the chocolate and pour it over the ice cream.**
melts—melting—melted—has melted

mem·ber ['membər] *noun*
person who belongs (to a club, etc.); **he is a member of the golf club; the club is limited to 250 members; she is a member of the House of Representatives.**

mem·o·ry ['meməri] *noun*
(*a*) ability to remember; **he has a very good memory for dates; I have no memory for names; he said the whole poem from memory.**
(*b*) thing which you remember; **I have wonderful memories of our last vacation.**
plural **memories**

mem·o·rize ['meməraɪz] *verb*
to learn something and remember it; **he memorized the whole poem.**
memorized—memorizing memorized—has memorized

men [men] *see* **man**

mend [mend] *verb*
to repair/to make something perfect which had a fault; **can you mend my watch? he's trying to mend his ways = improve his behavior; my pants are torn—can they be mended?**
mends—mending—mended—has mended

men·tion ['menʃn] *verb*
to refer to something in a few words; **he mentioned that he was going away for a few days; did she mention the results of the election? they don't know about the party—shall I mention it to them?**
mentions—mentioning— mentioned—has mentioned

men·u ['menjuː] *noun*
list of food in a restaurant; **do you have any fish on the menu?** the waiter brought us the menu; she always chooses the most expensive dish on the menu.

mer·ry ['merɪ] *adjective*
happy; **Merry Christmas;** he wished us a Merry Christmas.
merry—merrier—merriest

mess [mes] 1. *noun*
dirt; something which isn't neat; **the builders made a mess all over the floor; the room is in a mess**—you'll have to clear it up; he made a mess of fixing his car = he did it badly.
plural **messes**
2. *verb*
to mess something up = to make it dirty; **the room was all messed up after the children's party.**
messes—messing—messed— has messed

mes·sy, *adjective*
dirty/not neat; fixing the car was a messy job; clean up your room—it's very messy.
messy—messier—messiest

mes·sage ['mesɪdʒ] *noun*
news/instructions which are sent to someone; he received a message telling him to go to the police station; your boss has left a message for you; here's a phone message for you.

mes·sen·ger ['mesɪndʒər] *noun*
person who brings a message.

met [met] *see* **meet**

met·al ['metl] *noun*
solid material which can carry heat and electricity and is used for making things; **a metal teapot;** the spoons are plastic but the knives are metal; this table is made of metal.

me·ter ['miːtər] *noun*
measurement of length; **the room is four meters by three; one square meter =** area which is one meter by one meter;

the area of the stage is ten square meters.
Note: with figures **meter** *is usually written* **m** *and* **square meter** *is written* **m²** **(four meters = 4m; six square meters = 6m²)**

meth·od ['meθəd] *noun*
way of doing something; he showed me a new method of making bread.

mice [maɪs] *see* **mouse**

mid·dle ['mɪdl] *noun*
(a) center; he was standing in the middle of the room; Wisconsin is in the middle of the U.S.; I woke up in the middle of the night; she was in the middle of making the dinner when we called; the telephone rang in the middle of the meeting.
(b) waist; the water came up to my middle; he's getting fat around the middle.
mid·dle-aged, *adjective*
not very young, and not very old; he's middle-aged; three middle-aged women got on the bus.

mid·night ['mɪdnaɪt] *noun*
12 o'clock at night; you must go to bed before midnight; I heard the clock strike midnight and then went to sleep.

might [maɪt] *verb used with other verbs*
(a) *to mean* it is possible; **it might rain;** he might be waiting outside; you might have left your gloves on the train.
(b) *to mean* something should have been done; **he might have done something to help =** it would have been better if he had done something; you might have told me = I wish you had told me.
I might, you might, he might, we might, they might
Negative: **might not,** *usually* **mightn't**
Note: **might** *does not have* **to** *and is always used with other verbs.* **Might** *is the past of* **may,** *but can be used as a more polite form of the present when asking for something*
might·y ['maɪtɪ] *adjective & adverb*
strong; very; **a mighty army; he's mighty angry =** very angry.
mighty—mightier—mightiest

MENU

SOUPS AND JUICES
        vegetable soup $1.25
        chicken soup 1.25
        orange juice, tomato juice 75

LUNCH PLATES
        fried chicken, french fries, salad 4.50
        fried fish, french fries, salad. 4.50
        ham & cheese salad, roll & butter. 2.95

SANDWICHES
        hamburger. 1.95
        hot dog. 1.50
        egg salad. 1.25
        toasted cheese 1.15

SIDE ORDERS
        vegetable of the day (peas, beans) 85
        french fries 85
        small salad. 1.25

DESSERTS
        apple pie. 1.50
        chocolate cake 1.50
        ice cream. 1.50

DRINKS
        coffee, tea. 65
        milk .60
        soft drinks. 75

mild [maɪld] *adjective*
soft; not hard or cold; not serious; **we had a very mild winter; she's had a mild attack of measles; I like strong mustard**—this kind is too mild = it doesn't have a strong taste.
mild—milder—mildest

mild·ness ['maɪldnəs] *noun*
being soft/warm; **they enjoyed the mildness of the weather in England.**
no plural

mile [maɪl] *noun*
(*a*) measurement of length (= 1609 meters); **we walked for miles before we found the post office; the car was traveling at 60 miles per hour; it's 24 miles from here to the sea; it's a three-mile walk from here.**
(*b*) a long distance; **he missed it by a mile** = by a long way; **the nearest store is miles away.**
with figures **miles per hour** *is usually written* **mph: 60 miles per hour** = **60 mph**

milk [mɪlk] 1. *noun*
white liquid produced by female animals to feed their young, especially that produced by cows; **have you drunk your milk? can I have a glass of milk, please? I must buy some milk; do you have enough milk? we have no milk left.**
no plural: **some milk; a glass of milk/a bottle of milk**
2. *verb*
to take the milk from an animal; **the farmer was milking the cow; the cows haven't been milked yet.**
milks—milking—milked—has milked

milk·man, *noun*
man who delivers milk to each house in the morning; **tell the milkman to leave six quarts of milk today.**
plural **milkmen**

milk shake, *noun*
drink made by mixing milk with ice cream and sweet stuff; **he drank two chocolate milk shakes.**

mil·li·me·ter ['mɪlimiːtər] *noun*
very small measurement of length; **the wood is only 10 millimeters thick; there are ten millimeters in a centimeter, and a thousand in a meter.**
with figures **millimeter** *is usually written* **mm: 26 mm** = **26 millimeters**

mil·lion ['mɪljən] number 1,000,000
the population of the country is 60 million; millions of trees were burned in the forest fire; the country spends millions of dollars on oil; millions of people spend their vacation in Florida.
Note: no plural with figures: **sixty million;** *with figures* **million** *can be written* **m: $2m** = **two million dollars**

mil·lion·aire, *noun*
very rich man, who owns more than $1m.

mil·lionth, *adjective & noun*
referring to a million; **a millionth of a second; congratulations—you're our millionth customer!**

mind [maɪnd] 1. *noun*
place from which thoughts come; **what do you have in mind?** = what are you thinking of? **he's got something on his mind** = he's worrying about something; **let's try to take her mind off her exams** = to keep her from worrying about them.
state of mind = general feeling; **he's in a terrible state of mind.**
to make up your mind = to decide; **I can't make up my mind whether to go on vacation or stay here and work; she couldn't make up her mind what hat to wear.**
to change your mind = to decide to do something different; **I have decided to go on vacation, and nothing will make me change my mind; he took out his bike, but then changed his mind and went by bus.**
2. *verb*
(*a*) to be careful about; **mind your manners! the ceiling is low—mind your head!**

(b) to worry about; **never mind** = don't worry; **you must learn to mind your own business** = not to deal with other people's problems.

(c) to be bothered by; **do you mind if I close the window? they won't mind if you're late; I wouldn't mind a cup of coffee** = I'd like a cup of coffee; **do you mind if we sit down? I don't mind standing up.**

minds—minding—minded—has minded

mine [maɪn] 1. *pronoun*
thing/person belonging to me; **that bike is mine; can I borrow your pen?—I've lost mine; Paul is a friend of mine.**

2. *noun*
(a) deep hole in the ground where coal, etc., is taken out; **a coal mine; a gold mine.**

(b) type of bomb which is hidden under the ground or under water; **the truck went over a mine and was blown up.**

3. *verb*
to dig (coal, etc.) out of the ground; **they are mining gold here.**

mines—mining—mined—has mined

min·er, *noun*
person who works in a coal mine.

min·ing, *noun*
digging (coal, etc.) out of the ground; **mining is an important industry in some states.**

no plural

min·er·al ['mɪnərəl] *noun*
stone/coal, etc., which is taken out of the earth; **they mine coal and other minerals in the north of the country; mineral water** = water taken out of the ground and sold in bottles.

min·is·ter ['mɪnɪstər] *noun*
(a) man who is in charge of a church; **the minister spoke to everyone as they came out of church.**

(b) member of the government in charge of a department in some countries; **the Minister of Defense** = minister in charge of the armed forces.

mint [mɪnt] *noun*
small white candy with a sweet, cool taste; **they passed around a bowl of mints after dinner.**

mi·nus ['maɪnəs] *preposition*
from (in subtraction); **ten minus four equals six; he got A⁻ (A minus) on his exam** = less than A.

min·ute¹ ['mɪnɪt] *noun*
(a) a sixtieth part of an hour; **there are sixty minutes in an hour; 12 minutes to four** = 3:48; **12 minutes past three** = 3:12; **I'll meet you in fifteen minutes; the house is about five minutes' walk from the station/is a five-minute walk from the station; minute hand** = long hand which shows the minutes on a watch or clock.

(b) very short space of time; moment; **why don't you sit down for a minute? I'll just be a minute** = I'll be very quick; **can you wait a minute?**

mi·nute² [maɪ'nju:t] *adjective*
very small; **a minute piece of dust got in my eye.**

mir·ror ['mɪrər] *noun*
piece of glass with a dark back, so that when you look at it you can see yourself; **he looked at his face in the bathroom mirror; she carried a small mirror in her handbag.**

mis·be·have [mɪsbɪ'heɪv] *verb*
to behave badly; **the little boy misbehaved while his mother was away.**

misbehaves—misbehaving—misbehaved—has misbehaved

Miss [mɪs] *noun*
name given to young girl or unmarried woman; **Miss Jones; Miss Anne Jones; Miss, can I have the check, please?**

*Note: with a name, **Miss** can be followed by the last name or the first name and last name; without a name, **Miss** is used to call a waitress or a salesgirl*

miss [mɪs] 1. *noun*
not hitting; **he scored a goal and then had two misses.**

plural **misses**

2. *verb*

(*a*) not to hit; he missed the ball; they tried to shoot the rabbit but missed.

(*b*) not to see/ to catch, etc.; we missed the house in the dark; they missed the bus and had to walk home; I missed the article about farming in yesterday's paper; you didn't miss much = there wasn't much to see/the film, etc., wasn't very good; he just missed being the winner = he was almost the winner.

(*c*) to be sad because something is not there; do you miss your dog? I miss those long walks we used to take; they'll miss you if you go to work in another office; I haven't seen my brother in two years and I miss him a lot.

misses—missing—missed—has missed

miss·ing, *adjective*

which is not there/which has been lost; we're looking for my missing keys; there is a lot of money missing; the police searched for the missing children.

miss out on, *verb*

to be left out of something; they will miss out on all the fun if they don't come along.

mis·take [mɪ'steɪk] **1.** *noun*

action or thought which is wrong; I made a mistake; I got on the wrong bus by mistake; by mistake he tried to eat his soup with his fork; there are several mistakes in her work.

2. *verb*

to think wrongly; I mistook him for his brother = I thought he was his brother; he is mistaken in thinking I am your brother; if I'm not mistaken, Dr. Smith is your brother.

mistakes—mistaking—mistook [mɪ'stʊk]—has mistaken

mit·ten ['mɪtn] *noun*

type of glove without separate fingers; a pair of mittens.

mix [mɪks] *verb*

to put things together; mix the flour and

milk in a bowl; if you mix blue and yellow you will get green.

mixes—mixing—mixed—has mixed

mix·er, *noun*

machine for mixing; put the flour and eggs in the mixer.

mix·ture ['mɪkstʃər] *noun*

things mixed together; the walls are painted in a mixture of red and blue; after mixing together eggs, milk and butter, pour the mixture into a pot.

mix up, *verb*

to mistake; to put out of the right order; I'm always mixing him up with his brother; all the books got mixed up in the box.

mod·el ['mɒdl] *noun*

(*a*) small copy of something larger; he is making a model plane; have you seen his model trains?

(*b*) person who wears new clothes to show them to customers.

(*c*) style of car, etc., produced at a particular time; this is the latest model; he has a 1979 model Ford.

mod·ern ['mɒdərn] *adjective*

of the present time; their house is very modern = does not look old; modern languages = languages which are spoken today; he's studying French and Spanish in the modern languages department.

mom [mɒm] *noun*

child's name for mother; Mom, can I have another cookie, please?

mo·ment ['məʊmənt] *noun*

very short time; please wait a moment; I only saw him for a moment; we expect him to arrive at any moment = very soon; we only heard of it a moment ago = just recently.

at the mo·ment = right now; I'm rather busy at the moment.

for the mo·ment = for a little while; we won't bother you for the moment.

Mon·day ['mʌndɪ] *noun*

second day of the week, the day between Sunday and Tuesday; **the store is closed on Mondays; I saw her last Monday; we're going on vacation next Monday; will you be in the office on Monday afternoon? we go to the movies every Monday.**

mon·ey ['mʌniː] *noun*
coins or notes which are used for buying things; **how much money have you got? I don't have any money with me; we ran out of money** = we spent all our money; **you spent too much money last week; I want to change my dollars into Mexican money.**
no plural

month [mʌnθ] *noun*
one of twelve parts of a year; **January is the first month of the year; February is the shortest month; what day of the month is it today? I'm going on vacation next month; it rained a lot last month, in fact it rained all month; a month from today I'll be sitting on the beach** = in a month's time; **we haven't had any homework for months** = for a long time; **he's taken a month's vacation.**

moon [muːn] *noun*
star in the sky which goes around the earth and which shines at night; **it is hard to believe that men have walked on the moon; the moon is very bright tonight; there was no moon because there were too many clouds; it only happens once in a blue moon** = hardly ever; **new moon** = time when the moon is only a thin curve; **full moon** = time when the moon is a full circle.

moon·light, *noun*
light of the moon; **everything looked white in the moonlight.**

mop [mɒp] 1. *noun*
soft brush on a long stick used for cleaning floors; **she left the mop in a bucket of water.**
2. *verb*
to clean (a floor) with a soft brush on a long stick; **he mopped the kitchen floor.**
mops—mopping—mopped—has mopped

more [mɔːr] 1. *adjective*
extra/which is added; **do you want some more coffee? we need two more men to make a football team; there are many more trains on weekdays than on Sundays; $10—that's more than I can pay.**
2. *noun*
extra thing; **is there any more of this jam?**
3. *adverb used with adjectives to make the comparative*
he was more surprised than I was; she is more skilled than her brother; it was even more expensive than I had thought it would be.
more or less = roughly/not quite completely; **I've more or less finished my homework.**
not . . . an·y more = no longer; **he doesn't write to me any more; we don't go abroad on vacation any more.**
Note: **more** *is used to make the comparative of long adjectives which do not take* -**er**

morn·ing ['mɔːrnɪŋ] *noun*
first part of the day before 12 o'clock; **I go to the office every morning; tomorrow morning he's going to be on a radio program; we'll meet on Tuesday morning; I woke up at four in the morning** = at 4 a.m.; **have you read the morning paper? we must get the morning plane to Dallas.**

most [mɒʊst] 1. *adjective*
very large number of; **most people have breakfast at about 8:00; most children like watching TV; most apples are sweet.**
2. *noun*
very large number/amount; **most of the work has been done; he sits and writes most of the time; it rained for most of the day; most of the children are over 11.**
3. *adverb*
(*a*) *making the superlative* **he's the most sensitive child in his class; the most important thing is to be able to speak Russian.**
(*b*) *very;* **I find it most awkward to walk into a room which is full of strangers; most probably he will be held up by the**

bad weather; you are most kind.

Note: **most** *is used to form the superlative of long adjectives which do not take* **-est**

most·ly, *adverb*
most often; sometimes we go away for our vacation, but mostly we stay at home.

mo·tel [məʊ'tel] *noun*
hotel made especially for motorists; they stayed at a motel just off the highway.

moth·er ['mʌðər] *noun*
female parent; he lives with his mother; my mother's a doctor; Mother! there's someone asking for you on the telephone.
Note: **Mother** *is sometimes used as a name for a* **mother,** *but* **Mom** *or* **Ma** *are more usual*

mo·tor ['məʊtər] *noun*
engine/part of a machine which makes it work; switch on the motor; the boat has an electric motor.

mo·tor·bike, mo·tor·cy·cle, *noun*
two-wheeled cycle driven by a motor; he fell off his motorbike; I'm learning to ride a motorcycle.

mo·tor·boat, *noun*
boat driven by a motor.

mo·tor·cy·clist, *noun*
person who rides a motorcycle.

mo·tor·ist, *noun*
person who drives a car.

moun·tain ['maʊntn] *noun*
very high piece of land, much higher than the land which is around it; Everest is the highest mountain in the world; we go climbing in the mountains every weekend; are we nearly at the top of the mountain yet?

mouse [maʊs] *noun*
little animal with a long tail, often living in houses; a mouse ran under the bed; my sister is afraid of mice; John brought a white mouse to school.
plural **mice** [maɪs]

mouth [maʊθ] *noun*
opening below your nose through which you take in food and drink, and through which you speak; don't talk with your mouth full; she was sleeping with her mouth open; the cat was carrying a bird in her mouth.
plural **mouths** [maʊðz]

mouth·ful, *noun*
amount which you can hold in your mouth; he had a mouthful of bread.

move [muːv] **1.** *noun*
changing the place of something; we must make a move = we must go; get a move on! = hurry up; what's the next move? = what do we have to do next? on the move = active; she's always on the move = she is always doing something. **2.** *verb*
(a) to change the place of something; to change your own place; move the chairs away from the table; an animal was moving in the bushes; only the end of the cat's tail was moving; who has moved my book?—I left it on the table; he moved his head; don't move! = stand still.
(b) to leave one place to go to live in another; they moved from Washington to Pittsburgh; my husband has got a job in Atlanta, but I don't want to move; we are moving back to New York.
moves—moving—moved—has moved

move a·long, *verb*
to keep moving; the policeman told the crowd to move along.

move a·round *verb*
to change the place of something often; to change place often; he moved the boxes around; crowds of people were moving around in the street.

move a·way, *verb*
to change the place of something or your own place, to a place further away; the ship moved away from the rocks; we're moving away from Chicago = we are going to live in another town away from Chicago.

move in, *verb*
to put your furniture into a new house and start to live there.

move·ment, *noun*
changing of the place of something; not being still; there was a movement in the trees; all you could see was a slight movement of the cat's tail.

move out, *verb*
to leave to go live somewhere else; she's moving out of her apartment.

mov·ie ['muːvɪ] *noun*
moving picture shown in a theater; we're going to the movies tonight; did you see that old Charlie Chaplin movie? we stayed up late, watching an old movie on TV.

Mr. ['mɪstər] *noun*
name given to a man; Mr. Jones; Mr. John Jones; Dear Mr. Smith (*at beginning of a letter*); Mr. and Mrs. Smith.
Mr. is used with a last name, sometimes with a first name and last name

Mrs. ['mɪsɪz] *noun*
name given to a married woman; Mrs. Jones; Mrs. Anne Jones; Dear Mrs. Jones (*at beginning of a letter*); Mr. and Mrs. Smith.
Mrs. is used with a last name, sometimes with a first name and last name

Ms. [mɪz] *noun*
name given to any woman; Ms. Jones; Dear Ms. Jones (*at beginning of a letter*)
Ms. is used with a last name, sometimes with a first name and last name

much [mʌtʃ] 1. *adjective*
a lot of; with much love; how much bread do you want? I never carry much money with me; he eats too much meat; how much does it cost? = how much money? how much is that book?
as much as = the same amount; you haven't eaten as much as she has; he spends as much money as I do.
Note: much is used with nouns which you cannot count: not much money but not many boys

2. *adverb*
very; a lot; she's feeling much better today; it's much less cold in the south of the country; does it matter very much? that book is much too expensive.
much—more [mɔːr]**—most** [məʊst]
3. *noun*
a lot; much of the work has been done; you didn't write much while you were

away; do you see much of him? = do you see him often?

mud [mʌd] *noun*
earth and water mixed; we were up to our ankles in mud; the tractor got stuck in the mud.
no plural

mud·dy, *adjective*
full of mud; covered with mud; don't walk across the kitchen in your muddy boots; he dropped his hat into a pool of muddy water.
muddy—muddier—muddiest

mud·guard, *noun*
piece of metal over the wheel of a bicycle which protects it from mud or water.

muf·fin ['mʌfɪn] *noun*
small cake, often eaten warm with butter; blueberry muffins.

mul·ti·ply ['mʌltɪplaɪ] *verb*
to work out the sum of several numbers repeated several times; if you multiply 240 by 2 the answer is 480.
multiplies—multiplying—multiplied—has multiplied

mul·ti·pli·ca·tion [mʌltɪplɪ'keɪʃn] *noun*
sum when one number is multiplied by another; I can do division but I'm no good at multiplication.

mumps [mʌmps] *plural noun*
disease which makes the sides of your face become fat; he caught mumps from the children next door; she's in bed with mumps; he can't go to school—he has the mumps.

mur·der ['mɜrdər] 1. *noun*
killing of someone; he was arrested for murder; the police are looking for the knife used in the murder.
2. *verb*
to kill someone; he was charged with murdering the old man; she was murdered while she was sleeping.
murders—murdering—murdered—has murdered

mur·der·er, *noun*
person who kills someone.

mus·cle ['mʌsl] *noun*
meat part of the body, which makes the legs and arms, etc., move; **if you do a lot of exercises you develop strong muscles.**

mu·se·um [mju:'ziəm] *noun*
building in which a collection of interesting things are put on show; **a natural history museum; have you visited the city museum? a museum of modern art; the Metropolitan Museum of Art.**

mush·room ['mʌʃru:m] *noun*
small white plant eaten as a vegetable; **he put some fresh mushrooms into the salad; a can of mushrooms; she loves mushroom soup.**

mu·sic ['mju:zɪk] *noun*
(*a*) sound made when you sing or play an instrument; **do you like modern music? he's taking music lessons; her music teacher says she plays the piano very well.**
(*b*) written signs which you read to play an instrument; **here's some piano music—try and play it; he can play the piano without any music.**
no plural: **some music; a piece of music**
mu·si·cal, *adjective*
referring to music; **he doesn't play any musical instrument.**

must [mʌst] *verb used with other verbs*
(*a*) *to mean* it is necessary; **you must do your homework or the teacher will be mad at you; we mustn't be late or we'll miss the TV program; you must hurry up if you want to catch the bus; must you go so soon?**
Negative: **mustn't, needn't**
Note: **mustn't** = not allowed, **needn't** = not necessary: we **mustn't be late/you needn't hurry**

(*b*) *to mean* probably/it is likely; **I must have left my book on the train; there's a knock at the door—it must be the doctor; they must be wet after walking in the rain.**
Negative: **can't: it can't be the doctor.**
I must, you must, he must, we must, they must
Past: **had to: I must go to the dentist's/I had to go to the dentist's yesterday**
Negative: **didn't have to**
Perfect: **must have: I must have left it on the train**
Negative: **couldn't have: I couldn't have left it on the train**
Note: **must** *does not have* **to** *and is always used with other verbs*

mus·tache ['mʌstæʃ] *noun*
hair which grows above a man's mouth; **the cop had a big black mustache.**

mus·tard ['mʌstərd] *noun*
hot-tasting yellow paste; **do you want some mustard with your beef? have you put any mustard on the ham sandwiches?**
no plural

my [maɪ] *adjective*
belonging to me; **that's my pen you're using! have you seen my new car? I broke my leg when I was playing football.**
my·self, *pronoun referring to me*
I've hurt myself; I saw it myself; I enjoyed myself very much; I did it all by myself = with no one helping me; **I don't like being all by myself in the big house** = all alone.

mys·ter·y ['mɪstərɪ] *noun*
thing which cannot be explained; **it is a mystery how the burglar got into the house; the police are trying to clear up the mystery of the missing jewels.**
plural **mysteries**

Nn

nail [neɪl] **1.** *noun*
(*a*) hard part at the end of your fingers and toes; **she painted her nails red; nail scissors** = special curved scissors for cutting your nails; *see also* **finger-nail, toenail**
(*b*) small piece of pointed metal with a flat end, which you knock into wood, etc., with a hammer; **hang that picture on the nail; put in another nail—the piece of wood is loose.**
2. *verb*
to attach with nails; **she nailed the pieces of wood together; they were nailing the carpet to the floor; they nailed down the lid of the box.**
nails—nailing—nailed—has nailed

name [neɪm] **1.** *noun*
special word which you use to call someone or something; **his name's John; I've forgotten the name of the shoe store; first name/Christian name** = particular name given to someone; **last name** = name of a family; **her first name/her Christian name is Anne, but I don't know her last name; I know him by name** = I have never met him, but I know who he is; **don't call the teacher names** = don't be rude to the teacher.
2. *verb*
to call someone or something by a name; **he's named John after his grand-father** = his grandfather was called John too; **can you name the largest city in the U.S.A?**
names—naming—named—has named

nap [næp] **1.** *noun*
short sleep; **she takes a nap every after-noon.**
2. *verb*
to sleep for a short while; **he was nap-ping when the visitors arrived.**
naps—napping—napped—has napped

nap·kin [ˈnæpkɪn] *noun*
small cloth used to protect your clothes and to wipe your mouth when eating; **don't forget to put a napkin next to each plate when you set the table.**

nar·row [ˈnærəʊ] *adjective*
not wide; **the road is too narrow for two cars to pass; we had a narrow escape** = we almost didn't escape.
narrow—narrower—narrowest
nar·row·ly, *adverb*
only just; **we narrowly missed hitting the tree.**

na·tion [ˈneɪʃən] *noun*
country; **all the nations of the world.**
na·tion·al [ˈnæʃənəl] *adjective*
referring to a particular country; **she's wearing the national costume; they're singing a national song.**
na·tion·al·i·ty [næʃəˈnælɪtiː] *noun*
the state of belonging to a particular country; **he's of French nationality; what nationality is she?**

na·ture [ˈneɪtʃər] *noun*
plants and animals; **nature study** = learning about plants and animals at school.
nat·u·ral [ˈnætʃərəl] *adjective*
(*a*) normal/not surprising; **his behavior was quite natural; it's natural for old people to go deaf.**
(*b*) not made by men; (thing) which comes from nature; **do you think the color of her hair is natural? natural gas** = gas which is found in the earth and is not made in a factory; **natural history** = study of nature.

nat·u·ral·ly, *adverb*
(*a*) of course; **naturally the little boy was beaten by the big one; do you want to watch the game?—naturally!**
(*b*) because of nature, not made; **she has naturally curly hair.**

naugh·ty [ˈnɔːtɪ] *adjective*
badly behaved; **if you're naughty you won't get any ice cream; you naughty boy, stop pulling the cat's tail.**
naughty—naughtier—naughtiest
Note: **naughty** *is usually used of children or small animals*

na·vy [ˈneɪvɪ] *noun*
all of a country's ships for war, and the sailors who sail in them; **he's in the navy; we want to join the navy; navy blue** = very dark blue.
plural **navies**

near [nɪr] **1.** *adverb, preposition & adjective*
(*a*) close to/not far away from; **the store is near the post office; bring your chair nearer to the fire; the bus stop is nearer to our house than the city hall; which is the nearest police station? we had a near miss** = we were nearly hit.
(*b*) soon/not far in time; **my birthday is near Christmas; winter is drawing near** = will be here soon.
near—nearer—nearest
2. *verb*
to come close to; **the train was nearing the station.**
nears—nearing—neared—has neared

near·by [niːrˈbaɪ] *adverb & adjective*
not far away; **they live nearby; we met in a nearby restaurant.**

near·ly, *adverb*
almost; **he's nearly 20 years old; the war lasted nearly ten years; this film isn't nearly as good as the one we saw last week; hurry up, it's nearly time for the bus to come; the TV program is nearly over.**

neat [niːt] *adjective*
clean; **her room is always neat; why is his homework never neat?**
neat—neater—neatest

nec·es·sar·y [ˈnesəserɪ] *adjective*
which has to be done; **it's necessary to pay your taxes by April 15; if you are going abroad it's necessary to have a passport; is all this equipment really necessary?**

neck [nek] *noun*
(*a*) part of the body which joins your head to your body; **I've got a stiff neck; she wears a gold chain around her neck; he's breathing down my neck all the time** = he's always watching how I'm working; **they're neck and neck** = exactly equal in the race.
(*b*) part of a piece of clothing which goes around your neck; **a pullover with a V neck; he wears shirts with a size 13 neck.**
(*c*) narrow part; **the neck of a bottle; a neck of land** = narrow piece of land between two pieces of water.
neck·lace [ˈnekləs] *noun*
string of jewels, etc., which is worn around your neck.
neck·tie, *noun*
tie/long piece of cloth which men wear around their necks under the collar of their shirts; **he wore a blue necktie; you can't come into the restaurant if you're not wearing a necktie.**

need [niːd] **1.** *noun*
what is necessary or wanted; **there's no need for us to wait; to be in need of** = to want something/to be without something; **they're in need of food; are you in need of help?**
if need be = if it is necessary.
2. *verb*
to be necessary for something; to want; **we shall need foreign money for our vacation; painting needs a lot of skill; do you need help? the house needs painting; I'm afraid the TV needs to be fixed again; do you really need all this equipment? the police need to know who saw the accident; you don't need to come if you have a cold; will you be needing me any more or can I go home? I need you to help me with the cleaning; you**

can take the book—I don't need it any
more.

**needs—needing—needed—has
needed**

need·n't *verb used with other verbs*
to mean it isn't necessary; **you needn't
come if you have a cold; he needn't have
called; he needn't make so much noise
in the shower.**

needn't *is not used with* **to** *and is
only used with other verbs*

nee·dle ['ni:dl] *noun*
thin metal tool with a sharp point used
for sewing or knitting; **she has lost her
knitting needles; don't sit down, I've left
a needle on that chair.**

neg·a·tive ['negətɪv] *adjective & noun*
showing "no"; **"didn't" is the negative
of "did"; the answer's in the negative** =
the answer is "no."

neigh·bor ['neɪbər] *noun*
person who lives near you; **our next door
neighbors** = the people who live in the
house next to ours; **the Swedes and
Danes are neighbors** = their countries
are close together.

neigh·bor·hood, *noun*
area and the people who live in it; **this
is a quiet neighborhood; the mailman
knows everyone in the neighborhood.**

neigh·bor·ing, *adjective*
which is close to you; **we go to the
neighboring town to see the doctor as
there isn't one in our town; Brazil and
Peru are neighboring countries.**

neigh·bor·ly, *adjective*
friendly and helpful.

nei·ther ['ni:ðər] 1. *adjective & pronoun*
not either of two (people, etc.); **neither
of them guessed the right answer; neither
brother is tall/neither of the brothers is
tall.**

2. *adverb & conjunction*
not either; **he doesn't like fish and neither
do I** = I don't like fish either; **it's neither
too hot nor too cold—it's just right; he
isn't tall—but neither is he really very
short** = he isn't really very short either.

Note: verb comes before subject after
neither

neph·ew ['nefju:] *noun*
son of your brother or sister; **my sister
has two sons, so I have two nephews; an
uncle and his nephews.**

nerve [nɜrv] *noun*
one of the many threads in a body
which take messages to and from
the brain; **he gets on my nerves** = he
bothers me; **he had the nerve to tell me
to be quick when he's so slow himself** =
he was rude enough to tell me to be
quick.

nerv·ous, *adjective*
very easily worried; **she's nervous about
her exams; don't be nervous—the driving
test is quite easy.**

nest [nest] *noun*
place built by birds to lay their eggs;
**the birds have built a nest in the apple
tree.**

net [net] 1. *noun*
material made of string or thread with
very large holes; **a fishing net; a tennis
net; he hit the ball into the net.**

2. *adjective*
(*price/weight, etc.*) after taking away
anything extra; **net weight** = weight
without the container; **net income** =
income left after all the taxes have been
paid.

nev·er ['nevər] *adverb*
not at any time; not ever; **I'll never
forget our vacation in Mexico; I've never
been into that store although I've often
walked past it; she never eats meat;
never mind!** = don't worry/don't
bother about it.

new [nju:] *adjective*
(*a*) quite recently made/not used; **take a
new piece of paper; this is a new model
of car; this bike is new—I didn't buy it
secondhand.**

(*b*) recently arrived/fresh; **here are the
new boys in the class; we bought some
new potatoes** = the first potatoes of this
year's crop.

(*c*) which has just been got/just been
bought; **have you seen his new car? she**

introduced me to her new teacher.

new—newer—newest

New Year, *noun*
first few days of the year; **I start my new job in the New Year; Happy New Year** = good wishes for the New Year; **New Year's Day/New Year's** = January 1.

news, *singular noun*
spoken or written information about what has happened; **he was watching the 6 o'clock news on TV; did you hear the news on the radio? he told me the news about the fire; have you heard the news?** = have you heard what has happened? **have you gotten any news about your new job? we always like to hear good news.**

Note: **news** *is singular, not plural*

news·boy, *noun*
boy who delivers or sells newspapers.

news·pa·per, *noun*
sheets of paper (which usually come out each day) with news of what has happened; **a daily newspaper/a weekly newspaper; has today's newspaper been delivered? have you finished the crossword puzzle in today's newspaper? yesterday's newspaper was full of news of the election.**

Note: **a newspaper** *is often called* **a paper**

news·stand, *noun*
small wooden store in the street, where newspapers and magazines are sold.

next [nekst] *adjective & adverb*
(*a*) coming after in time; **on Wednesday we arrived in Los Angeles and the next day we left for Seattle; what shall we do next? first the teacher came into the classroom, and next came a policeman; next Monday I start my vacation; the next time you go to the post office, can you buy me some of the new stamps? come to see me the week after next; next please!** = asking the next person in the line to step forward for service in a bank or post office.
(*b*) nearest (in place); **the walls are thin—we can hear everything that is said in the next room; he sat down next to me;** **it costs next to nothing** = very little.

next door, *adjective & adverb*
in the house next to this one; **she lives next door to my aunt; our next door neighbors are Germans; they have a lot of flowers next door.**

nice [naɪs] *adjective*
pleasant/fine; **what a nice time we had at the party! come and see us if the weather's nice; it was rainy today, so we hope it'll be nicer tomorrow; he had a nice sleep after lunch; we went for a nice ride in his new car; that wasn't a very nice thing to say** = that wasn't very pleasant.

nice—nicer—nicest

nick·el [ˈnɪkl] *noun*
5-cent coin; **can you give me two nickels for a dime?**

niece [niːs] *noun*
daughter of your brother or sister; **I've got three nieces—they're my brother's children; the niece looks like her aunt.**

night [naɪt] *noun*
part of the day when it is dark; **I don't like going out alone late at night; it rained a lot during the night; we stayed at home last night, but tomorrow night we're going to a party; if you travel by night you pay less.**

night·mare [ˈnaɪtmeər] *noun*
frightening dream; **he had a nightmare about falling off a bridge.**

night·time, *noun*
whole period of the night; **burglars usually come during the nighttime; we took a nighttime flight to the West Coast.**

nine [naɪn] number 9
he's nine (years old); come to see me tomorrow morning at nine o'clock; you've eaten nine cookies! nine times out of ten = very often.

nine·teen, number 19
she's nineteen (years old); the two-nineteen train = the train leaving at 2:19; **in**

the 1950s = during the years 1950–1959.

Note: **1950s:** *say* "the nineteen fifties"

nine·teenth, 19th, *adjective & noun*
referring to nineteen; he came nineteenth in the race; it's her nineteenth birthday tomorrow; the nineteenth century = the period from 1800 to 1899; **June (the) nineteenth (June 19).**

nine·ty, number 90
she is ninety (years old); her husband is ninety-two; they are both in their nineties.

Note: **ninety-one (91), ninety-two (92),** *etc., but* **ninety-first (91st), ninety-second (92nd),** *etc.*

nine·ti·eth, 90th, *adjective & noun*
referring to ninety; **a ninetieth of a second;** she was ninetieth in the competition; it will be grandmother's ninetieth birthday next month.

ninth, 9th, *adjective & noun*
referring to nine; at least a ninth of the children are ill; she was ninth in her class; today is September (the) ninth (September 9); tomorrow is his ninth birthday.

no [nəʊ] *adjective & adverb*
(*a*) (*showing the opposite of* **yes**) we asked him if he wanted to come, and he said "no"; do you want some more coffee?—no, thank you.
(*b*) not any; there's no butter left; there are no stores for miles around; I've gotten no reply to my letter; no parking/no smoking/no exit = do not park/smoke/go out.
(*c*) not at all; this book is no better than the last one I read; he's no longer here; he's no good at his job.

no·bod·y [ˈnəʊbədɪ] *pronoun*
no one/no person; there's nobody in the bathroom; I saw nobody I knew; nobody likes sour milk; nobody else wears red socks like you.

nod [nɒd] 1. *noun*
moving your head forward to show you agree/to greet someone; he gave me a

nod; when we asked if he wanted some ice cream, he gave a nod.
2. *verb*
to move your head forward to show you agree/to greet someone; he nodded to me in the street; when she asked if anyone wanted ice cream, all the children nodded.
nods—nodding—nodded—has nodded

nod off, *verb*
to begin to go to sleep; he nodded off in his chair; give me a tap if I nod off; she's nodding off over her book.

noise [nɔɪz] *noun*
sound which is often loud or not pleasant; don't make so much noise—I'm trying to work; the car's making strange noises—perhaps something's wrong with the engine; I thought I heard a noise in the kitchen; he's making so much noise that he can't hear the telephone; we were woken up by noises in the night.
nois·y, *adjective*
which makes a lot of noise; a noisy car; a crowd of noisy children.
noisy—noisier—noisiest

none [nʌn] *pronoun*
(*a*) not any; a little money is better than none at all; none of the houses has a red door; he was none the worse for his accident = not at all hurt; her health is none too good = not very good.
(*b*) not one; none of the teachers has a beard; none of the guests left the party early.

non·sense [ˈnɒnsens] *noun*
something which does not make sense; silly behavior; you're talking nonsense; it's nonsense to say that money doesn't matter; take an umbrella!—nonsense, it won't rain; stop that nonsense at once!

noon [nuːn] *noun*
12 o'clock in the middle of the day; she won't be back in the office before noon.

no one [ˈnəʊwʌn] *pronoun*
nobody/no person; there's no one in the room; I saw no one I knew; no one here

likes sour milk; no one else wears red
socks like you.

nor [nɔ:r] *conjunction*
neither . . . nor = not one . . . and not the
other; she's neither English nor American;
neither you nor she looks very well.

nor·mal ['nɔ:rml] *adjective*
usual; ordinary; wet weather is quite
normal at this time of year; after the
strike the trains went back to their
normal service.
nor·mal·ly, *adverb*
usually; I normally have a cup of
hot chocolate before going to bed; we
normally go on vacation in August.

north [nɔ:rθ] **1.** *noun*
direction when you are facing away
from the sun at noon; snow fell in the
north of the country; the wind is blowing
from the north.
2. *adjective*
referring to the north; the north coast of
Alaska; the north side of the house
never gets any sun.
3. *adverb*
towards the north; we were traveling
north; the house faces north.
North A·mer·i·ca, *noun*
part of America containing the U.S.A.
and Canada.
north·ern, ['nɔ:rðərn] *adjective*
of the north; they live in the northern
part of the country.
North Pole, *noun*
furthest point at the north of the earth.
north·ward, *adverb*
towards the north; they traveled north-
ward for six hours.

nose [nəʊz] *noun*
part of your face which you breathe
through and smell with; he has a red
nose; dogs have wet noses; she must have
a cold—her nose is running = liquid is
dripping from her nose; don't wipe your
nose on your sleeve—use a handkerchief;
he blew his nose several times = blew
through his nose into a handkerchief to
get rid of liquid in his nose; to speak
through your nose = as if your nose is

blocked, so that you say "b" instead of
"m" and "d" instead of "n"; to look
down your nose at something = to look
as if you don't think it is very good; to
turn up your nose at something = to
refuse something because you don't feel
it is good enough.

not [nɒt] *adverb*
(*a*) (*used with verbs to show that the
action is the opposite—short form is
n't) he won't come; she isn't there; he
didn't eat his meat; they couldn't go
home because of the snow; the service
charge is not included.
(*b*) (*used to make sentences and words
have the opposite meaning*) it is not at
all funny; is he coming?—I hope not; I
don't want to go—why not? the whole
family was there—not forgetting old
Aunt Jane = even including; not a few
= many; not very well = sick; I'm not
sorry to leave = I'm glad to leave; not
yet = not until later.
not . . . ei·ther = and not . . . also; I
don't like meat and I don't like fish
either; it wasn't sunny but it wasn't raining either.
not on·ly . . . but al·so = not just
this . . . but this as well; he isn't only
blind, but he's also deaf; the book is not
only very long but it's also very bad.

note [nəʊt] **1.** *noun*
(*a*) very short letter; a few words written
down; I sent him a note to say I was
sick; he made some notes before giving
his speech; we must make a note of what
we need before we go on vacation; students take notes during classes.
(*b*) musical sound; written sign meaning
a musical sound; key on a piano; he
can't sing the high notes; he only played
the black notes on the piano.
2. *verb*
(*a*) to write down quickly; the policeman
noted down the details of the accident.
(*b*) to take notice of; please note that
the movie starts at 7 o'clock.
**notes—noting—noted—has
noted**
note·book, *noun*
small book for making notes.

note·pa·per, *noun*
paper for writing letters.
no plural: **some notepaper; a piece of notepaper**

noth·ing [ˈnʌθɪŋ] *noun*
not anything; **there's nothing in the box; when asked about the accident he said nothing; he said nothing about the accident; he thinks nothing of riding his bike ten miles to work** = he does it easily; **it has got nothing to do with you** = it is not your problem; **nothing much happened** = not very much; **there was nothing interesting on the news; there's nothing more to be done; he has nothing left in the bank** = no money left; **the car gave us nothing but trouble** = only caused trouble.
for nothing = free; **I got the tickets for nothing—they were a present from my boss.**

no·tice [ˈnəʊtɪs] **1.** *noun*
(*a*) piece of writing giving information, usually put in a place where everyone can see it; **he put up a notice about the meeting.**
(*b*) warning; **they had to leave with ten minutes' notice; it had to be done at short notice** = with very little warning time; **if you want to quit your job, you have to give a month's notice.**
(*c*) attention; **take no notice of what he says** = pay no attention to it/don't worry about it.
2. *verb*
to see; to take note of; **nobody noticed that I was wearing one blue and one white sock; did you notice what the time was when I started boiling the egg?**
notices—noticing—noticed—has noticed

no·tice·a·ble, *adjective*
easily noticed/seen; **it was noticeable that he had lost a lot of weight.**

noun [naʊn] *noun*
word used to show a person or thing or idea; "**man**," "**stone**" and "**color**" are all nouns.

No·vem·ber [nəʊˈvembər] *noun*

eleventh month of the year; **today is November 5; he was born in November; we didn't go away last November.**
Note: **November 5:** say "November fifth," "November the fifth" *or* "the fifth of November"

now [naʊ] **1.** *adverb*
at this moment; **I can hear the car coming now; can we go to the beach now? he ought to be in Arkansas by now; now's the best time for picking apples; a week from now we'll be on vacation; until now she has never had to see a doctor.**
2. *conjunction*
at this moment; **now that I know how to drive I can go on vacation by myself; now that you've reminded me, I do remember seeing him last week.**
3. *interjection*
(*a*) (*showing warning*) **now then, let's get ready; come on now, pull hard!**
(*b*) (*getting someone's attention*) **now, let's begin.**
now·a·days, *adverb*
at the present time; **everything is very different nowadays from what it was fifty years ago; nowadays most people have cars and refrigerators.**
now and then, *adverb*
from time to time; **now and then, we all go to the movies.**

no·where [ˈnəʊweər] *adverb*
(*a*) not in any place/not to any place/not anywhere; **the cat was nowhere to be found; where are you going?—nowhere! there is nowhere else to put the typewriter.**
(*b*) **nowhere near** = not at all; **the house is nowhere near finished; he is nowhere near completing his homework.**

nui·sance [ˈnjuːsəns] *noun*
something/someone who causes trouble; **what a nuisance—I've lost my front door key! that little boy is a real nuisance.**

num·ber [ˈnʌmbər] *noun*
(*a*) name of a figure; **13 is my lucky number; they live in apartment number 48b; what is your telephone number? I**

can't remember the number of our bank account.

(b) how many people/things; **a large number/large numbers of people are looking for work; a large number of houses were damaged in the fire; numbers of lives were lost in the accident; only a small number of people were there; I've seen that film a number of times** = several times; **I've been to San Francisco any number of times** = so many times I cannot count them; **you could take your driving test any number of times but you still wouldn't pass it.**

(c) piece of music played or sung; **would you do that number again?**

Note: when **number** *refers to a plural noun it is followed by a plural verb:* **a number of houses were damaged**

nurse [nɜrs] 1. *noun*
person (usually a woman) who takes care of sick people; **she works as a nurse in the local hospital; she's training to be a nurse; male nurse** = man who takes care of sick people.
2. *verb*
to take care of sick people; **when he was sick, his sister nursed him until he was better; I'm staying home to nurse my cold.**
nurses—nursing—nursed—has nursed

nurs·er·y school, *noun*
school for little children; **now that she is three, we may send her to nursery school in the mornings.**

nut [nʌt] *noun*
fruit of a tree, with a hard shell and a softer center which you can eat; **he was eating a bar of milk chocolate with nuts.**

Oo

oak [əʊk] *noun*
type of large tree; wood of this tree; **there is an oak in front of the library; the house has oak floors.**

oar [ɔːr] *noun*
long wooden pole with a wide flat end, used for rowing a boat.

oats [əʊts] *noun*
type of grain; **he fed the horse some oats.**
no plural

oat·meal [ˈəʊtmiːl] *noun*
ground oats used in making a hot cereal; **she had a bowl of oatmeal for breakfast.**
no plural

o·bey [əˈbeɪ] *verb*
to do what someone or a rule tells you to do; **you ought to obey your father; you must obey the rules.**
obeys—obeying—obeyed—has obeyed

ob·ject 1. *noun* [ˈɒbdʒekt]
(a) thing; **a big black object fell into the middle of the field.**
(b) something which you try to do; **what's the object of your plan? the object of the game is to throw the ball between the posts.**
(c) noun or pronoun which follows immediately after a verb or a preposition; **in the sentence "the dog chased the cat," the word "cat" is the object of the verb "chased."**
2. *verb* [əbˈdʒekt]
to refuse to agree to something/not to like something; **I object to having to attend long meetings; he objected to my going on vacation; does anyone object if I smoke my pipe?**
objects—objecting—objected—has objected

ob·serve [əbˈzɜrv] *verb*
to notice/to see something and understand it; **a policeman observed**

them putting the boxes into a truck.

**observes—observing—
observed—has observed**

ob·vi·ous ['ɒbviəs] *adjective*
which can easily be seen/be noticed; it's
obvious that the car is no good; he made
a very obvious mistake.
ob·vi·ous·ly, *adverb*
naturally; obviously he was very pleased
when he passed the test.

oc·cu·py ['ɒkjʊpaɪ] *verb*
to fill up/to take up space or time; the
table occupies the whole corner of the
room; how do you occupy your time
when you are on vacation? the soldiers
occupied the town; is this seat occupied?
I'm afraid the manager is occupied at
the moment = busy.

**occupies—occupying—
occupied—has occupied**

oc·cu·pa·tion [ɒkjʊ'peɪʃn] *noun*
job; what is his occupation?

o·cean ['əʊʃən] *noun*
very large sea which lies around the
main areas of land on the earth; the
Pacific Ocean; the Atlantic Ocean.

o'clock [ə'klɒk] *adverb phrase*
(*used with numbers to mean the exact
hour*) it's 6 o'clock; I never get up before
8 o'clock; by 10 o'clock everyone was
asleep.
*Note: o'clock is only used for the
exact hour, not for times which include minutes. It can also be left out:
we got home at eleven = we got
home at eleven o'clock*

Oc·to·ber [ɒk'təʊbər] *noun*
tenth month of the year; were you born
in October? today is October 21; last
October we went to Germany.
*Note: October 21: say "October
twenty-first," "October the twenty-
first" or "the twenty-first of October"*

odd [ɒd] *adjective*
(*a*) strange; I find it odd that he hasn't
written to us; how odd that the door
wasn't locked; isn't it odd that he is
afraid of the telephone?

(*b*) (number) which cannot be divided
by 2; 3, 5, 7 are all odd numbers; the
houses with odd numbers are on this side
of the street.
(*c*) not one of a group; I have two odd
socks = two socks which are not the
same; there was an odd glove left on the
table.
(*d*) not regular; he does odd jobs in the
house; she writes the odd article for the
newspaper.

odd—odder—oddest

of [ʌv] *preposition*
(*a*) (*showing connection*) he's the son of
the man who fixed my car; she's a
friend of mine; where's the lid of the
black saucepan? what are the dates of
Henry VIII?
(*b*) (*showing a part/an amount*) how
much of it do you want? today is the
first of June; there are six of them; half
of the children were sick with flu; a pint
of milk; two pounds of potatoes.
(*c*) of = who/which is; a child of ten
= a child who is ten years old; the
city of Detroit is an important city in the
Midwest.
(*d*) (*showing position/material/cause*) he
lives south of the town; the sweater is
made of wool; he died of his wounds; of
course = yes naturally; of course I'll go
shopping with you!
*Note: of is often used after verbs or
adjectives: to think of; to be fond
of; to be tired of; to smell of; to
be afraid of, etc.*

off [ɔːf] *adverb & preposition*
(*a*) (*showing movement away from a
place*) I'm off to California tomorrow; the
post office is just off Green Street; she
got off the bus; take your shoes off if
they are wet; take the cloth off the table;
he fell off his horse; she gets off work
at 5 = she finishes work at 5 o'clock;
he's taking a day off = a day away from
work; the picnic is off = the picnic
won't be held.
(*b*) not switched on; turn all the lights
off; is the TV off?
(*c*) wrong (when you are calculating); I

am $10 off = I have $10 too much or too little; **you are off by 50 cents.**

off and on = now and then/from time to time.

Note: **off** *is often used after verbs:* **to keep off; to take off; to fall off; to break off,** *etc.*

of·fer ['ɔːfər] **1.** *noun*
showing that you are ready to give something; **$10 is the best offer I can make** = I'm not ready to pay more; **we had offers of help from everyone in the neighborhood; special offer** = goods which are on sale at a reduced price.
2. *verb*
to say that you are ready to do or give something; **did he offer to help? they didn't even offer me a cup of coffee; I offered to go with her to the bus stop.**
offers—offering—offered—has offered

of·fice ['ɔːfɪs] *noun*
room/building where a business is carried on or where something is organized; **he works in an office in Omaha; I'll be staying late at the office this evening; she's the manager of our Toronto office; Miss Jones's office is next door to mine;** *see also* **post office**

of·fi·cer ['ɔːfɪsər] *noun*
person in command in the army, navy, air force, etc.; **he's an army officer; a police officer came to look at the damage.**

of·fi·cial [ə'fɪʃl] **1.** *adjective*
as used by government or people in charge; **an official report; his official title is Manager of the Sales Department.**
2. *noun*
person in an important government job; **an official from the Tax Office came to look at our accounts; she's an official in the Department of Education.**

of·ten ['ɔːfn] *adverb*
many times/frequently; **I often go to St. Louis on business; do you often have chicken for dinner? how often are there trains to Chicago? I go to the movies every so often** = not very frequently.

oh [əʊ] *interjection*
(*showing surprise/interest/excitement*) **Oh look, there's the train! Oh, Mr. Jones, can you come here, please? You must come to the police station—Oh no I won't!**

oil [ɔɪl] **1.** *noun*
any of various kinds of thick liquid used in cooking/engineering/painting etc.; **cooking oil; vegetable oil; he's fond of painting in oils; an oil painting; an oil well; an oil field** = large area where oil is found underground.
2. *verb*
to put oil on a machine, etc.; **you should oil the car door because it makes a noise.**
oils—oiling—oiled—has oiled

OK, okay [əʊ'keɪ] *noun & interjection*
all right; **shall we start now?—OK, let's go; I was ill yesterday, but I'm OK now; he gave our plan the OK** = he said the plan was fine.

old [əʊld] *adjective*
(*a*) having lived/existed for a long time; not young; **my grandfather is an old man —he's eighty; my mother's getting old; an old church; I don't like this old music—play something modern; we're old friends.**
(*b*) having been used for a long time/ not new; **I'll have to wear my old clothes to paint the house; she sold her old car and bought a new one.**
(*c*) having a certain age; **she's ten years old today; how old are you?** = what is your age?
(*d*) (*used as a pleasant way of talking about someone*) **the old man** = your father/the boss, etc.
(*e*) past/former; **our old house was on the other side of the town.**
old—older—oldest

on [ɒn] **1.** *preposition*
(*a*) touching or lying on the top or outside of something; **put the book on the table; flies can walk on the ceiling.**
(*b*) hanging from; **hang the picture on the hook.**
(*c*) (*showing movement or position*) **he**

Office

1. book	13. notice
2. calculator	14. package
3. card	15. page
4. cassette	16. pen
5. check	17. pencil
6. computer	18. ruler
7. desk	19. safe
8. envelope	20. telephone
9. ink	21. telephone book
10. letter	22. thumbtack
11. magazine	23. typewriter
12. notebook	

got on the train; it's on page 4; the house is on the right side of the road.

(*d*) belonging to; **she's on the staff of the school; he's on the committee.**

(*e*) busy doing something; **he's gone to Germany on business; they're on vacation.**

(*f*) (*showing time/day/date*) **on Sundays; on Monday we went to the zoo; on December 25; on my arrival = when I arrived.**

(*g*) (*showing means of travel*) **he went away on foot; she's going on her bike.**

(*h*) about; **he wrote a book on African animals.**

(*i*) (*showing an instrument/machine which is used*) **he played a piece of music on the piano; she was on the telephone for half an hour; the play was on the radio yesterday; I watched the football game on TV.**

2. *adverb*

(*a*) in position; being worn; **put the kettle on; have you put your boots on? because it was cold he kept his coat on in the house.**

(*b*) working; **the gas is on; you've left the light on; turn the engine on; switch the TV on; what's on at the movies?**

(*c*) continuing/not stopping; **he worked on until the evening; she went on talking; go on—don't stop; the play went on and on = lasted for a long time.**

(*d*) (*showing that time has passed*) **later on; from that time on.**

Note: **on** *is often used after verbs:* **to sit on; to jump on; to put on; to lie on,** *etc.*

once [wʌns] **1.** *adverb*

(*a*) one time; **take the medicine once a day; the magazine comes out once a month; how many times did you see the dentist?—only once.**

(*b*) at a time in the past; **I knew him once; once, when I was going home, I fell off my bike.**

2. *conjunction*

as soon as; **once you start you can't stop; once I'm on vacation, I'll swim every day.**

at once, *adverb*

(*a*) immediately; **do it at once! the doctor came at once.**

(*b*) at the same time; **don't all speak at once.**

one [wʌn] **1.**

(*a*) number 1; **our little boy is one year old; his grandfather is a hundred and one.**

(*b*) single thing; **there's only one left; this is the last page but one = the page before the last.**

2. *adjective & pronoun*

(*a*) single (thing); **there's only one cake left; which one do you want—the green one or the black one? one of the boys will help you; I've lost my pen—do you have one?**

(*b*) you; **one can't afford to drive a large car these days.**

(*c*) **one another = each other; you should write to one another more often.**

Note: **one (1)** *but* **first (1st)**

one-way street, *noun*

street where the traffic only goes in one direction; **you can't turn left—it's a one-way street.**

on·ion [ˈʌnjən] *noun*

vegetable with a round white root which makes you cry when you cut it; **we had onion soup for dinner.**

on·ly [ˈəʊnlɪ] **1.** *adjective*

one single (thing or person); **it's the only watch I've got; she's an only child = there are no other children in her family.**

2. *adverb*

(*a*) and no one/nothing else; **I only have three dollars; only you can help us; employees only can use this elevator; only children are allowed in free.**

(*b*) as recently as; **only yesterday I got a postcard from her.**

if on·ly (*phrase showing a strong wish*) **if only I had known; if only she had phoned the police.**

on·ly too = extremely; I'm only too happy to help.

on·to [ˈɒntuː *or* ˈɒntə] *preposition*

to a place on; **she's getting onto the bus;**

the dog jumped onto the boat as it moved away from the dock.

o·pen [ˈəʊpən] 1. *adjective*
(*a*) not shut; **that box is open; leave the door open—it's hot in here; why is the oven door open?**
(*b*) which you can go into; **are the stores open on Sundays? the museum is open from 10 a.m. to 5 p.m.; the meeting is open to the public** = anyone can go to it.
(*c*) without any walls/any protection; **the field is open on three sides; I like being out in the open air; the competition is open to everyone** = anyone can enter it.
2. *verb*
(*a*) to make open; **open the door—the cat wants to go out; can you open that box?**
(*b*) to start up; **a new store is going to open next door to us; the stores open early in the morning.**
opens—opening—opened—has opened
3. *noun*
in the open = not hidden; **the story about the president is now out in the open.**
no plural

o·pen·er, *noun*
tool for opening; **a can opener; a bottle opener.**

o·pen·ing, *noun*
(*a*) the action of opening; **opening time for the library is 10:00 a.m.**
(*b*) place where something opens; **the sheep got out through an opening in the fence.**

o·pen·ly, *adverb*
without hiding anything; **he openly admitted taking the radio.**

op·er·a·tion [ɒpəˈreɪʃən] *noun*
act of cutting open someone's body to cure something; **she's had an operation on her foot; the operation was successful.**

op·er·a·tor [ˈɒpəreɪtər] *noun*
telephone company employee who helps you to make calls; **to make a long-distance call, first call the operator.**

o·pin·ion [əˈpɪnjən] *noun*
what people think about something; **what's your opinion of the situation? ask the manager for his opinion about what we should do; he has a very high/a very low opinion of his assistant** = he thinks he is very good/very bad.

op·po·site [ˈɒpəzɪt] 1. *adjective & preposition*
facing/on the other side; **their house is just opposite the post office; it's not on this side of the street—it's on the opposite side; his car hit a truck going in the opposite direction; will you sit opposite my mother?**
2. *noun*
something which is completely different; **"big" is the opposite of "small"; what's the opposite of "black"? he's just the opposite of his brother; he said one thing, and then did the opposite.**

or [ɔːr] *conjunction*
(*a*) (*showing something else which is possible*) **you can come with us or you can stay at home; I don't mind if I have tea or coffee; did she die in an accident or was she murdered?**
(*b*) (*showing a rough figure*) **six or seven people came; it costs $4 or so** = roughly $4.
or else = if not; **you must wear a coat or else you'll catch cold; he has to get up early or else he'll miss his train.**

or·ange [ˈɔːrɪndʒ] 1. *noun*
sweet juicy fruit, colored between yellow and red; **I have an orange for breakfast; can I have a glass of orange juice?**
2. *adjective & noun*
the color of an orange/a color between yellow and red; **does he always wear an orange tie? they painted the kitchen ceiling orange; I'd like to paint the front door a dark orange.**

or·chard [ˈɔːrtʃərd] *noun*
group of planted fruit trees; **apple orchard.**

or·ches·tra [ˈɔːrkɪstrə] *noun*

large group of people who play music together; **the school orchestra played music by Beethoven.**

or·der [ˈɔːrdər] **1.** *noun*

(*a*) saying that something has to be done; **he gave an order to the soldiers; if you can't obey orders, you shouldn't be a policeman.**

(*b*) asking for something to be served/ to be sent; **we have a large order for machinery from Japan; he gave the waiter his order; the waiter brought him the wrong order.**

(*c*) arrangement of things in a special way; **the names on the list are in alphabetical order; the books in the library are all in the wrong order/all out of order** = not in the right places.

(*d*) correct running of a machine, etc.; **the elevator is out of order** = it is not working; **are your papers in order?** = are they correct?

in or·der that = so that; **people on bikes should wear orange coats in order that drivers can see them in the dark.**

in or·der to = to/so as to; **he ran fast in order to catch the bus; she bent down in order to pick up her book.**

2. *verb*

(*a*) to say that something has to be done; to tell someone to do something; **he ordered the school to be closed; the doctor ordered three weeks' rest; I don't like being ordered around** = I don't like people always telling me what to do.

(*b*) to ask for something to be served/to be sent; **he ordered a hamburger and a can of beer; we've ordered a new electric typewriter.**

orders—ordering—ordered—has ordered

or·di·nar·y [ˈɔːrdnerɪ] *adjective*

normal/not special; **I'll wear my ordinary suit to the office; he leads a very ordinary life; the film is quite out of the ordinary** = quite different from other films.

or·gan·ize [ˈɔːrgənaɪz] *verb*

to arrange things/to put things into a special order; **you must organize your**

work better than that; **she organized a meeting to fight the rent increase.**

organizes—organizing— organized—has organized

or·gan·i·za·tion, *noun*

(*a*) way of organizing; **you have to have good organization if you want the business to succeed.**

(*b*) group which is organized; **a church organization; an organization which sends food to poor people; she belongs to an organization which helps old people.**

oth·er [ˈʌðər] *adjective & pronoun*

(*a*) not the same/different (person or thing); **the two boys went swimming while the other members of the family sat on the beach; some of my relatives live in New York while the others live in Boston; I don't like these sandwiches—can I have one of the other ones/one of the others? which others do you want? any other kind would do; can't we go to some other place on vacation next year?**

(*b*) second one of two; **one pencil is red, and the other (one) is blue; one girl is tall, but the other (one) is short.**

(*c*) (*showing an idea which is not clear*) **he went to stay in some little town or other on the coast; she met some boy or other at the party; the other day/the other week** = a day or two ago/a week or two ago.

one af·ter the oth·er = following in line; **they fell down one after the other; they all got colds one after the other.**

eve·ry oth·er = every second; **the police stopped every other car** = the first, third, fifth cars, etc.; **he wrote a letter every other day** = on Tuesday, Thursday, Saturday, etc.

ought [ɔːt] *verb used with other verbs*

(*a*) *to mean* it would be a good idea to; **you ought to see that movie; he ought to see a doctor; she ought to have told you before she went away.**

(*b*) *to mean* it is probable that; **he ought to pass his exams easily; she ought to get** home by 6 o'clock; the party ought to be over soon.

I ought, you ought, he ought, we ought, they ought
Past: **ought to have**
Negative: **ought not, ought not to have,** *usually* **oughtn't, oughtn't to have**
Note: **ought** *is followed by* **to. ought** *and* **ought to have** *do not follow* **to** *and are only used with other verbs*

ounce [auns] *noun*
measure of weight; **there are sixteen ounces in a pound; a four-ounce jar of coffee.**
Note: with figures **ounce** *is often written* **oz. (7 oz.** = seven ounces)

our ['aur] *adjective*
belonging to us; **our house is near the post office; we have lost our dog; one of our children has measles.**

ours, *pronoun*
thing/person belonging to us; **that house is ours; is that their son?—no, he's ours; some friends of ours told us to go; can we borrow your car?—ours won't start.**

our·selves, *pronoun*
referring to us **we organized ourselves into two groups; we were enjoying ourselves; we did it all by ourselves** = with no one to help us; **we don't like being (all) by ourselves** = all alone.

out [aut] *adverb*
(*a*) not in; away from; **no one answered the phone—they must all be out; the rabbit got out of its cage; he pulled out a gun; take the camera out of its box; the water came out of the hole in the pipe; the telephone is out of order** = not working.
(*b*) away; **the manager is out; the ship is out at sea.**
(*c*) not burning; **the fire has gone out.**
(*d*) among (in a total); **he got 10 out of 12 on the test; nine times out of ten she's wrong** = nearly all the time.

(*e*) **out of** = without; **we are out of sugar; she is out of work.**
Note: **out** *is often used with verbs:* **to jump out; to get out; to come out,** *etc.*
Note: **out** *is often followed by* **of**

out·door, *adjective*
in the open air; **an outdoor swimming pool; outdoor furniture.**

out·doors, *adverb*
in the open air; **you should sit outdoors instead of sitting in the house.**

out·er, *adjective*
further out; which is not inside; **the outer layer of an orange; outer space** = space beyond the earth.

out·num·ber, *verb*
to have greater numbers than; **our factories outnumber yours; they were outnumbered by the enemy soldiers.**

outnumber—outnumbering—outnumbered—have outnumbered

out·put, *noun*
amount which a company/a person/a machine produces; **output is falling; the factory has an output of 200 tons per day.**

out·side 1. *noun*
surface of something/part which is not inside; **the outside of the house is painted white; the apple looked nice on the outside, but the inside was rotten.**
2. *adjective*
which is on the outside; **the outside walls of the house.**
3. *adverb & preposition*
not inside/beyond the walls of something; **I left my bike outside the front door; come and sit outside in the yard; his coat's all wet—it must be raining outside.**

ov·en ['ʌvən] *noun*
inside part of a stove which is heated and which you cook food in; **I've put a cake in the oven; your dinner's in the oven.**

o·ver ['əuvər] 1. *preposition*
(*a*) on top of; higher than; **she spread a cloth over the table; the plane flew over**

our house; the water was soon over her ankles.

(b) on the other side; to the other side; she threw the bottle over the wall; they jumped over the railroad tracks.

(c) from the top of; he fell over the edge; she looked over the edge.

(d) during; over the last few months he has grown quite tall; we talked about it over dinner.

(e) more than; children over 5 years old; it costs over $50; we've been waiting for over two hours.

2. *adverb*

(a) everywhere; he's dirty all over.

(b) several times; he played the record over and over again; they did it ten times over.

(c) down from standing up; the bottle fell over; he knocked the bottle over; she leaned over and picked up the cushion.

(d) finished; is the game over yet? when the war was over we had more food to eat.

(e) more than; children of 14 and over pay full price; there are reduced prices for groups of 30 and over.

(f) not used/left behind; you can keep what's left over.

Note: over *is used after many verbs:* to run over; to fall over; to come over; to look over, *etc.*

o·ver·alls, *plural noun*
one-piece sleeveless suit often worn when working; he was wearing a red shirt and a pair of blue overalls.

o·ver·coat, *noun*
thick coat which you wear over other clothes outside; put on your overcoat—it's snowing.

o·ver·crowd·ed, *adjective*
with too many people inside; the building is overcrowded; an overcrowded bus.

o·ver·night, *adverb & adjective*
lasting all night; for the night; we stayed overnight in Boston; will the food stay fresh overnight? they took the overnight train to St. Louis.

o·ver·pow·er, *verb*
to get control over; the thief was overpowered by the policeman.
overpowers—overpowering—overpowered—has overpowered

o·ver·seas, *adjective & adverb*
across the ocean; his relatives live overseas; an overseas shipment.

o·ver·sleep, *verb*
to sleep longer than you had planned; he was late for work because he overslept.
oversleeps—oversleeping—overslept—has overslept

o·ver·time, *noun, adjective & adverb*
more than the normal hours of work; he gets paid double for working overtime.

o·ver·weight, *adjective*
weighing too much; she has been overweight since childhood.

owe [əʊ] *verb*
(a) to have money which you should pay someone; he owes me $5; how much do I owe you for the gas?

(b) to have something because of what someone has done; I owe him my life = I am alive because he saved my life; he owes a lot to his father = his father has helped him a lot.
owes—owing—owed—has owed

owl [aʊl] *noun*
large bird which hunts for food at night; owls sometimes eat mice.

own [əʊn] 1. *adjective*
belonging to you alone; I have my own car; he has his own store.

2. *noun*
(a) my own/his own, etc. = mine/his; he has a car of his own; she has a house of her own; they have a garden of their own.

(b) on my own/on his own, etc. = alone; I'm on my own today; he did it on his own.

3. *verb*
to have; I don't own a car; who owns this land?
owns—owning—owned—has owned

own·er, *noun*
person who owns; the police are looking for the owner of the car; who's the owner of this house?

own up (to), *verb*
to say that you have done something wrong; she owned up to having stolen the jewels; he owned up to his mistake; the teacher asked who had drawn pictures on the board, but no one would own up.

Pp

pa [pɑ:] *noun*
child's name for father; **my pa owns a farm.**

pack [pæk] 1. *noun*
group of things put together (in a box); **a pack of cards; a pack of gum.**
2. *verb*
(*a*) to put things into a suitcase/to put things in boxes ready for sending; **she has packed her suitcase; have you finished packing yet? I packed my toothbrush at the bottom of the bag; the glasses are packed in boxes to keep them from being broken.**
(*b*) to squeeze a lot of people or things into something; **how can you pack ten people into that little car? the planes are packed with people going on vacation; the shelves were packed with books.**
packs—packing—packed—has packed

pack·age [ˈpækɪdʒ] *noun*
something wrapped up; **the mailman brought this package for you; open the package of cookies; package deal =** offer or agreement in which several things are included in one price.

pack up, *verb*
to put things away (before leaving); **they packed up the picnic things when the rain started; let's pack up and go home.**

pad [pæd] *noun*
(*a*) small cushion; **the players wore shoulder pads.**
(*b*) many sheets of paper glued together; **a pad of paper; a note pad.**

page [peɪdʒ] *noun*
one of the sides of the sheets of paper used in books, newspapers, etc.; **the paper has 32 pages; turn the page; look at the next page; the answer to the** crossword puzzle is on page 23; open the book to page 24.
Note: with numbers, the word "the" is left out: **on the next page; on page 50**

paid [peɪd] *see* **pay**

pail [peɪl] *noun*
large round container with a handle on top, used for carrying liquids; **the cow kicked over a milk pail.**

pain [peɪn] *noun*
(*a*) feeling when you are hurt; **I have pains in my legs after playing tennis; she says she has a pain in her back.**
(*b*) **to take pains =** to be very careful when you are doing something; **he took pains with his homework; they took great pains to be at the meeting on time.**
pain·ful, *adjective*
which hurts; **his foot is so painful he can hardly walk; your eye looks very red—is it painful?**
pain·less, *adjective*
without hurting; **the doctor said the treatment would be painless.**

paint [peɪnt] 1. *noun*
colored liquid which you use to give something a color/to make a picture; **we gave the front door two coats of paint; she got a box of paints for her birthday; I need a 1-gallon can of blue paint; the paint is coming off the ceiling.**
2. *verb*
(*a*) to cover something with paint; **he's painting the outside of the house; we painted the front door red.**
(*b*) to make a picture of something using paint; **he painted a picture of his mother;**

she's painting the old church; the sea is very difficult to paint.

paints—painting—painted—has painted

paint·brush, *noun*
brush used when painting a picture or covering something with paint; **be sure to clean your paintbrush when you are finished with it.**

plural **paintbrushes**

paint·er, *noun*
person who paints; **the painter is coming today to paint the bathroom; Rembrandt was a famous painter.**

paint·ing, *noun*
picture; **do you like this painting of my mother?**

pair [peər] *noun*
(*a*) two things taken together; **she bought a new pair of shoes; these socks are a pair = they go together.**
(*b*) two things joined together to make one; **I'm looking for a clean pair of pajamas; he needs a pair of brown pants; this pair of scissors isn't very sharp.**

pa·ja·mas [pə'dʒɑːməz] *plural noun*
light shirt and pants which you wear in bed; **I must buy another pair of pajamas; he ran into the street in his pajamas.**
Note: **a pair of pajamas** *means one shirt and one pair of pants*

pale [peɪl] *adjective*
light colored; **she turned pale at the sight of blood = her face turned white; he was wearing pale gray pants; this blue is too dark—do you have something paler?**
pale—paler—palest

palm [pɑːm] *noun*
(*a*) soft inside part of your hand; **he held the egg in the palm of his hand; if you look at the lines on your palm you can see what will happen to you in the future.**
(*b*) type of tall tree with a bare trunk and long leaves at the top, found in warm climates; **he climbed up a palm tree.**

pan [pæn] *noun*
metal container which you heat on a stove and use for cooking; **put the**

potatoes into a pan of boiling water; use a larger pan if you're boiling lots of eggs; the handle of the frying pan is hot; *see also* **frying pan, saucepan**

pan·cake, *noun*
thin soft cake made in a frying pan, using a mixture of eggs, flour, milk, etc.; **we usually have pancakes on Sunday morning; who wants another pancake?**

pants [pænts] *plural noun*
clothes which cover your legs and the bottom part of your body; **he tore his pants; he was wearing a blue jacket and brown pants; I've bought two pairs of pants.**
Note: to show one piece of clothing say **a pair of pants**

pa·pa ['pɑːpə] *noun*
child's name for father; **Papa, can we go to the baseball game?**

pa·per ['peɪpər] *noun*
(*a*) thin sheet of material which you write on, and which is used to make books/newspapers, etc.; **she uses pink paper when she writes to her friend; the book was wrapped up in brown paper; can you give me another piece of paper/another sheet of paper? this paper's too thin to write on; I bought a box of paper napkins; he floated a paper boat on the lake.**
(*b*) newspaper; **I read the paper on the train on my way to work; did you see the picture of our school in yesterday's paper? the local paper comes out on Fridays; has the evening paper been delivered yet? Sunday papers are so big that it takes me all day to read them.**
(*c*) long report; **he had to write a paper on Andrew Jackson for his history class.**
Note: no plural for (a); **some paper; a sheet of paper/a piece of paper**

pa·per·back (book), *noun*
book with a paper cover; **does this book come in paperback?**

pa·per·boy, *noun*
boy whose job is to deliver newspapers to houses.

pa·per·clip, *noun*
small metal loop used to hold papers together; **a box of paperclips.**

pa·rade [pə'reɪd] *noun*
event in which bands play while marching down a street; **a Christmas parade.**

par·a·graph ['pærəgræf] *noun*
group of several sentences in a book/letter/newspaper, etc., which starts with a small space at the beginning of the first line; **look at the second paragraph on page 2; start a new paragraph.**

par·al·lel ['pærəlel] *adjective*
(lines) which are side by side and the same distance apart, but which never join; **the rails of a railroad track are parallel; the lines of writing should be parallel to the top of the page.**

par·don ['pɑːrdn] 1. *noun*
action of forgiving; **pardon me** = please let me pass/please forgive me; **pardon?** = what did you say?
2. *verb*
to forgive.
pardons—pardoning— pardoned—has pardoned

par·ents ['peərənts] *plural noun*
father and mother; **my parents live in Miami; she went to live with her parents; did your parents tell you they had sold their house?**
Note: **parent** *is not often used in the singular*

park [pɑːrk] 1. *noun*
(*a*) open public place with grass and trees; **Central Park is in the middle of New York; they plan to visit several National Parks on their vacation; she took her dog for a walk in the park.**
(*b*) field where games are played; **they went to the ball park to watch a game.**
2. *verb*
to leave your car in a place while you are not using it; **you can park your car at the back of the hotel; don't park on the grass; the bus ran into a parked car; no parking** = sign showing that you must not park your car.
parks—parking—parked—has parked

park·ing lot, *noun*
special place where you can leave a car when you are not using it; **he left his car in the parking lot behind the hotel.**

part [pɑːrt] 1. *noun*
(*a*) piece; **parts of the book are good; we live in the southern part of the state; part of the year he works in Canada.**
(*b*) **to play a part** = to do something (in an action); **he played an important part in putting out the fire; to take part** = to be active; to join in; **he took part in the battle; did she take part in the fight?**
(*c*) place where hair divides on your head.
2. *verb*
(*a*) to divide the hair on your head; **she parts her hair in the middle.**
(*b*) to go away from each other; **after spending two weeks together they parted at the train station.**
part·ly, *adverb*
not completely; **the house is partly finished; I'm only partly happy with the way the cake turned out.**

par·tic·u·lar [pər'tɪkjələr] *adjective*
special and different from all others; **I don't like that particular restaurant.**
in par·tic·u·lar = especially; **he's good at languages, in particular Italian and Greek; she likes Shakespeare's plays, "Hamlet" in particular.**
par·tic·u·lar·ly, *adverb*
especially; **he is interested in sports, particularly baseball and football.**

part·ner ['pɑːrtnər] *noun*
person with whom you share something; **do you have a partner for this dance? they are business partners/partners in business.**
part·ner·ship, *noun*
sharing (a business) with someone; **the two friends formed a partnership.**

par·ty ['pɑːrtɪ] *noun*
(*a*) meeting of several people on a special occasion; **we're having a party on Saturday night; can you come to our**

party next Saturday? she had fifteen people at her birthday party.

(b) group of people; there were several parties of Canadians visiting the museum.

(c) group of people who believe in a certain type of politics; he joined a political party; which party does the President belong to?

plural **parties**

pass [pæs] *verb*

(a) to go past; on the way to the bank you pass a church on your left; I passed him on the stairs; when you're passing the post office, can you mail this letter?

(b) to move something towards someone; can you pass me the sugar? he passed the ball to another player; they passed the empty plates to the person at the end of the table.

(c) to be successful in an exam or a course; he passed math, but failed English; she passed her driving test.

(d) to make a law; Congress has passed a law against drugs.

passes—passing—passed—has passed

pass out, *verb*

to faint; when we told her her father was sick, she passed out.

pas·sen·ger ['pæsɪndʒər] *noun*

person who is traveling in a car/bus/ plane, etc., but who is not the driver or member of the crew; the plane is carrying 125 passengers and a crew of 6.

pass·port ['pæspɔːrt] *noun*

official book which shows who you are and allows you to go from one country to another.

past [pæst] 1. *preposition*

(a) after; it's past ten o'clock; it was past dinnertime; the train leaves at twenty past two; it's already half past three; it's five past twelve—we've missed the news on TV.

(b) from one side to the other in front of something; go past the post office and turn left; he walked past me without saying hello; the car drove past at 50 miles an hour.

2. *adjective*

(time) which has passed; she has spent the past hour talking about her vacation.

3. *noun*

(a) time before the present; in the past we always went to Florida for our vacation.

(b) (*also* past tense) form of a verb which shows something which happened before now; "he went" is the past of the verb "to go."

Note: past is used for times between o'clock and half past: 4:05 = five past four; 4:15 = quarter past four; 4:25 = twenty-five past four; 4:30 = half past four. For times after half past, see to

past *is also used with many verbs:* to go past; to drive past; to fly past, *etc.*

paste [peɪst] 1. *noun*

(a) thin glue for sticking paper; put some paste on the back of the picture before you stick it in the book.

(b) soft material, esp. food; we need a can of tomato paste to make the sauce; *see also* **toothpaste**

2. *verb*

to glue; he pasted the pictures into his book; they pasted the picture onto the wall.

pastes—pasting—pasted—has pasted

pas·ture ['pæstʃər] *noun*

field of grass where cows and sheep can feed; the cows were put to pasture.

pat [pæt] 1. *noun*

(a) light tapping; he got a pat on the back = sign of thanks.

(b) small square of butter.

2. *verb*

to tap lightly; the boy patted the dog.

pats—patting—patted— has patted

path [pæθ] *noun*

(a) narrow way for walking; the path goes across the field; follow the path until it comes to the river.

(b) direction in which something moves; the house stood in the path of the freeway = where the freeway was going to be built.

path·way, *noun*
narrow way for walking; **a pathway leads to the campground.**

pa·tient ['peɪʃənt] 1. *adjective*
(person) who can wait a long time without getting bothered; **you have to be patient if you are at the end of a long line.**
2. *noun*
person who is in a hospital, or who is being treated by a doctor; **the patients are all asleep in their beds; the doctor is taking the patient's temperature.**

pa·tient·ly, *adverb*
without getting bothered; **they waited patiently for two hours.**

pat·tern ['pætərn] *noun*
(*a*) something which you copy to make something; **to knit this sweater, you have to follow the pattern.**
(*b*) lines/flowers, etc., repeated again and again on cloth, etc.; **her dress has a pattern of white and red spots; I don't like the pattern on this carpet.**

pave [peɪv] *verb*
to cover a piece of ground with a hard material; **they paved the driveway with concrete.**
paves—paving—paved—has paved

paw [pɔ:] *noun*
foot of an animal like a dog or cat; **the cat stuck a paw into the paint can.**

pay [peɪ] 1. *verb*
(*a*) to give money for something; **I paid $100 for my watch; did he pay for the coffee? how much do you pay for gasoline? I'll pay for both of us** = I will pay for the tickets, etc., for both.
(*b*) to give money to someone for doing something; to give money to someone who sells you something; **please pay the waiter for your meal; I paid him a dollar for washing the car; I'll pay you a dollar to wash the car; they paid him $10 for his old bike.**

(*c*) **to pay a visit** = to visit; **we'll pay my mother a visit when we are in town.**
pays—paying—paid [peɪd]—has paid
Note: you **pay him to wash the car** *before he washes it, but you* **pay him for washing the car** *after he has washed it*
2. *noun*
money you get for doing work; **did you pick up your pay at the office?**
no plural

pay back, *verb*
to give someone money which you owe them; **I lent you the money—when will you pay me back?**

pay·check, *noun*
regular check or cash which you get for working; **I must take my paycheck to the bank.**

pay·day, *noun*
day of the week on which you get paid for working.

pay·ment, *noun*
sum of money which you pay on a debt; **she has to make a car payment this week.**

pay up, *verb*
to pay all the money which you owe; **he paid up quickly when they started to take out their guns.**

pea [pi:] *noun*
green vegetable with little round green seeds which you eat; **with the meat we'll have potatoes and peas; don't eat your peas with your knife!**

peace [pi:s] *noun*
(*a*) not being at war; **after the long war, there were thirty years of peace.**
(*b*) being quiet; **I like the peace of the country better than the noise of the city.**
no plural

peace·ful, *adjective*
quiet; **the park is so peaceful.**

pea·nut ['pi:nʌt] *noun*
type of small nut which you often eat with salt; **he bought a bag of peanuts to eat during the movie; peanut butter** =

paste made from ground peanuts which you can spread on bread.

ped·al ['pedl] *noun*
thing which you push with your foot and which makes a piece of machinery work; **bicycle pedal; he took his feet off the pedals as he was riding down the hill; brake pedal** = pedal which works a brake.

peel [pi:l] **1.** *noun*
skin on a fruit or vegetable; **put the apple peel into the garbage can; I need some orange peel to make this dessert.**
no plural
2. *verb*
to take the peel or skin off a fruit or vegetable; **he was peeling an orange; peel the potatoes before you cook them.**
peels—peeling—peeled—has peeled

pen [pen] *noun*
thing for writing which uses ink; **I've lost my pen—can I borrow yours? if you don't have a pen you can write in pencil.**

pen·cil ['pensəl] *noun*
thing for writing with, made of wood with a lead in the center; **can I borrow your knife?—I want to sharpen my pencil; you must not write your answers in pencil.**

peo·ple ['pi:pəl] *plural noun*
men, women or children; **how many people are there in the room? there were thirty people waiting to see the doctor; so many people tried to see the movie that they had to go on showing it for several months; several people in our office went to California on vacation; here's a photo of the people we met on vacation.**

pep·per ['pepər] *noun*
hot-tasting food used in cooking, made from ground black or white seeds; **pepper makes me sneeze; don't put so much pepper in your soup.**
no plural

per [pər] *preposition*
(*a*) out of; **ten per thousand** = ten out of every thousand; **there are about six bad eggs per hundred.**
(*b*) in each/for each; **the car can't go faster than sixty miles per hour; we eat about 10 loaves of bread per week; tomatoes cost 60¢ per pound; we paid her $3 per hour.**

per·cent, *adverb & noun*
out of each hundred; **fifty percent of the people (50%) voted in the election** = half of them; **seventy-five percent (75%) of the cars are less than two years old** = three quarters of them.
Note: **percent** *is written % when used with figures*

per·fect ['pərfikt] **1.** *adjective*
without any mistakes; exactly right; **he speaks perfect English; she drew a perfect circle; it's a perfect day for a picnic.**
2. *noun* (*also* **perfect tense**)
form of a verb which shows something which happened before now; **"he has gone" is the perfect of "to go."**
per·fect·ly, *adverb*
without any mistakes; completely; **she can speak English perfectly; it was a perfectly wonderful vacation.**

per·form [pər'fɔ:rm] *verb*
(*a*) to sing/dance/act in front of people who are watching; **the students performed Shakespeare's "Hamlet."**
(*b*) to work well; to get good results; **our football team performed very well; the car hasn't been performing very well.**
performs—performing—performed—has performed

per·form·ance, *noun*
showing of a film/a play; **did you enjoy the performance of "Hamlet"?**
per·form·er, *noun*
person who sings/dances/acts in front of people who are watching; **all the performers gathered on stage after the show.**

per·fume ['pərfju:m] *noun*
liquid with a pleasant smell which you

put on your body; **he gave her a bottle of perfume for Christmas.**

per·haps [pər′hæps] *adverb*
possibly; it may be; **perhaps he'll come; they're late—perhaps the snow is very deep; do you think it's going to rain?—perhaps not, I can see some blue sky.**

pe·ri·od [′pɪrɪəd] *noun*
(*a*) length of time; **I can swim under the water for short periods; this happened at a period when food was in short supply.**
(*b*) time for a lesson in school; **we have three periods of math a week; I had to leave during sixth period for a doctor's appointment.**
(*c*) dot (.) at the end of a written sentence.

per·mit 1. *noun* [′pɜrmɪt]
written paper which allows you to do something; **he has a permit to use the library; you must have a permit to park in the college parking lot; the store has a permit to sell alcohol.**
2. *verb* [pər′mɪt]
to allow someone to do something; **smoking is not permitted in the theater; this ticket permits you to park at any time.**
**permits—permitting—
permitted—has permitted**

per·son [′pɜrsən] *noun*
man/woman; **this ticket admits three persons; she's a very interesting person; he was there in person** = he was there himself.
per·son·al, *adjective*
referring to a person/belonging to a person; **he lost all his personal property in the fire.**

pet [pet] *noun*
animal which you keep in your home; **we have a lot of pets—a cat, two dogs and a white mouse.**

phone [fəʊn] 1. *noun*
telephone/machine which you use to speak to someone a long distance away; **the phone is ringing; can you answer the phone for me—I'm in the bathtub; he picked up the phone and called the police.**
on the phone = speaking by telephone; **don't make noise—Daddy is on the phone; there's someone on the phone who wants to speak to you.**
2. *verb*
to call someone by telephone; **your sister phoned yesterday; phone the doctor—the baby is ill; can you phone me tomorrow morning? I want to phone New York.**
phones—phoning—phoned—has phoned

phone back, *verb*
to reply by telephone; **Mr. Smith is out—can you phone back in an hour? she phoned back very late at night.**

phone book, *noun*
book which gives the names of people and businesses in an area in alphabetical order, with their addresses and phone numbers; **this restaurant isn't in the phone book.**

phone booth, *noun*
tall square box with windows, with a public telephone inside; **you can call from the phone booth at the corner of the street; I wanted to use the phone booth, but I didn't have any dimes.**

phone num·ber, *noun*
number which refers to a particular phone; **what's your phone number? my phone number is 405-9935.**

pho·to [′fəʊtəʊ] *noun*
picture taken with a camera; **here's a photo of our house; let me show you our vacation photos.**
pho·tog·ra·pher [fə′tɒgrəfər] *noun*
person who takes pictures.
pho·tog·ra·phy [fə′tɒgrəfiː] *noun*
study of taking pictures; **she's interested in photography.**

phrase [freɪz] *noun*
group of words, not usually containing

a verb; "the big green door" and "along the road" are phrases.

pi·an·o [ˈpjænəʊ] *noun*
musical instrument with black and white keys which you press to make music; **he's learning to play the piano; she plays the piano all day long; she played the song on the piano.**

pick [pɪk] 1. *noun*
(*a*) what you choose; **take your pick** = choose which one you want.
(*b*) sharp tool for breaking up hard material; **ice pick.**
2. *verb*
(*a*) to choose; **the captain picked his team; he was picked to play pitcher.**
(*b*) to take fruit or flowers from plants; **we've picked all the apples; she was picking roses in the garden.**
(*c*) to take away small pieces of something with your fingers/with a tool; **he picked the blades of grass off his coat; she was picking her teeth with a pin** = taking away little bits of food which were stuck between her teeth.
(*d*) **to pick someone's pocket** = to steal something from someone's pocket; **my pocket has been picked!**
(*e*) **to pick a lock** = to open a lock by using a wire or other tool instead of the key.
picks—picking—picked—has picked

pick on, *verb*
to choose someone in order to attack them; **why do you always pick on children who are smaller than you? stop picking on me all the time.**
pick out, *verb*
to choose; **he picked out all the good apples in the box.**
pick up, *verb*
(*a*) to lift something up which is lying on the ground; **she picked up the books which had fallen on the floor; he dropped his money and bent down to pick it up.**
(*b*) to learn something easily without being taught; **I was never taught to**

type—**I just picked it up; she picked up some Chinese when she was living in China.**
(*c*) to give someone a ride in a car; **I'll pick you up at your office; can you come to pick me up at six o'clock?**
(*d*) to meet and make friends with someone by chance; **he picked up a girl in a coffee shop.**
(*e*) to catch; **the police picked him up at the airport.**
(*f*) to get stronger/better; to increase; **he was sick for months, but he's picking up now; the car began to pick up speed; business is picking up.**
Note: **pick your money up** *or* **pick up your money** *but only* **pick it up**

pic·nic [ˈpɪknɪk] 1. *noun*
party with a meal eaten in the open air; **let's go on a picnic on Saturday; we went on a picnic last week and it rained; they stopped the car and had a roadside picnic.**
2. *verb*
to eat while on a picnic; **we were picnicking by the side of the road.**
picnics—picnicking—picnicked—has picnicked

pic·ture [ˈpɪktʃər] *noun*
(*a*) drawing/painting/photo, etc., of something; **he's painting a picture of the church; have you seen the picture she drew of the house? the book has several pictures of wild flowers; he cut out the picture of the President from the newspaper.**
(*b*) **pictures** = movies; **we go to the pictures every Friday evening.**

pie [paɪ] *noun*
cooked food with a shell made of flour, water and fat and a filling inside; **we had apple pie and ice cream; she made a chicken pie for dinner.**

piece [piːs] *noun*
(small) bit of something; **can I have another piece of cake? I want two pieces of paper; the watch came to pieces in my hand** = broke into several bits; **he dropped the plate and it broke into**

tiny pieces; to fix the clock, he had to take it to pieces = to put it into pieces to see what was wrong with it.

Note: piece is often used to show one bit of something which has no plural: furniture: a piece of furniture; wood: a piece of wood; toast: a piece of toast; news: a piece of news; advice: a piece of advice

pig [pɪg] *noun*
fat farm animal which gives meat; the pigs were lying in the mud.
Note: the meat from a pig is called pork, bacon or ham
pig·pen, *noun*
small fenced area in which pigs are kept.

pi·geon [ˈpɪdʒən] *noun*
common gray bird; he was feeding the pigeons in the park.

pile [paɪl] 1. *noun*
lots of things put on top of each other; there were piles of old books on the floor; throw those bricks onto the pile.
piles of = a lot of; we've got piles of work to do.
2. *verb* (*also* to pile up)
to put things on top of each other; he piled (up) the bricks by the side of the house; the books were piled (up) on the table; she was piling boxes on top of each other.
piles—piling—piled—has piled

pill [pɪl] *noun*
small round cake of medicine; the doctor said to take two pills after each meal.

pil·low [ˈpɪloʊ] *noun*
soft cushion on a bed which you put your head on when you lie down.
pil·low·case, *noun*
cover for a pillow; matching sheets and pillowcases.

pi·lot [ˈpaɪlət] *noun*
(*a*) person who flies a plane; don't talk to the pilot when the plane is landing.
(*b*) person who guides boats into or out of a harbor.

pin [pɪn] 1. *noun*
small sharp piece of metal for attaching papers, etc., together; he kept his pants up with a safety pin; fasten the papers together with a pin.
2. *verb*
to attach with a pin; the papers were pinned together; the material is pinned to the pattern; the notices are pinned to the wall of the office.
pins—pinning—pinned—has pinned

pin up, *verb*
to attach something to a wall with a pin; the notice is pinned up outside the entrance; he was pinning the sign up on a tree.
Note: pin the notice up or pin up the notice but only pin it up

pine [paɪn] *noun*
type of tree with leaves like needles, which stays green all year long; they walked through a pine forest; he cut down a small pine to have as a Christmas tree.

pink [pɪŋk] *noun & adjective*
of a color like very pale red; these pink roses smell nice; her hat was a dark pink.

pint [paɪnt] *noun*
measure of liquids (equal to half a quart); please buy a pint of cream for me.

pipe [paɪp] *noun*
(*a*) long round tube for water, gas, etc.; the water pipes are under the street; he made a hole in the gas pipe and the gas started to come out.
(*b*) thing with a small bowl and a tube which you put in your mouth, used for smoking tobacco; he was smoking a pipe; can I have another match—my pipe has gone out; it's difficult to light a pipe when it is windy.

pit [pɪt] *noun*
very deep hole in the ground; he fell into a pit.

pitch [pɪtʃ] *verb*
(*a*) to throw (a ball); he pitched a fast ball.

(*b*) to put up (a tent); **they pitched their tent near the stream.**
(*c*) **to pitch in** = to help with something; to give money along with others.
pitches—pitching—pitched— has pitched

pitch·er, *noun*
(*a*) (*in baseball*) player who throws the ball to the player at bat.
(*b*) large container for pouring liquids; **he brought out a pitcher of lemonade and two glasses.**

pit·y ['pɪtɪ] 1. *noun*
(*showing that you are sorry*) **it's a pity that . . .** = it is sad that . . .; **it's a pity that it rained when we went on the picnic; what a pity that she was sick and couldn't run in the race.**
no plural
2. *verb*
to feel sorry for someone who has had bad luck/who is not well/who has done badly, etc.; **I pity you having to baby-sit while we all go to the movies.**
pities—pitying—pitied— has pitied

pit·i·ful ['pɪtɪfəl] *adjective*
sad; badly done; **it's pitiful to see how sick the child is; the play was pitiful.**

place [pleɪs] 1. *noun*
(*a*) spot; where something is; where something happens or happened; **this is the place where we had the accident; put the books back in the right place; there were papers lying all over the place** = everywhere; **Greenville is a good place to live if you like small towns.**
(*b*) home; **why don't we all go back to my place for a cup of coffee?**
(*c*) seat; **this is Mr. Smith's place; I'm afraid this place is taken; I changed places with Jane** = we each took the other's seat.
(*d*) position (in a race); **the German runners were in the first three places** = they were first, second and third in the race; **he's in first place** = he is winning.
(*e*) page where you have stopped reading a book; **I used a piece of paper to mark my place; I've lost my place**

and can't remember where I left off.
to take place = to happen; **the argument took place in the restaurant; the story takes place in Russia.**
2. *verb*
to put; **he placed his hat carefully on the table; can you place the books in the right order?**
places—placing—placed— has placed

plain [pleɪn] 1. *adjective*
(*a*) easy to see/easy to understand; **it's plain to see that he doesn't know anything about motorcycles; I want to make it plain that we will not pay you any more money.**
(*b*) simple/ordinary; **I like plain country cooking best; a plain black dress.**
plain—plainer—plainest
2. *noun*
large flat area of land; **the wind whistled across the plain.**
plain·ly, *adverb*
clearly; **they could plainly see that he was in trouble.**

plan [plæn] 1. *noun*
(*a*) way of doing things which you arrange before starting; **we've drawn up plan for saving money each week; the burglars made a plan to get into the house by the kitchen window.**
(*b*) drawing of the way something is built/is arranged; **here are the plans for the new school; this is a plan of the office; I can't find our street on the town plan** = on the map of the town.
2. *verb*
to arrange how you are going to build something/to do something; to intend to do something; **she planned her kitchen herself; they've planned a whole new town; we are planning to go on vacation in August; I wasn't planning to stay up late** = I thought I would go to bed early.
plans—planning—planned—has planned

plane [pleɪn] *noun*
(*a*) airplane/machine which flies; **when does this plane leave for Copenhagen? the plane to Boston is full—you will**

have to wait for the next one; there are six planes a day to New York.
(b) tool for making wood smooth.

plan·et ['plænət] *noun*
large ball which moves around the sun; the earth is one of the nine planets.

plant [plænt] 1. *noun*
living thing which grows in the ground and has leaves and flowers; **a tomato plant; these plants are growing very tall; house plants** = plants which you grow in pots in the house.
2. *verb*
to put a plant in the ground; **I've planted an apple tree in the yard.**
plants—planting—planted—has planted

plant·er, *noun*
(a) person who plants; **a tobacco planter.**
(b) special container for growing plants.

plas·ter ['plæstər] *noun*
white dust which is mixed with water and used to make inside walls/to cover broken legs, etc.; **the ceiling is made of plaster.**
no plural: **some plaster**

plas·tic ['plæstɪk] *adjective & noun*
hard material made from oil, and used to make many objects; **take the plastic plates on the picnic; I need a plastic bag to put my sandwiches in; don't put that plate in the oven—it's made of plastic; these seats in the car are made of plastic and get very hot in the summer.**
no plural: **it's made of plastic**

plate [pleɪt] *noun*
(a) flat round thing for putting your food on; **put the sausages on a plate; pass your empty plates to the person at the end of the table.**
(b) food which is on a plate; **she held out a plate of cookies; he ate two plates of salad.**
(c) flat sheet of metal/glass, etc.; **a plate glass window** = a very large window, such as in a store; **license plate** = plate on the front and back of a car which shows its number.

plat·form ['plætfɔːrm] *noun*
(a) high flat surface by the side of the railroad tracks at a station, so that passengers can get on or off the trains easily, **there were crowds waiting on the platform; the train to Pittsburgh will leave from platform 6; the Boston train is leaving from the next platform; I was in such a hurry that I left my suitcase on the platform.**
(b) high place in a hall for speakers to stand on; **the speaker went up onto the platform; someone in the crowd threw a tomato at the speaker on the platform.**

play [pleɪ] 1. *noun*
(a) something written, which is acted in a theater/ on TV; **did you watch the play last night? we're going to see a new play at the National Theater; we have to read two of Shakespeare's plays for our English class.**
(b) way of amusing yourself; taking part in a game; **play will start at 3 o'clock** = the game will start; **the ball went out of play** = went off the field; **it's child's play** = it is very easy.
2. *verb*
(a) to amuse yourself; **he was playing with his sister; the children were playing in the yard; let's play hospital** = let's act as if we are to be doctors and nurses.
(b) to take part in a game; **he plays football for the school team; can you play baseball? I don't play tennis in the winter.**
(c) to make music on a musical instrument or to put on a record; **don't talk while he's playing the guitar; I can't play the piano very well; let me play you my new record.**
(d) to act as a person in a film/play; **he played Harry Lime in "The Third Man."**
plays—playing—played—has played

play·er, *noun*
person who plays; **you need eleven players for a football team; tennis players have to be in good condition; three of our players are sick.**
play·ful, *adjective*
liking play; **a playful dog.**

play·ground, *noun*
place (usually around a school) where children can play; if it's raining you can't go into the playground during the break; they were playing quietly in the playground.

play·house, *noun*
(*a*) theater; what's on at the playhouse this weekend?
(*b*) small house for children to play in; they built a playhouse near the garage.

play·ing cards, *noun*
set of pieces of stiff paper with pictures or patterns on them, used for playing various games; *see also* **card.**

play·ing field, *noun*
large field where sports can be played; the football team ran out onto the playing field.

pleas·ant ['plezənt] *adjective*
which makes you happy/which you like; what a pleasant surprise; the weather is very pleasant.
**pleasant—pleasanter—
pleasantest**

pleas·ant·ly, *adverb*
in a pleasant way; he answered me pleasantly.

please [pliːz] *interjection*
used to make an order polite; shut the door, please; please come in; can I have another cup of coffee, please? do you want some more cake?—yes, please.
pleased, *adjective*
happy; I'm very pleased with my new car; she isn't pleased with her test scores; he wasn't pleased when we broke his bedroom window; I'd be pleased to help you if I can; was she pleased to get your letter?
pleas·ing, *adjective*
which makes you happy; a pleasing performance.
pleas·ure ['pleʒər] *noun*
pleasant feeling; working in the garden is my greatest pleasure; I'll do the job with pleasure = I will be very glad to do it; it gives me great pleasure to be here today.

plen·ty ['plentɪ] *noun*
large amount/lots; you have plenty of time; we have plenty of food left after the party; plenty of people were waiting for the bus; do you have enough milk?—yes, we've got plenty.
no plural

plow [plaʊ] 1. *noun*
farm machine for turning over the soil.
2. *verb*
to turn over the soil with a plow; the farmer was plowing the field.
**plows—plowing—plowed—has
plowed**

plug [plʌg] 1. *noun*
(*a*) electric object on the end of a wire, with pins which go into holes to allow the electricity to go into a machine; the refrigerator has stopped working—I think that a wire has broken in the plug.
(*b*) rubber object used to keep water from running out of a bathtub, etc.
2. *verb* (*usually* to plug in)
(*a*) to attach an electric machine to the electricity supply with a plug; have you plugged the radio in? the light won't work—it isn't plugged in!
(*b*) to plug up = to block; the pipe is plugged up with dirt.
**plugs—plugging—plugged—has
plugged**

plu·ral ['plʊrəl] *adjective & noun*
form of a word showing there is more than one; "children" is the plural of "child"; "is" is the third person singular of the verb "to be" and "are" is the plural; "they" is a plural pronoun.

plus [plʌs] *preposition*
in addition to; three plus five equals eight; he bought six shirts and three ties, plus a pair of shoes.

P.M., p.m. ['piː'em] *adverb*
after 12 o'clock noon; the meeting will start at 2 P.M.; she's catching the 7 p.m. train to Pittsburgh.
Note: **P.M.** *is used to show the exact hour and the word* **o'clock** *is left out*

pock·et ['pɒkɪt] *noun*
small bag attached to the inside of a

coat, etc., which you can keep your wallet/your keys, etc., in; **I've looked in my coat pockets but I can't find my keys; there's a hole in my pocket, and all my money fell out; he was walking along with his hands in his pockets; put your hands in your pockets if you want to keep them warm.**

pock·et·book, *noun*
woman's small bag for carrying money, keys, etc.

pock·et cal·cu·la·tor = small calculator which you can put in your pocket.

pock·et mon·ey = small amount of money which you can spend as you please; **I don't have any pocket money this week; I spent all my pocket money on magazines.**

po·em ['pəʊəm] *noun*
piece of writing, especially with lines of the same length which rhyme; **do you like this poem about autumn? he spends all his time writing poems.**

po·et, *noun*
person who writes poems; **Byron and Keats are famous English poets.**

po·et·ry, *noun*
type of writing done by a poet; **we have to study American poetry of the nineteenth century; he was reading a poetry book.**
no plural

point [pɔɪnt] **1.** *noun*
(*a*) sharp end; **he broke the point of his pencil; this needle hasn't got a very sharp point.**
(*b*) dot used to show the division between whole numbers and parts of numbers; **3.256** *say* "three point two five six."
(*c*) particular time/place; **we walked for miles and came back to the point where we'd started from; the lights went off at that point** = at that moment.
(*d*) meaning/reason; **there's no point in trying to call him—he has gone away; the point of the meeting is to discuss how we can save money; I see your point** = I see what you mean.

(*e*) score in a game; **he scored three points; that shot gives you ten points.**
(*f*) mark in a group of numbers; **what's the freezing point of water?**
2. *verb*
to aim (a gun/your finger) at; to show with your finger; **the policeman is pointing at you; he pointed his gun at the door; don't point at people—it's rude.**
points—pointing—pointed—has pointed

point·ed, *adjective*
with a sharp point; **a pointed stick.**

point out, *verb*
to show; **he pointed out all the mistakes in my homework.**
Note: **he pointed the mistakes out** *or* **he pointed out the mistakes** *but only* **he pointed them out**

poi·son ['pɔɪzən] *noun*
something which can kill you if you eat or drink it; **I think someone has put poison in my soup; try putting some poison on the floor if you want to kill the mice.**

poi·son·ous, *adjective*
full of poison; **don't eat those seeds—they're poisonous; I wish I knew which mushrooms are good to eat and which are poisonous.**

pole [pəʊl] *noun*
(*a*) long wooden or metal stick; **the flag is attached to a tall pole; the tent is held up by two poles; the car ran into a telephone pole.**
(*b*) one of the two points at the ends of the earth; **who was the first man to get to the North Pole?**

po·lar, *adjective*
referring to the North or South Pole; **a polar bear.**

po·lice [pə'liːs] *noun* (*usually plural*)
group of people (in uniform) who control traffic, who try to stop crimes and who try to catch criminals; **the police are looking for three armed men; if someone steals your car, you must tell the police; call the police—someone's taken all my money! he was run over by a police car.**

po·lice·man, po·lice·wom·an, *noun*
member of the police; **three policemen were hiding behind the wall; if you don't know how to find the post office—ask a policeman.**
plural **policemen, policewomen**

po·lice sta·tion, *noun*
building with the offices of the police in it; **they arrested two men and took them to the police station.**

po·lite [pə'laɪt] *adjective*
not rude; behaving in a pleasant way; with good manners; **you should always be polite to your teacher; it wasn't very polite to leave without saying thank you; it is polite to say "please" when you are asking for something; he's a very polite little boy.**
po·lite·ly, *adverb*
in a polite way; **if you ask her politely she will give you some cake.**

po·lit·i·cal [pə'lɪtɪkəl] *adjective*
referring to a certain way of running a country; **political party** = group of people who believe the country should be run in one particular way.
pol·i·ti·cian [pɒlɪ'tɪʃən] *noun*
person who is an active member of a political party, especially an elected official.
pol·i·tics, *noun*
study of how a country should be governed; **he is going into politics** = he is going to be an active member of a political party.

pool [puːl] *noun*
(*a*) small amount of liquid not contained in anything; **there was a pool of blood on the floor.**
(*b*) (**swimming**) **pool** = special pool of water built for swimming in; **the competition will be held in the outdoor pool; our school has an indoor pool; come out—you've been in the pool long enough; we have a heated swimming pool in our yard.**
(*c*) game in which you hit balls with a long stick on a special table.

poor [pʊr] *adjective*
(*a*) (person) who has little or no money; **they are very poor, now that their father is out of work; poor people can get extra money from the government; it is one of the poorest countries in the world.**
(*b*) not very good; **this soil is poor—it's not good for growing fruit trees; their football team is very poor this year—they haven't won a single game; these bananas are very poor quality; he's in poor health.**
(*c*) (*showing you are sorry*) **poor John—he's got to stay in bed while we're going on a picnic; my poor feet—I've been walking all day!**
poor—poorer—poorest

pop [pɒp] *noun*
soft drink; **a bottle/a can of pop.**
no plural: **some pop; a can of pop**

pop·corn ['pɒpkɔːrn] *noun*
corn which has been heated till it bursts; **we ate popcorn at the movies.**
no plural: **some popcorn; a box of popcorn**

pop·u·lar ['pɒpjələr] *adjective*
which is liked by a lot of people; **Cape Cod is a popular place for summer vacation; this movie has been very popular; cold milk is a popular drink with children.**

pop·u·la·tion [pɒpjə'leɪʃən] *noun*
number of people who live in one place; **the population is increasing by 2% each year; what is the population of Denmark?**

porch [pɔːrtʃ] *noun*
covered platform just outside a door; **we sat on the front porch all afternoon.**
plural **porches**

pork [pɔːrk] *noun*
meat from a pig; **we're having roast pork for dinner; would you like some more pork? can I have another pork chop, please? pork sausages** = sausages made from pork.
no plural: **some pork; a piece of pork/a slice of pork**

po·si·tion [pəˈzɪʃən] *noun*
(*a*) place (where something is); the way something is held/the way something stands/lies, etc.; it was a difficult job putting the piano into position; she found herself in a very difficult position; he was in third position in the race; you need to have the brush in the right position to paint well.
(*b*) job; she's applying for a teaching position.

pos·i·tive [ˈpɒzətɪv] *adjective*
(*a*) meaning yes; a positive answer.
(*b*) certain; I'm positive that he was born in 1923.

pos·si·ble [ˈpɒsɪbəl] *adjective*
which can happen/which is likely to happen; that field is a possible place for a house; it's possible that the train will be late because of the fog.
as pos·si·ble (*used to make a superlative*) go as far away as possible; I would like it done as quickly as possible; give me as much time as possible; this is the cheapest possible way of going to Europe.
pos·si·bil·i·ty [pɒsɪˈbɪləti:] *noun*
chance/being likely to happen; is there any possibility that the plane will be late?
pos·si·bly, *adverb*
(*a*) perhaps; it is possibly the worst weather we have ever had.
(*b*) (*used to make a word stronger*) you can't possibly eat all those sausages!

post [pəʊst] 1. *noun*
(*a*) large wooden pole put in the ground; the gate is attached to a gate post; he kicked the ball but it bounced off the post.
(*b*) job; she has applied for a post in the library.
2. *verb*
to send a letter, etc., by mail; the letter was posted ten days ago.
posts—posting—posted—has posted

post·age [ˈpəʊstɪdʒ] *noun*
money which you pay to send something by mail; what is the postage for a letter to Australia?
no plural

post·card, *noun*
piece of card (often with a picture on one side) which you send to someone with a message on it; send me a postcard when you get to Italy; she sent me a postcard of the hotel where she was staying.

post·man, *noun*
person who delivers letters to houses; has the postman come yet?
plural **postmen**

post of·fice, *noun*
building where you can buy stamps/send letters and packages/where letters and packages are picked up, etc.; can you take this package to the post office for me? the post office is closed on Saturday afternoons.

pot [pɒt] *noun*
container made of china/metal, etc.; plant the flowers in a bigger pot; she made the tea in the pot; I've just made a pot of coffee.

po·ta·to [pəˈteɪtəʊ] *noun*
common vegetable which grows under the ground; boiled potatoes; do you want any more potatoes?
plural **potatoes**

po·ta·to chip, *noun*
thin slice of fried potato which is eaten cold; a bag of potato chips; they serve potato chips with the sandwiches at this restaurant.

pound [paʊnd] *noun*
measure of weight equal to 16 ounces; I want a pound of onions and three pounds of potatoes; the baby only weighed four pounds when he was born; how much is sugar?—it's 40¢ a pound.
Note: with numbers **pound** *is usually written* **lb.; it weighs 26 lbs.; take 6 lbs. of sugar**

pour [pɔːr] *verb*
(*a*) to make liquid go from a container; she poured the tea into my cup; pour the dirty water down the sink; he poured out

two glasses of water; can you pour me another cup of coffee?

(b) (*of liquid, etc.*) to come out fast/to come onto something fast; **smoke poured out the window; oil was pouring out of the hole in the pipe; it was pouring** = it was raining hard.

pours—pouring—poured—has poured

pow·er ['pauər] *noun*

(a) force which drives something; **the engine runs on electric power; the wheel is turned by water power; power cut** = break in the supply of electricity.

(b) control; **the party has a lot of power in the city council; the general came to power in 1962** = became the president.

pow·er·ful, *adjective*

very strong; **the motor isn't powerful enough to drive the car up steep hills.**

prac·ti·cal ['præktɪkəl] *adjective*

which works in practice; **she gave me some practical advice; he's a practical man** = he's reasonable/he's good at getting things done.

prac·ti·cal·ly, *adverb*

almost; **I've practically finished my homework.**

prac·tice ['præktɪs] 1. *noun*

(a) actual working; **it's a good idea, but will it work in practice?**

(b) exercises; **he has football practice every day; with practice, you should be able to play tennis quite well.**

2. *verb*

to do exercises; to do something over and over again to become good at it; **he practices the piano every day; she's practicing her Spanish; if you don't practice you'll never play tennis well.**

practices—practicing—practiced—has practiced

pray [preɪ] *verb*

to speak to God/to ask God for something; to hope very much that something will happen; **they are praying for fine weather; we prayed for his sister** = we asked God to save her.

prays—praying—prayed—has prayed

prayer [preər] *noun*

words spoken to God; **he said his prayers before he went to bed.**

prefer [prɪ'fɜr] *verb*

to like something/to like to do something better than something else; **I don't want to sit on the porch—I prefer watching TV inside; which do you prefer —chocolate or orange ice cream? I prefer American cars to foreign ones; we prefer to go on vacation in June because the weather is better; I don't want to go to the movies—I'd prefer to stay at home.**

prefers—preferring—preferred— has preferred

pre·fix ['pri:fɪks] *noun*

word which goes in front of another word and is joined to it; **in the word "impossible," "im-" is a prefix which means "not."**

pre·pare [prɪ'peər] *verb*

to get ready; to get something ready; **they are preparing to go on vacation next week; she was preparing the dinner when the salesman called.**

prepares—preparing— prepared—has prepared

pre·pared, *adjective*

ready; **are you prepared to leave immediately? they weren't prepared for the letter from the bank** = they were surprised to get it.

prep·o·si·tion [prepə'zɪʃən] *noun*

word which is used with a noun or pronoun to show how it is connected to another word; **prepositions are words such as "near," "next to," "through," in the sentences "his house is near the Post Office," "she sat down next to me," "he drove through the town."**

pres·ent 1. *noun* ['prezənt]

(a) thing which you give to someone; **he gave me a watch as a present; do you give your children big presents at Christmas? how many birthday presents did** you get? all the Christmas presents are under the tree.

(b) the time we are in now; **at present** = now.

(c) form of a verb which shows the time we are in now; **the present of "to give" is "he gives" or "he is giving."**

2. adjective ['prezənt]

(a) being at the time we are in now; **what is your present address? the present situation; present tense** = form of a verb which shows the time we are in now; **the present tense of "to sit" is "he sits" or "he is sitting."**

(b) being there when something happened; **were you present when the old man died? Mr. Smith?—present** = I'm here.

3. verb [prɪ'zent]

(a) to give; **when he retired, the company presented him with a watch.**

(b) to introduce a show (on TV, etc.); **he's presenting a program on wild animals.**

presents—presenting—presented—has presented

pres·i·dent ['prezɪdənt] noun
head of a country/a club, etc.; **the President of the United States; we've elected him president for the next year.**
Note: can be used with names: **President Kennedy, etc.**

presidential, adjective
referring to a president; **a presidential election.**

press [pres] 1. noun

(a) **printing press** = machine which prints letters on paper.

(b) newspapers and magazines; **the British press reported a plane crash in Africa; the press has not mentioned the problem; I read about it in the press.**
no plural

2. verb

(a) to push/ to squeeze; **press the button if you want a cup of coffee; they all pressed around him; I'm pressed for time** = I'm in a hurry.

(b) to iron; **your pants need pressing.**

presses—pressing—pressed—has pressed

pres·sure ['preʃər] noun
action of squeezing/of forcing; force of something which is pushing down, etc.; **there is not enough air pressure in your tires; to put pressure on someone to do something** = to try to force someone to do something; **he is under a lot of pressure** = he is having many difficulties now; **blood pressure** = force of the blood as it is being pumped around the body.

pret·ty ['prɪtɪ] adjective
pleasant to look at; **he has two pretty daughters; she is prettier than her sister; what a pretty little garden! it was a pretty good movie** = a fairly good movie.

pretty—prettier—prettiest
Note: used of things or girls, but never of men

pre·vent [prɪ'vent] verb
to keep something from happening; **the fog prevented the planes from taking off; something must have prevented her from coming; cars have red lights to try to prevent accidents.**

prevents—preventing—prevented—has prevented

price [praɪs] 1. noun
amount of money which you have to pay to buy something; **the price of meat is going up; we can't pay such a high price; don't go to that butcher's—his prices are too high; that TV is very cheap—at that price you could buy two.**

2. verb
to give something a price; **the table is priced at $25; it won't sell—it is too highly priced.**

prices—pricing—priced—has priced

pri·ma·ry ['praɪmərɪ] adjective

(a) basic; most important; **the primary colors** = simple colors like red, blue and yellow which can be mixed to make all the other colors.

(b) referring to the first years of school; **primary education** = education for small children; **primary school** = the first three grades of school, for children between five and eight years old.

prin·ci·pal ['prɪnsɪpəl] *noun*
head of a school; he was sent to the principal's office for misbehaving.

print [prɪnt] 1. *noun*
(*a*) letters marked on a page; the print in that book is so small that I can't read it.
(*b*) photo; can you develop this film and make black and white prints of it?
2. *verb*
(*a*) to mark letters on paper with a machine; the book was printed in the U.S.A.; this newspaper is printed on pink paper.
(*b*) to write using only capital letters; please print your name and address.
prints—printing—printed—has printed

print·ing, *noun*
way of writing in which the letters are not joined; his printing is very neat.

pris·on ['prɪzən] *noun*
place where people are kept when they have been found guilty of a crime; he was sent to prison for four years; his mother is in prison; they escaped from prison.
Note: often used without the

pris·on·er, *noun*
person who is in prison; the prisoners tried to escape by climbing over the wall.

pri·vate ['praɪvɪt] *adjective*
personal/belonging to one person, not to the public; this is a private park; he won't talk about his private life = about what he does at home, away from the office, etc.; we were having a private talk = we were talking together without anyone else listening.

prize [praɪz] *noun*
something given to someone who wins; the person with the highest marks gets a prize of $10; there are several good prizes in the contest; a prize pig = pig which has won prizes in shows.

prob·a·ble ['prɒbəbəl] *adjective*
likely; it's probable that the ship sank in a storm; this horse is a probable winner.
prob·a·bly, *adverb*
likely to happen; they're probably going to be late because of the snow; he has probably forgotten about the meeting; we'll probably see you next week.

prob·lem ['prɒbləm] *noun*
something which is difficult to find an answer to; I couldn't do the problems in the math exam; the government is trying to deal with the problem of crime/with the crime problem.

pro·duce [prə'djuːs] *verb*
to make; the company is producing a new kind of toothpaste; he hit the piano hard, but only produced a little noise; if you bring the two electric wires together you'll produce a flash; the country doesn't produce enough oil; we produce so many vegetables that we sell them to our neighbors.
produces—producing—produced—has produced

prod·uct ['prɒdəkt] *noun*
thing which is produced; we sell electrical products; coal is an important product in the northern parts of the country.
pro·duc·tion [prə'dʌkʃən] *noun*
making of something; production of cars was held up by the strike; we are trying to increase production.
no plural

pro·gram ['prəʊgræm] *noun*
(*a*) show on TV or radio; we watched a program on wild animals of the desert; did you see that funny program last night? there's a sports program after the news.
(*b*) paper in a theater or at a sports event, etc., which gives information about the play or game and the names of the people acting or playing in it; can I look at your program? the program costs 50¢.

prom·ise ['prɒmɪs] 1. *noun*
saying that you will certainly do some-

thing; he gave his promise that he would work harder; she broke her promise that she would pay us the money = she did not pay although she said she would.

2. *verb*

to say that you will certainly do something; he promised to send us a postcard when he arrived; promise me you'll go to bed early; she promised she would pay back the money.

promises—promising— promised—has promised

prom·is·ing, *adjective*

(person) who seems likely to be successful; he's a promising student.

pro·noun ['prəʊnaʊn] *noun*

word used instead of a noun; "I," "you," "they," etc., are pronouns; "he," "it" and "me" are pronouns in the sentence "he gave it to me."

pro·nounce [prə'naʊns] *verb*

to say a word; he didn't pronounce the name very clearly; how do you pronounce the word "l-a-u-g-h"?

pronounces—pronouncing— pronounced—has pronounced

pro·nun·ci·a·tion [prənʌnsɪ'eɪʃn] *noun*

way of speaking (a word); the pronunciation is given for the words in this dictionary; what's the correct pronunciation of "t-h-r-o-u-g-h"?

proof [pru:f] *noun*

something which shows that something is true; the police have proof that he was not at home when the old woman was murdered; you say he stole your bicycle— but do you have any proof of it?

prop·er ['prɒpər] *adjective*

right/correct; what is the proper way to hold a baseball bat? the envelope did not have the proper address.

prop·er·ly, *adverb*

rightly/correctly; they didn't put the wheel on the car properly; the envelope wasn't properly addressed.

prop·er·ty ['prɒpərtɪ] *noun*

(*a*) thing which belongs to someone; that piano is my property.

(*b*) buildings and land; he has a lot of property in northern Montana; not much private property was destroyed in the war.

pro·tect [prə'tekt] *verb*

to stop something which might harm; the house is protected from the wind by a row of tall trees; they were protected from the cold by their thick coats; the harbor is protected by a high wall; the white coat will protect your clothes in the factory; the police were protecting the President against attack.

protects—protecting— protected—has protected

pro·tec·tion, *noun*

thing which protects; that thin coat is no protection against the rain; the President has police protection = is protected by the police.

proud [praʊd] *adjective*

feeling pleased because of something you have done/because of something which belongs to you; she was proud of her grades; hitting an old lady is nothing to be proud of; he's very proud of his cooking; she's proud of her children; I'm proud to be here today.

proud—prouder—proudest

proud·ly, *adverb*

in a proud way; he proudly showed us his new car.

prove [pru:v] *verb*

(*a*) to show that something is true/correct; the police think he's a burglar, but they can't prove it; can you prove that you were at home on the day the old woman was murdered?

(*b*) to happen; the weather proved to be even worse than they had expected; the film proved to be very bad.

proves—proving—proved—has proved

pro·vide [prə'vaɪd] *verb*

to supply; the hotel will provide us with sandwiches; they'll bring the food, but we'll have to provide the drinks.

provides—providing—provided— has provided

pro·vid·ed that, *conjunction*
on condition that; **I will come provided that the weather is warm; he said he would make a speech provided that someone told him what to say.**

prov·ince [ˈprɒvəns] *noun*
part of a country; **Alberta is one of the provinces of Canada.**

pub·lic [ˈpʌblɪk] *adjective*
used by people in general; not private; **go to the public library to see if there is a book on sailing; the last Thursday in November is a public holiday.**

pull [pʊl] *verb*
to move something towards you; to move something which is coming behind you; **you have to pull that door to open it, not push; the plow is pulled by a tractor; he pulled a piece of paper out of his pocket; I don't like people who pull my hair.**
to pull some·one's leg = to make them believe something which is wrong as a joke; **don't believe what he says—he's pulling your leg.**
pulls—pulling—pulled—has pulled

pull in(to), *verb*
to arrive; **the train pulled into the station; we pulled into the parking lot and stopped.**
pull off, *verb*
to make a success of something; **the burglars pulled off a big crime; you'll have to get 80 percent on this exam in order to pass the course—do you think you can pull it off?**
pull out, *verb*
to drive a car away from the side of the road.
pull o·ver (to) *verb*
to drive close to the side the road and stop; **he pulled over to the side of the road when he saw the ambulance coming.**
pull·o·ver, *noun*
sweater which you pull over your head to put it on; **I like your new pullover.**
pull to·geth·er, *verb*
to pull yourself together = to become

calmer; **although he was very angry he soon pulled himself together.**
pull up, *verb*
(*a*) to bring something closer; **pull your chair up to the table.**
(*b*) to stop (in a car, etc.); **a car pulled up and the driver asked us the way to the zoo.**

pump [pʌmp] **1.** *noun*
machine which forces liquids or air into or out of something; **gasoline pump** = machine (at a gas station) which provides gasoline.
2. *verb*
to force liquid or air with a pump; **he was pumping up his tires; I can't pump any more air into this balloon; they tried to pump the water out of the boat.**
pumps—pumping—pumped—has pumped

punch [pʌntʃ] **1.** *noun*
hit with the hand closed; **he got a punch in the nose.**
plural **punches**
2. *verb*
to hit with the hand closed; **someone punched him in the stomach.**
punches—punching—punched—has punched

pun·ish [ˈpʌnɪʃ] *verb*
to make someone feel pain because he has done something wrong; **you will be punished for talking in class; I'll punish him by taking away his chocolate.**
punishes—punishing—punished—has punished
pun·ish·ment, *noun*
action of punishing; **as a punishment, you can't watch TV for three days.**

pup [pʌp], **pup·py** [ˈpʌpɪ] *noun*
young dog; **her parents gave her a puppy for Christmas.**
plural **puppies**

pu·pil [ˈpjuːpəl] *noun*
child at school; **how many pupils are there in your school?**

pure ['pjʊr] *adjective*

very clean; not mixed with other things; this gold is 100% pure; this sweater is made of pure wool; is the water pure?

pure—purer—purest

pure·ly, *adverb*

only; he was reading the book purely for pleasure.

pur·pose ['pɜrpəs] *noun*

aim/plan; what's the purpose of going by plane when it's much cheaper by car? I think he set fire to the house on purpose = because he planned to do it.

pur·pose·ly, *adverb*

on purpose; she purposely stayed at home instead of coming to work.

purse [pɜrs] *noun*

small bag for carrying money; she dropped her purse on the floor of the bus; I put my ticket in my purse so that I wouldn't forget it.

push [pʊʃ] *verb*

(*a*) to make something move away from you; to make something which is in front of you move; they had to push their car to get it to start; we can't lift the piano, we'll have to push it into the corner; I had to push my bike home because I had a flat tire; did he fall into the river, or was he pushed?
(*b*) to press with your finger; push button A to make the machine start; (*in an elevator*) which floor number do you want me to push? = which button.

pushes—pushing—pushed—has pushed

put [pʊt] *verb*

(*a*) to place; put your books down on the table; he put the milk in the refrigerator; do you want me to put another record on? can you help me put up the curtains?
(*b*) to say (in words); if you put it like that, it sounds very pleasant; I want to put a question to the speaker.

puts—putting—put—has put

put a·way, *verb*

to clear things away; put your toys away before you go to bed.

put back, *verb*

to put something where it was before; put that book back on the shelf; shall I put the milk back in the refrigerator?

put off, *verb*

to arrange for something to take place later; the meeting has been put off until next week.

Note: **we put the meeting off** *or* **we put off the meeting** *but only* **we put it off**

put on, *verb*

(*a*) to dress yourself with a piece of clothing; put your coat on; put on your coat if you're going out.
(*b*) to switch on; put the light on, it's getting dark.

Note: **put your coat on** *or* **put on your coat** *but only* **put it on**

put out, *verb*

to stop (a fire); the fire spread so quickly that they could not put it out.

Note: **put the fire out** *or* **put out the fire** *but only* **put it out**

put up, *verb*

(*a*) to attach to; she put up the curtains = she hung them in place over the window.
(*b*) to build; they put up a new gas station on the corner.
(*c*) to give someone a place to sleep in your house; can you put me up for the night?

put up with, *verb*

to accept someone/something even though he or it is not pleasant; if you live near an airport you have to put up with a lot of noise; how can you put up with all those children?

puz·zle ['pʌzəl] *noun*

problem; game where you have to find the answer to a problem; it's a puzzle to me why he doesn't sell his house; she finished the crossword puzzle.

Qq

qual·i·ty [ˈkwɒlɪtɪ] *noun*

(*a*) how good something is; **the cloth is of very high quality; those tomatoes are of poor quality.**

(*b*) particular way of behaving; **he has many good qualities.**

plural **qualities**

quart [ˈkwɔːrt] *noun*

liquid measure equal to two pints; **would you pick up a quart of milk at the store?**

quar·ter [ˈkwɔːrtər] *noun*

(*a*) one of four parts which make a whole/ a fourth; **cut the apple into quarters; the bottle is only a quarter full; a quarter of the club members were absent; I want a quarter of a pound of coffee.**

(*b*) 25-cent coin; **I would like to change these four quarters for a dollar bill; you must put a quarter in the machine to get a cup of coffee.**

(*c*) **a quarter of an hour** = 15 minutes; **it's (a) quarter to four** = it's 3:45; **at (a) quarter past seven** = at 7:15.

Note: **a quarter and three quarters are often written ¼ and ¾**

quar·ter·back, *noun*

important player in football.

queen [kwiːn] *noun*

wife of a king; woman who rules a country; **the Queen of England lives in Buckingham Palace; Queen Victoria was queen for many years.**

Note: **queen** *is spelt with a capital when used with a name or when referring to a particular person*

ques·tion [ˈkwestʃən] *noun*

(*a*) sentence which needs an answer; **he asked the teacher a question; the teacher couldn't answer all our questions; I didn't answer two of the questions on the exam.**

(*b*) problem or matter; **the question is— do we want to spend a lot of money on a new car? it is out of the question** = it is impossible.

ques·tion mark, *noun*

sign (?) used in writing to show that a question is being asked.

quick [kwɪk] *adjective*

fast; **which is the quickest way to get to the post office? I had a quick lunch and then got back to work; she is much quicker at arithmetic than her sister; if you went by air it would be quicker than taking the train.**

quick—quicker—quickest

quick·ly, *adverb*

without taking much time; **he finished his dinner very quickly because he wanted to watch a TV program; the firemen quickly put the fire out.**

qui·et [ˈkwaɪət] *adjective*

with no noise/no excitement; **the children are very quiet—they must be doing something naughty; please keep quiet— I'm trying to work; we had a quiet weekend working in the garden; it's a quiet little town.**

quiet—quieter—quietest

qui·et·ly, *adverb*

without making any noise; **the burglar went quietly upstairs; he shut the door quietly.**

quit [kwɪt] *verb*

to leave your job; to stop doing something; **she quit her job; he told the boss he was quitting; he quit working for the day; quit blowing that horn!**

quits—quitting—quit—has quit

quite [kwaɪt] *adverb*

(*a*) more or less; **it's quite a good film;**

she's quite a fast typist; the book is quite interesting, but I liked the TV program better.

(*b*) completely; you're quite right; I couldn't quite understand what he meant; have you finished?—not quite.

quite a few = several/many; quite a

few people were sick.

quite a bit = much; it took quite a bit of time for her to finish the test.

Note the order of words: **he's quite a good student** *but* **he's a fairly good student**

Rr

rab·bit [ˈræbɪt] *noun*
common wild animal with brown fur, long ears and a short white tail, also kept as a pet; **the rabbit went down its hole.**

race [reɪs] **1.** *noun*
(*a*) competition to see which person/ horse/car, etc., is the fastest; **he won the mile race; we watched a bicycle race; I like watching horse races on TV.**
(*b*) group of people with similar bodies; **the white races.**
2. *verb*
to run/ride, etc., to see who is the fastest; **let's race to see who gets to school first; I'll race you to the candy store.**
races—racing—raced—has raced

race·track, *noun*
track where horse or car races are held; **he likes to go to the racetrack on weekends.**

ra·di·o [ˈreɪdɪəʊ] *noun*
way of sending out and receiving messages using waves that travel through the air; machine which does this; **he got the message by radio; did you hear the program on the radio about Germany? turn on the radio—it's time for the news; I was listening to the news on the car radio.**

rag [ræg] *noun*
piece of old, torn cloth; **dressed in rags** = wearing old, torn clothes.

rail [reɪl] *noun*
(*a*) bar set across two posts; **the cowboy tied his horse to the rail.**

(*b*) metal bar of a train track; **don't step on that rail—it's electric.**
(*c*) trains used as a means of travel/of carrying goods; **they traveled by rail when they were in Europe.**

rail·ing, *noun*
fence made of metal bars; **he looked through the railing at the animals in the zoo.**

rail·road
(*a*) track with two rails along which trains run; **he helped to build the railroad.**
(*b*) organization which uses trains to carry passengers and goods; **a railroad station; he works for the railroad.**

rain [reɪn] **1.** *noun*
drops of water which fall from the clouds; **the ground is very dry—we haven't had any rain for weeks; last week Chicago had two inches of rain; don't go out in the rain without an umbrella; the rain will help the plants grow.**
no plural: **some rain; a drop of rain**
2. *verb*
to fall as drops of water from the clouds; **it started to rain as soon as we sat down on the grass; you can't have a picnic when it's raining; it rained all day yesterday.**
rains—raining—rained—has rained
Note: **to rain** *is only used with* **it**

rain·bow, *noun*
colored half circle which shines in the

sky when it is sunny and raining at the same time.

rain·coat, *noun*
coat which keeps off water, which you wear when it is raining; **put on your raincoat if it's raining; he took off his raincoat and hung it in the hall.**

rain·drop, *noun*
small amount of rain which falls from a cloud; **the raindrops left spots on the windows.**

rain·storm, *noun*
storm with a lot of rain; **the streets were flooded in the rainstorm last night.**

rain·y, *adjective*
when it rains; **the rainy weather interfered with our vacation.**
rainy—rainier—rainiest

raise [reɪz] 1. *verb*
(*a*) to lift; **he raised his arm; don't raise your voice.**
(*b*) to increase; **they've raised the bus fares again.**
(*c*) to bring up (children/animals); **they raise cattle on the farm; she was raised by her grandmother.**
raises—raising—raised—has raised
2. *noun*
increase in pay; **he asked his boss for a raise.**

ran [ræn] *see* **run**

rang [ræŋ] *see* **ring**

rap·id [ˈræpɪd] *adjective*
fast; **we heard rapid footsteps on the stairs; the enemy made a rapid attack.**
rap·id·ly, *adverb*
quickly; **he read the names out rapidly.**

rat [ræt] *noun*
common small gray animal with a long tail, which lives under houses and eats garbage.

rate [reɪt] *noun*
amount of something compared to something else; **a high rate of interest; birth rate** = number of children born per 1,000 of population.

at an·y rate = whatever may happen; **are you going to the party?—we're going, at any rate.**

rath·er [ˈræðər] *adverb*
(*a*) quite; **it's rather cold outside.**
(*b*) *used with* would *to mean* prefer; **I'd rather stay at home than go to the party; are you going to pay for everybody?— I'd rather not.**
(*c*) (*showing that something is preferred*) **rather than wait for a bus, we decided to walk home; rather than have to pay, he said he had no money.**
or rath·er = or to be more correct; **his father is English, or rather Scottish.**

rat·tle [ˈrætəl] 1. *noun*
(*a*) sound of several sharp noises coming one right after the other; **the car engine made a loud rattle.**
(*b*) child's toy which makes a rattling sound.
2. *verb*
to make several sharp noises, one right after the other; **the old bicycle rattles when you ride it.**
rattles—rattling—rattled—has rattled

rat·tler [ˈrætlər], **rat·tle·snake,** *noun*
poisonous American snake which makes a rattling sound with its tail; **watch out for rattlesnakes in the desert.**

raw [rɔː] *adjective*
not cooked; **he eats his meat raw; too much raw fruit can make you sick.**

ra·zor [ˈreɪzər] *noun*
sharp knife or small machine for cutting off the hair on your face; **he was shaving with his electric razor; she used a razor blade to sharpen her pencil.**

reach [riːtʃ] 1. *noun*
distance which you can stretch out your hand to; distance which you can travel easily; **you should keep medicines out of the reach of the children; the house is within easy reach of the station.**

2. verb
(*a*) to stretch out your hand to; **he reached across the table and put a potato on my plate; the little boy is tall enough to reach the cupboard; can you reach the box on the top shelf** = stretch out your hand and bring down the box.
(*b*) to arrive at; **we reached the hotel at midnight; what time are we supposed to reach Los Angeles? the letter never reached him** = he never received it; **the amount in my bank account has now reached $1000.**
reaches—reaching—reached—has reached

read [ri:d] *verb*
to look at and understand written words; **I can read Russian but I can't speak it; he was reading the newspaper; I can't read the instructions on the medicine bottle—the letters are too small; he plays the piano by ear, but he can't read music; I'm reading about the British elections; the teacher read out all our grades** = read them in a loud voice.
reads—reading—read [red]**—has read** [red]

read·er, *noun*
person who reads; **the magazine has thousands of readers.**

read·y ['redɪ] *adjective*
prepared to do something; prepared to be used or eaten; **we can't eat yet—dinner isn't ready; wait for me, I'll be ready in two minutes; are you ready to go to school? the children are ready for bed** = have their pajamas on, etc.; **he's ready for anything** = prepared to do anything.

re·al [ri:l] *adjective*
(*a*) which does not copy; **is your watch real gold? this plastic fruit looks very real/looks like the real thing.**
(*b*) which exists; **have you ever seen a real live elephant?**
re·al·ly, *adverb*
(*a*) in fact; **is he really English? did she really mean what she said? he really believes that the earth is flat; did the**

house really belong to your father?
(*b*) (*used to show surprise*) **he doesn't like chocolate—really?**

re·al·ize ['ri:əlaɪz] *verb*
to understand; **he realized that he was becoming deaf; did she realize that the car was going too fast? I realize that the vacation will be expensive.**
realizes—realizing—realized—has realized

rear [rɪr] 1. *noun*
(*a*) back part; **please move to the rear of the bus.**
(*b*) buttocks.
2. adjective
which is in the back; **one of the rear tires on my car is flat.**
rear view mir·ror, *noun*
mirror inside a car above the windshield, through which you can see cars behind you.

rea·son ['ri:zən] *noun*
thing which explains why something happens; **what was the reason for the train being late? they said the train would be late, but didn't give any reason; the reason he has gone to live in Florida is that it's warmer there than here.**
rea·son·a·ble, *adjective*
acting in a normal/fair way; **the manager was very reasonable when I said I had left all my money at home.**

re·ceipt [rɪ'si:t] *noun*
piece of paper showing that you have paid for something; **keep your receipt—you'll have to show it if you want to change your sweater for another one.**

re·ceive [rɪ'si:v] *verb*
to get something which has been sent or given to you; **he received a lot of cards on his birthday; did you ever receive the check I sent you? he received a gold watch when he retired.**
receives—receiving—received—has received

re·cent ['ri:sənt] *adjective*
which happened not very long ago; **his recent film about the war; the President's recent speech.**

re·cent·ly, *adverb*
not long ago; lately; **have you ever been to Sweden?—I was there just recently;** he recently joined the tennis club.

rec·og·nize ['rekəgnaız] *verb*
to know something/someone because you have seen it/him before; **the police recognized the writing on the letter; I recognized her by the hat she was wearing; you've had your hair cut—I didn't recognize you!**
recognizes—recognizing—recognized—has recognized

rec·ord 1. *noun* ['rekərd]
(*a*) flat, round piece of black plastic which has sound printed on it, and which you play on a special machine; **I bought her an Elvis Presley record for her birthday; I don't like his new record—do you? some records are expensive, so I borrow them from the record library; put another Beethoven record on.**
(*b*) success in a sport which is better than any other; **he holds the world record for the 1000 meters; she broke the world record/she set a new world record in the last Olympics** = she did better than the last record; **they're trying to set a new record for eating sausages.**
2. *verb* [rı'kɔ:rd]
to fix a sound on a flat round piece of plastic or on a plastic tape; **he recorded the speech on his pocket tape recorder; this music has been badly recorded.**
records—recording—recorded—has recorded

re·cord·er, *see* **tape recorder**
rec·ord play·er, *noun*
machine for playing records; **why don't you put your new record on the record player? turn the record player off—I want to watch TV.**

red [red] *adjective & noun*
of a color like the color of blood; **he has red hair; they live in a house with a red door; I'm painting the chair red; he turned red when we asked him what he had done with the money; do you have** any paint of a darker red than this one? you have to stop when the traffic lights are red; the pan is red hot = extremely hot.
red—redder—reddest

Red Cross, *noun*
international organization which provides medical help.
red·head, *noun*
person with red hair; **all of her children are redheads.**

re·duce [rı'dju:s] *verb*
to make something smaller or lower; **you must reduce your speed when you come to the traffic lights; we've reduced the temperature in the office; he's trying to reduce** = to lose weight.
reduces—reducing—reduced—has reduced

re·fer to [rı'fɜrtu:] *verb*
to talk about or write about something/someone; **are you referring to me? he referred to the letter he had just received.**
refers—referring—referred—has referred

re·fill ['ri:fıl] *noun*
container with a fresh supply of liquid; **you can have free refills of coffee; I need a refill for my pen.**

re·fresh [rı'freʃ] *verb*
to make fresh again; **the nap refreshed me.**
refreshes—refreshing—refreshed—has refreshed
re·fresh·ing, *adjective*
which makes you fresh again; **a refreshing shower.**
re·fresh·ments, *plural noun*
food and drink served at a party/a sports event, etc.; **refreshments will be served after the meeting.**

re·frig·er·a·tor [rı'frıdʒəreıtər] *noun*
machine in the kitchen for keeping food cold; **put the milk in the refrigerator; we need to have our refrigerator repaired; close the refrigerator door.**

re·frig·er·ate [rɪˈfrɪdʒəreit] *verb*
to keep in the refrigerator; the paper on the jar reads "refrigerate after opening"; milk should be refrigerated.
refrigerates—refrigerating—refrigerated—has refrigerated

re·fuse [rɪˈfjuːz] *verb*
to say that you will not do something; not to accept; he came to the party but he refused to talk to anyone; they refused my offer of a ride home; we asked them to come to dinner, but they refused.
refuses—refusing—refused—has refused

re·gion [ˈriːdʒən] *noun*
area; the Great Lakes region; the southern region of Africa; they live in the region of Los Angeles = in the Los Angeles area.

reg·u·lar [ˈregjələr] *adjective*
which takes place again and again after the same period of time; which happens at the same time each day; 11 o'clock is my regular time for going to bed; if you don't have regular meals you may become ill; regular visits to the dentist are important; is this your regular train? = the train you catch each day.
reg·u·lar·ly, *adverb*
happening often after the same period of time; he finds it difficult to exercise regularly; you should go to the dentist regularly.

re·lat·ed [rɪˈleitɪd] *adjective*
belonging to the same family; they are related—his mother is her aunt; she is related to the family who run the local grocery store.

re·la·tion [rɪˈleiʃən], **rel·a·tive** [ˈrelətɪv] *noun*
member of a family; all our relations came for grandmother's birthday party; she doesn't speak to any of her relatives; we have relatives in Australia but I've never met them.
rel·a·tive·ly, *adverb*
quite/more or less; this train is relatively

fast; the tickets were relatively cheap.

re·lax [rɪˈlæks] *verb*
to rest; he was relaxing with a good book; you must learn to relax.
relaxes—relaxing—relaxed—has relaxed

re·li·gion [rɪˈlɪdʒən] *noun*
believing in gods or in one god; he's a follower of the Christian religion.
re·li·gious, *adjective*
referring to religion; they held a religious ceremony to mark the town's birthday.

re·main [rɪˈmein] *verb*
(*a*) to stay; several people remained behind when the speaker left; the weather will remain cold for several days.
(*b*) to be left; two problems remain to be dealt with.
remains—remaining—remained—has remained
re·mains, *plural noun*
things left behind; after the fire the remains of the house had to be torn down; the dog can have the remains of the meat.

re·mem·ber [rɪˈmembər] *verb*
to bring back into your mind something which you have seen or heard before; do you remember the football game where we lost 20–0? my grandfather can remember seeing the first planes flying; I can't remember where I put my book; I don't remember having been to this restaurant before; I remember her very well; it's strange that she can never remember how to get to their house.
remembers—remembering—remembered—has remembered

re·mind [rɪˈmaind] *verb*
to make someone remember something; remind me to write to my aunt; he reminds me of someone I used to know in Africa = he looks like someone I knew in Africa.
reminds—reminding—reminded—has reminded

re·move [rɪˈmuːv] *verb*
to take away; they removed the TV set

when we couldn't pay the bill; the police came to remove my car because it was parked in a no parking area.
removes—removing—removed— has removed

re·mov·er, *noun*
liquid or cream which removes something; paint remover; spot remover.

rent [rent] 1. *noun*
money which you pay to live in or use a house/an apartment which belongs to someone else; they had to get out of their apartment when they couldn't pay the rent.
2. *verb*
(a) to pay money to live in or use a house/an apartment, etc.; we rent this office from the government; when I go on vacation I'll rent a car.
(b) to allow someone to borrow a house for a time and pay for it; we are renting our house to an English family for the summer; this apartment is for rent at $200 a week; they live in a rented house.
rents—renting—rented—has rented

rent·al, *noun*
paying money to use something; allowing someone to pay money to use something; what is the charge for skate rental? he had a car rental business = business in which customers pay you for the use of cars.

re·pair [rɪˈpeər] *verb*
to fix; to make something good again; my shoes need repairing; the workmen have repaired the broken gas pipe.
repairs—repairing—repaired— has repaired

re·pairs, *plural noun*
fixing of something; they have done some repairs to the roof.

re·peat [rɪˈpiːt] *verb*
to say something again; could you repeat the address so that I can write it down? he kept repeating that he wanted a drink; she keeps repeating herself =

she keeps saying the same thing again and again.
repeats—repeating—repeated— has repeated

re·ply [rɪˈplaɪ] 1. *noun*
answer; we haven't received a reply to our letter; I've gotten so many replies that I can't answer them all.
plural **replies**
2. *verb*
to answer; when I asked him how to get to the post office, he replied that he didn't know; she wrote to the company three weeks ago, but they still haven't replied.
replies—replying—replied—has replied

re·port [rɪˈpɔːrt] 1. *noun*
(a) description of what has happened; the department manager must write a weekly report to give to his boss.
(b) statement by a government committee; they presented a report on the problem of crime in large cities.
2. *verb*
to tell (the police) about someone or something; we had better report this accident to the police.
reports—reporting—reported— has reported

re·port card, *noun*
written statement by a teacher about a pupil's work; she had a very good report card this term.

re·port·er, *noun*
person who writes about news in a newspaper; a crime reporter/a sports reporter.

rep·re·sent [reprɪˈzent] *verb*
to speak for someone else; to be an example of; the lawyer is representing her in court; the painting represents the Baroque period in art.
represents—representing— represented—has represented

rep·re·sent·a·tive [reprɪˈzentətɪv] *noun*
person who speaks for someone else; she was elected to the House of Representatives; the president of the company

couldn't attend the meeting so he sent his representative.

re·quire [rɪ'kwaɪr] *verb*
to need; to demand; **you are required to take this course in order to get a degree.**
requires—requiring—required—has required

re·quire·ment, *noun*
something which is needed; **medical knowledge is just one of the requirements of being a good doctor.**

res·cue ['reskju:] **1.** *noun*
saving (of someone from danger); **the rescue of the school children lost on the mountain; six policemen took part in the rescue.**
2. *verb*
to save (from danger); **the firemen rescued ten people from the burning house; he tried to rescue his cat which was up a tree.**
rescues—rescuing—rescued—has rescued

re·serve [rɪ'zɜrv] **1.** *noun*
something kept in case it will be needed later; **our reserves of oil are low; we're keeping these sandwiches in reserve in case more people come to the party.**
2. *verb*
(*a*) to keep something for someone; **I'm reserving the seat next to me for my sister.**
(*b*) to arrange to have a seat/a table; **I've reserved a table for six people; can I reserve some seats by telephone?**
reserves—reserving—reserved—has reserved

rest [rest] **1.** *noun*
(*a*) lying down/being calm; **what you need is a good night's rest; I had a few minutes' rest and then I started work again.**
(*b*) not moving; **the car came to rest at the bottom of the hill.**
(*c*) what is left; **here are John and Jim, but where are the rest of the children; the cat drank the rest of the milk; he put the rest of his dinner in the garbage can; she gave away three**

apples and ate the rest herself.
Note: **rest** *takes a singular verb when it refers to a singular:* **here's the rest of the milk; where's the rest of the string? the rest of the money has been stolen;** *it takes the plural when it refers to a plural:* **here are the rest of the children; where are the rest of the bricks? the rest of the books have been stolen**

2. *verb*
(*a*) to lie down/ to be calm; **don't bother your mother—she's resting; they walked for ten miles, then rested for ten minutes, then walked again.**
(*b*) to lean something against something; **he rested his bike against the wall.**
rests—resting—rested—has rested

rest room, *noun*
public bathroom; **could you tell me where the rest room is, please?**

res·tau·rant ['restərənt] *noun*
place where you can buy a meal; **let's not stay at home tonight—let's go to the restaurant on the corner; he's waiting for me at the restaurant.**

re·sult [rɪ'zʌlt] **1.** *noun*
(*a*) something which happens because of something; **I repeated that the price was too high, but with no result; as a result of the accident, six people had to go to the hospital; the result of all our discussions was that nothing was decided; what were the election results?**
(*b*) score (in a game)/grade (on an exam); **the result of the game was a draw; what was the result of your math test?**
2. *verb*
to happen because of something; **the accident resulted in a traffic jam; his illness resulted in his being away from work for several weeks.**
results—resulting—resulted—has resulted

re·tire [rɪ'taɪr] *verb*
to stop work at a certain age; **most people retire at 65; he retired after twenty years**

Restaurant

1. bottle	12. pepper
2. candle	13. plate
3. chair	14. salt
4. check	15. saucer
5. coffeepot	16. spoon
6. cup	17. table
7. fork	18. tablecloth
8. glass	19. waiter
9. knife	20. waitress
10. menu	21. wine
11. napkin	

one hundred and ninety-five

in the factory; both my parents are retired.

retires—retiring—retired—has retired

re·turn [rɪ'tɜrn] 1. *noun*
(*a*) coming back/ going back; **on his return to work he was given a present; put your return address on the back of the envelope; can you send me your reply by return mail** = immediately; **many Happy Returns** = best wishes for a happy birthday.
(*b*) something which is sent back; **he mailed in his income tax return; election returns** = election results.
2. *verb*
(*a*) to come back/to go back; **they returned from vacation last week; he hasn't returned to work since he had the accident.**
(*b*) to give back; **I must return my books to the library; she borrowed my knife and never returned it.**

returns—returning—returned—has returned

re·view [rɪ'vjuː] 1. *verb*
to go over something again; **let's review our last French lesson.**

reviews—reviewing—reviewed—has reviewed

2. *noun*
going over something again; written opinion of a book, play, etc.; **we will have a review of the words you've already learned before going on to new ones; an excellent review of his book appeared in yesterday's paper.**

re·ward [rɪ'wɔːrd] 1. *noun*
prize you get for doing something; **they are offering a $1000 reward for information about the crime.**
2. *verb*
to give someone a prize for doing something; **the girl brought home a good report card and her father rewarded her with a bicycle.**

rewards—rewarding—rewarded—has rewarded

re·write ['riː'raɪt] *verb*
to write something again; **please rewrite**

this report—it's not complete.

rewrites—rewriting—rewrote—has rewritten

rhyme [raɪm] 1. *noun*
same sound in two words used in poetry; "blow" isn't a rhyme for "cow"; I can't finish my poem because I can't think of a rhyme for "scissors."
2. *verb*
to have the same sound (in poetry); "blow" doesn't rhyme with "cow"/ "blow" and "cow" don't rhyme.

rhymes—rhyming—rhymed—has rhymed

rib [rɪb] *noun*
one of several long bones in the chest; **she punched him in the ribs; spare ribs** = cooked ribs of pork served with a sauce.

rib·bon ['rɪbən] *noun*
long, thin piece of material; **she tied a ribbon in her hair; he tied the package with blue ribbon; do you know how to change this typewriter ribbon?**

rice [raɪs] *noun*
common food plant, grown in hot countries, of which you eat the seeds; **he was eating a bowl of rice.**
no plural: **some rice; a bowl of rice/a spoonful of rice.**

rich [rɪtʃ] *adjective*
(*a*) having a lot of money; **he's so rich that he doesn't know what to do with his money; if I were a rich man, I'd go to warm places in the winter; she doesn't spend any money and so gets richer and richer.**
(*b*) dark (color); **he painted the ceiling a rich chocolate color.**
(*c*) with many minerals/treasures, etc.; **the country is rich in coal; the city is rich in old churches; the museum has a rich collection of Italian paintings.**
(*d*) very sweet (food); **this cake is too rich for me.**

rich—richer—richest

rid [rɪd] *verb*
to get rid of something = to throw something away/to make something go away; **to be rid of something** = not to have something which causes a problem any

more; **I'm trying to get rid of my old car; he can't get rid of his cold—he's had it for weeks; I'm very glad to be rid of my cold.**

ride [raɪd] 1. *noun*
trip on a horse/on a bike/in a car, etc.; **I'm going for a ride on my bike; do you want to come for a bike ride? can I have a ride on the black horse? we all went for a ride in his new car; the shopping center is only a short bus ride from our house.**
2. *verb*
to go for a trip on a horse/on a bike, etc.; **I was riding my bike when it started to rain; have you ever ridden (on) an elephant? she's learning to ride a bicycle.**
rides—riding—rode [rəʊd]—**has ridden** ['rɪdən]

right [raɪt] 1. *adjective*
(*a*) correct/not wrong; **you're right— they didn't win; he's always right; he gave the right answer every time; I think the answer is 240—right! is your watch right? is that the right time? this isn't the right train for Pittsburgh; put the books back in the right place; if you don't put the bottle right side up, all the milk will run out of it; is this the right way to get to the post office?** *see also* **all right.**
(*b*) not left/referring to the hand which most people use to write with; **in England, you mustn't drive on the right side of the road; she was holding her bag in her right hand; my right arm is stronger than my left.**
2. *noun*
(*a*) the side opposite the left/the side of the hand which most people write with; **in England you mustn't drive on the right; in Germany you must keep to the right; when you get to the traffic lights, turn to the right; who was that girl sitting on your right?** = at the right side of you; **take the second street on the right.**
(*b*) what you should be allowed to do or to have; **you have no right to read my letters; everyone has the right to say what they like about the government.**
3. *adverb*
(*a*) straight; **she bumped right into a policeman; instead of turning he went right on into a tree.**

(*b*) (*also* **right away**) immediately; **he phoned the police right after the accident; the doctor came right away.**
(*c*) exactly/completely; **his house is right at the end of the road; the TV broke down right in the middle of the program; go right along to the end of the hall; don't stand right in front of the TV—no one can see the picture.**
(*d*) correctly; **he guessed right; nothing seems to be going right.**
(*e*) to the right-hand side; **turn right at the traffic lights; look right and left before you cross the street.**
right now = at the present time; **right now, we have no sugar in stock.**
right-hand, *adjective*
on the right side; **look in the right-hand drawer; he lives on the right-hand side of the street.**
right-hand·ed, *adjective*
using the right hand more often than the left; **he's right-handed.**

ring [rɪŋ] 1. *noun*
(*a*) circle of metal, etc.; **she has a gold ring on her finger.**
(*b*) circle of people or things; **we all sat in a ring.**
(*c*) noise of an electric bell; **there was a ring at the door.**
(*d*) call on the phone; **I'll give you a ring tomorrow.**
(*e*) square place with ropes around it where boxers fight.
2. *verb*
to make a sound with a bell; **he rang the doorbell; the bells were ringing; ring your bicycle bell and people will get out of the way; is that your phone ringing? that rings a bell** = it reminds me of something.
rings—ringing—rang [ræŋ] **—has rung** [rʌŋ]

rip [rɪp] 1. *noun*
tear; **there was a rip in the skirt.**
2. *verb*
to make a hole or a tear in something by pulling; **she ripped her coat on the fence; he ripped up the piece of paper** = tore it into pieces.
rips—ripping—ripped—has ripped

ripe [raɪp] *adjective*
(fruit) which is ready to eat; **that apple isn't ripe—it will make you sick; are oranges ripe in the winter?**
ripe—riper—ripest

rise [raɪz] *verb*
to go up; **the sun rises in the east; the road rises steeply; prices have risen this year.**
rises—rising—rose [rəʊz]**—has risen** [ˈrɪzən]

risk [rɪsk] 1. *noun*
possible harm or bad result; **is there any risk of being caught by the police? they ran the risk of being caught** = they did it, even though they might have been caught; **there's not much risk of rain** = it is not likely to rain.
2. *verb*
to do something which may possibly harm or have bad results; **I'll risk going out without a coat; he risked his life to save the little girl.**
risks—risking—risked—has risked

riv·er [ˈrɪvər] *noun*
wide stream of water which goes across land and into the sea or a lake; **he's trying to swim across the river; don't fall into the river—it's very deep; St. Louis is on the Mississippi River.**
riv·er·side, *noun & adjective*
on the land beside a river; **he owns a riverside house.**

road [rəʊd] *noun*
hard way used by cars/trucks, etc., to travel along; **in England, you drive on the left side of the road; be careful—the road is covered with ice; he lives in a house across the road; where do you live?—15 State Road.**
Note: often used in names: State Road, York Road, etc., and often written Rd.: Birch Rd., etc.
road·side, *noun & adjective*
land beside a road; **roadside fruit stand; they stopped along the roadside to have lunch.**

roast [rəʊst] 1. verb
to cook meat in an oven; **the pork is roasting in the oven; I like roast chicken.**
roasts—roasting—roasted—has roasted
Note: as an adjective, use roast: roast beef/roast pork, etc.
2. *noun*
meat to be cooked in the oven; **when should the roast come out of the oven?**

rob [rɒb] *verb*
to steal from someone or a place; **he was robbed of all his money; three men robbed the bank.**
robs—robbing—robbed—has robbed
rob·ber, *noun*
person who steals from someone; **they were attacked by robbers.**
rob·ber·y [ˈrɒbəriː] *noun*
stealing from someone or a place; **a robbery took place yesterday at the bank.**
plural **robberies**

rob·in [ˈrɒbən] *noun*
common brown bird with a red underside; **seeing a robin is a sign that spring is coming.**

rock [rɒk] 1. *noun*
(*a*) stone as part of the earth; **the house is built on hard rock; the road is cut out of the rock.**
(*b*) large piece of stone; **rocks fell down the mountain; the ship hit some rocks and sank.**
2. *verb*
to move from side to side instead of standing still; **the waves are rocking the boat; he rocked backwards and forwards on his chair.**
rocks—rocking—rocked—has rocked
rock·er, rock·ing chair, *noun*
chair fixed on curved pieces, so that it can rock backwards and forwards.
rock·y, *adjective*
full of rocks; **it's difficult to grow crops in rocky soil; the Rocky Mountains.**
rocky—rockier—rockiest

rock·et ['rɒkət] *noun*
vehicle shot into space; **they sent a rocket to the moon.**

rode [rəʊd] *see* **ride**

roll [rəʊl] **1.** *noun*
something which has been turned over and over on itself; **a roll of paper; (dinner) roll** = small loaf of bread for one person, often served at dinner.
2. *verb*
to make something go forward by turning it over and over; to go forward by turning over and over; **he rolled the ball across the table; the football rolled down the stairs; the penny rolled under the piano.**
rolls—rolling—rolled—has rolled

roll up, *verb*
to turn something flat over and over until it is a tube; **he rolled up the carpet; she rolled the newspaper up.**
Note: she rolled up the carpet *or* she rolled the carpet up *but only* she rolled it up

roll·er skates *plural noun*
boots with wheels for rolling along on a flat surface; **he bought a pair of roller skates.**

roll·er-skat·ing, *noun*
rolling along on a flat surface wearing skates; **we went roller-skating yesterday.**

roof [ru:f] *noun*
part of a building/a car, etc., which covers it and protects it; **the cat walked across the roof of the house; the roof needs to be repaired—the rain is coming in; put your suitcases on the roof of the car.**

room [ru:m] *noun*
(*a*) part of a house, divided with walls; **here's the dining room; our apartment has five rooms, and a kitchen and bathroom.**
(*b*) room in a hotel or bedroom; **I want to reserve a room for two nights; here's your room—it's just opposite mine.**
(*c*) space for something; **this table takes up a lot of room; there isn't enough room for three people; we can't have a piano in**

our house—there just isn't any room. no plural for (c): some room; no room; too much room

room·mate ['ru:meɪt] *noun*
person who shares a room or apartment with you; **her new roommate moved in yesterday.**

room·y, *adjective*
full of space; **it's a very roomy apartment.**
roomy—roomier—roomiest

roost·er ['ru:stər] *noun*
male chicken; **we saw a rooster and four hens in the yard.**

root [ru:t] *noun*
part of a plant which goes down into the ground; **root crops** = vegetables like carrots where you eat the roots but not the leaves.

root beer, *noun*
soft drink made with liquid from a certain root; **a glass of root beer; she'd like some root beer.**

rope [rəʊp] *noun*
very thick string made of several thin pieces twisted together; **they pulled the car out of the river with a rope; he climbed down from the window on a rope.**

rose [rəʊz] **1.** *noun*
common garden flower which grows on a bush; **she was picking a bunch of roses; this red rose has a beautiful smell.**
2. *verb see* **rise**

rose·bush *noun*
rose plant; **a large rosebush grew near the door.**
plural rosebushes

rot·ten ['rɒtən] *adjective*
(food) which has become bad; **all these apples are rotten; don't eat that potato—it's rotten; a bag of rotten oranges.**

rough [rʌf] *adjective*
(*a*) not smooth; **a rough road led to the farm; the sea was rough—we were all sick.**
(*b*) not finished/not very correct; **he made a rough drawing of the scene of the accident; I can only make a rough guess at what happened.**

(c) violent; **we had a rough game of football.**

rough—rougher—roughest

rough·ly, *adverb*

(a) in a violent way; **they played roughly.**

(b) more or less; **the cost will be roughly $25; I can't say exactly, but I can tell you roughly how big it is.**

round [raʊnd] 1. *adjective*

shaped like a circle; **a round carpet; we sat at a round table; round trip =** traveling to a place and back again.

2. *adverb & preposition*

in a circle; **the wheels went round and round; the flowers grow all year round =** throughout the whole year.

3. *noun*

(a) regular trip; **the mailman's round =** the streets he goes down every day; **a newspaper round =** the houses which one boy delivers newspapers to.

(b) **round of drinks =** drinks bought for several people by one person; **I'll buy the next round.**

(c) part of a competition; **if you answer all the questions, you will go on to the next round.**

round up, *verb*

to gather together; **they rounded up the cows.**

Note: **she rounded the children up** *or* **she rounded up the children** *but only* **she rounded them up**

route [ruːt] *noun*

(a) way to take to reach a certain place; **you could take the country route or the city route.**

(b) regular trip; **the paperboy had a long route.**

(c) long highway; **take Route 43 out of the town until you come to a gas station.**

row [rəʊ] 1. *noun*

line of things/people, etc.; **there were rows of empty seats in the theater; try and find a seat in the front row; stand in a row facing the camera.**

2. *verb*

to make a boat go forward by using

oars; **we rowed the boat across the river.**

rows—rowing—rowed—has rowed

row·boat, *noun*

small boat for rowing; **let's rent a rowboat and go on the river.**

roy·al [ˈrɔɪəl] *adjective*

referring to a king or queen; **when we were in Copenhagen we visited the royal gardens; the Royal Family =** the family of a king or queen.

rub [rʌb] *verb*

to move something backwards and forwards across the surface of something; **he rubbed cream into his skin; she rubbed her knee after she knocked it against the corner of the table; he was rubbing his hands in excitement.**

rubs—rubbing—rubbed—has rubbed

rub out, *verb*

to remove something which has been written; **rub out those pencil marks.**

rub·ber [ˈrʌbər] *noun*

(a) material which we can stretch, made from liquid which comes from a tree; **cars have rubber tires; they were blowing up a rubber boat; some boots are made of rubber.**

(b) **a pair of rubbers =** low boots which fit over your shoes.

no plural for (a)

rub·ber band, *noun*

thin circle of rubber used to attach things together; **the cards were held together with a rubber band.**

rude [ruːd] *adjective*

not polite; **he was rude to his customers; you mustn't be rude to your teachers; he's the rudest man I know.**

rude—ruder—rudest

rug [rʌg] *noun*

small carpet, often one on top of a large carpet; **he sat on the rug in front of the fire.**

rule [ruːl] 1. *noun*

general way of behaving; statement of what you should or should not do in a game, etc.; **I make it a rule not to smoke before breakfast; you have to play the game according to the rules; the teacher tries to keep the children from breaking the rules.**

as a rule = in a general way/ usually; **as a rule he gets to the office before 9 a.m.**

2. *verb*

to control a country; **the new country is ruled by a president.**

rules—ruling—rules— has ruled

rul·er [ˈruːlər] *noun*

flat piece of wood/plastic/metal, etc., which you use to draw straight lines; **this line isn't straight—use a ruler next time.**

run [rʌn] 1. *noun*

(a) going quickly on foot; **he went for a run before breakfast; I was tired out after that long run.**

(b) short trip by car; **let's go for a run in your new car.**

(c) point made in baseball; **he made three runs in the game.**

2. *verb*

(a) to go quickly on foot; **he ran upstairs; don't run across the road; he's running in the 100-yard race; she runs two miles a day.**

(b) (*of buses/trains, etc.*) to be working; **the trains aren't running today because of the strike; the bus is running late because of the traffic; this bus doesn't run on Sundays.**

(c) (*of machines*) to work; **he left his car engine running.**

(d) to go; **the main street runs north and south; the play ran for two years.**

(e) to direct a business; to organize a club, etc.; **he runs a shoe shop; I want someone to run the sales department for me; she runs the ladies' club; the army is running the country.**

(f) to be up for election; **he's running for president.**

(g) to drive; **I'll run you down to the station** = I will take you there in my car.

runs—running—ran [ræn]—**has run**

run a·way, *verb*

to go away fast; to escape; **he's running away from the police; she threw a stone through the window and ran away; he ran away from school when he was 14.**

run in·to, *verb*

(a) to go fast and hit something (usually in a vehicle); **he ran into a tree; the bus ran into the mailbox.**

(b) to meet; **I ran into your brother yesterday.**

run·ner, *noun*

person who runs; **there are ten runners in the race.**

run out of, *verb*

to have none left of something; **we've run out of gasoline; I must go to the store—we're running out of milk.**

run o·ver, *verb*

to knock someone down by hitting them with a vehicle; **he was run over by a bus; he drove without looking and ran over a dog.**

run·way, *noun*

track on which planes land and take off at an airport.

rung [rʌŋ] *see* **ring**

rush [rʌʃ] 1. *noun*

going fast; **there was a rush for the door** = everyone ran towards the door.

2. *verb*

to go fast; **he rushed into the room; she was rushed to the hospital; why was everyone rushing to the door?**

rushes—rushing—rushed—has rushed

rush hour, *noun*

time of day when everyone is trying to travel to work or back home from work; **you can't drive fast in the rush hour traffic; if we leave the office early we'll avoid the rush hour.**

Ss

sack [sæk] **1.** *noun*

(*a*) bag, often a large one made of strong rough cloth; **we bought a sack of potatoes; I've ordered three sacks of coal.**

(*b*) being told to leave your job; **he got the sack because he was always late for work.**

2. *verb*

to tell someone to leave his job; **she was sacked because she was always late.**

sacks—sacking—sacked—has sacked

sad [sæd] *adjective*

not happy; **she's sad because her little cat has died; it was such a sad film that we cried; reading poetry makes me sad.**

sad—sadder—saddest

sad·ness, *noun*

being unhappy; **the sadness of the story made her cry.**

safe [seɪf] **1.** *adjective*

not in danger; not likely to hurt you or cause damage; **the town is safe from attack; you should keep medicines high up so that they are safe from children; I keep my money in a safe place; even if the school is on fire, all the children are safe; is this snake safe to touch? it isn't safe to touch the bomb; is it safe to go into the house now? don't play with the stove—it isn't safe.**

safe—safer—safest

2. *noun*

strong box for keeping money/jewels, etc., in; **he puts his gold coins in the safe every night.**

safe·ly, *adverb*

without danger; without being hurt; **although the plane was on fire, all the passengers got out safely; he stopped the car safely although the brakes weren't working.**

safe·ty, *noun*

being safe; **traffic safety** = care taken by people on the roads to avoid accidents; **safety belt** = belt which you wear in a car or a plane to keep you from being hurt if there is an accident; **safety pin** = pin whose point fits into a little cover when it is fastened, and so can't hurt you.

no plural

said [sed] *see* **say**

sail [seɪl] **1.** *noun*

(*a*) large piece of cloth which makes a boat go forward when it is blown by the wind; **the wind blew so hard it tore our sails; look at those little boats with their blue sails.**

(*b*) short trip on a boat; **let's go for a sail across the harbor.**

2. *verb*

to travel on water; to control a sailboat; **hurry up—the ferry sails at 11:30; she was the first woman to sail alone around the world; the children were sailing their little boats in the park; we go sailing every weekend.**

sails—sailing—sailed—has sailed

sail·boat, *noun*

boat which uses sails rather than a motor.

sail·or, *noun*

person who sails; **the sailors and the passengers stood on the deck; he wants to be a sailor, so he's going to join the navy; I'm a bad sailor** = I feel sick when I travel on a boat.

sal·ad [ˈsæləd] *noun*

dish of cold vegetables, often raw; cold meat or fish served with cold vegetables; **I'll have a chicken salad; we had a ham and tomato salad; fruit salad** = various fresh fruit cut up and mixed together.

sal·ad dress·ing *noun*
liquid which you pour over salad; **what
kinds of salad dressing do you have? she
would like some salad dressing.**

sal·a·ry [ˈsæləɪ] *noun*
money given to a worker every month;
**he has a very good salary; he has applied
for a job with a salary of $20,000 a year.**
plural **salaries**

sale [seɪl] *noun*
(*a*) giving something to someone for
money; **this house is for sale; some of
these towels are on sale in the department
store.**
(*b*) selling things at cheap prices; **our
store is having a sale on china this week;
I bought this hat for $1.00 in a sale.**
(*c*) **sales** = money which a business
receives; **our sales have gone up this year.**

sales·clerk, *noun*
person who sells; **the store was advertising for salesclerks.**

sales·girl, *noun*
girl who sells; **the salesgirl will help you
find the right dress.**

sales·man, sales·wo·man, *noun*
person who sells; **ask the salesman to
show you the new car.**
plural **salesmen, saleswomen**

salt [sɔːlt] *noun*
white powder used to make food,
especially meat, fish and vegetables,
taste better; **did you put any salt in this
soup? put some more salt on your fish;
fish which live in the sea can only live in
salt water.**
no plural: **some salt; a spoonful of
salt**

salt·y, *adjective*
tasting of salt; **sea water is very salty;
this soup is very salty—I think you've put
too much salt in it.**
salty—saltier—saltiest

same [seɪm] *adjective & pronoun*
looking/tasting/sounding, etc., exactly
alike; showing that two things are of
one kind; **you get very bored having
to do the same work day after day; she
was wearing the same dress she wore last**

year; **they all live on the same street;
everyone else was looking tired—but
he stayed the same; these two drinks
taste the same; coffee looks the same as
tea, but has quite a different taste.**

all the same, *adverb*
anyway; **I don't like parties, but I will
come to yours all the same.**

sand [sænd] *noun*
very small pieces of stone which you
find on a beach or in the desert; **the
children were playing in the sand; they
raced across the sand on their horses.**
no plural

sand·y, *adjective*
coverered with sand; **a sandy beach.**

san·dal [ˈsændəl] *noun*
light shoe which is open on the top,
which you wear in the summer; **he
bought a new pair of sandals for his
vacation; she was wearing blue sandals.**

sand·wich [ˈsændwɪtʃ] *noun*
two slices of bread with meat, etc., in
between; **a ham sandwich; two cheese
sandwiches; what kind of sandwiches do
you want me to make for the picnic? we
had a sandwich and some beer in the
restaurant.**
plural **sandwiches**

sang [sæŋ] *see* **sing**

sank [sæŋk] *see* **sink**

sat [sæt] *see* **sit**

Sat·ur·day [ˈsætərdɪ] *noun*
seventh day of the week/day between
Friday and Sunday; **we go shopping on
Saturdays; I saw him at a party last
Saturday; today is Saturday, September
20; we'll go to the movies next Saturday.**

sauce [sɔːs] *noun*
liquid which you eat with food or pour
over it; **we eat applesauce with pork; do
you want any chocolate sauce on your
ice cream? he poured a can of
tomato sauce into the bowl.**

sauce·pan, *noun*
metal pan with high sides and a long
handle in which you cook things on a

stove; **put the potatoes in the saucepan; the soup has stuck to the bottom of the saucepan.**

sau·cer ['sɔːsər] *noun*
small plate which you stand a cup on; **he poured so much coffee into his cup that it all ran into the saucer; get out another cup and saucer—your uncle is coming for dessert.**

sau·sage ['sɔːsɪdʒ] *noun*
food made of chopped meat in a long tube which you eat; **we had sausages and fried eggs for breakfast; when you go to the butcher shop can you buy me a pound of pork sausages?**

save [seɪv] *verb*
(*a*) to stop someone from being hurt or killed; to stop something from being damaged; **the policeman saved the little boy from being burned in the fire; how many people were saved when the ship sank? he saved my life** = he stopped me from being killed.
(*b*) to keep (money, etc.) so that you can use it later; **I'm saving to buy a car; they save all the old pieces of bread to give to the birds; if you save $1 each week, you'll have $52 in a year's time.**
(*c*) not to waste (time, money, etc.); **if you walk to work you will save $5 a week on bus fares; he delivered the letter himself so as to save buying a stamp; if you travel by air you'll save a lot of time; if you have your car fixed now it will save you a lot of trouble later.**
saves—saving—saved—has saved
save up, *verb*
to keep money so that you can use it later; **I'm saving up to buy a new car.**
sav·ings, *plural noun*
money which you have saved; **he put all his savings in the bank; she spent all her savings on a vacation in Australia; savings account** = bank account in which your money draws interest.
Note: **I've saved my money up** *or* **I've saved up my money** *but only* **I've saved it up**

saw¹ [sɔː] **1.** *noun*
tool with a long metal blade with teeth

along its edge, used for cutting wood, etc.; **he cut his hand on the saw; this saw doesn't cut well—it needs to be sharpened; chain saw** = saw made of a chain with teeth in it, which turns very fast when driven by a motor.
2. *verb*
to cut with a saw; **he was sawing wood; they sawed the tree into small pieces; he said he was going to saw the piece of wood in half.**
saws—sawing—sawed—has sawed/has sawn [sɔːn]

saw² *see* **see**

say [seɪ] *verb*
(*a*) to speak words; **he said he wanted to come with us; don't forget to say "thank you"; I was just saying that we never hear from Uncle John, when he phoned; can you understand what he said? the newspaper says it will be sunny tomorrow.**
(*b*) to put in writing; **their letter says that they will arrive on Monday; the timetable says that there are no trains on Sundays.**
(*c*) to suggest; **choose a number—let's say sixteen; let's meet next week—shall we say Thursday?**
says [sez]**—saying—said** [sed]**—has said**

scale [skeɪl] *noun*
machine for weighing; **he weighed the sugar on the kitchen scale; the bathroom scale must be wrong—I'm heavier than I was yesterday.**

scare [skeər] **1.** *noun*
becoming frightened; **she had a scare when her son didn't come home.**
2. *verb*
to make someone frightened; **the loud noise scared her; don't scare me like that!**
scares—scaring—scared—has scared
scar·y, *adjective*
frightening; **a scary movie.**
scary—scarier—scariest

scene [siːn] *noun*
place where something happens; **five**

minutes after the accident, an ambulance arrived on the scene; the police were at the scene of the crime.

sched·ule ['skedʒʊl] 1. *noun*
list of appointments/times of classes in school; do you like your class schedule? he has a heavy schedule.
2. *verb*
to make a list of times to do certain things; the meeting is scheduled for next Thursday.
schedules—scheduling—scheduled—has scheduled

school [sku:l] *noun*
(a) place where people (usually children) are taught; he's four, so he'll be going to school this year; do you like school? what did you do at school today? she ran away from school; he left school and joined the navy; which school do you go to? there are two schools near our house.
(b) part of a university; he's going to medical school; she has a degree from the School of Engineering.
(c) group of fish; a large school of fish passed by the boat.
el·e·men·ta·ry school = school for small children.
high school/sec·ond·ar·y school = school for children after the age of eleven or twelve.
school·boy, school·girl, school·chil·dren, *nouns*
boy or girl or children who go to school.
school·yard, *noun*
area around a school building; the children are playing in the schoolyard.

sci·ence ['saɪəns] *noun*
study which is based on looking at and noting facts, especially facts which are arranged into a system; he's no good at languages, but very good at science.
sci·en·tif·ic [saɪən'tɪfɪk] *adjective*
referring to science; he carried out scientific experiments.
sci·en·tist ['saɪəntɪst] *noun*
person who studies science.

scis·sors ['sɪzərz] *plural noun*
thing for cutting, made of two blades

and two handles; the hairdresser was cutting my hair with his scissors; I must buy another pair of scissors; someone has borrowed my scissors and hasn't given them back.
Note: you can say **a pair of scissors** *if you want to show that there is only one tool*

score [skɔ:r] 1. *noun*
(a) number of points made in a game/ on a test; the football game ended with a score of 6–0; what's the score in the game so far?
(b) set of 20; a score of sailboats floated in the harbor; scores of = many; scores of people caught measles; I've seen that film scores of times.
2. *verb*
to make a point in a game; he scored three goals; she scored twenty-five!
scores—scoring—scored—has scored

scratch [skrætʃ] *verb*
to move a sharp point across a surface; they scratched the top of the table as they were carrying it upstairs; be careful not to scratch yourself on that rosebush; he scratched his name on the wall of the school.
from scratch = from the beginning; we'll have to start again from scratch.
scratches—scratching—scratched—has scratched

scream [skri:m] 1. *noun*
loud sharp cry; you could hear the screams of the people in the burning building.
2. *verb*
to make a loud sharp cry; she screamed when a man suddenly opened the door; all the children screamed with laughter.
screams—screaming—screamed—has screamed

screen [skri:n] *noun*
net-like piece in a window which lets air in but keeps insects out.

sea [si:] *noun*
salt water which covers a large part

of the earth; I like swimming in the sea better than in a river; the sea's rough— I hope I won't be sick; to get to Germany from England you have to cross the North Sea; she couldn't decide whether to send the package by sea or by air.
Note: in names **Sea** *is written with a capital letter.* **Sea** *is usually used with* **the**: **the sea's too cold; the North Sea,** *etc.*

sea·man, *noun*
man who works on a ship.
plural **seamen**

sea·shell, *noun*
hard shell of a small animal that lives in the ocean; **they collected many different kinds of seashells as they walked along the beach.**

sea·shore/sea·side, *noun*
land on the edge of the sea; **we go to the seashore for our vacation; I like a seaside vacation; this seaside town is empty in the winter.**

sea·sick, *adjective*
ill because of the movement of a ship; **she didn't enjoy the trip because she was seasick all the time; I'll stay on deck because I'm feeling seasick.**

sea·weed, *noun*
plant which grows in the sea; **the beach is covered with seaweed.**
no plural: **some seaweed; a piece of seaweed**

search [sɜrtʃ] 1. *noun*
trying to find something; **we went to every store in search of a German book, but couldn't find it; the police sent out search parties to look for people lost in the snow; we all joined in the search for his wallet** = we all tried to find it.
2. *verb*
to look for something; **we've searched everywhere but can't find mother's watch; they're searching the mountains for people lost in the snow; the customs man searched my suitcase.**
searches—searching— searched—has searched

sea·son ['siːzən] *noun*
(*a*) one of four parts of a year; **spring, summer, autumn and winter are the four seasons.**
(*b*) any part of the year when something usually happens; **the baseball season lasts from April to September; the town is very crowded during the skiing season; when are pears in season? apples are out of season right now.**

sea·son tick·et, *noun*
train/bus/theater ticket which you can use for a whole year or several months.

seat [siːt] *noun*
something which you sit on; **sit in the front seat of the car; I want two seats in the front row; I couldn't find a seat on the bus, so I had to stand; this chair isn't very comfortable—it has a wooden seat; why is your bicycle seat so narrow? take a seat, please, the doctor will see you in a few minutes.**

seat belt, *noun*
belt which you wear in a car or plane to prevent you from being hurt if there is an accident.

sec·ond ['sekənd] 1. *noun*
(*a*) one of the sixty parts of a minute; **the bomb will go off in ten seconds.**
(*b*) very short time; **I saw him a second ago; wait for me—I'll only take a second to get ready.**
(*c*) something/someone that comes after the first thing or person; **the German runner was first, the British runner was second; today is the second of January/January (the) second (January 2); Charles the Second (Charles II) was king at the time of the fire of London.**
Note: in dates **second** *is usually written* **2: April 2, 1973; November 2, 1980;** *with names of kings and queens* **second** *is usually written* **II: Queen Elizabeth II**

2. **2nd** *adjective*
coming after the first; **February is the second month in the year; it's Mary's second birthday next week; B is the second letter in the alphabet; men's clothes are on the second floor; this is**

the second tallest building in the world = there is one building which is taller; she's the second most powerful woman in the company; that's the second time the telephone has rung while I'm in the bathtub.

sec·ond·ar·y, *adjective*
which is not the most important; which comes second; **secondary school** = high school; school for children after the age of eleven or twelve.

sec·ond class, *noun*
(*a*) ordinary seats in a train/on a ship; **a second class ticket to Pittsburgh; she travels second class because it is so much cheaper.**
(*b*) class of mail used for newspapers and magazines; **we can send this paper second class** = by second class mail.

sec·ond hand, *noun*
long hand on a watch which turns around fast and shows the seconds.

sec·ond·hand, *adjective & adverb*
not new/which someone else has owned before; **he just bought a secondhand car; I bought this car secondhand.**

se·cret ['si:krət] *noun & adjective*
something which is hidden/which is not known; **I won't tell you what your birthday present will be—it's a secret; he hid his money in a secret place; can you keep a secret?** = can you not tell anyone if I tell you a secret?

sec·re·tar·y ['sekrəterı] *noun*
person who writes letters/answers the telephone, etc., for someone else; **my secretary will tell you when you can come to see me.**
plural **secretaries**

sec·tion ['sekʃən] *noun*
part; **he likes to read the sports section of the newspaper; I think our seats are in this section of the theater.**

see [si:] *verb*
(*a*) to use your eyes to notice things; **can you see that house over there? cats can see in the dark; I can see the bus coming; we saw the car hit the tree.**
(*b*) to watch a film, etc.; **have you seen the movie at the Pine Theater? I saw**

the football game on TV.
(*c*) to go with someone; **the policeman saw the old lady across the road; my secretary will see you to the door; they saw me off at the airport** = they went with me to say goodbye.
(*d*) to understand; **I don't see why you need so much money; don't you see that we have to be at the station by ten o'clock? I see—you want to borrow a lot of money; I see your point** = I understand what you are saying.
(*e*) to make sure that something happens; to check; **can you see that the children are in bed by nine o'clock? would you see if the mail has arrived? I'll see if dinner is ready.**
(*f*) to meet/to visit; **I see him often, because he lives very close to me; see you on Thursday! see you again soon! I saw him last Christmas; you should see a doctor about your cough.**
sees—seeing—saw [sɔ:]**—has seen**

see through, *verb*
to understand everything about someone/something; **I saw through his plan.**

see to, *verb*
to arrange to deal with/to make sure that something happens; **can you see to it that the children are in bed by nine o'clock? will you see to the Christmas cards?** = will you deal with them?

seed [si:d] *noun*
part of a plant which you put in the ground so that it will grow into a new plant; **I'll plant some carrot seeds; these seeds are so small that you can hardly see them.**

seem [si:m] *verb*
to appear/to look as if; **he seems to like his new job; they seem to be having a good time; I seem to have lost my wallet; it seems that they got lost in the snow; they seem very nice; it seems strange that no one answered your letter; it seems to me that we ought to buy a new car** = I think that we ought to buy one.
seems—seeming—seemed—has seemed

seen [si:n] *see* **see**

self- [self] *prefix referring to yourself*
  self·de·fense, *noun*
defending yourself.
  self·ish, *adjective*
doing things only for yourself; keeping things for yourself; **don't be selfish—let me have one of your chocolates.**
  self-serve, self-serv·ice, *noun &*
adjective
store, etc., where you take things yourself and pay for them as you go out; **self-service restaurant** = restaurant where you take the food to the table yourself; **self-service gas station** = one where you put the gas into the car yourself.

sell [sel] *verb*
to give something to someone for money; **I sold my bike to my brother; we sold our car for $500; they sold him their house; they sell vegetables in that store, but you can't buy meat there.**
sells—selling—sold [səʊld]**—has sold**
  sell out, *verb*
to sell all of something; **we've sold out of potatoes** = we have no potatoes left.

se·mes·ter [sə'mestər] *noun*
half of a school year; **how many classes do you have this semester?**

send [send] *verb*
to make something/someone go from one place to another; **he sent me to the supermarket to buy some meat; we send 100 cards to our friends every Christmas; I'll send you a card when I get home.**
sends—sending—sent—has sent
  send a·way for, *verb*
to write to ask someone to send you something, usually when you have seen an advertisement; **I sent away for a watch which I saw advertised in the paper.**
  send back, *verb*
to return something; **if you don't like your present, send it back and I'll buy you something different.**
Note: **send the present back** *or* **send back the present** *but only* **send it back**

  send off, *verb*
to mail; **I sent the letter off without a stamp.**
Note: **send the letter off** *or* **send off the letter** *but only* **send it off**

sense [sens] *noun*
(*a*) one of the five ways in which you notice something (seeing, hearing, touching, smelling and tasting); **he lost his sense of smell.**
(*b*) way of feeling; **he has no sense of humor** = he doesn't often think things are funny.
(*c*) meaning; **this letter doesn't make sense** = it doesn't mean anything.
(*d*) reasonable behavior; **it makes sense to save money** = it's wise.

sen·si·tive ['sensɪtɪv] *adjective*
(*a*) (person) who is easily upset; **don't mention her hair—she's very sensitive about it.**
(*b*) which hurts easily; **his arm is still sensitive where he hurt it.**

sent [sent] *see* **send**

sen·tence ['sentəns] *noun*
words put together to make a complete statement, usually ending in a period; **the second sentence in his letter doesn't mean anything.**

sep·a·rate 1. *adjective* ['seprət]
not together; **keep the water and the oil separate; I am sending you the book in a separate package; can we have two separate bills, please?**
2. *verb* ['sepəreɪt]
to make things or people be separate; **you must separate the big stones from the sand; the family got separated in the crowd; let's separate, and meet again in thirty minutes; her parents separated two years ago** = they stopped living together.
separates—separating—separated—has separated
  sep·a·rate·ly, *adverb*
not together; **we want to pay for the two meals separately.**

Sep·tem·ber [sep'tembər] *noun*
ninth month of the year; **my birthday is**

in September; today is September 21; we're going on vacation next September. *Note:* **September 21**: *say* "September twenty-first," "September the twenty-first" *or* "the twenty-first of September"

se·ri·ous ['sɪrɪəs] *adjective*

(*a*) not funny; **I'm being serious** = I am not joking.

(*b*) very important/very bad; **he has had a serious illness; there was a serious accident on the highway.**

se·ri·ous·ly, *adverb*

in a serious way; **he is seriously thinking of moving to Canada; she is seriously ill.**

serve [sɜrv] *verb*

(*a*) to be used/to be of help; **this box will serve as a chair; the game served the purpose of keeping the children busy.**

(*b*) to give people food at a meal; **let me serve the potatoes; he is serving dinner at 7:00.**

(*c*) to work for; **he served in the Police Force for twenty years.**

(*d*) to help a customer in a store, etc.; to provide a service; **are you being served? the bus serves the villages in the hills.**

(*e*) (*in games like tennis*) to start the game by hitting the ball.

serves—serving—served—has served

serv·ant, *noun*

person who is paid to work for a family.

serv·ice, *noun*

(*a*) working for someone/helping someone in a store or restaurant; **service charge** = money which you pay for service in addition to the charge for goods; **can I be of service? the food in the restaurant was good but the service was terrible.**

(*b*) group of people working together; **health service** = doctors, nurses who treat students who are ill at a school/university; **the services** = the army, the navy and the air force.

(*c*) providing things which people need; **the bus service is very bad; the mail service could be improved.**

(*d*) regular religious ceremony; **I'm going to the nine o'clock service on Sunday.**

serv·ice sta·tion, *noun*

business which sells gasoline, oil, etc. for cars; **we'll have to pull into the next service station for gas.**

set [set] **1.** *noun*

(*a*) group of things which are used together; **a set of tools; a tea set** = cups, saucers, teapot, etc.

(*b*) machine; **a TV set.**

2. *verb*

(*a*) to put in a special place; **he set the table** = he put the knives and forks, plates, cups, etc., on the table.

(*b*) to arrange; **I've set my watch to the correct time; the bomb was set to go off at ten o'clock.**

(*c*) to make something happen; **the house was set on fire; the prisoner was set free.**

(*d*) to go down; **the sun sets in the west.**

(*e*) to write music to go with words; **the poem was set to music.**

(*f*) to be ready; **I was all set to leave the house when the telephone rang.**

sets—setting—set—has set

set back, *verb*

(*a*) to make late; **the bad weather has set the crops back by three weeks.**

(*b*) to place back; **the house is set back from the road** = is not built near the road.

set off, *verb*

to begin a trip; **we're setting off for Italy tomorrow; he set off on a long walk over the mountains.**

set out, *verb*

to begin a trip; **they set out to find the lost child; we're setting out early tomorrow.**

set up, *verb*

to make/to build; **they set up an exhibit on local plant life; they set up a baby-sitting service.**

Note: **set up the exhibit** *or* **set the exhibit up** *but only* **set it up**

set·tle ['setəl] *verb*

(*a*) to come to rest; **they've settled in Colorado; the animals settled down for the night.**

(b) to come to an agreement; **have they settled on which car they're going to buy? I'll settle the bill** = I'll pay the bill.
settles—settling—settled—has settled

sev·en ['sevən] number 7
there are seven bottles of milk in the refrigerator; she's seven (years old); the train leaves at seven (o'clock).
sev·en·teen, number 17
she's seventeen (years old); the train leaves at six seventeen (6:17).
sev·en·teenth, 17th, adjective & noun
today is the seventeenth of September/September seventeenth (September 17); the seventeenth letter of the alphabet; it's my seventeenth birthday next week.
sev·enth, 7th, adjective & noun
the seventh of June/June seventh (June 7); a seventh of the bottle; Charles the Seventh (Charles VII); it's his seventh birthday on Wednesday.
Note: in dates **seventh** is usually written 7: August 7, 1980; May 7, 1965; with names of kings and queens **seventh** is usually written VII: King Henry VII
sev·en·ti·eth, 70th, adjective & noun
the seventieth film which I have seen this year; tomorrow is grandfather's seventieth birthday.
sev·en·ty, number 70
he's seventy (years old); she's in her seventies = she is between 70 and 79 years old.
Note: **seventy-one (71), seventy-two (72)**, etc., but **seventy-first (71st), seventy-second (72nd)**, etc.

sev·er·al ['sevrəl] adjective & pronoun
more than a few, but not very many; I've met him several times; several of us are going to the theater; several houses were damaged in the storm.

sew [səʊ] verb
to attach or make using a needle and a thread; can you sew this button on my coat? she's sewing some curtains.
sews—sewing—sewed—has sewn

sew·ing ma·chine, noun
small machine which is used in the house or in factories to sew clothes, etc.

sex [seks] noun
one of two groups (male and female) into which animals and plants can be divided; please write on the form your name, age, and sex.
plural sexes

shade [ʃeɪd] noun
(a) dark place which is not in the light of the sun; we'll sit in the shade of the apple tree; the sun is too hot—let's sit in the shade.
(b) type of color; another shade of blue; a darker shade of red.
(c) something which blocks out light; pull down the window shade.

shad·ow ['ʃædəʊ] noun
shade made by something which is in the light; I can see the shadow of a man on the sidewalk; what a strange shadow the tree makes!

shake [ʃeɪk] 1. noun
(a) action of moving quickly up and down or from side to side; give your watch a good shake to start it.
(b) drink made by mixing milk, ice cream and sweet stuff; a milk shake; can I have a chocolate milk shake?
2. verb
to move quickly from side to side or up and down; he shook his watch to see if it would work; the buildings shook in the storm; don't shake the box—you'll break the glasses; she shook her head = she moved her head from side to side to mean "no"; he shook hands with me = he greeted me by shaking my right hand with his.
shakes—shaking—shook [ʃʊk]—has shaken

shak·er, noun
small container with holes in the top for shaking out salt, etc.; would you please pass the pepper shaker?

shall [ʃæl] *verb used with other verbs*
(*a*) *to make the future:* **we shall leave for Italy on Saturday.**
(*b*) *to show a suggestion:* **shall I shut the door? shall we go to the theater tonight?**
Past: **should, should not,** *usually* **shouldn't**
Note: **shall** *is mainly used with* **I** *and* **we**

sham·poo [ʃæm'puː] 1. *noun*
liquid soap used to wash your hair; **a bottle of shampoo.**
2. *verb*
to wash your hair with liquid soap; **she shampooed her hair after her bath.**
shampoos—shampooing— shampooed—has shampooed

shape [ʃeɪp] *noun*
form/how something looks; **she has a ring in the shape of the letter A; my sweater is beginning to lose its shape** = beginning to stretch; **the car is in bad shape** = old/broken down; **he's trying to get in shape** = to lose weight/to become healthier.
shaped, *adjective*
with a particular shape; **her hat is shaped like a beehive.**
shape·less, *adjective*
with no particular shape; **she was wearing a shapeless dress.**

share [ʃeər] 1. *noun*
(*a*) part of a whole which belongs to someone; **don't eat my share of the cake! has he done his share of the work?**
(*b*) small part of a company; **he bought 300 shares in Atlantic Richfield.**
2. *verb*
(*a*) to divide something between several people; **all seven of us have to share the cake; he doesn't want to share his candy.**
(*b*) to use something which someone else also uses; **we share a bathroom with the apartment next door; he doesn't want to share his toys with the other children; we only have one room**

empty in the hotel—do you mind sharing it?
shares—sharing—shared—has shared

sharp [ʃɑːrp] *adjective*
(*a*) which cuts easily; **be careful with that knife—it's very sharp; I cut my foot on the sharp stones.**
(*b*) which bends suddenly; **a sharp corner; the car made a sharp turn across the road.**
(*c*) with a high sound; **he gave a sharp cry.**
sharp—sharper—sharpest
sharp·en, *verb*
to make sharp; **he sharpened his pencil with a knife; this knife doesn't cut well— it needs sharpening.**
sharpens—sharpening— sharpened—has sharpened

shave [ʃeɪv] 1. *noun*
cutting off the hair on your face with a razor; **he hasn't had a shave for two days; I need a shave.**
2. *verb*
to cut off the hair on your face with a razor; **he cut himself while shaving; he hasn't shaved for two days.**
shaves—shaving—shaved—has shaved
shav·er, *noun*
object/machine for shaving; **he uses an electric shaver.**

she [ʃiː] *pronoun referring to a female person, a female animal and sometimes to machines and countries.*
she's my aunt; she and I are going on vacation together; I'm angry with Anne—she has taken my bike; she's a nice little cat; get off the ship—she's sinking.
Note: when it is the object, **she** *becomes* **her: she hit the ball/the ball hit her;** *when it follows the verb* be, **she** *usually becomes* **her: who's that?—it's her, the girl we met yesterday**

sheep [ʃiːp] *noun*
farm animal, kept to give wool and also

used as meat; **he's watching his sheep; the sheep are in the field.**
no plural: **one sheep; ten sheep**
Note: the meat from a **sheep** *is called* **lamb**

sheet [ʃiːt] *noun*
(*a*) large piece of cloth which you put on a bed; **she pulled the sheet over her head and went to sleep.**
(*b*) large flat piece; **a sheet of glass; give me two sheets of paper.**

shelf [ʃelf] *noun*
flat piece of wood attached to a wall or inside a cupboard which things can be put on; **put the books back on the shelves; the jam is on the top shelf.**
plural **shelves** [ʃelvz]

shell [ʃel] **1.** *noun*
(*a*) hard outside of an egg, a nut or of some animals; **to eat a boiled egg you have to take off the shell; they collected different kinds of shells as they walked along the beach.**
(*b*) type of bomb fired from a gun; **the shells were falling near the church.**
2. *verb*
to hit something with a shell from a gun; **the guns shelled the town.**
shells—shelling—shelled—has shelled

she'll [ʃiːl] *see* **she**

shel·ter [ˈʃeltər] **1.** *noun*
place where people or things can be protected (usually from bad weather); **food, clothing and shelter are basic needs; he took shelter from the rain; you should keep your new bike under shelter; bus shelter** = small building with a roof where you can wait for a bus; **the people stood in the bus shelter out of the rain.**
2. *verb*
to provide a shelter for; to stand in a shelter; **he sheltered (himself) from the rain under a big tree; she led a sheltered life** = protected against bad experiences.
shelters—sheltering—sheltered—has sheltered

she's [ʃiːz] *see* **she is, she has**

shine [ʃaɪn] *verb*
to be bright with light; **the sun is shining so I think it'll be hot today; he cleaned his shoes until they shone; the glasses shone in the sunshine; why do cats' eyes shine in the dark?**
shines—shining—shone [ʃəʊn]**— has shone**

shin·y, *adjective*
which shines; **the table has a shiny surface.**
shiny—shinier—shiniest

ship [ʃɪp] *noun*
large machine which floats on water and carries cargo and passengers; **we traveled to Europe by ship; she's a fine passenger ship; the navy has many ships.**
Note: a **ship** *is often referred to as* **she/her**

ship·ment [ˈʃɪpmənt] *noun*
(*a*) sending; **shipment of guns is not allowed.**
(*b*) something which is sent; **we are getting in a new shipment of books today.**

ship·yard, *noun*
place where ships are built; **there is a large shipyard near the harbor.**

shirt [ʃɜrt] *noun*
light piece of clothing which you wear on the top part of your body; **he wore a dark suit and a white shirt; when he came home his suitcase was full of dirty shirts; it's so hot that I'm going to take my shirt off.**

shoe [ʃuː] *noun*
piece of clothing made of leather or hard material which you wear on your foot; **he bought a new pair of shoes; she put her shoes on and went out; I must take my shoes off—my feet hurt.**
shoe·lace [ˈʃuːleɪs] *noun*
long, thin piece of material for tying up a shoe; **he broke one of his shoelaces.**
shoe·mak·er, *noun*
person who makes and repairs shoes; **I must take these shoes to the shoemaker—the heels have worn down.**

shone [ʃəʊn] *see* **shine**

shook [ʃʊk] *see* **shake**

shoot [ʃuːt] *verb*

(*a*) to fire a gun; to hit someone by firing a gun; **the soldiers were shooting into the houses; he was shot by a policeman as he tried to run away; he shot two rabbits.**

(*b*) to go very fast; **she shot up the stairs; the car shot out of the garage.**

shoots—shooting—shot [ʃɒt]—has shot

shoot down, *verb*

to make an aircraft crash by hitting it with a shell; **we shot down three airplanes.**

shop [ʃɒp] 1. *noun*

small store; **she owns a gift shop in Chicago; I buy my meat at the butcher's shop on the corner.**

2. *verb*

to buy things in a shop or store; **we've been shopping; he's out shopping.**

shops—shopping—shopped—has shopped

shop a·round, *verb*

to go to various stores to find which one is the cheapest before you buy what you want; **if you want a cheap radio, you ought to shop around.**

shop·keep·er, *noun*

person who owns a shop.

shop·per, *noun*

person who buys things in a shop or store.

shop·ping, *noun*

(*a*) buying things in a shop or store; **I do all my shopping on Saturday mornings; she's doing her shopping; have you done any shopping?**

(*b*) things which you have bought in a shop or store; **put all your shopping on the table.**

no plural: **some shopping; a lot of shopping**

shop·ping cen·ter, *noun*

large group of stores with a parking lot for customers; **I'm going to the shopping center tomorrow to look for a new dress.**

shore [ʃɔːr] *noun*

land at the edge of the sea or lake; **we**

walked along the shore; these plants grow on the shores of the lake.

short [ʃɔːrt] *adjective*

(*a*) not long in space; **I need a short piece of string—about six inches; the shortest way to the station is to go up Pearl Street.**

(*b*) not long in time; **he was here a short time ago; they had a short vacation in Greece; I had a short nap on the train.**

(*c*) not tall; **John is shorter than his brother.**

(*d*) **short of** = with not enough of; **we're short of sugar; I'm short of money now, so I can't pay you till next week.**

(*e*) (word) which is written or spoken with fewer letters than usual; **Co. is short for Company; his name is Robert, but we call him Bob for short.**

short—shorter—shortest

short·en [ˈʃɔːrtən] *verb*

to make less in length; **she will shorten the skirt for you.**

shortens—shortening—shortened—has shortened

short·ly, *adverb*

soon; **he left the house shortly after breakfast.**

shorts, *plural noun*

short pants which end above your knees; **tennis players wear white shorts; you can't go into the church in shorts.**

shot [ʃɒt] *noun*

action of shooting; **the police fired a shot at the car;** *see also* **shoot.**

should [ʃʊd] *verb used with other verbs*

to mean ought to *when you think something is correct or when you expect something to happen;* **you shouldn't eat so many chocolates; he should go to see the doctor if his cold gets worse; we shouldn't have come to this party—it's terrible; they should have arrived by now.**

Negative: **should not,** *usually* **shouldn't**

Note: **should** *is the past of* **shall: shall we go to the theater?—I suggested we should go to the theater**

shoul·der [ˈʃəʊldər] *noun*

(*a*) top part of the body between the top of the arm and the neck; **he carried his gun over his shoulder; the policeman touched him on the shoulder; his shoulders are very wide; she looked over her shoulder to see who was following her.**

(*b*) part of a piece of clothing which covers the shoulder; **the shoulders of this shirt are too narrow.**

(*c*) area along the edge of a road; **do not drive on the shoulder.**

shout [ʃaʊt] 1. *noun*

loud cry from someone; **I heard a shout for help; there were shouts of surprise when the winner was announced.**

2. *verb*

to say something very loudly; **they shouted for help; they were shouting at each other in anger.**

shouts—shouting—shouted—has shouted

shov·el [ˈʃʌvəl] 1. *noun*

tool for digging in the ground; **snow shovel** = tool for removing snow from the sidewalk.

2. *verb*

to dig up soil/snow and place it somewhere else; **they shoveled snow all morning; he shoveled sand into the box.**

shovels—shoveling—shoveled—has shoveled

show [ʃəʊ] 1. *noun*

(*a*) things which are put out for people to look at; **we are going to the flower show; did you go to the boat show last year?**

(*b*) something which is on at a theater; program on TV; **"My Fair Lady" is a wonderful show; we're going to a show tonight; this is my favorite TV show.**

2. *verb*

to let someone see something/to point out something to someone; **can I show you my stamp collection? he showed her his new car; show me where you fell down; ask the salesclerk to show you the way to the manager's office; can you show me how to get to the post office? he showed me how the camera worked; my**

watch shows the date as well as the time.

shows—showing—showed—has shown

show a·round, *verb*

to lead a visitor around a place; **the guide showed us around the museum.**

show off, *verb*

to show how much better you are than others; **don't look at her—she's showing off; he's showing off his new car.**

show up, *verb*

(*a*) to arrive; **we invited twenty people to the party, but no one showed up.**

(*b*) to make something be seen or known; **her singing performance showed up her lack of practice.**

(*c*) to be seen clearly; **this orange jacket shows up in the dark when I ride my bike.**

show·er [ˈʃaʊər] *noun*

(*a*) small amount of rain or snow which falls for a short time; **we often have showers in April; the TV says that there will be snow showers tonight.**

(*b*) arrangement in a bathroom for washing your body under drops of water; **we've put a shower over the bathtub; each room in the hotel has a toilet and a shower; shower curtain** = curtain to pull when you are having a shower.

(*c*) washing your body under a shower of water; **she has a shower every morning before breakfast; I don't like cold showers!**

shut [ʃʌt] 1. *adjective*

closed/not open; **all the banks are shut on Sundays; we tried to go in, but the door was shut.**

2. *verb*

to close something which is open; **please shut the window—it's getting cold; I brought you a present—shut your eyes and guess what it is.**

shuts—shutting—shut—has shut

shut down, *verb*

to close completely; **the factory shut down for the Christmas holiday.**

shut off, *verb*

to switch something off; **can you shut off the electricity?**

Note: **he shut the electricity off** *or* **he shut off the electricity** *but only* **he shut it off**

shut up, *verb*

(*a*) to close something inside; **shut the dog up in the kitchen.**

(*b*) to stop making noise/to stop speaking; **shut up! I'm trying to listen to the news.**

sick [sɪk] *adjective*

(*a*) ill/not well; **she's sick in bed.**

(*b*) having an illness where you bring up food from your stomach to your mouth; **when I got up this morning I felt sick; he ate too many pieces of cake and was sick all over the floor.**

(*c*) **to be sick of** = to have had too much of; **I'm sick of hearing all that noise; I'm sick and tired of taking care of all these children.**

(*d*) **to make someone sick** = to bother someone; **the way he spends money makes me sick.**

sick·en·ing [ˈsɪkənɪŋ] *adjective*

which makes you sick; **she thought the movie was sickening.**

sick·ness, *noun*

not being well; **there is a lot of sickness in the winter.**

side [saɪd] 1. *noun*

(*a*) one of the parts which (with the top and bottom) make a box or (with the front and back) make a house; **turn the box on its side; the garden is by the side of the house.**

(*b*) flat surface; **write on only one side of the piece of paper.**

(*c*) one of two parts/two edges of something; one of two parts separated by something; **he lives on the other side of the street; she jumped over the wall to get to the other side; in England cars drive on the left-hand side of the road; we live on the south side of Chicago; their house is on the sunny side of the street.**

(*d*) sports team; **our side was beaten 3–0; which side does he play for?**

(*e*) part of the body between the top of the legs and the shoulder; **lie down on**

your side; she stood by my side; all the soldiers stood side by side** = one next to the other.

(*f*) **to be on someone's side** = to have the same point of view; **I'm on your side; whose side are you on?**

2. *adjective*

at the side; **if your shoes are dirty, use the side door, not the front door.**

side·walk, *noun*

hard path at the side of a street; **the sidewalks are slippery after yesterday's snow; the children were playing on the sidewalk.**

side·ways, *adverb*

to the side/from the side; **they all walked sideways; if you look at him sideways you'll see how big his nose is; would you turn sideways while I take this picture?**

sight [saɪt] *noun*

(*a*) one of the five senses/being able to see; **he lost his sight in the war** = he became blind.

(*b*) seeing; **she can't stand the sight of blood; I caught sight of the mountain in the distance** = I saw it for a moment; **there wasn't a policeman in sight** = there were no policemen around; **they waved until the ship was out of sight** = until they couldn't see it any more.

(*c*) something which you see (especially something famous or strange); **the guide took us to see the sights of the town; she looks a sight in that red hat.**

sight·see·ing, *noun*

visiting the sights of a city or area; **on their first two days in New York they went sightseeing.**

no plural: **some sightseeing**

sign [saɪn] 1. *noun*

(*a*) movement/drawing, etc., which means something; **he made a sign with his hand and the cars began to go forward; go straight until you come to a sign marked "business district"; the house has a big sign outside it saying "for sale."**

(*b*) mark/something which shows; **is there any sign of the snow stopping? there's no sign of how the burglar got into the house.**

2. *verb*
to write your name on a form/check, etc., or at the end of a letter; **he forgot to sign the check; the manager signed the letter; sign here, please.**
signs—signing—signed—has signed

sign up, *verb*
to write your name on a list; **he signed up for a class in photography.**

sig·nal [ˈsɪgnəl] **1.** *noun*
movement/flag/light, etc., which shows that you should do something; **he waved a flag which was the signal for the race to start; the traffic signals aren't working; always use your turn signal before making a turn.**
2. *verb*
to make a sign; **always signal before turning; the policeman signaled to us to stop.**
signals—signaling—signaled—has signaled

sig·na·ture [ˈsɪgnətʃər] *noun*
name which someone writes when he signs; **I can't read his signature; her signature is easy to recognize; they need your signature on this tax form.**

si·lence [ˈsaɪləns] *noun*
absence of noise/not talking; **the crowd waited in silence; the teacher asked for silence.**
si·lent, *adjective*
not making any noise; not talking; **they kept silent for the whole meeting.**
si·lent·ly, *adverb*
without any noise; **they walked silently into the church.**

silk [sɪlk] *noun*
soft, expensive material made from a thread produced by an insect; **she was wearing a silk shirt; this tie is made of silk.**
no plural: **some silk; a piece of silk**
silk·y, *adjective*
soft and smooth; **the dog had a silky coat.**
silky—silkier—silkiest

sil·ly [ˈsɪlɪ] *adjective*
stupid; **don't be silly—you can't eat raw potatoes; what a silly question!**
silly—sillier—silliest

sil·ver [ˈsɪlvər] *noun*
(a) valuable white metal; **a silver teapot; this ring is silver; the handle of the knife is made of silver.**
(b) things made of silver; **don't forget to clean the silver.**
(c) silver coins; **I don't have any silver in my pocket—just bills.**
no plural
sil·ver·ware, *noun*
forks, spoons and knives with which you eat, often made of silver; **would you get the silverware out of the drawer? you've put the dishes out on the table but you've forgotten the silverware.**
sil·ver wed·ding, *noun*
day when you have been married for twenty-five years.

sim·i·lar [ˈsɪmələr] *adjective*
which looks/tastes, etc., the same; **the two houses are very similar; his job is similar to mine; do you have something similar but not as expensive?**

sim·ple [ˈsɪmpəl] *adjective*
(a) easy; **the answer is very simple; I didn't think the exam was very simple.**
(b) ordinary/not very special; **we had a simple meal of bread and soup; it's a very simple plan.**
simple—simpler—simplest
sim·ply, *adverb*
(a) in a simple way; **he described what happened very simply.**
(b) only; **he did it simply to see what you would say.**

since [sɪns] **1.** *adverb & preposition*
from that time on; **he was rude to the teacher and has had bad grades ever since; we've been working since 2 o'clock; since we got home, it has rained every day.**
2. *conjunction*
because; **he can't come with us since he's**

ill; since it's such a nice day, let's go for a picnic.

sin·cere [sɪnˈsiːr] *adjective*
very honest; **was he sincere when he promised he would work better?**
sin·cere·ly, *adverb*
in a sincere way; **Sincerely yours** = words which you put at the end of a letter before your signature.

sing [sɪŋ] *verb*
to make music with your voice; **he was singing as he worked; can you sing that song again? she was singing a song about roses.**
sings—singing—sang [sæŋ]—**has sung** [sʌŋ]
sing·er, *noun*
person who sings.

sin·gle [ˈsɪŋɡəl] 1. *adjective*
(*a*) one/for one person; **I haven't seen a single newspaper; I want a single room for one night; do you want a double bed or two single beds?**
(*b*) not married; **he's still single.**
2. *noun*
(*a*) one of something; **the baseball player hit a single** = he reached first base; **may I have five singles instead of a five-dollar bill?** = five one-dollar bills.
(*b*) **singles** = tennis game played between two people; **the men's singles.**
sin·gu·lar [ˈsɪŋɡjələr] *adjective & noun*
form of a word showing that there is only one; **"mouse" is the singular, and "mice" is the plural; "is" is the singular of the verb "to be" and "are" is the plural; "he" is a singular pronoun.**

sink [sɪŋk] 1. *noun*
place in a kitchen where you wash the dishes; **put the dirty plates in the sink.**
2. *verb*
(*a*) to go to the bottom of water/not to float; **get off the ship—she's sinking; the boat sank because there were too many people in it; they sank the ship with a bomb.**
(*b*) to go down; **he sank into an armchair; the sun is sinking in the west; my**

heart sank = I felt very sad because something I had hoped would happen did not happen.
sinks—sinking—sank [sæŋk]—**has sunk** [sʌŋk]

sir [sɜr] *noun*
(*a*) (*usually used by someone working in a store or restaurant*) polite way of referring to a man who you are talking to; **would you like to order your lunch, sir? please sit here, sir.**
(*b*) polite way of writing to a man who you do not know; **Dear Sir.**

sis·ter [ˈsɪstər] *noun*
female who has the same father and mother as another child; **she's my sister; he has three sisters; his sister works in a bank.**

sit [sɪt] *verb*
(*a*) to be resting with your buttocks on something; **he was sitting on the floor; you can sit on the table if you like; sit next to me; she was sitting in bed eating her breakfast.**
(*b*) to be at rest somewhere; **the car is just sitting in the driveway.**
sits—sitting—sat [sæt]—**has sat**
sit down, *verb*
to take a seat; **everyone sat down and the meeting began; don't sit down—that chair has just been painted.**
sit up, *verb*
(*a*) to sit with your back straight; to move from a lying to a sitting position; **he sat up in bed; sit up straight!**
(*b*) to stay up without going to bed; **we sat up until 2 a.m.**

sit·u·a·tion [sɪtjʊˈeɪʃən] *noun*
how things are; position; **we're in a difficult situation; this has made the situation very difficult for us.**

six [sɪks] number 6
she's six (years old); come and have a cup of coffee at six (o'clock); there are six chocolates left.
six·teen, number 16
he's sixteen (years old).
six·teenth, 16th, *adjective & noun*
he was sixteenth in the race; August sixteenth/the sixteenth of August (August

16); his sixteenth birthday is next week.

sixth, 6th, *adjective & noun*
they live on the sixth floor; F is the sixth letter of the alphabet; he spent a sixth of the money; ten minutes is a sixth of an hour; the sixth of February/February sixth (February 6); Henry the Sixth (Henry VI); tomorrow is my son's sixth birthday.

Note: in dates **sixth** *is usually written* **6: April 6, 1980; December 6, 1976;** *with names of kings and queens* **sixth** *is usually written* **VI: King Henry VI**

six·ty, number 60
he's sixty (years old); I bought sixty books yesterday; she's in her sixties = she is between 60 and 69 years old.

Note: **sixty-one (61), sixty-two (62)** *etc., but* **sixty-first (61st), sixty-second (62nd),** *etc.*

six·ti·eth, 60th, *adjective & noun*
he was sixtieth out of 120; a minute is a sixtieth of an hour; it's father's sixtieth birthday tomorrow.

size [saɪz] *noun*
how big something is; that onion is the size of a tennis ball; he has a garage about the same size as our house; what's the size of a normal swimming pool? she takes size 7 in shoes; what size shirts do you wear?

skate [skeɪt] 1. *noun*
sharp blade worn under a boot to slide on ice; shoe with small wheels for roller-skating; she was putting on her skates.
2. *verb*
to slide on ice wearing skates; to roll along a flat surface in roller skates; we went skating on the ice; there is a big skating competition next week; she skates very well.
skates—skating—skated—has skated

skat·er, *noun*
person who skates; she and her brother are very good skaters.

skel·e·ton [ˈskelɪtən] *noun*
all the bones which make your body or an animal's body.

ski [skiː] 1. *noun*
long piece of wood which you attach to a boot, to allow you to slide on snow.
2. *verb*
to slide on snow wearing skis; he skied down the mountain; we go skiing every weekend.
skis—skiing—skied [skiːd]—**has skied**

skill [skɪl] *noun*
being able to do something which is difficult; something which you get by training; you need special skills to become a doctor.
skilled, *adjective*
having a particular skill by training; he's a skilled workman.

skin [skɪn] *noun*
outside surface of a human's or an animal's body or of a fruit; his skin turned brown in the sun; the skin of a cow can be used to make leather; a banana skin.
skin·ny, *adjective*
very thin; his mother thinks he should eat more because he's so skinny.
skinny—skinnier—skinniest

skip [skɪp] *verb*
to miss on purpose; we skipped the chapter on the Canadian government; I skipped lunch today.
skip—skipping—skipped—has skipped

skirt [skɜrt] *noun*
piece of clothing worn by women covering the lower part of the body from the waist to the knees or ankles; I like wearing jeans better than wearing a skirt; her skirt is so long it touches the ground.

sky [skaɪ] *noun*
space above the earth which is blue (or gray) during the day and black at night; look at all the clouds in the sky; when the sky is gray it means it'll be wet; the birds are flying high in the sky.
plural **skies**

sky·scrap·er [ˈskaɪskreɪpər] *noun*

very tall building; **the city was full of skyscrapers.**

slacks [slæks] *plural noun*
pants; **she bought a pair of blue slacks; he wore a green sweater and brown slacks.**
Note: to show one piece of clothing, say **a pair of slacks**

slam [slæm] *verb*
to make a loud noise when closing something; **he slammed the door.**
slams—slamming—slammed—has slammed

slap [slæp] 1. *noun*
hit with the hand flat; **he got a slap in the face.**
2. *verb*
to hit with the hand flat; **she slapped him on the wrist.**
slaps—slapping—slapped—has slapped

sleep [sli:p] 1. *noun*
resting (usually at night) when your eyes are closed and you do not know what is happening; **she needs eight hours' sleep a night; get a good night's sleep—we have a lot of work to do tomorrow; to go to sleep** = to start sleeping; **I'm trying to go to sleep; he went to sleep in front of the TV set.**
2. *verb*
to be asleep/ to rest with your eyes closed and not knowing what is happening; **he always sleeps for eight hours each night; she slept through the whole TV program; don't bother him—he's trying to sleep.**
sleeps—sleeping—slept [slept]**—has slept**

sleep in, *verb*
to sleep later than usual in the morning.
sleep·less, *adjective*
without resting; **he had a sleepless night.**
sleep·y, *adjective*
feeling ready to go to sleep; **I'm feeling sleepier and sleepier; the children are very sleepy by ten o'clock.**
sleepy—sleepier—sleepiest

sleeve [sli:v] *noun*
part of a piece of clothing which you put your arm into; **one sleeve of this coat is longer than the other; I often wear shirts with short sleeves in the summer.**
sleeve·less, *adjective*
without sleeves; **she wore a sleeveless blouse and a pair of shorts.**

slept [slept] *see* **sleep**

slice [slaɪs] *noun*
thin flat piece of food which has been cut off something larger; **cut me another slice of bread; he ate six slices of ham.**

slide [slaɪd] 1. *noun*
(*a*) colored photo on plastic which you can see through; **turn out the lights—I'll show you my vacation slides.**
(*b*) fall of rock or soil; **their house was damaged in a mud slide.**
2. *verb*
to move smoothly across a slippery surface; **the door slid open; the truck has sliding doors; let's go sliding on the ice.**
slides—sliding—slid [slɪd]**—has slid**

slight [slaɪt] *adjective*
not very large/not very serious; **there has been a slight frost; he has a slight temperature; she has had a slight accident.**
slight—slighter—slightest
slight·ly, *adverb*
not very much; **the new box is slightly larger than the old one; I only know him slightly.**

slip [slɪp] 1. *noun*
(*a*) underwear which you wear under a skirt or dress; **her slip was showing** = was hanging down below her skirt.
(*b*) small piece of paper; **he attached slips of paper to several pages in the book.**
2. *verb*
(*a*) to slide by mistake; **he slipped on the ice and fell down.**
(*b*) to go quickly; **she slipped upstairs**

when no one was watching; I'll just slip out to the store for a moment; she slipped past the guard very easily.

slips—slipping—slipped—has slipped

slip·per, *noun*
comfortable light shoe which is worn indoors; he took off his shoes and put on his slippers.

slip·per·y, *adjective*
so smooth that you may easily slip; watch out—the ice is slippery!

slope [sləʊp] 1. *noun*
surface which is neither flat nor standing straight up; a steep slope; the house is built on the slope of the mountain.
2. verb
to be neither flat nor standing straight up; the path slopes upwards; the road sloped down to the river.

slopes—sloping—sloped—has sloped

slow [sləʊ] *adjective*
(*a*) not fast; taking a long time to do something; the car was going at a slow speed; the train was very slow; he's very slow at answering my letters.
(*b*) showing a time which is earlier than the right time; my watch is three minutes slow.

slow—slower—slowest

slow down, *verb*
to go more slowly; to make something go more slowly; the snow slowed down the cars; the bus slowed down as it came to the traffic lights.

slow·ly, *adverb*
in a slow way/not fast; the car was going very slowly when it hit the wall; we walked slowly around the museum; the teacher must speak slowly so that the children can understand.

small [smɔ:l] *adjective*
little/not big; small cars use less gasoline than big ones; I'm selling my house and buying a smaller one; he only paid a small sum of money; she's smaller than her brother, but her mother is the smallest person in the family; this book isn't small enough to put in your pocket; my son is

too small to ride a bike = he is too young.

small—smaller—smallest

smart [smɑ:rt] *adjective*
clever/able to learn quickly; you're a very smart little girl; don't act smart = don't try to be so clever.

smart—smarter—smartest

smell [smel] 1. *noun*
one of the five senses/something which you can feel through your nose; dogs have a good sense of smell; the smell of roses makes me sneeze; do you like the smell of onions? what an awful smell! there's a smell of burning/there's a burning smell; there's a funny smell in the kitchen.
usually used in the singular
2. verb
(*a*) to notice the smell of something; I can smell smoke; dogs can smell strangers; can you smell cooking? I can't smell anything when I have a cold; smell these flowers!
(*b*) to produce a smell; this cheese smells very strong; the dinner smells good; the air smells fresh; there's something which smells funny in the kitchen; it smells of gas in here.

smells—smelling—smelled/ smelt [smelt]**—has smelled/has smelt**

smell·y, *adjective*
which has a bad smell; a smelly river; a smelly old dog.

smelly—smellier—smelliest

smile [smaɪl] 1. *noun*
way of showing that you are pleased/ happy by turning your mouth up at the corners; she gave me a friendly smile; he had a big smile on his face when he left the store with his new bike.
2. verb
to show that you are pleased by turning your mouth up at the corners; she smiled at me; stop smiling—this is very serious; smile please—I'm taking a picture.

smiles—smiling—smiled—has smiled

smoke [sməʊk] 1. *noun*

white, gray or black gas which is given off by something burning; **the room was full of cigarette smoke; do you smell smoke? I like the smell of cigar smoke; clouds of smoke poured out of the burning ship.**

2. *verb*

(*a*) to give off smoke; **the remains of the house are still smoking.**

(*b*) to breathe smoke into your mouth from a cigarette/cigar/pipe, etc.; **she was smoking a cigarette; he only smokes a pipe; she doesn't smoke; we always sit in the "no smoking" area; smoking can make you sick; if you want to play tennis, you shouldn't smoke.**

smokes—smoking—smoked—has smoked

smok·er, *noun*

person who often smokes cigarettes.

smok·y, *adjective*

full of smoke; **a smoky room.**

smooth [smuːð] 1. *adjective*

flat/not rough; **the table is quite smooth; we had a very smooth ride in our new car.**

smooth—smoother—smoothest

2. *verb*

to make something smooth; **she smoothed down the sheets on the bed; he tried to smooth over the problem** = to make things easier.

smooths—smoothing—smoothed—has smoothed

smooth·ly, *adverb*

in a smooth way; **the car came to a stop very smoothly.**

snack [snæk] *noun*

very small meal; **let's have a snack at the station; I always have a snack at 11 o'clock in the morning.**

snack bar, *noun*

small shop where you can buy snacks.

snake [sneɪk] *noun*

long smooth animal with no legs which moves by sliding; **she's afraid of snakes; some snakes can kill you.**

sneak [sniːk] *verb*

to move without being seen; **he sneaked past the guard and entered the building; she sneaked some cookies out of the kitchen** = took them without being seen.

sneaks—sneaking—sneaked—has sneaked

sneak·ers, *plural noun*

soft shoes with rubber bottoms, worn for sports etc., **he wore a pair of old sneakers when he went to help paint the house.**

sneak·y, *adjective*

without being seen; secret; **how could she do such a sneaky thing to her brother?**

sneaky—sneakier—sneakiest

sneeze [sniːz] 1. *noun*

sudden blowing out of air through your nose and mouth when you have a cold, etc.; **she gave a loud sneeze; his sneezes woke me up!**

2. *verb*

to blow air suddenly out of your nose and mouth because you have a cold, etc.; **she sneezed three times; the smell of flowers makes me sneeze.**

sneezes—sneezing—sneezed—has sneezed

snow [snəʊ] 1. *noun*

light white pieces of frozen water which fall from the sky when it is cold; **look at all the snow which has fallen during the night; the mountains are covered with snow; the trains will be late because the tracks are covered with snow; three inches of snow had fallen during the night.**

no plural; **some snow; a lot of snow**

2. *verb*

to fall as snow; **it's snowing! it snowed all night; do you think it's going to snow? it never snows here.**

snows—snowing—snowed—has snowed

Note: **to snow** *is always used with* **it**

snow·ball, *noun*

ball made with snow; **they threw snowballs at the teacher; he broke a window with a snowball.**

snowed in, *adjective*
having so much snow all around, that
you cannot travel; **we were snowed in
for six days.**

snow·fall, *noun*
amount of snow which has fallen; **the
snowfall has been very light this year.**

snow·man, *noun*
shape of a man made of snow; **they made
a snowman in the school playground; if
the sun comes out, your snowmen will
melt.**
plural **snowmen**

snow·storm, *noun*
storm when the wind blows and snow
falls.

snow·y, *adjective*
covered with snow; (weather) when it is
snowing; **snowy weather; if it's snowy,
you should stay indoors; this is the
snowiest winter I can remember; they
walked through the snowy streets to the
grocery store.**
snowy—snowier—snowiest

so [səʊ] **1.** *adverb*
(*a*) (*showing how much*) **it's so cold
that the river has frozen; we enjoyed ourselves so much that we're going to the
same place for our vacation next year;
the cake was so sweet that it made me
feel sick.**
(*b*) also; **he was late and so was I; we all
came down with colds, and so did the
teacher; I like fish—so do I; he can cook
well—so can his wife.**
(*c*) (*showing that the answer is "yes"*) **is
this the train for New York?—I think so;
did the burglars steal all your records?—
I'm afraid so; are you coming to the
party?—I hope so; will you be at the meeting?—I guess so.**
2. *conjunction*
(*a*) for this reason; **it was raining, so we
didn't go for a walk; she caught a cold,
so she couldn't come to the party.**
(*b*) **so that** = in order that; **so as to** =
in order to; **people on bicycles should
wear bright colors so that drivers can see
them in the dark; we ran to the station
so as not to miss the train.**
so far, *adverb*

until now; **he said he would call me, but
so far he hasn't done so; how do you like
your new job so far?**

so long, *interjection used when leaving
someone*
so long—I'll see you next week.

soap [səʊp] *noun*
stuff which you use to wash with,
made from oils and usually with a
pleasant smell; **I must buy some more
soap; they went camping and forgot to
take any soap with them; I've put a new
bar of soap in the bathroom; this soap has
a strong smell—it makes me sneeze.**
no plural: **some soap; a bar of
soap/a piece of soap**

so·ci·e·ty [sə'saɪətɪ] *noun*
people in general and the way in which
they live together; **money is too important in our society; society has to be protected from dangerous criminals.**
plural **societies**

sock [sɒk] *noun*
piece of clothing which you wear on
your foot inside your shoe; **he's wearing
blue socks and a blue tie; I'm almost
ready—I just have to put my socks and
shoes on; knee socks** = long socks which
go up to your knee.

so·fa ['səʊfə] *noun*
long soft seat for several people; **we sat
on the sofa and watched TV.**

soft [sɒft] *adjective*
(*a*) not hard; **the seats in this car are too
soft; he was sitting in a big soft armchair;
babies have soft skin; do you like soft ice
cream? soft drink** = drink which is not
alcoholic.
(*b*) not loud; **she talked in such a soft
voice that we could hardly hear her.**
(*c*) not bright; **the soft lighting made the
room look warm.**
soft—softer—softest

soft·ly, *adverb*
in a gentle way; quietly/not loudly; not
brightly; **I touched her hair softly; she
speaks very softly; the lights were shining
softly.**

soil [sɔil] *noun*

earth in which plants grow; **put some soil in a pot and plant your seeds in it.** *no plural:* **some soil; a bag of soil**

sold [səʊld] *see* **sell**

sol·dier [ˈsəʊldʒər] *noun*

man who is in the army; **the soldiers attacked the railroad station; soldiers wear brown uniforms.**

sol·id [ˈsɒlɪd] *adjective*

(*a*) hard/not liquid; **water turns solid when it freezes.**

(*b*) made all of one material; **the table is made of solid metal; a solid gold plate.**

solve [sɒlv] *verb*

to find the answer to; **how did he solve that problem? he's good at solving crossword puzzles.**
solves—solving—solved—has solved

some [sʌm] *adjective & pronoun*

(*a*) certain; **some people drive much too fast; some days it was so hot that we had to stay indoors.**

(*b*) several/not many; **can you cut some slices of bread? some of these apples are green; there are some people waiting by the door; I've bought some oranges.**

(*c*) a certain amount; **can you buy some gasoline when you go to town? do you want any sugar?—no, I've already taken some.**
some *is used with plural nouns and with nouns which have no plural:* **some people; some apples; some bread,** *etc.*

some·bod·y [ˈsʌmbədiː], **some·one** [ˈsʌmwʌn] *pronoun*

a certain person; **somebody/someone has stolen my car; there's somebody/someone in the telephone booth; if somebody/someone phones, say I will be back at 4 o'clock; I know somebody/someone who's a policeman.**

some·how, *adverb*

in one way or another; **we must get to Los Angeles somehow.**

some·place, *adverb*

in/at a certain place; **the book must be someplace in this library; we want to go someplace warm for our vacation.**

some·thing, *pronoun*

a certain thing; **there's something at the bottom of the bag; something's wrong with the engine; can I have something to eat?**

some·times, *adverb*

at certain various times; at a particular time; **sometimes it is cold in the summer; sometimes the car runs well, and sometimes it doesn't run at all; I sometimes go to Columbus on business.**

some·where, *adverb*

in/at a certain place; **I left my keys somewhere in the office; this restaurant is full—let's go somewhere else; he lives somewhere in Scotland.**

son [sʌn] *noun*

male child of a parent; **they have two sons and one daughter; her son is studying in France; my son Simon likes football.**

song [sɔːŋ] *noun*

words and music which are sung; **she was singing a song in the bathtub; have you heard his latest song?**

soon [suːn] *adverb*

(*a*) in a short time from now; **we'll soon be home; it will soon be dinnertime; I want to see you as soon as possible; I'll see you next week—can't you come any sooner? when did the fire start?—soon after 9 o'clock; sooner or later** = at some time in the future; **he drives so badly that sooner or later the police will catch him.**

(*b*) **would sooner** = would rather/prefer; **I'd sooner stay at home than go to the party;** *see also* **rather.**

as soon as = immediately; **as soon as he sat down the telephone rang.**
soon—sooner—soonest

sore [sɔːr] **1.** *adjective*

(*a*) which hurts; **she has a sore throat; his feet were sore after the long walk.**

(*b*) angry; **he's sore about losing the game.**
sore—sorer—sorest

2. *noun*
spot on the skin which hurts; **if you have an open sore you shouldn't go into the swimming pool.**

sor·ry ['sɔːrɪ] **1.** *adjective*
feeling bad about something which has happened; **I'm sorry it rained when you went on vacation; she stepped on my toe and didn't say she was sorry; we were all sorry to hear you had been ill; to feel sorry for someone** = to pity someone; **I feel sorry for her—her husband is very ill.**
2. *interjection*
used to pardon yourself; **sorry! I didn't see that you were in the bathroom; sorry! I've got the wrong number; can you give me a cigarette?—sorry! I don't have any left.**

sound [saʊnd] **1.** *noun*
something which you can hear; **the sound of music came through the open window; do you hear the sound of a train? I don't like the sound of that** = I don't like that/I don't think that is a good idea.
2. *verb*
to make a sound; **he sounded his horn when he came to the corner; that sounds strange** = what I hear seems strange; **it sounds like a car** = I think I can hear a car; **that sounds like my father** = (i) it is similar to the way my father talks; (ii) I think I can hear my father coming.
sounds—sounding—sounded—has sounded

soup [suːp] *noun*
liquid which you eat hot in a bowl at the beginning of a meal; **I don't like onion soup; do you want some soup? we had vegetable soup for dinner; open a can of soup—I'm hungry; soup bowl/soup spoon** = special bowl/spoon for eating soup.
no plural: **some soup; a bowl of soup**

sour [saʊər] *adjective*
(a) not sweet; **these oranges are as sour as lemons.**
(b) **sour milk** = milk which has gone bad; **you need sour cream to make this salad dressing.**
sour—sourer—sourest

south [saʊθ] **1.** *noun*
direction of where the sun is at noon; **the town is to the south of the mountains; the wind is blowing from the south.**
2. *adjective*
referring to the south; **the south coast of England; the south side of the river.**
3. *adverb*
towards the south; **birds fly south in the winter; go due south for ten miles.**
South A·mer·i·ca, *noun*
part of America containing Brazil, Argentina, Chile and several other countries.
south·ern ['sʌðərn] *adjective*
of the south; **they live in the southern part of the country; it's a southern wind** = coming from the south.
South Pole, *noun*
furthest point at the south of the earth.
south·ward, *adjective & adverb*
toward the south; **they traveled in a southward direction; he was moving southward into the desert when the police caught him.**

space [speɪs] *noun*
place/empty area between things; **park your car in that space over there; write your name and address in the space at the top of the paper; this table takes up a lot of space; (outer) space** = area beyond the earth where there are stars, etc.
space·craft, space·ship, *noun*
rocket in which men travel in space; **the spaceship returned to earth yesterday.**
no plural for **spacecraft**

spar·row ['spærəʊ] *noun*
small brown and gray bird; **several sparrows flew over to the table to eat the small pieces of bread.**

speak [spiːk] *verb*
to say words; to talk; **he walked past me without speaking; she was speaking to the mailman; can he speak English? I must speak to him about his son.**
speaks—speaking—spoke [spəʊk] **—has spoken**

speak·er, *noun*
(*a*) person who speaks; **he is a funny speaker** = he makes funny speeches.
(*b*) *see also* **loudspeaker**.

speak out, *verb*
to speak freely; **he spoke out against crime.**

speak up, *verb*
to speak louder; **speak up—I can't hear you!**

spe·cial [ˈspeʃəl] *adjective*
which refers to one particular thing; not ordinary; **this is a very special day—it's my birthday; he has a special pair of scissors for cutting his hair; there is nothing very special about his new car** = it is fairly ordinary.

sped [sped] *see* **speed**

speech [spiːtʃ] *noun*
(*a*) talk given in public; **she made a short speech at the dinner; all the speeches were much too long.**
(*b*) language; **the parts of speech** = different types of words which are used in different ways (like nouns/verbs, etc.).
plural **speeches, but no plural for (b)**

speed [spiːd] 1. *noun*
how fast you move; **the car was traveling at high speed; if you go at a speed of 30 miles per hour you'll use less gasoline; the ship was going at full speed.**
2. *verb*
to go fast; **the car sped across the road; he was arrested for speeding** = for going too fast.
speeds—speeding—sped [sped]/ **speeded—has sped/has speeded**

speed lim·it, *noun*
highest speed at which you are allowed to drive; **the speed limit here is 30 miles per hour.**

speed up, *verb*
to go faster; to make something go faster; to do something faster; **can't you speed it up? I'm in a hurry to get to work.**

spell [spel] 1. *noun*
short period; **the cold spell lasted a week.**

2. *verb*
to write or say correctly the letters which make a word; **how do you spell your name? you've spelled his name wrong; L-A-U-G-H spells "laugh"; his name is Steven, but I don't know if it's spelt PH or V** = if it is Stephen or Steven.
spells—spelling—spelled/spelt— has spelled/has spelt

spell·ing, *noun*
way in which words are spelled; **he writes very well, but his spelling is bad.**

spend [spend] *verb*
(*a*) to pay money in a store, restaurant, etc.; **I spent $6 on a new tie; I don't like spending too much money on food; he has saved up all his pocket money and is going to spend it on Christmas presents.**
(*b*) to pass time; **we spent our vacation in Maine last year; he spent two hours fixing the car; why don't you spend the weekend with us? don't spend hours doing your homework.**
spends—spending—spent—has spent

spi·der [ˈspaɪdər] *noun*
small animal with eight legs, which makes a net to catch flies; **she's afraid of spiders; help! there's a spider in the bathtub.**

spill [spɪl] *verb*
to let liquid fall by mistake; **I spilled some soup down my shirt; the cat knocked over the bottle and the milk spilled all over the table.**
spills—spilling—spilled/spilt [spɪlt] **—has spilled/has spilt**

splash [splæʃ] 1. *noun*
noise made by liquid being thrown; **he fell into the swimming pool with a big splash; you could hear the the splash of the waves on the rocks.**
plural **splashes**
2. *verb*
to make a noise of liquid being thrown; to cover with drops of liquid; **the waves splashed against the rocks; the children were splashing around in the pool; the bus**

splashed me with dirty water; when you're painting the ceiling, be careful not to splash paint on the rug.

splashes—splashing—splashed—has splashed

split [splɪt] 1. *noun*
thin crack in something solid; **there is a split in this piece of wood; do you know that you've got a split in the back of your pants? banana split** = dessert made with bananas, ice cream, sweet sauce and nuts.
2. *verb*
to divide something into parts; to make something crack or tear; **if you get any fatter, you'll split your pants; my pants split when I bent down; the committee has split into three groups; let's split the money between us.**

splits—splitting—split—has split

split up, *verb*
to divide into parts; to separate; **the students split up into two groups; let's split up and meet at the post office in half an hour; her parents split up after living together for years.**

spoke [spəʊk], **spoken** ['spəʊkən] *see* **speak**

spoon [spuːn] 1. *noun*
long tool with a handle at one end and a small bowl at the other, used for eating; **eat your dessert with your spoon, not with your knife; do you have a big spoon to serve the peas? soup spoon** = special spoon for eating soup.
2. *verb*
to move something with a spoon; **she was spooning out ice cream onto all the plates.**

spoons—spooning—spooned—has spooned

spoon·ful, *noun*
amount which a spoon can hold; **he put two spoonfuls of sugar into his coffee.**

sport [spɔːrt] *noun*
game which you play; all games; **I like watching sports on TV; do you like the sports programs on TV? the only sport**

I play is football; he doesn't like any sport at all.

sports car, *noun*
fast open car.

sports·cast·er ['spɔːrtskæstər] *noun*
person who gives news about sports on radio or TV; **the sportscaster gave the scores for all the baseball games.**

spot [spɒt] 1. *noun*
(a) place; **this is a good spot for a picnic; this is the spot where the accident took place; he was killed on the spot** = immediately.
(b) small round mark; **he has a blue tie with red spots; you've got spots of mud on your coat; he must be sick—his face is covered with red spots.**
2. *verb*
to notice; **he spotted a mistake in my homework; did you spot the color of the car?**

spots—spotting—spotted—has spotted

sprang [spræŋ] *see* **spring**

spread [spred] *verb*
(a) to send out/to go out over a wide area; **don't spread the news—it's supposed to be a secret; the soldiers spread out across the fields; the fire spread to the house next door.**
(b) to cover with; **she spread a cloth over the table; he was spreading butter on his bread; don't spread too much glue on the paper.**

spreads—spreading—spread—has spread

spring [sprɪŋ] *noun*
(a) season of the year between winter and summer; **in spring, the trees grow new leaves; we always go on vacation in the spring; they started work last spring/in the spring of last year; what beautiful spring flowers!**
(b) wire which is twisted round and round and which goes back to its first shape after you have pulled it; strong pieces of metal which allow a car to go easily over bumps; **there are no springs in this bed; there's a spring to**

keep the door closed; my car needs new springs.

square [skweər] *noun & adjective*
(*a*) shape with four equal sides and four corners of 90°; **the floor is covered with black and white squares; it's difficult to fit six people around a small square table; this piece of paper isn't square; ten square feet** = area of 10 feet × 10 feet.
(*b*) open area in a town, surrounded by big buildings; **I'll meet you on Public Square; Red Square is in the middle of Moscow.**
Note: **ten square meters** *is usually written* **10m²**

squash [skwɒʃ] 1. *noun*
large green or yellow vegetable with hard skin; **they grow summer squash in their garden; we're having yellow squash and chicken for dinner.**
plural **squashes** *or* **squash**
2. *verb*
to make something flat; to press together; **he sat on my hat and squashed it; don't put the cake at the bottom of the bag—it'll get squashed.**
squashes—squashing— squashed—has squashed

squeeze [skwiːz] *verb*
to press hard; to press together; **he squeezed the juice out of the lemon; they all squeezed into the little car.**
squeezes—squeezing— squeezed—has squeezed

squir·rel [ˈskwɜrəl] *noun*
common brown or gray animal with a bushy tail; **the squirrel gathered nuts in the grass.**

staff [stæf] *noun*
group of people who work in a school/ business, etc.; **the company has a staff of 100; the staff don't like the new offices.**
Note: when used as a subject, **staff** *often takes a plural verb;* **a staff of 25** *but* **the staff work very hard**

stage [steɪdʒ] *noun*
part of a theater where the actors act; **he came onto the stage and started to sing.**

stairs [steərz] *plural noun*
steps which go up or down from one floor of a building to the next; **he ran up the stairs to his bedroom; she fell down the stairs and broke her leg;** *see also* **downstairs, upstairs.**
Note: **stair** *is sometimes used in the singular for one step:* **she was sitting on the bottom stair**

stair·case, *noun*
several stairs which go from one floor in a building to another; **he fell down the staircase; this staircase goes down to the ground floor.**

stamp [stæmp] 1. *noun*
(*a*) small piece of paper with a price printed on it which you stick on a letter to show that you have paid for it to be sent by mail; **you need a 20¢ stamp for that letter; did you remember to put a stamp on my letter before you mailed it? he collects stamps and old coins.**
(*b*) machine for making a mark on something; mark made on something; **he has a stamp for marking the date on letters; there was a government stamp at the top of the letter.**
2. *verb*
(*a*) to stick a stamp on something; to mark something with a stamp; **did they stamp your passport when you entered the country? send a stamped self-addressed envelope for a reply** = an envelope with your address and a stamp on it.
(*b*) to bang your foot on the ground; **they stamped on the floor and shouted; he stamped out of the room.**
stamps—stamping—stamped— has stamped

stand [stænd] 1. *noun*
(*a*) something which holds something up; **put the pot back on the stand; refreshment stand** = small building or table where light food and drinks are sold.

(b) seats where you watch a football game, etc.; **the stands were crowded.**

2. *verb*

(a) to be straight up; to put straight up; **stand the ladder against the wall; the box was standing in the middle of the room.**

(b) to be on your feet/not to be sitting or lying; **I'm so tired I can hardly stand; there are no seats left, so we'll have to stand; don't just stand there—come and help; stand on a chair if you want to reach the top of the cupboard.**

(c) not to be upset by; **I can't stand all this noise; what a dirty office—I don't know how you can stand it; she stopped going to her German class because she couldn't stand the teacher.**
stands—standing—stood [stʊd]—**has stood**

stand a·round, *verb*
to stand without doing anything; **they just stood around and watched.**

stand back, *verb*
to take a step or two backwards; **the police told the crowd to stand back as the president rode by.**

stand for, *verb*
to mean; **what do the letters U.S.A. stand for?**

stand out, *verb*
to be very clear against a background; **the blue picture stands out very well against the white wall.**

stand up, *verb*
(a) to get up from being on a seat; **when the teacher came into the room all the children stood up; please don't stand up!**

(b) to hold yourself on your feet; **stand up straight.**

(c) to put something straight up; **stand all those books up; he stood his umbrella up in the corner of the room.**

stand up for, *verb*
to try to defend someone/something in an argument; **you must stand up for your rights.**

star [stɑːr] *noun*
(a) small bright light which you see in the sky at night; **look at all those stars—the weather will be nice tomorrow.**

(b) famous person who acts in a play or

movie; **she's the star of the new movie; a TV star.**

stare [steər] *verb*
to look straight at someone/something for a long time; **he stared at his plate; it's rude to stare at people; she kept staring at me.**
stares—staring—stared—has stared

start [stɑːrt] 1. *noun*
beginning; **it took 3 hours from start to finish; we must get an early start** = we must leave early.

2. *verb*

(a) to begin; **he started eating his sandwiches; it's starting to rain; have you started your new job yet? we'll start by learning the alphabet; we must start to get ready or we'll miss the train; when does the movie start?**

(b) to begin to work; to make something begin to work; **I can't start the car/the car won't start.**
starts—starting—started—has started

start off, start out, *verb*
to begin; to leave; **we'll start off for the city early in the morning; they started out with no money but now they are very rich; we'll start off with soup and then have some fish.**

state [steɪt] 1. *noun*
(a) way in which something is; **the house isn't in a very good state; his state of health is getting worse.**

(b) independent country or part of a country with its own government; **the African states; the United States of America; the State of California; the electricity industry is owned by the state; she was active in state and local government; he was arrested by the state police.**

2. *verb*
to say clearly; **she stated that she had never been to Paris; the form states the details of the job.**
states—stating—stated—has stated

state·ment, *noun*
clear description of something; **he made**

a statement to the police; the president made a statement about prices; bank statement = paper showing how much money you have in your bank account.

sta·tion ['steɪʃən] *noun*
(a) place where trains stop for passengers to get on or off; **can you tell me the way to the station? the train doesn't stop at the next station; we can have something to eat at the station while we wait for the train to arrive.**
(b) **bus station** = place where buses begin and end their journeys; **we had to wait at the bus station for an hour.**
(c) large building for some service; **fire station/police station; the policeman said we would have to go down to the station; power station** = factory which makes electricity; **service station** = garage which sells gasoline and repairs cars; **TV station/radio station** = main building where TV or radio programs are produced.

stay [steɪ] 1. *noun*
time which you spend in a place; **I'm only here for a short stay.**
2. *verb*
to stop in a place for some time; **I'll stay at home tomorrow; we'll stay in Los Angeles on our way to San Francisco; how long will you be staying in New York? she's sick and has to stay in bed; they came for dinner and stayed until ten o'clock.**
stays—staying—stayed—has stayed

stay out, *verb*
not to come home; **don't stay out after ten o'clock.**

stay put, *verb*
to remain in a place for a long time; **they've lived in several different cities, but now they plan to stay put.**

stay up, *verb*
not to go to bed; **we stayed up very late last night; little children shouldn't stay up watching TV; I'm staying up to watch the late movie on TV.**

steak [steɪk] *verb*
thick slice of meat, usually beef, cut

from the best part of the animal; **he took me out for a steak dinner; can I have some more steak?** = another piece of steak.

steal [stiːl] *verb*
to take something which does not belong to you; **the burglar stole all the jewelry; someone has stolen my car.**
steals—stealing—stole [stəʊl]—**has stolen**

steam [stiːm] *noun*
hot gas which comes off boiling water; **steam was coming out of the kettle; the train was pulled by an old steam engine.**

steel [stiːl] *noun*
strong metal used for making knives/cars, etc.; **he works in the steel industry; he has glasses with steel frames; you need a pair of steel scissors—those plastic ones won't cut paper!**
no plural

steep [stiːp] *adjective*
which slopes up or down a lot; **the car had trouble going up the steep hill; there has been a steep increase in prices.**
steep—steeper—steepest

steer [stɪr] *verb*
to make a car/a boat go in a certain direction; **he steered the boat into the harbor; steer towards that rock.**
steers—steering—steered—has steered

steer·ing wheel, *noun*
wheel in a car which you hold, and turn to make the car turn.

step [step] 1. *noun*
(a) movement of your foot when walking; **he took two steps forward; she took a big step sideways; step by step** = little by little.
(b) regular movement of feet; **out of step/in step** = moving at a different rate/at the same rate as everyone/everything else; **try to keep in step; wages are out of step with the rise in prices.**
(c) place where you walk going up or down; **there is a step down into the kitchen; be careful, there are two steps**

up into the bathroom; to go from the house into the yard you have to go down some steps.
(d) action; we must take steps to make sure that we do not lose money; the first step is to find out how much money we are spending = the first thing to do.
2. *verb*
to move forward on foot; he stepped out into the street; she stepped off the bus; step over that pile of garbage.
steps—stepping—stepped—has stepped

step up, *verb*
to increase; we are trying to step up production.

stick [stɪk] 1. *noun*
(a) piece of wood; collect some dry sticks to light a fire.
(b) **walking stick** = long piece of wood which you use to help you to walk; the blind man had a white stick.
2. *verb*
(a) to push something sharp into something; he stuck a pin into me; the nurse stuck a needle into my arm.
(b) to attach (with glue); he stuck the stamp on the envelope; she tried to stick the handle onto the cup with glue.
(c) to stay and not to move; stick close to me and you won't get lost; the car got stuck in the mud; the door is stuck and we can't open it.
(d) to push/to put; he stuck the letter in his pocket; stick all those books in the back of the car.
sticks—sticking—stuck [stʌk]—**has stuck**

stick a·round, *verb*
to stay here; he didn't stick around long enough to learn the job.

stick out, *verb*
to push out; to be further out; the doctor asked him to stick out his tongue/to stick his tongue out; his wallet was sticking out of his pocket.
Note: **he stuck his tongue out** *or* **he stuck out his tongue** *but only* **he stuck it out**

stick up for, *verb*
to try to defend someone/something in an argument; he stuck up for her when the manager wanted to fire her; *see also* **stand up for.**

stick·y, *adjective*
which is covered with glue; there's something sticky on the table; don't sit on that chair—the paint is still sticky.
sticky—stickier—stickiest

stiff [stɪf] *adjective*
(a) which cannot be bent or moved easily; my knee is stiff after playing football; brush your coat with a stiff brush; he's frozen stiff = very cold.
(b) difficult; you have to take a stiff driving test.
stiff—stiffer—stiffest

still [stɪl] 1. *adjective*
not moving; stand still while I take your picture; the surface of the water was completely still.
2. *adverb*
(a) until now/until then/continuing; they came for lunch and they were still here at ten o'clock; I've still got some money left; they're still talking about the election.
(b) even; there were fifty people in the room and still more tried to get in; it has been cold all day, and it will be still colder tonight.
(c) however; it wasn't very sunny—still, it didn't rain; he still went on vacation although he had no money.

stock [stɒk] *noun*
(a) supply of goods; do you have any envelopes in stock? we're out of stock right now = we don't have any.
(b) shares in a company; his father owns stock in the telephone company.

stock·ing [ˈstɒkɪŋ] *noun*
long light piece of clothing worn by women which covers all your leg and your foot; she was wearing blue stockings and white shoes.

stole [stəʊl], **stolen** [ˈstəʊlən] *see* **steal**

stom·ach ['stʌmək] *noun*
part of the front of the body lower than the chest; **he hit him in the stomach; he slid across the room on his stomach; stomach ache** = pain in the stomach caused by eating too much food, etc.

stone [stəʊn] *noun*
(*a*) hard material, found in the ground, and used for building; **a big stone bridge; the houses in the town are all built of stone; these stone floors are very cold.**
(*b*) small piece of stone; **don't throw stones at the cars; she's got a stone in her shoe; the beach is covered with sharp stones.**
ston·y, *adjective*
covered with stones; **a stony beach.**
stony—stonier—stoniest

stood [stʊd] *see* **stand**

stop [stɒp] 1. *noun*
(*a*) end of something, especially of a movement; **the car came to a stop at the bottom of the hill; we must put a stop to crime; all work came to a stop when the company couldn't pay the workers.**
(*b*) place where a bus lets passengers get on or off; **we waited for twenty minutes at the bus stop; the bus stop is right in front of the post office; I must get off at the next stop.**
2. *verb*
(*a*) not to move any more; to make something not move any more; **the policeman stopped the traffic to let the children cross the street; the car didn't stop at the red light; some trains don't stop at this station; the bus just went past without stopping; stop him! he has stolen my watch!**
(*b*) not to do something any more; **can't you stop that noise? the clock stopped at 3:30; it has stopped raining; last week it rained for three days without stopping; he stopped work and went home.**
(*c*) to stay in a place for a time; **we'll be stopping in Rome for a few days on our way to Greece; can you stop at the butcher shop on your way home and buy some meat for dinner?**

(*d*) **to stop someone/something from doing something** = to prevent someone/something from doing something; **the weather stopped us from playing baseball; can the police stop the children from stealing candy?**
stops—stopping—stopped—has stopped

stop·light, *noun*
traffic light; **he raced through the stoplight.**

stop off, stop o·ver, *verb*
to spend a night in a place on a long journey; **we'll stop over in Amsterdam on the way to Moscow.**

stop up, *verb*
to block; **you can stop up the hole with a piece of wood.**
Note: **stop the hole up** *or* **stop up the hole** *but only* **stop it up**

store [stɔːr] 1. *noun*
(*a*) place where you can buy things; **there are three department stores at the shopping center; the furniture store is next to the bookstore; all the stores are closed on Sundays; does this store have a restaurant?**
(*b*) food, etc., kept to use later; **we have a big store of wood for the winter.**
2. *verb*
to keep food, etc., to use later; **we'll store all our apples in that cupboard.**
stores—storing—stored—has stored

store·keep·er, *noun*
person who owns a store.

store·room, *noun*
room in which things are kept for use later; **would you put these boxes in the storeroom?**

storm [stɔːrm] *noun*
very bad weather with a high wind; **two ships sank in the storm; the storm blew down two trees; we often have storms in March.**
storm·y, *adjective*
with storms; **a period of stormy weather.**
stormy—stormier—stormiest

sto·ry ['stɔːrɪ] *noun*
(*a*) telling of what happened; **tell the**

Streets

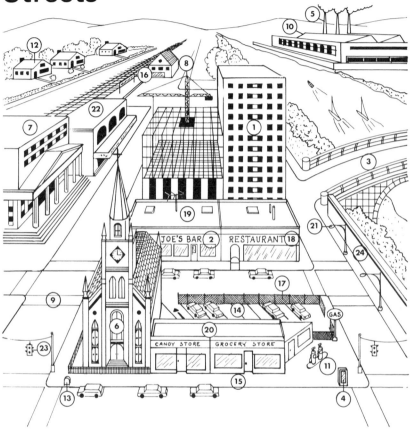

1. apartment
2. bar
3. bridge
4. phone booth
5. chimney
6. church
7. city hall
8. crane
9. crosswalk
10. factory
11. gas station
12. house
13. mailbox
14. parking lot
15. sidewalk
16. railroad station
17. railing
18. restaurant
19. roof
20. stores
21. streetlight
22. theater
23. traffic light
24. wall

policeman your story; it's a long story =
it is difficult to explain what happened;
the film is the story of two children and
a little white dog; he writes stories about
the war.
(b) lie/something which is not true; **don't
tell stories.**
(c) floor of a building; **this building has
15 stories; a ten-story building.**
plural **stories**

stove [stəʊv] *noun*
machine for cooking or heating; **we
have a gas stove in the kitchen; please
take that pan off the stove.**

straight [streɪt] 1. *adjective*
(a) not curved; **a straight road; draw a
straight line; he has long straight hair.**
(b) neat/in its proper place; **your tie isn't
straight; now that you've moved it, the
picture is straight; let's get it straight** =
let us understand clearly what
happened/understand the situation.
straight—straighter—straightest
2. *adverb*
(a) in a straight line/not curving; **keep
going straight until you come to the traffic
lights; see if you can walk straight after
going on this ride.**
(b) immediately; **I'll come straight back;
he went straight to the police.**
(c) without stopping or changing direction; **he drank the milk straight out of
the bottle; he ran straight across the road
without looking; she looked him straight
in the face.**
straight·en, *verb*
to make straight or neat; **you'd better
straighten up your room before your
mother gets home; I must straighten that
picture on the wall.**
**straightens—straightening—
straightened—has straightened**

strange [streɪndʒ] *adjective*
(a) odd/not usual; **the car engine is
making a strange sound; he said some
very strange things about his boss.**
(b) which you have never seen before/
where you have never been before; **it's
difficult to get to sleep in a strange room;**

we went to Hong Kong and had lots of
strange food to eat.
strange—stranger—strangest
stran·ger, *noun*
person whom you have never met;
person in a place where he has never
been before; **he's a complete stranger;
don't accept presents from strangers; I'm
a stranger here—I'm afraid I don't know
where the post office is.**

straw·ber·ry [ˈstrɔːberɪ] *noun*
small red fruit growing on low plants;
**we will have strawberries and whipped
cream for dessert; he likes strawberry ice
cream.**
plural **strawberries**

stream [striːm] *noun*
(a) small river; **he jumped over the
mountain stream.**
(b) large numbers of cars/people, etc.,
all going in the same direction; **streams
of cars were going toward the coast;
you can't cross the stream of traffic.**

street [striːt] *noun*
road in a city or town, with houses or
stores on each side; **the main street is
very busy on Saturday mornings; go
down the street to the traffic lights; the
post office is on the other side of the
street; where do you live?—16 Oxford
Street.**
Note: often used in names: **Oxford
Street, Main Street,** *etc., and
usually written* **St.: Oxford St**.
street·light, *noun*
light at the top of a tall post along a
street; **the streetlights come on just
before sunset.**

strength [streŋθ] *noun*
being strong; **he kicked the ball with all
his strength; he doesn't know his own
strength** = he doesn't know how strong
he really is.
no plural

stretch [stretʃ] *verb*
(a) to pull out; to make longer; **the wire
was stretched between two poles; you've
stretched your sweater by pulling it over**

your head = made it become too big.

(*b*) to put out your arms and legs as far as they will go; **he stretched out his hand and took a book from the shelf; the cat got up from the chair and stretched; she lay stretched out on the floor.**

(*c*) to go on for a great distance; **the sea stretched all around us; the road stretches for miles.**

stretches—stretching— stretched—has stretched

strike [straɪk] **1.** *noun*

(*a*) stopping of work by workers; **the office workers are on strike; the strike by the bus drivers lasted two weeks.**

(*b*) missing the ball when you are at bat in a baseball game; **he has got two strikes so far.**

2. *verb*

(*a*) to hit; **he struck a policeman with a bottle; the car went down the hill and struck a tree.**

(*b*) to surprise; to make someone think; **I was struck by what she said; it strikes me that she was telling a lie** = it seems to me.

(*c*) to stop work; **the employees are striking for more money.**

(*d*) (*of a clock*) to ring a bell to show the hour; **the church clock struck ten.**

(*e*) to light (a match).

strikes—striking—struck [strʌk]— **has struck**

strike out, *verb*

to set off; **he struck out towards the top of the hill.**

string [strɪŋ] *noun*

(*a*) thin threads twisted together; **tie the package up with a piece of string; I bought a ball of string; this string isn't strong enough; do you have any more string?**

(*b*) long thread on a musical instrument which makes a note when you hit it; **a guitar has six strings.**

no plural for (*a*): **some string; a piece of string**

strong [strɔːŋ] *adjective*

(*a*) who/which has a lot of force/a lot of strength; **is he strong enough to pick up that box? the rope is broken—we need something stronger; the strong wind blew all the leaves off the trees; he's feeling stronger now that the worst part of the illness is over** = he's feeling healthier.

(*b*) with a powerful smell/taste, etc.; **this cheese is too strong; this tea is too strong—put some water in it; what I want is a cup of strong black coffee; there was a strong smell of onions.**

strong—stronger—strongest

struck [strʌk] *see* **strike**

stuck [stʌk] *see* **stick**

stu·dent [ˈstjuːdənt] *noun*

person who is studying at a school, college or university; **all the students are preparing for their exams.**

stud·y [ˈstʌdɪ] **1.** *noun*

learning about something; **she has finished her studies** = has finished her education at a college/university, etc.; **he's making a study of diseases of fish.**

plural **studies**

2. *verb*

to learn about something; **he's studying math; don't make any noise—we're all studying for our exams; she studied very hard at college.**

studies—studying—studied—has studied

stuff [stʌf] **1.** *noun*

material/things (especially when you don't know what it is); **put some of that stuff in the bottom of the box; there's some green stuff on the table—I don't know what it is; there's still some stuff left in the car.**

no plural

2. *verb*

to push hard into; **he stuffed the papers into his pocket; she was stuffing her clothes into a suitcase.**

stuffs—stuffing—stuffed—has stuffed

stu·pid [ˈstjuːpɪd] *adjective*

silly/not very smart; **don't be stupid—**

you can't drive a car if you haven't passed your test; he's a stupid boy—he spends all his time watching TV instead of doing his homework; that was a stupid thing to do.

sub·ject [ˈsʌbdʒekt] *noun*
(*a*) word which shows the person or thing doing an action; **in the sentence "the dog fell into the water" the word "dog" is the subject.**
(*b*) thing which is being talked about, written about or studied; **I have to study three subjects—English, math and science; what subject does Mr. Smith teach?—he teaches English; the subject of his book is American history; she's talking on the subject "the place of women in Congress"; let's change the subject** = let's talk about something else.

sub·tract [sʌbˈtrækt] *verb*
to take one number away from another; **subtract 24 from 86 and the answer is 62.**
subtracts—subtracting subtracted—has subtracted
sub·trac·tion [sʌbˈtrækʃən] *noun*
taking one number from another; **I'm good at subtraction, but I can't do division.**

suc·ceed [səkˈsiːd] *verb*
to do well; to do what you have been trying to do; **he tried to climb up the tree but didn't succeed; she succeeded in finding a good job; this book tells you how to succeed in business.**
succeeds—succeeding succeeded—has succeeded
suc·cess [səkˈses] *noun*
(*a*) doing something well; doing what you have been trying to do; **I've been trying to get a job, but with no success.**
(*b*) somebody/something which does well; **the party was not a success; his new play is a great success.**
plural **successes**
suc·cess·ful, *adjective*
which does well; **a successful party; he's a successful businessman.**
suc·cess·ful·ly, *adverb*
well; **he manages to do everything successfully.**

such [sʌtʃ] *adjective*
(*a*) like; of this kind; **people such as doctors need to study for many years; there is no such thing as a plastic frying pan; there is no such day as February 30; he was asking for Miss Jones, but there is no such person working here.**
(*b*) so large/so great; **there was such a crowd of people that there were not enough chairs; he's such a slow worker; people can't afford to drive such large cars.**

sud·den [ˈsʌdən] *adjective*
which happens quickly and without warning; which surprises; **there was a sudden bang and smoke poured out of the engine; don't drive too fast—there's a sudden bend in the road.**
all of a sudden = happening quickly and making you surprised; **all of a sudden the lights went out.**
sud·den·ly, *adverb*
happening quickly and making you surprised; **the car stopped suddenly; suddenly a police car appeared behind us.**

sug·ar [ˈʃʊɡər] *noun*
white or brown sweet stuff which you use to make food sweet; **do you take sugar in your coffee? there's too much sugar in this cake; can you buy a bag of sugar—we don't have any left.**
no plural: **some sugar; a bag of sugar; a lump of sugar**

sug·gest [səˈdʒest] *verb*
to mention an idea; **I suggest we stop for a cup of coffee; she suggested that we should ask John to the party; we've suggested to the principal that he should talk to the parents.**
suggests—suggesting suggested—has suggested
sug·ges·tion, *noun*
idea which has been mentioned; **I don't agree with your suggestion that we should stop for coffee; can I make a suggestion? it was my suggestion that we should all go for a walk.**

suit [suːt] **1.** *noun*
(*a*) various pieces of clothing (jacket and

pants or skirt) made of the same cloth and worn at the same time; **he had a dark gray suit on; she was wearing a blue suit.** (*b*) one of the four groups of cards with the same pattern in a pack of cards; **you must draw two cards of the same suit; to follow suit** = to do what everyone else does; **he ran up the stairs and we all followed suit.**

2. *verb*

(*a*) to fit; **I don't think he's suited for this type of work.**

(*b*) to be convenient; **he only works when it suits him** = when he wants to; **that suits me fine** = that is very convenient; **suit yourself** = do whatever you want.

suits—suiting—suited—has suited

suit·a·ble, *adjective*

which fits/which is convenient; **the most suitable date for the meeting would be October 18; they're trying to think of a suitable title for the book.**

suit·case, *noun*

box with a handle which you carry your clothes in when you are traveling; **she was putting her clothes into a suitcase; your suitcase is very heavy.**

sum [sʌm] *noun*

(*a*) problem in math; **he's no good at sums; I can't do this sum; she tried to do the sum in her head** = without writing it down.

(*b*) total amount (of money); **she received the sum of $25.**

sum·mer [ˈsʌmər] *noun*

hottest season of the year, the season between spring and autumn; **most people go on vacation in the summer; last summer we went to Greece; summer is the hottest time of the year; I don't have any summer clothes—it is never very warm here.**

sun [sʌn] *noun*

very hot star around which the earth travels and which gives light and heat; **we can go for a walk now that the sun is shining again; the sun is so hot that we'll have to sit in the shade; you can't spend all day just sitting in the sun** = sitting in the sunshine; **the sun rises in the east.**

sun·burn, *noun*

having red skin from being in the sun too long; **she got a bad sunburn at the beach today.**

sun·flow·er, *noun*

very large yellow flower with seeds you can eat; **the sunflower was five feet tall.**

sun·glass·es, *plural noun*

dark glasses which you wear to protect your eyes from the sun; **he kept bumping into the chairs because he wore his sunglasses in the house.**

sun·light, *noun*

light from the sun; **this plant needs a lot of sunlight to grow well.**

no plural: **some sunlight**

sun·ny, *adjective*

with the sun shining; **a sunny day; the sunny side of the street.**

sunny—sunnier—sunniest

sun·rise, *noun*

time when the sun comes up in the morning.

sun·set, *noun*

time when the sun goes down in the evening.

sun·shine, *noun*

light from the sun; **the sunshine hurts my eyes.**

no plural: **some sunshine**

sun·tan, *noun*

having brown skin after being in the sun; **she got a good suntan on her vacation in Hawaii.**

Sun·day [ˈsʌndɪ] *noun*

day between Saturday and Monday; **last Sunday we went on a picnic; the stores are closed on Sundays; shall we meet next Sunday? today is Sunday, October 18.**

sung [sʌŋ] *see* **sing**

sunk [sʌŋk] *see* **sink**

su·per·mar·ket [ˈsuːpərmɑːrkɪt] *noun*

large store which sells mainly food, where you take things from the shelves and pay for them as you leave; **go to the supermarket and get me some coffee; the supermarket stays open late on Friday evenings.**

sup·per ['sʌpər] *noun*
meal which you eat in the evening; **what did you eat for supper? we have supper at about seven o'clock; come and have supper with us tomorrow.**
see note at **dinner**

sup·ply [sə'plaɪ] 1. *noun*
(*a*) something which is provided; **the electricity supply has broken down; the army dropped supplies to the farms which were cut off by the snow; the store sells school supplies** = pencils, paper, etc., needed by schoolchildren.
(*b*) something which is kept for later use; **we have a good supply of wood for the winter; eggs are in short supply now** = there are not many eggs in the stores.
plural **supplies**
2. *verb*
to provide/to give something which is needed; **the army is supplying the farms with food; bread is supplied by the local bakery; the town is supplied with water from the river; can you supply me with information about the accident? he couldn't supply any information about vacations in Germany.**
supplies—supplying—supplied—has supplied

sup·pose [sə'pəʊz] *verb*
(*a*) to think; to imagine; **I suppose she will be late as usual; are you going to the party tonight?—I suppose so; he's supposed to be a good doctor** = people say he is a good doctor.
(*b*) **to be supposed to** = ought to; **you're supposed to be in bed.**
(*c*) **suppose/supposing** = if we imagine/what happens if; **suppose/supposing it rains tomorrow, shall we still go on the picnic? suppose/supposing he has had an accident?**
supposes—supposing—supposed—has supposed

sure [ʃʊr] 1. *adjective*
certain; **I'm sure he'll come to the party; are you sure she'll lend you her car? are you sure you haven't lost the key? it's sure to be cold in Canada in January; make sure/be sure you lock all the doors.**

2. *adverb*
yes, of course; **will you come to the store with me? Sure!**
sure·ly, *adverb*
of course (*used mostly in questions where a particular answer is expected*) **surely you don't expect him to go out in the rain? surely his name is John not James?**

sur·face ['sɜrfɪs] *noun*
top part of something which the air touches; **the fish came to the surface of the water to breathe; the table has a shiny surface.**

sur·prise [sər'praɪz] 1. *noun*
feeling caused by something which you did not expect to happen; **let's hide behind the door and give him a surprise; they made her a big birthday cake as a surprise; what a surprise to meet him in the supermarket!**
2. *verb*
to give someone a surprise; **I'm surprised to hear that he is in prison; I wouldn't be surprised if it snows.**
surprises—surprising—surprised—has surprised

swal·low ['swɒləʊ] *verb*
to make food go down from your mouth to your stomach; **chew your food well or you won't be able to swallow it; give him a glass of water—he has swallowed a fly.**
swallows—swallowing—swallowed—has swallowed

swam [swæm] *see* **swim**

sweat·er ['swetər] *noun*
knitted piece of clothing for the top part of the body and arms; **her mother knitted her a sweater; he wore a gray sweater.**

sweep [swi:p] *verb*
(*a*) to clean with a brush; **he swept the dead leaves into a pile; don't forget to sweep the kitchen floor.**
(*b*) to go fast; **the crowd swept into the street; the flood swept away many houses** = took them away.
sweeps—sweeping—swept—has swept

sweet [swiːt] 1. *adjective*
tasting like sugar; not sour/bitter; **my coffee is too sweet—I put two spoonfuls of sugar in it; do you like sweet drinks? oranges are sweeter than lemons; he has a sweet tooth** = he likes sweet things.
sweet—sweeter—sweetest

2. *noun*
candy; sweet food, made with sugar; **he likes sweets; eating sweets is bad for your teeth.**

sweet·en, *verb*
to make sweet; **she sweetened her tea with honey.**
sweetens—sweetening—sweetened—has sweetened

sweet po·ta·to, *noun*
sweet vegetable which grows under the ground; **they had ham and sweet potatoes for dinner.**
plural **sweet potatoes**

swept [swept] *see* **sweep**

swim [swɪm] 1. *noun*
moving in the water, using your arms and legs to push you along; **we went for a swim before breakfast; it's too cold to have a swim.**

2. *verb*
to move in water using your arms and legs to push you along; **he can't swim; she's learning to swim; I swam across the river twice; can you swim under the water? let's go swimming this afternoon.**
swims—swimming—swam [swæm]—has swum [swʌm]

swim·mer, *noun*
person who swims.

swim·ming pool, *noun*
special pool of water built for swimming in; **our school has an indoor swimming pool; we have a little swimming pool in the yard; he swam two lengths of the swimming pool.**

swim·suit, *noun*
light piece of clothing you wear for swimming; **she bought a new swimsuit before going on vacation.**

swing [swɪŋ] 1. *verb*
(a) to move from side to side or forwards and backwards; **he was swinging on a rope; the door swung open.**
(b) to turn suddenly; **he swung around and shouted something; the car swung across the road and hit a tree.**
swings—swinging—swung [swʌŋ]—has swung

2. *noun*
small seat on the end of two ropes which you can sit on and swing through the air; **the little girl wanted to go on the swing; there was a large swing hanging from the tree.**

switch [swɪtʃ] 1. *noun*
button which you push to stop or start something electric; **push the red switch to start the engine; the light switch is behind the door.**
plural **switches**

2. *verb*
to switch on/off = to make an electric machine start/stop; **can you switch the TV off when you go to bed? he forgot to switch off his car lights/to switch his car lights off; switch on the radio/switch the radio on—it's time for the news.**
switches—switching—switched—has switched
Note: **he switched the radio off** *or* **he switched off the radio** *but only* **he switched it off**

swum [swʌm] *see* **swim**

swung [swʌŋ] *see* **swing**

syl·la·ble [ˈsɪləbəl] *noun*
part of a word with a single sound; **divide this word into syllables; "traffic" has two syllables; the first syllable of "notice" is "no."**

sys·tem [ˈsɪstəm] *noun*
arrangement of things so that they work together; **the country's railroad system; I don't understand the tax system; he has a special system for organizing his record collection.**

Tt

ta·ble [teɪbəl] *noun*

piece of furniture with a flat top and legs, which is used to eat at/to work at, etc.; **a dining room table; a kitchen table; can you set the table please?** = put the knives/forks/spoons/plates, etc., on a table ready for a meal; **let me help you clear the table** = take away the dirty knives/forks/spoons/plates, etc., after a meal.

ta·ble·cloth, *noun*

cloth which you put on a table for a meal.

ta·ble·spoon, *noun*

large spoon used for measuring or serving food; **add two tablespoons of sugar to the mixture.**

tag [tæg] *noun*

small piece of paper attached to an object; **look at the price tag on the dress.**

tail [teɪl] *noun*

(*a*) back part of an animal at the end of the body just above the legs, usually sticking out; **the cat was moving its tail from side to side; some birds have very long tails; a fish swims with its tail.**

(*b*) side of a coin opposite the head; **let's play heads or tails** = let's throw the coin in the air to see which side comes down on top.

take [teɪk] *verb*

(*a*) to pick something up; **he took the book from the shelf; she took the newspaper off the table.**

(*b*) to go with something to another place; **can you take this letter to the post office? she was taking her children to school; he has taken the car to the garage.**

(*c*) to steal; **who took my pen? someone has taken my car.**

(*d*) to fill (a space); **this seat is taken; please take a seat.**

(*e*) to do an examination or test; **he's taking his exams tomorrow so he has to go to bed early; she took her driving test three times before she passed.**

(*f*) to eat/to drink (often); **do you take sugar in your coffee? he has to take the medicine three times a day.**

(*g*) to accept; to choose; **if he offers you the job, take it; what kind of ice cream do you want?—I'll take chocolate.**

(*h*) to do certain actions; **I'm going to take a vacation; has he taken a bath yet? he took a picture of the White House; hurry up and take the picture, it's starting to rain; you should go and take a rest.**

(*i*) to need; **it took three men to lift the car; it took us three days to walk to Niagara Falls; how long does it take to get to school by bus? he must have been hungry—it didn't take him long to eat all his dinner.**

(*j*) to accept/to hold; **this machine only takes quarters; his car can take four passengers.**

takes—taking—took [tʊk]—**has taken**

take af·ter, *verb*

to be like (a parent); **he takes after his father.**

take a·way, *verb*

(*a*) to remove something/someone; **take that knife away from him; the police came and took him away.**

(*b*) to subtract one number from another; **if you take six away from ten, you have four.**

take back, *verb*

(*a*) to go back with something; **this shirt is too small—I'll take it back to the store.**

(*b*) to accept something which someone has returned; **I went to the store with the** shirt which I had just bought, but they wouldn't take it back.

take care of, *verb*
to watch; to look after; **who is taking care of the children?**

take in, *verb*
(*a*) to understand; **are you taking in all he is saying?**
(*b*) to trick; **don't be taken in by what he says.**
(*c*) to sew a piece of clothing so that it is smaller; **now that she has lost weight she'll have to take in her skirts.**

take off, *verb*
(*a*) to remove (especially clothes); **he took off all his clothes/he took all his clothes off; take your shoes off before you come into the house.**
(*b*) to fly into the air; **the plane took off at 4:30.**

take on, *verb*
to agree to do a job/to agree to have someone as a worker; **he has taken on two more jobs; the company has taken on three new secretaries.**

take out, *verb*
(*a*) to carry something away from a place; **she took some money out of her bank account; he took out some books on his library card.**
(*b*) to go to a restaurant, theater, etc. with someone and pay for it; **he took me out to dinner.**

take over, *verb*
(*a*) to get control of; **the soldiers took over the government; the business was taken over by a larger company last year.**
(*b*) to start to be in charge of something in place of someone else; **I'll take over from you now; when the math teacher was ill, the history teacher had to take over his class.**

take turns, *verb*
to share a job with someone by doing it every other time; **we'll take turns washing the dishes.**

take up, *verb*
(*a*) to occupy; **this table takes up a lot of room; playing football takes up too much time.**
(*b*) to start to do (a sport, etc.); **he has taken up tennis.**

(*c*) to shorten; **he will have to get these pants taken up.**
Note: **he took his shoes off** *or* **he took off his shoes; she took the shirt back** *or* **took back the shirt** *but only* **took them off, took it back,** *etc.*

talk [tɔːk] *verb*
to speak; **I don't understand what they're talking about; I must talk to the man at the garage about the car engine; he's talking of going to Alaska on his vacation.**
talks—talking—talked—has talked

talk into, *verb*
to get someone to do something by talking to him/her; **we talked her into going to the party with us.**

talk over, *verb*
to discuss; **go and talk things over with your teacher.**

tall [tɔːl] *adjective*
high (usually higher than others); **a tall building; can you see that tall tree over there? he's the tallest in his class—he's taller than all the others; how tall are you? I'm five foot seven inches (5′7″) tall.**
tall—taller—tallest
Note: **tall** *is used with numbers:* **the tree is 10 meters tall; he's 6 feet tall**

tan [tæn] *noun & adjective*
(*a*) very light brown color; **he's wearing a tan shirt.**
(*b*) having brown skin from being in the sun; **she has a deep tan from spending so much time at the beach.**
tan—tanner—tannest

tap [tæp] *verb*
to hit lightly; **he tapped her on the shoulder and asked her to dance.**
taps—tapping—tapped—has tapped

tape [teip] 1. *noun*
(*a*) long thin flat piece of plastic/of cloth; **tape measure/measuring tape = tape with marks on it showing inches or centimeters.**

(b) long thin piece of plastic on which sound is recorded; **have you heard this tape? let me play you the tape I bought today.**

(c) long thin piece of plastic with glue on it for sticking pieces of paper together; **put this note up on the door with a piece of tape.**

2. *verb*

(a) to record sound on plastic tape; **he's going to tape the speech for me since I can't go to hear it myself.**

(b) to attach with tape; **she taped the sign to the wall.**

tapes—taping—taped—has taped

tape re·cord·er, *noun*

machine which records sound on tape; **he recorded the radio program on his tape recorder.**

taste [teɪst] 1. *noun*

one of the five senses, which you notice through your tongue; **I don't like the taste of onions; this ice cream has no taste at all.**

2. *verb*

to notice the taste of something with your tongue; to have a taste; **can you taste the salt in this soup? this cake tastes very sweet; I have a cold so I can't taste anything; what is it?—it tastes like milk.**

tastes—tasting—tasted—has tasted

tast·y, *adjective*

which has a good taste; **what a tasty pie!**

tasty—tastier—tastiest

taught [tɔːt] *see* **teach**

tax [tæks] *noun*

money which is paid to the government; **there's a 10% tax on gasoline; you always have to pay tax on the money you earn; no one likes paying taxes.**

plural **taxes**

tea [tiː] *noun*

(a) drink made from water which has been poured onto the dried leaves of a plant which grows in hot countries; the dried leaves of this plant; **put some tea into the pot and add boiling water; would**

you like another cup of tea/some more tea? **I don't like tea—can I have coffee instead?**

(b) a cup of tea; **we'll have two teas, please.**

no plural for (a); **teas** *means* **cups of tea**

tea bag, *noun*

small paper bag with tea in it which you put into the pot with hot water.

tea·cup, *noun*

cup for drinking tea.

tea·pot, *noun*

special pot which is used for making tea; **put some tea into the teapot and add boiling water.**

tea·spoon, *noun*

small spoon for mixing hot drinks; amount which a teaspoon can hold; **put a teaspoon of sugar into her coffee.**

teach [tiːtʃ] *verb*

to give lessons; to show someone how to do something; **he taught me how to drive; she teaches French in our school; she taught herself typing; who taught you to swim?**

teaches—teaching—taught [tɔːt] **—has taught**

teach·er, *noun*

person who teaches; **Mr. Smith is our English teacher; the music teacher is sick today.**

team [tiːm] *noun*

group of people who play a game together/who work together; **there are eleven people on a football team; she plays for the school team; which baseball team is your favorite? our team played badly last Saturday.**

team·mate [ˈtiːmeɪt] *noun*

person who is on the same team you are on; **all of his teammates congratulated him on his performance in the game.**

team·work, *noun*

working together as a group; **fixing up this house is going to require teamwork.**

tear¹ [tɪr] *noun*

drop of water which comes in your eye

when you cry; **tears ran down her face;
he burst into tears** = he suddenly
started to cry; **she ran out of the room in
tears** = she was crying.

tear² [teər] *verb*
(*a*) to make a hole in something by
pulling; **he tore a hole in his pants/he tore
his pants.**
(*b*) to pull something (especially paper
or cloth) to pieces; **I tore the letter into
little pieces.**
(*c*) to go fast; **he tore across the room;
the cars were tearing past.**
tears—tearing—tore [tɔːr]—**has
torn** [tɔːrn]
tear down, *verb*
to knock down (a building); **they are
tearing down these houses to make room
for the freeway.**
tear off, *verb*
to pull off by tearing; **he tore off the
next page in his notebook.**
tear out, *verb*
to pull something out by tearing; **he tore
a page out of his notebook.**
tear up, *verb*
to pull something to pieces; **she tore up
the letter; they tore up the old newspapers; they used torn up newspapers to
pack the cups into the box.**

teen·ag·er [ˈtiːneɪdʒər] *noun*
person between the ages of 12 and 20;
**three teenagers helped rescue the family
from the burning house; he liked loud
music when he was a teenager.**

teeth [tiːθ] *see* **tooth**

tel·e·gram [ˈtelǝgræm] *noun*
message sent along wires; **we've gotten a
telegram which says he's coming; send a
telegram to your mother.**

tel·e·phone [ˈtelǝfəʊn] 1. *noun*
machine which you use to speak to
someone a long distance away; **the telephone's ringing; can you answer the telephone for me—I'm in the bathtub; he
picked up the telephone and called the
police.**
on the tel·e·phone = speaking by

telephone; **please be quiet—Daddy's
on the telephone; there's someone on the
telephone who wants to speak to you.**
2. *verb*
to call someone by telephone; **your
sister telephoned yesterday; telephone the
doctor—the baby is sick; can you telephone New York from here?**
**telephones—telephoning—
telephoned—has telephoned**
Note: **call** *is nearly always used
instead of* **telephone**

tel·e·phone book, *noun*
book which gives the names of people
in a city or area in alphabetical order
with their addresses and phone numbers; **this restaurant isn't in the telephone
book.**
tel·e·phone booth, *noun*
tall square box with windows, with a
public telephone inside; **I'm calling from
the telephone booth outside the post
office.**
tel·e·phone num·ber, *noun*
number which refers to a particular
phone; **what's your telephone number?
his telephone number's 405-9935.**

tel·e·vi·sion [ˈtelǝvɪʒən] *noun*
(*a*) pictures which are sent through the
air and appear on a special machine; **we
watch television every night; are there
any sports programs on television
tonight? some television programs are
repeated too often.**
(*b*) machine which shows television
pictures; **I bought a color television; the
television has broken down; turn off the
television—that program is awful! when
he comes home in the evening he just
turns on the television and goes to
sleep.**
Note: **television** *is often written or
spoken as* **TV** [ˈtiːˈviː]
tel·e·vi·sion set, *noun*
machine which shows television pictures; **we bought a new television set.**

tell [tel] *verb*
(*a*) to say something to someone; **he told
me a long story; she told the police she
had seen the accident; do you think he is**

telling the truth? don't tell your mother
you've seen that movie!
(b) to give information/to order; can
you tell me how to get to the post office?
the teacher told the children to sit down;
tell me when to start; nobody told me
about the picnic.
(c) to notice the difference between two
things; can you tell the difference between butter and margarine? you can tell
he's angry by the way his ears turn red.
tells—telling—told [tɔʊld] **—has
told**

tell·er, noun
employee in a bank who counts,
receives and pays out money; the teller
gave me $50 instead of $40.

tem·per·a·ture [ˈtempərtʃər] noun
(a) heat measured in degrees; what's the
temperature of boiling water? the temperature in the desert is very hot; the car
won't start when the temperature is very
low; put the thermometer in your
mouth—I want to take your temperature.
(b) illness when your body is hotter than
normal; he's in bed with a temperature;
the doctor says she's got a temperature.

ten [ten] number 10
he bought ten oranges for $1; he's ten
(years old); the train leaves at ten
(o'clock).
tenth [tenθ] **10th** adjective & noun
the tenth of June/June (the) tenth (June
10); that's the tenth letter I've written
today; he spends a tenth of his money on
food; her tenth birthday is on Wednesday.

ten·nis [ˈtenɪs] noun
game for two or four people, where a
ball is hit backwards and forwards over
a net; would you like a game of tennis?
I'm no good at tennis; he's taking tennis
lessons.
no plural

ten·nis shoe, noun
soft sports shoe with a rubber bottom;
she needs a new pair of tennis shoes.

tent [tent] noun
small shelter made of cloth, held up by
poles and attached to the ground with

ropes; when we go camping we take our
tent in the back of our car; his tent was
blown down by the wind.

term [tɜrm] noun
(a) length of time; during his term as
President; he was sent to prison for a
five-year term.
(b) part of a school year when classes
are held; there are three terms in the
school year; the term ends on June 12;
next term, I'm going to take German.
(c) something which has to be agreed
before something else is done; what are
the terms of the agreement?
(d) way of getting along with someone;
we're on good terms with the people next
door.

ter·ri·ble [ˈterəbəl] adjective
very bad; he had a terrible accident; the
last meal I had in that restaurant was
terrible.
ter·ri·bly, adverb
very; these chocolates are terribly expensive.

test [test] 1. noun
examination to see if something works
well/to see if you can do something,
etc.; we had a math test this morning; he
passed his driving test; the doctor is going
to do a blood test.
2. verb
to examine to see if something is working well/if you can do something, etc.; I
must have my eyes tested; the teacher
tested his French; they tested the brakes
of the car.
**tests—testing—tested—has
tested**

text·book [ˈteksbʊk] noun
book which is used by children at
school/by students at a college or university.

than [ðæn or ðən] conjunction
used to show a second thing which is
being compared; my house is bigger than
yours; it's colder today than it was yesterday; I know Boston better than Chicago; more than thirty people were waiting for the bus.

thank [θæŋk] *verb*
to show that you are pleased with someone for doing something; he thanked me for having helped him; she thanked them for coming to see her; I must thank him for his present.

thanks—thanking—thanked—has thanked

thanks, *plural noun & interjection*
words which show you are pleased with someone for doing something; please give him my thanks for his present; we got no thanks for all our help; do you want some more coffee?—no thanks, I've had plenty; do you want a lift to the station?—thanks, it's a long way to walk.

Thanks·giv·ing, *noun*
holiday when you give thanks for the good things you have; in the United States, Thanksgiving Day is the fourth Thursday in November; they always have a big turkey dinner at his grandmother's on Thanksgiving.

thanks to, *adverb*
because of/as a result of; thanks to your father's map, we found our way to the house.

thank you, *interjection*
(*showing that you are pleased with what someone has done*) thank you for the present; did you say thank you to your mother for the book? do you want some more coffee?—no thank you, I've had plenty; do you want a lift to the station?—thank you, it's a long way to walk.

that [ðæt *or* ðət] 1. *adjective & pronoun*
(*a*) (*used to show something which is further away—the opposite of* **this**) that book is the one I was talking about, not this one; can you see that tall man standing by the door? what's the name of that restaurant where we had dinner yesterday? who's that sitting at the next table?

plural **those**

(*b*) (*used to join a subject or object to a verb*) where is the letter that he sent you? they live in a house that has red windows;

here's the box that you left in the bedroom.

Note: with an object **that** *can be left out:* **the letter he sent you? here's the box you left in the bedroom**

With a subject **that** *can be changed to* **which** (*for things and animals*) *or* **who** (*for people*); **a house that has red windows/a house which has red windows; the man that stole the car/the man who stole the car**

2. *conjunction*
(*a*) (*after verbs like* **hope, know, tell, say** *and adjectives like* **glad, sorry, happy**) he told me that she was out; she said that she was tired; he didn't know that we were coming; I'm glad that you were able to come.
(*b*) (*after* **so/such** + *adjective or noun*) it's so hot here that it makes me thirsty; the meat was so good that I ate all of it; it was raining so hard that we couldn't have our picnic; we had such bad weather that we ended up staying at a motel instead of camping; there was such a crowd that we couldn't get into the theater.

Note: **that** *is often left out:* **he didn't know we were coming; it's so hot here it makes me thirsty**

3. *adverb*
so very; the fish wasn't that big.

the [ðə; ði: *before a vowel*] *article*
(*a*) (*meaning something in particular*) where's the package which came today? there's the dog from next door.
(*b*) (*used with something of which only one exists*) the sun was shining; men have walked on the moon.
(*c*) (*meaning something in general*) do you like listening to the radio? the streets are crowded at Christmas.
(*d*) [ði:] (*meaning something very special*) that's the store for men's clothes = the best store; he's the doctor to see for skin problems; that's not the Charlie Chaplin is it? = not the real Charlie Chaplin?
(*e*) (*used to compare*) the less you work the fatter you get; the sooner you do it

the better; that's the best way to do it; he's the tallest boy in our school.

the·a·ter *or* **the·a·tre** [ˈθiːətər] *noun*
building in which plays or movies are shown; we're going to the theater tonight; is there a good play at the theater this week? what's playing at the movie theater?

their [ðeər] *adjective*
belonging to them; here's their house; they were eating their dinner.
theirs, *pronoun*
belonging to them; which house is theirs? he's a friend of theirs; they want to borrow my car—theirs won't start.

them [ðem] *object pronoun*
(*referring to a plural*) do you like chocolates?—no, I don't like them very much; the children are waiting outside—tell them to come in; if you are going to visit your parents can you take them this present?
them·selves, *plural pronoun*
(*referring to a plural subject*) cats clean themselves very carefully; the old ladies were all by themselves in the house = all alone; they did it all by themselves = with no one to help them; the doctors were ill themselves/the doctors themselves were ill.

then [ðen] 1. *adverb*
(*a*) at that time; the police said he killed his sister in Detroit on April 23, but he was in Florida then; can you come to a party next week?—no, I'll be on vacation then. (*b*) after that; he sat down and then they were served coffee; we had a busy vacation—we went to France, and then to Italy and then to Germany.
2. *conjunction*
and so; if you don't like fish then you'll have to eat meat; then you already knew that he had died?

there [ðeər] 1. *adverb*
in that place/to that place; we'll arrive there at 10 o'clock; is the car still there? where's the tea?—there, on the top shelf; have you ever been to Canada?—yes, I went there three years ago.

2. *interjection*
(*a*) (*showing pity*) there, there, don't cry; there, now try to get some sleep.
(*b*) (*showing you were right*) there, what did I tell you, we've missed the train.
(*c*) (*making a decision*) I'll go to the party all by myself, so there!
(*d*) (*used when giving something to someone*) there you are!
3. *pronoun*
(*used as the subject of verbs, usually with the verb* to be, *when the real subject follows the verb*) there's a big dog in the garden; there's a page missing in this book; were there many people at the meeting? is there anything to drink? there seems to have been an accident; there isn't any sugar left.

there·fore [ˈðeərfɔːr] *adverb*
for this reason; there's a lot of snow, therefore the trains might be late; the children are grown up and therefore can take care of themselves.

ther·mom·e·ter [θərˈmɒmɪtər] *noun*
instrument for measuring temperature; the thermometer showed only 2°—it was very cold.

these [ðiːz] *see* **this**

they [ðeɪ] *plural pronoun*
(*a*) (*referring to people or things*) where are the cups and saucers?—they're in the cupboard; who are those people in uniform?—they're army officers; the children went out in the snow with no coats on, so they all caught colds; they'd better be careful walking on that thin ice; if the police find out, they'll be caught.
(*b*) (*referring to people in general*) they say it's going to be hot; they tell me you've gotten married.
Note: when it is the object, **they** *becomes* **them:** *we gave it to* **them;** *he hit* **them** *with a stick; when it follows the verb* **be,** *they usually becomes* **them:** *who's that?—it's* **them!**

thick [θɪk] *adjective*
(*a*) not thin/with a lot of space between

the two surfaces; **a thick slice of cake; the walls are two feet thick; this orange has a very thick skin.**

(*b*) close together; **a thick forest** = forest whose trees are very close together; **the lawn was covered with thick grass.**

(*c*) (liquid) which does not flow easily; **this paint is too thick—add some water to it; a bowl of good thick soup.**

(*d*) which you can't see through easily; **the plane couldn't land because of thick fog.**

thick—thicker—thickest

thick·ness, *noun*
distance between two surfaces of an object; **what is the thickness of that board?**
plural **thicknesses**

thief [θiːf] *noun*
person who steals; **thieves broke into the store and stole 100 watches.**
plural **thieves** [θiːvz]

thin [θɪn] *adjective*
(*a*) not fat; **his legs are very thin; she's getting too thin—she should eat more.**
(*b*) not thick; **a thin slice of bread; a thin sheet of paper; a thin piece of string.**
(*c*) not close together; **the ground was covered with thin grass.**
(*d*) (liquid) which flows easily; **thin soup; add water until the paint is thin.**
(*e*) which you can see through; **thin curtains.**

thin—thinner—thinnest

thing [θɪŋ] *noun*
(*a*) something which is not living/not a plant or animal; **what's that black thing in the garden? what's that green thing for?**
(*b*) **things** = clothes/equipment; **have you brought your things? I left my painting things in the car.**
(*c*) something which is referred to in general; **how are things going? don't take things so seriously; it was a good thing the train was late** = it was lucky for us that the train was late; **she just sat there and didn't say a thing; the first thing to do is call the police; what a silly thing to do!**

think [θɪŋk] *verb*
(*a*) to use your mind; **think before you say anything; he never thinks about what people might say.**
(*b*) to believe/to have an opinion; **I think she is prettier than her sister; what do you think we should do now? everyone thought he was rich; what do you think of the film? he's thought to be in Canada** = people believe he is in Canada; **he's in Canada, isn't he?—I don't think so.**
(*c*) to expect; **I think it's going to rain; I didn't think the train would be late.**
(*d*) to plan; **he's thinking of going to live in Canada; have you thought about moving to Canada? she thought of everything for the party** = she remembered all the little things that make a good party.

thinks—thinking—thought [θɔːt]—**has thought**

think o·ver, *verb*
to think about a plan very carefully; **think it over, and give me your answer tomorrow.**

think up, *verb*
to invent; **he thought up a plan for making money.**

third [θɜːrd] **3rd,** *noun & adjective*
referring to three; **my birthday is on the third of September/September third (September 3); he was third in the race; they live in the third house on the left; King James the Third (James III); it's his third birthday on Friday.**
Note: with dates **third** *is usually written* **3: September 3, 1974; March 3, 1981;** *with names of kings and queens* **third** *is usually written* **III: King Charles III**

thirst [θɜːrst] *noun*
feeling that you want to drink.
thirst·y, *adjective*
wanting to drink; **I'm thirsty, give me a drink of water; if you're thirsty, have some orange juice.**
thirsty—thirstier—thirstiest

thir·teen [θɜːrˈtiːn] *number* 13
she's thirteen (years old).
thir·teenth, 13th, *adjective and noun*

she came thirteenth in the race; the thirteenth of August/August thirteenth
(August 13); it's his thirteenth birthday
on Monday.

thir·ty [ˈθɜrtɪ] number 30
he's thirty (years old); she has thirty
pairs of shoes; he's in his thirties = he is
between 30 and 39 years old.
Note: **thirty-one** (31), **thirty-two**
(32), *etc., but* **thirty-first** (31st),
thirty-second (32nd), *etc.*

thir·ti·eth, **30th**, *adjective & noun*
he was thirtieth in the race; the
thirtieth of June/June thirtieth (June
30); it was her thirtieth birthday last
week.

this [ðɪs] *adjective & pronoun*
(*a*) (*used to show something which is
nearer—the opposite of* **that**) this is the
book I was talking about; this little girl
is my sister's daughter; I think I have
been to this restaurant before; this is Mr.
Martin; these apples are bad.
(*b*) (*used to refer to a part of today, the
recent past or a period of time which will
soon arrive*) I saw him this morning; they
are coming for lunch this afternoon; I'll
be seeing him this week; she's retiring
this year; we're going to Greece this
summer.
plural **these**

those [ðəʊz] *see* **that**

though [ðəʊ] *conjunction*
even if; though he's small, he can hit
very hard; we wanted to go for a walk
even though it was raining very hard;
see also **although**.
as though = as if; it looks as though
it will rain.

thought [θɔːt] *see* **think**

thou·sand [ˈθaʊzənd] number 1000
I paid two thousand dollars for it
($2,000); thousands of people escaped
from the fire = very many people.
Note: after numbers **thousand** *does
not have an* **-s**: two thousand; ten
thousand

thread [θred] 1. *noun*
thin piece of cotton, etc.; I need some
strong thread to sew on my button.
2. *verb*
to put a thread/string, etc., through a
hole; can you thread this needle for me?
**threads—threading—threaded—
has threaded**

three [θriː] number 3
she's three (years old); can you see me at
three (o'clock)? three men stole my car.
Note: **three** (3) *but* **third** (3rd)

threw [θruː] *see* **throw**

throat [θrəʊt] *noun*
front part of your neck below the chin;
tube which goes down from your mouth
inside your neck; he held her by the
throat; a piece of meat got stuck in his
throat; he cleared his throat = gave a
little cough.

through [θruː] *adverb & preposition*
(*a*) crossing the inside of something/
going in at one side and coming out of
the other side; he went through the door;
she looked through the window; the water
runs through the pipe; the air comes in
through the hole in the wall; the road
goes straight through the center of the
town; she pushed the needle through the
ball of yarn.
(*b*) during a period of time; she talked
all through the movie; the store is open
Monday through Friday = all days from
Monday up to and including Friday.
(*c*) by; I sent the letter through the
office mail; we heard of it through my
sister.
(*d*) speaking by telephone; I'm trying to
get through to Germany; can you put me
through to the manager?
(*e*) finished; are you through with the
broom yet? = are you finished using the
broom?
Note: **through** *is often used after
verbs:* **to go through; to fall
through; to see through,** *etc.*

through·out, *preposition & adverb*
everywhere; all through; roads are
blocked by snow throughout the country;
heavy rain fell throughout the night.

throw [θrəʊ] *verb*
to send something through the air; **how far can you throw this ball? she threw the stone through the window; he threw the letter into the wastebasket; he threw the pillow at his sister.**
throws—throwing—threw [θruː] **—has thrown**

throw a·way, *verb*
to get rid of something which you don't need; **don't throw away that old bike—we can fix it; she threw away all her old clothes.**
Note: **throw that paper away** *or* **throw away that paper** *but only* **throw it away**

throw out, *verb*
(*a*) to put outside using force; **when he couldn't pay for the meal, he was thrown out of the restaurant.**
(*b*) to get rid of something which you don't need; **we're throwing out this old carpet.**

throw up, *verb*
to be sick; **the dog has thrown up all over the kitchen floor.**

thumb [θʌm] *noun*
short thick finger which is separated from the other four fingers on your hand; **he hit his thumb with the hammer; the baby put her thumb in her mouth.**
thumb·tack [ˈθʌmtæk] *noun*
small pin with a large, flat top for pinning paper on a wall, etc.; **she used four thumbtacks to pin the sign to the door.**

thun·der [ˈθʌndər] *noun*
loud noise in the air caused by lightning; **listen to the thunder! when there's thunder, the cat hides under the bed.**
thun·der·storm, *noun*
storm with rain and thunder and lightning; **we were caught on the mountain by a thunderstorm.**

Thurs·day [ˈθɜrzdɪ] *noun*
day between Wednesday and Friday, the fifth day of the week; **she was sick last Thursday; I have an evening class on Thursdays; shall we meet next Thursday? today is Thursday, October 27.**

tick [tɪk] *verb*
to make a small sound; **the room was so quiet—all we could hear was the clock ticking; run away—the bomb's ticking!**
ticks—ticking—ticked—has ticked

tick·et [ˈtɪkət] *noun*
(*a*) piece of paper/card which allows you to travel; **you can't get on the train without a ticket; I've lost my plane tickets—how can I get to New York?**
(*b*) piece of paper which allows you to go into a theater/an exhibit, etc.; **two tickets for the 6:30 show please; I went to several theaters but there were no tickets left anywhere.**
(*c*) paper which you get when you leave a car parked wrongly, telling you that you will have to pay a fine; **don't leave your car in front of the driveway—you'll get a ticket!**
(*d*) small piece of paper attached to an object and showing its price, size, etc.; **there's no ticket on this skirt, so I don't know how much it is.**

tie [taɪ] 1. *noun*
(*a*) long piece of cloth which men wear in a knot around their necks under the collar of their shirts; **he wore a blue tie with white spots; you can't come into the restaurant if you don't have a tie on.**
(*b*) game with no winner; **the game was a tie; it was a tie game.**
2. *verb*
(*a*) to attach with a knot; **the package is tied with string; he was tying his horse to the fence; the burglars tied her hands behind her back.**
(*b*) not to have a winner in a game; **the teams tied.**
ties—tying—tied—has tied

tie up, *verb*
(*a*) to attach tightly; **the package is tied up with string; that dog ought to be tied up or it will bite someone.**
(*b*) **to be tied up** = to be busy; **I'm rather tied up at the moment—can I call you tomorrow?**

tight [taɪt] 1. *adjective*
which fits closely; not loose; **the lid is so**

tight I can't open it; my pants are so
tight I can't zip them up; her shoes are
too tight.
2. adverb
closely; **shut the door tight; hold (on)
tight!**
tight—tighter—tightest

tight·en, *verb*
to make tight; **can you tighten this
handle? the lid needs tightening.**
**tightens—tightening—
tightened—has tightened**

tight·ly, *adverb*
in a tight way; **he put the lid on tightly;
hold on to the handle tightly.**

till [tɪl] *preposition*
until/up to the time when; **I won't be
home till nine o'clock; he worked from
morning till night.**

time [taɪm] 1. *noun*
(*a*) number of hours/days/weeks, etc.;
**you don't need to hurry—you have plenty
of time; do you have time for a cup of
coffee? he spends all his time reading the
newspaper; don't waste time putting your
shoes on—jump out of the window now.**
(*b*) certain period; **I haven't seen him for
a long time; it didn't take him much time
to get here; it took her a long time to get
better; we got a letter from her a short
time ago.**
(*c*) particular point in the day shown in
hours and minutes; **what time is it?/
what's the time? the time is exactly 6:35;
can you tell me the time please? he's only
four—he can't tell time yet** = he can't
read the time on a clock.
(*d*) particular point when something
happens; **I didn't hear the bang as I was
asleep at the time; by the time the police
arrived the burglars had run away; you
can't sing and drink at the same time.**
(*e*) hour at which something usually
happens; **closing time is 10:30; it's dinner
time—I'm hungry; is it time to go to bed?**
see also **bedtime, daytime, dinnertime, lunchtime, nighttime.**
(*f*) period when things are pleasant or
bad; **we had a good time at the party.**
(*g*) one of several moments/periods

when something happens; **I've seen that
film three times; that's the last time I'll
ask you to sing a song; next time you
come, bring your football.**
(*h*) **times** = multiplied by; **six times four
is twenty-four; this box is ten times as
heavy as that one; she's a hundred times
prettier than her sister.**
in time = not late; **we ran fast and
got to the station in time to catch the
train; hurry if you want to be in time for
the beginning of the movie; we were just
in time to see the soldiers march past.**
on time = happening at the right
time; **the train arrived on time; he's never
on time.**
2. verb
to count how many hours and minutes;
**if you run around the football field, I'll
time you; can you time these eggs?—they
have to cook for three minutes.**
**times—timing—timed—has
timed**

time·ta·ble, *noun*
list which shows the times when trains
or buses leave or arrive; list of the times
of classes; **look up the trains to New
York in the timetable; there are ten
French classes listed in the timetable.**

ti·ny [ˈtaɪnɪ] *adjective*
very small; **a tiny baby; this plant has
tiny blue flowers.**
tiny—tinier—tiniest

tip [tɪp] 1. *noun*
(*a*) end of something long; **she touched
it with the tips of her fingers; he used a
stick with a rubber tip to point at the
blackboard.**
(*b*) money given to someone who has
provided a service; **I gave the cab driver
a $1 tip; should I give the waiter a tip? is
a tip included in the bill?**
(*c*) small piece of useful information; **she
gave me some tips on saving money at
the supermarket.**
2. verb
(*a*) to make something empty/to pour
something out; **he picked up the bucket
and tipped the apples onto the floor; she
tipped the money out of her bag.**

(b) to give money to someone who has helped you; **I tipped the waiter $1; shall I tip the driver?**

tips—tipping—tipped—has tipped

tip o·ver, *verb*
to lean and fall over; to make something lean so that it falls over; **he tipped over the bottle; my cup tipped over and all my tea spilled onto the table.**

tip·toe, *noun & verb*
to go quietly on your toes; **he entered the room on tiptoe; she tiptoed past the sleeping guard.**

tiptoes—tiptoeing—tiptoed—has tiptoed

tire ['taɪr] *noun*
rubber cover which goes around a wheel and which is filled with air; **my bike has a flat tire.**

tired ['taɪrd] *adjective*
(a) feeling sleepy; feeling that you need rest; **I'm tired—I'll go to bed; if you feel tired, lie down on my bed; I'm tired after that long walk.**
(b) **to be tired of something** = to be bored with something, to have had enough of something; **I'm tired of hearing the baby cry; she's tired of having to do all the work; can't we play another game—I'm tired of this one.**

tired out, *adjective*
feeling very sleepy/feeling that you must have rest; **I'm tired out after that long walk; let her sit down—she's tired out.**

tis·sue ['tɪʃuː] *noun*
handkerchief made out of soft paper; **she kept a box of tissues in her car; would you hand me a tissue please?**

ti·tle ['taɪtəl] *noun*
name of a book/play/film, etc.; **the title of his next film was "The Third Man"; what's the title of that book you're reading?**

to [tuː *or* tə] **1.** *preposition*
(a) *(showing direction/place)* **he went to the station; I'm going to the library; is this the way to the post office? the church**

is to the east of the town; take one step to the left.
(b) *(showing time)* **from Monday to Saturday; he slept from ten to eight o'clock; it's ten to six; the time is a quarter to seven.**
(c) *(showing person/animal who gets something)* **give the book to the teacher; pass the sugar to your father; you must be kind to old people.**
(d) *(showing connection)* **she's an assistant to the Vice President; there are two dollars to the pound; there are three keys to the front door; in this class there are 35 children to one teacher.**
(e) *(showing that you are comparing)* **I prefer butter to margarine; you can't compare canned fruit to fresh fruit.**
2. *used before a verb*
(a) *(following verbs)* **he remembered to switch off the light; they tried to run away; she agreed to come with us; we decided to leave the office early.**
(b) *(showing purpose)* **they came to help us; the doctor left to go to the hospital.**
(c) *(used after adjectives)* **she was too tired to walk; are these apples good to eat? I'm sorry to be late.**
Note: **to** *is used for times between* **half past** *and* **o'clock: 4:35 = twenty-five to five; 4:45 = a quarter to five; 4:50 = ten to five**

toast [toʊst] *noun*
slices of bread which have been cooked until they are brown; **do you want toast and coffee for your breakfast? I want some more toast; can you make another piece of toast?**

no plural: **some toast; a piece of toast**

toast·er, *noun*
small machine for making toast; **put these slices of bread in the toaster; we must get the toaster fixed—the toast keeps coming out burned.**

to·bac·co [tə'bækoʊ] *noun*
dried leaves of a plant which are used to make cigarettes and cigars, and which you can smoke in a pipe; **these**

cigarettes are made of fine tobacco; I must buy some pipe tobacco.

no plural: **some tobacco**

to·day [təˈdeɪ] *adverb & noun*
this day; he said he was coming to see me today, but he hasn't come yet; today is my birthday; what's the date today? have you read today's newspaper?

no plural
Note: to refer to the morning/afternoon, etc. of **today**, *say* **this morning/this afternoon,** *etc.*

toe [təʊ] *noun*
part of the body—one of the five parts at the end of your foot; he stepped on my toe; big toe/little toe = biggest/smallest of the five toes.

toe·nail, *noun*
thin hard part covering the end of a toe.

to·geth·er [təˈgeðər] *adverb*
(a) in a group; we must stay together or we'll get lost; let's go to the movies together.
(b) one thing with another; tie the two chairs together; can you stick the pieces of the cup together again? add all these numbers together.

toi·let [ˈtɔɪlət] *noun*
place or room where you get rid of water or solid waste from your body; this toilet isn't working; I have to go to the toilet.

toi·let pa·per, *noun*
special paper for wiping yourself when you go to the toilet.

told [təʊld] *see* **tell**

to·ma·to [təˈmeɪtəʊ] *noun*
red fruit which is used in salads and cooking; have another tomato; a lettuce and tomato salad; tomato sauce = red sauce made with tomatoes.

plural **tomatoes**

to·mor·row [təˈmɒrəʊ] *adverb & noun*
the day after today; today is Tuesday, so tomorrow must be Wednesday; can you meet me tomorrow morning? tomorrow is my birthday; we are going to the theater tomorrow evening.

ton [tʌn] *noun*
very large measure of weight; that piece of metal weighs three tons.

tongue [tʌŋ] *noun*
part of the body—the long piece inside your mouth which can move and is used for tasting and speaking; don't stick your tongue out at the teacher; he said it tongue in cheek = he was not really serious.

to·night [təˈnaɪt] *adverb & noun*
the night/evening of today; we're having a party tonight; can you call me at 11:30 tonight? is there anything interesting on TV tonight? tonight's programs look very boring.

too [tuː] *adverb*
(a) more than necessary; he has too much money; it's too cold for you to play outside; these shoes are too small; she's not too happy about his grades = she's not very happy about them.
(b) also; he had some cake and I had some too; she, too, has a cold/she has a cold too.

took [tʊk] *see* **take**

tool [tuːl] *noun*
thing which you use with your hands for doing work; she got him a box of tools for Christmas; do you have the proper tool for taking the wheels off a car?

tooth [tuːθ] *noun*
(a) one of a set of bones in the mouth, which you use to chew food with; don't forget to brush your teeth after breakfast; I must see the dentist—one of my teeth hurts; he had to have a tooth out = had to have a bad tooth taken out by the dentist; he has a sweet tooth = he likes eating sweet things.
(b) one of the row of pointed pieces on a saw or comb.

plural **teeth** [tiːθ]

tooth·ache, *noun*
pain in your teeth; I must see the dentist—I've got a toothache.

no plural

tooth·brush, *noun*
small brush which you use to clean your teeth.
plural **toothbrushes**
tooth·paste, *noun*
soft material which you spread on a toothbrush and then use to clean your teeth; **I must buy some toothpaste; here's a tube of toothpaste.**
no plural: **some toothpaste; a tube of toothpaste**

top [tɒp] **1.** *noun*
(*a*) highest point; **he climbed to the top of the mountain; the bird is sitting on the top of the tree.**
(*b*) flat upper surface; **he sat on the top of his car; take the top off the box; the table has a black top; the cake has sugar and fruit on top; on top of** = on; **put the book on top of the others.**
(*c*) most important place; highest place; **look at the top of the next page; our team is at the top in the competition.**
2. *adjective*
in the highest place; **my office is on the top floor of the building; the coffee is on the top shelf; he's the top boy in the class** = he has the best grades; **he's one of the top players in the world** = he's one of the best players.

tore [tɔːr], **torn** [tɔːrn] *see* **tear**

to·tal [təʊtəl] **1.** *adjective & noun*
complete/whole (amount); **what's the total cost? the total which you have to pay is at the bottom of the bill; the room was a total wreck.**
2. *verb*
to add up; to amount to; **he totaled up the bill; the number of patients totaled 293.**
totals—totaling—totaled—has totaled
to·tal·ly, *adverb*
completely; **the house was totally destroyed.**

touch [tʌtʃ] **1.** *noun*
(*a*) passing of news and information; **I'll be in touch with you next week** = I'll call/write, etc.; **we've lost touch with him**

now that he has gone to live in Australia.
(*b*) feeling gently; **I felt a touch on my arm.**
(*c*) very small amount; **add a few touches of green to the picture; there's a touch of frost in the air.**
plural **touches, but no plural for** (*a*)
2. *verb*
(*a*) to feel with your fingers; to be so close to something that you press against it; **the policeman touched me on the shoulder; don't touch that door—the paint isn't dry yet; he's so small that his feet don't touch the floor when he sits on a chair; there is a mark on the wall where the chair has touched it.**
(*b*) **I never touch coffee** = I never drink it.
touches—touching—touched—has touched

touch up, *verb*
to add a small amount of paint; **I must touch up the car where it has been scratched.**
touch·y, *adjective*
easily bothered; **he's very touchy about that subject.**
touchy—touchier—touchiest

tough [tʌf] *adjective*
(*a*) hard; **this steak is tough** = hard to chew; **it's a tough problem.**
(*b*) strong; **a tough material.**
tough—tougher—toughest

to·ward *or* **to·wards** [tɔːrd, tɔːrdz] *preposition*
(*a*) in the direction of; **he ran toward the policeman; the car was going toward Rockford; the ship is sailing toward the rocks.**
(*b*) near (in time); **can we meet toward the end of next week? we went on vacation toward the middle of August.**
(*c*) as part of the money to pay for something; **they gave me $10 a week towards the cost of food.**
(*d*) to; **he behaved very kindly towards me.**

tow·el [ˈtaʊəl] *noun*
piece of soft cloth which is used for drying; **she rubbed her hair with a towel;**

she picked up a dish towel and began drying the glasses.

tow·er [ˈtaʊər] *noun*
very tall building; **let's climb to the top of the church tower; control tower** = tall building at an airport from which the movements of aircraft are controlled.

town [taʊn] *noun*
place where people live and work, with houses, stores, offices, factories, etc.; **we usually do our shopping in the next town; which is the nearest town to your farm? this town has an interesting history; his office is in town.**
Note: **to town, into town** *and* **in town** *do not need* **the**

town hall, *noun*
government offices of a town; **are you going to the meeting at the town hall tonight?**

toy [tɔɪ] *noun*
thing for children to play with; **he's playing with his toy soldiers; put all your toys away before you go to bed; our children love going to the toy store.**

trace [treɪs] 1. *noun*
(*a*) very small amount; small mark; **there's a trace of onion in the soup; the police found traces of blood in the shop.**
(*b*) **there's no trace of** = there are no signs of; **there's no trace of a car having been past here; there's no trace of your letter—it must have been lost by the Post Office.**
2. *verb*
to follow tracks to try to find where someone has gone; **the police have traced her to New York; I can't trace your letter.**
traces—tracing—traced—has traced

track [træk] *noun*
(*a*) mark left by an animal/a car, etc., which has gone past; **look—there are bicycle tracks in the sand; I'm trying to keep track of the money we're spending** = trying to count how much money; **I've lost track of how many times I've seen that movie** = I can't count how many times.

(*b*) path, especially for racing; **he's running around the track.**
(*c*) line of rails; **the engine went off the track; she warned the boys not to play on the railroad track.**

track suit, *noun*
warm suit made of pants and a jacket, worn when running.

trac·tor [ˈtræktər] *noun*
farm vehicle with large wheels, used for pulling a plow or other machines; **he drove his tractor across the field.**

trade [treɪd] *verb*
to give something in return for something else; **I'll trade you this baseball for that record; he's trading in his old car** = giving it to partly pay for a new car.
trades—trading—traded—has traded

traf·fic [ˈtræfɪk] *noun*
cars/trucks/buses, etc., traveling on a road; **there's a lot of traffic on Friday nights; the lights turned red, and the traffic stopped; there's so much traffic that it's quicker to ride a bike.**
no plural: **some traffic; a lot of traffic**

traf·fic jam, *noun*
too much traffic on the road, which means that it cannot move; **the accident caused a big traffic jam; there are traffic jams every Friday evening.**

traf·fic light, *noun*
set of red, green and orange lights for making traffic stop and start; **turn right at the next traffic light; he went across the street when the traffic lights were red.**

trail [treɪl] 1. *noun*
path; **you won't get lost if you follow the trail.**
2. *verb*
to follow behind; **the police trailed him.**
trails—trailing—trailed—has trailed

trail·er [ˈtreɪlər] *noun*
vehicle which you can live in and which you pull behind a car; **they go camping with their trailer every fall.**

Travel

1. airplane	13. helicopter
2. airport	14. motorcycle
3. bicycle	15. mudguard
4. bus	16. passenger
5. car	17. roof
6. control tower	18. seat
7. door	19. tire
8. driver	20. train
9. engine (of train)	21. truck
10. fender	22. wheel
11. handlebars	23. window
12. headlight	

train [treɪn] 1. *noun*
set of cars pulled by an engine on a
railroad track; **the train to Chicago
leaves from platform 3; I go to work
every day by train; hurry up if you want
to catch the next train; we missed the
last train and had to take a cab.**
2. *verb*
(*a*) to teach someone or an animal how
to do something; **he has trained his dog
to bring the newspaper in from the porch;
he's training to be a pilot.**
(*b*) to practice for a sport; **she's training
for the 100-meter race.**
**trains—training—trained—has
trained**

trans·fer [ˈtrænsfər] *verb*
to change over; **she transferred some
money from one bank account to another; we have to transfer to another
bus.**
**transfers—transferring—
transferred—has transferred**

trap [træp] 1. *noun*
something which catches an animal or
person; **we caught the wild cat in a
trap; the burglars were caught in a
police trap.**
2. *verb*
to catch someone/an animal, so that
they can't move; **we were trapped in the
elevator for two hours; the police trapped
the burglars inside the bank.**
**traps—trapping—trapped—has
trapped**

trap door, *noun*
small door in a ceiling or floor.

trash [træʃ] *noun*
things which are not needed and are
thrown away; **put all that trash in the
wastebasket.**
no plural

trash can, *noun*
container for trash; **he carried the trash
cans out to the street.**

trav·el [ˈtrævəl] *verb*
to move from one country to another/
from one place to another; **he travels to
work by car; they're traveling to India**

by boat; **they traveled across the country
by bicycle.**
**travels—traveling—traveled—
has traveled**

trav·el a·gent, *noun*
person who sells tickets/organizes trips,
etc.; **I bought my plane tickets at the
travel agent's.**
trav·el·er, *noun*
person who travels.
trav·el·er's check, *noun*
check which you buy at a bank and
which you can then use while you are
traveling.

trea·sure [ˈtreʒər] *noun*
store of money/jewels/gold, etc.; **they
found some treasure when they were
digging in the garden; the burglars hid
the treasure in a garage.**
no plural: **some treasure; a piece
of treasure; treasures** *means* **valuable things**

treat [tri:t] *verb*
(*a*) to deal with; **he was badly treated by
the police; she treats her dogs very
kindly.**
(*b*) to help a sick or hurt person; **after
the accident the passengers were treated
in the hospital for cuts; he's being treated
by his doctor for heart disease.**
(*c*) to give someone a special present;
**I'll treat you all to some ice cream; he
treated himself to a long vacation in
Africa.**
**treats—treating—treated—has
treated**

treat·ment, *noun*
(*a*) way of dealing with someone; **the
treatment of prisoners by the police.**
(*b*) way helping a sick or hurt person;
**this is a new treatment for heart disease;
she's in the hospital for treatment to her
back.**

tree [tri:] *noun*
very large plant, with a trunk and
branches; **he climbed up a tree; birds
make their nests in trees; we have six
apple trees in the yard; let's have our
picnic under this tree.**

tribe [traɪb] *noun*
group of people ruled by a chief; **he belonged to an Indian tribe.**

trick [trɪk] **1.** *noun*
clever action which can confuse someone; **he did some card tricks; she did a trick and made a handkerchief come out of his ear; they played a trick on the teacher.**
2. *verb*
to confuse someone; **he was tricked into signing the paper; she was tricked out of her money** = she was made to lose her money.
tricks—tricking—tricked—has tricked
trick·y, *adjective*
difficult; **a tricky math problem.**
tricky—trickier—trickiest

tried [traɪd], **tries** [traɪz] *see* **try**

trip [trɪp] **1.** *noun*
journey; **we went on a boat trip down the Thames; he's on a business trip to Canada; they're taking a trip to Germany this summer.**
2. *verb*
to knock your foot on something, so that you fall down; **he tripped over the piece of wood; she tripped and fell down in the mud.**
trips—tripping—tripped—has tripped

trou·ble [ˈtrʌbəl] *noun*
problem/difficult situation; **the trouble is that the car won't start; it's no trouble—I can do it easily; the children are no trouble at all; he has money troubles; they got into trouble with the police; it's asking for trouble** = it is likely to cause problems; **he got his friend into trouble** = he made his friend do something wrong.

truck [trʌk] *noun*
large motor vehicle for carrying goods; **he was loading the boxes onto the truck; the big trucks make a lot of noise as they go past the house.**
truck·driv·er, truck·er, *noun*
person who drives a truck.

true [truː] *adjective*
correct/right; **what he says is true; it's true that she is married; is it true that you went to Scotland on your vacation?**

trunk [trʌŋk] *noun*
(*a*) main part of a tree; **the tree trunk is 3 feet around; can you jump over that tree trunk?**
(*b*) long nose of an elephant; **the elephant picked up the banana with its trunk.**
(*c*) large box for sending clothes, books, etc.; **I have two suitcases and a trunk.**
(*d*) place for carrying things in the back of a car; **he put his suitcase in the trunk.**
(*e*) **trunks** = men's shorts for various sports; **don't forget your swimming trunks; he bought a new pair of trunks.**

truth [truːθ] *noun*
something which is correct/right; **always tell the truth.**

try [traɪ] *verb*
(*a*) to make an attempt to do something; **he tried to climb up the tree; don't try to drive if you've never driven before; let me try to start the car.**
(*b*) to test/to see if something is good; **try one of my cookies; have you tried this new toothpaste? have you tried skating backwards yet?**
tries [traɪz]—**trying—tried** [traɪd]—**has tried**
try on, *verb*
to put on a piece of clothing to see if it fits; **try the shoes on before you buy them; did you try on the shirt?**
try out, *verb*
to test/to see if something is good; **try out the car before you buy it.**
Note: **try this hat on** *or* **try on this hat; try out the car** *or* **try the car out,** *but only* **try it on, try it out**

tube [tjuːb *or* tuːb] *noun*
(*a*) long pipe; **a plastic tube takes the gasoline from here to the engine.**
(*b*) soft pipe with a lid, which is filled with some sort of liquid; **a tube of toothpaste; a tube of glue.**

Tues·day ['tju:zdɪ *or* tu:zdɪ] *noun*
day between Monday and Wednesday, the third day of the week; **he came to see me last Tuesday; I go to the library on Tuesdays; shall we meet next Tuesday? today is Tuesday, October 28.**

tur·key ['tɜrkɪ] *noun*
large bird raised on a farm, often eaten at Thanksgiving; **have some more turkey; they bought a 20-pound turkey for Thanksgiving dinner.**
no plural for the meat of a turkey: **some turkey; a slice of turkey/a piece of turkey**

turn [tɜrn] 1. *noun*
(*a*) movement in a circle; **he gave the handle two turns.**
(*b*) change of direction; **the car made a sudden turn to the right; the car did a U-turn** = turned around and went back in the opposite direction.
(*c*) chance to do something in order; **wait for your turn to see the doctor; it's your turn to play now; let me go first—it's my turn, not yours; don't go out of turn** = when it is not your turn; **they took turns carrying the box** = each of them carried it for a while and then passed it to the next person.
2. *verb*
(*a*) to go around in a circle; to make something go around in a circle; **the wheels are turning slowly; turn the key to the left to open the door; the hands of the clock turned slowly to ten o'clock; the boat turned upside down.**
(*b*) to change direction; **turn right at the next traffic light; he turned the corner; the road turns to the left.**
(*c*) to move your head or body so that you face in another direction; **he turned to look at the camera.**
(*d*) to change into something different; **the leaves turn brown in the autumn; his hair is turning gray; we are turning this area into a football field.**
(*e*) to go past a time; **he turned fifty last week** = he had his 50th birthday last week.
turns—turning—turned—has turned

turn a·way, *verb*
(*a*) to send people away; **the parking lot is full, so we have to turn people away.**
(*b*) to move away; **she turned away because she didn't want her picture taken.**
turn back, *verb*
to go back in the opposite direction; **the weather was so bad that we had to turn back and go home.**
turn down, *verb*
(*a*) to refuse; **he was offered a job, but he turned it down; she turned down a job/ turned a job down in the library.**
(*b*) to make less strong; **turn down the radio—it's too loud; turn down the heat/ turn the heat down—it's too hot.**
turn in, *verb*
(*a*) to go to bed; **it's time to turn in.**
(*b*) to give back; **she turned in her uniform and quit her job.**
turn off, *verb*
(*a*) to switch off; **don't forget to turn the TV off; turn off the lights/turn the lights off—I'm going to show my film.**
(*b*) to leave a road you are traveling on; **he turned off Main Street into a parking lot.**
turn on, *verb*
to switch on; **turn the lights on/turn on the lights—it's getting dark; can you turn on the TV/turn the TV on—it's time for the news.**
turn out, *verb*
(*a*) to produce; **the factory turns out 2,000 cars a week.**
(*b*) to switch off; **turn out the lights/turn the lights out—I'm going to show a film.**
(*c*) to happen; **it turned out that he knew my sister; everything turned out all right.**
(*d*) to come out; **the whole school turned out to see the race.**
turn o·ver, *verb*
to roll over; **the truck turned over; the boat turned over.**
turn up, *verb*
(*a*) to arrive; to be found; **half the people didn't turn up until nine o'clock; the little boy finally turned up in St. Louis** = he was finally found in St. Louis; **my pen turned up in my coat pocket.**

(b) to make stronger; **can you turn up the radio/turn the radio up**—I can't hear it; **turn up the gas/turn the gas up, the water hasn't boiled yet.**

Note: **turn the radio down** *or* **turn down the radio; turn the light off** *or* **turn off the light,** *etc., but only* **turn it down, turn it off,** *etc.*

TV ['ti:'vi:] *noun, short for* **television**
do you watch TV every night? are there any games on TV tonight? he bought a color TV; our TV set has broken down; some TV programs make me go to sleep.

twelve [twelv] number 12
he's twelve (years old); come for a cup of coffee at twelve o'clock; there are twelve months in a year.

Note: **twelve o'clock** *is also called* **noon; twelve o'clock at night** *is* **midnight**

twelfth [twelfθ] **12th,** *adjective & noun*
he came twelfth in the race; today is the twelfth of November/November twelfth (November 12); it's her twelfth birthday next week.

twen·ty ['twentı] number 20
she's twenty (years old); he's in his **twenties** = he is between 20 and 29 years old.

Note: **twenty-one** (21), **twenty-two** (22), *etc., but* **twenty-first** (21st), **twenty-second** (22nd), *etc.*

twen·ti·eth, 20th, *adjective & noun*
she was twentieth in her class; today is the twentieth of December/December twentieth (December 20); it's her twentieth birthday on Tuesday.

twice [twaıs] *adverb*
two times; I've already seen that film twice; twice two is four; he's twice as old

as I am; she earns twice as much money as her sister; this book is twice as big as that one/is twice the size of that one.

twist [twıst] *verb*
(a) to turn round and round; to bend; the road twisted around the mountain; he twisted the metal bar into the shape of an S; threads are twisted together to make string.
(b) to bend something in a wrong way; the fire twisted the metal roof; he twisted his ankle = hurt it by bending it in an odd direction.

twists—twisting—twisted—has twisted

two [tu:] number 2
there are only two chocolates left in the box; his son is two (years old); they didn't come home until two (o'clock).
one or two = some/a few; there were only one or two people in the store.

Note: **two** (2), *but* **second** (2nd)

ty·ing [taıŋ] *see* **tie**

type [taıp] 1. *noun*
kind; you can have two types of cloth for your chairs; this is a new type of apple; what type of car are you looking for?
2. *verb*
to write with a typewriter; he's learning to type; I can only type with two fingers; she types all day long; he typed a letter.

types—typing—typed—has typed

type·writ·er, *noun*
machine which prints letters onto a piece of paper when you press the keys; she has a new electric typewriter; do you know how to change the ribbon in this typewriter?

typ·ist, *noun*
person who types.

Uu

ug·ly [ˈʌglɪ] *adjective*
not beautiful/not pleasant to look at;
she was wearing an ugly hat; they live in
an ugly little house.
ugly—uglier—ugliest

um·brel·la [ʌmˈbrelə] *noun*
round cover of folded cloth which you
open up and hold over your head to
keep the rain off; can I come under your
umbrella? he has an umbrella with red,
white and blue stripes; the wind broke my
umbrella.

un·a·ble [ʌnˈeɪbəl] *adjective*
not able; he was unable to come to the
meeting; after her accident, she was
unable to walk.

un·at·trac·tive [ʌnəˈtræktɪv] *adjective*
not nice-looking; it's an unattractive
part of town.

un·cle [ˈʌŋkəl] *noun*
brother of your father or mother; husband of your aunt; look, here's Uncle
John.

un·der [ˈʌndər] *preposition*
(*a*) in or to a place where something else
is on top or above; he hid under the
table; my pencil rolled under the piano;
can you swim under water? = below the
surface of the water.
(*b*) less than; she's under thirty = she is
less than 30 years old; the car was sold
for under $200; he ran the race in under
six minutes.
*Note: under is often used with verbs:
to look under; to go under, etc.*

un·der·ground, *adverb & adjective*
under the ground; the railroad track
goes underground for a short distance;
he went through an underground
hallway to the next building.

un·der·line, *verb*
to put a line under a word or words;
underline that sentence in the letter.
**underlines—underlining—
underlined—has underlined**

un·der·side, *noun*
side opposite the top of something;
pieces of old chewing gum were stuck to
the underside of the table.

un·der·wear, *noun*
clothing which you wear under your
other clothes; he needs some new underwear; she's washing her underwear.
no plural: **some underwear; a piece
of underwear**

un·der·stand [ʌndərˈstænd] *verb*
(*a*) to know; to see what something
means; do you understand how this
machine works? he doesn't understand
English, so don't try to talk to him; I
hardly speak any Chinese, but I made
myself understood.
(*b*) to have information; I understood
you were going to be late? we understand
he's getting married next week.
**understands—understanding—
understood—has understood**

un·dress [ʌnˈdres] *verb*
to take your clothes off; he undressed
and got into bed; before you get undressed, can you see if the garage door is
shut?
**undresses—undressing—
undressed—has undressed**

un·e·ven [ʌnˈiːvən] *adjective*
not straight/not equal; your haircut is
uneven.

un·fin·ished [ʌnˈfɪnɪʃt] *adjective*
not complete; we have some unfinished
business to take care of.

two hundred and fifty-nine

un·fold [ʌnˈfəʊld] *verb*
to spread out; he unfolded the letter and
read it aloud.
**unfolds—unfolding—
unfolded—has unfolded**

un·hap·py [ʌnˈhæpɪ] *adjective*
sad/not happy; she's unhappy because
her cat is sick; he looked very unhappy
when he came out of the principal's
office.
**unhappy—unhappier—
unhappiest**

un·hap·pi·ly, *adverb*
sadly; she stared unhappily out of the
window.

u·ni·form [ˈjuːnɪfɔːrm] *noun*
special clothes worn by everyone in a
group, especially soldiers, policemen,
etc.; the policemen were in uniform; was
he wearing a uniform? the children all
have to wear school uniforms.

u·nite [juːˈnaɪt] *verb*
to bring together/to join together; the
United States (of America) = very large
country south of Canada in North
America; the United Kingdom =
country formed of England, Scotland,
Wales and Northern Ireland.
**unites—uniting—united—has
united**
Note: **the United States of
America** *is usually called* **the U.S.**
or **the U.S.A.; the United Kingdom** *is usually called* **the U.K.**

u·ni·ver·si·ty [juːnɪˈvɜrsɪtɪ] *noun*
place where you can study after leaving
high school; the university is on the south
side of the town; he's studying history at
the state university; she goes to Columbia
University.
plural **universities**

un·less [ʌnˈles] *conjunction*
if not; **unless you leave now, you'll be
late** = if you do not leave now; **don't
call unless the message is important** = if
the message isn't important; **we'll have
our picnic in the field, unless it rains** =
if it doesn't rain; **don't come unless you
want to** = if you don't want to.

un·lock [ʌnˈlɒk] *verb*

to open the lock on something; she
unlocked the front door.
**unlocks—unlocking—unlocked—
has unlocked**

un·luck·y [ʌnˈlʌkɪ] *adjective*
not lucky; it's unlucky to walk under a
ladder; Friday the 13th is my unlucky day.
unlucky—unluckier—unluckiest

un·nat·u·ral [ʌnˈnætʃərəl] *adjective*
not normal/not natural; her hair looks
so unnatural.

un·nec·es·sar·y [ʌnˈnesəserɪ] *adjective*
not needed; these extra cups on the table
are unnecessary.

un·safe [ʌnˈseɪf] *adjective*
dangerous; it's unsafe to cross the street
here.

un·tie [ʌnˈtaɪ] *verb*
to open something which is tied; your
shoelace is untied; she untied the package.
**unties—untying—untied—has
untied**

un·til [ʌnˈtɪl] *preposition*
till/up to the time when; I won't be home
until after eleven o'clock; until yesterday,
I felt fine.

un·u·su·al [ʌnˈjuːʒʊəl] *adjective*
which does not happen often/strange;
we're having an unusual amount of rain
this month; what an unusual hat!

up [ʌp] *adverb & preposition*
(*a*) in or to a high place; he climbed up the
stairs; she was going up a ladder; lift your
hands up; why is the cat up there on the
roof?
(*b*) to a higher level; the temperature has
gone up; prices seem to go up every day.
(*c*) along; go up the street to the traffic
lights and then turn left.
(*d*) not in bed; he's still up—he should
be in bed; she stayed up all night.
(*e*) towards the north; I'll be going up to
Alaska next week.
(*f*) what's up? = what is the matter?
(*g*) your time is up = you have had all
the time allowed.
Note: up is often used after verbs: **to
keep up; to look up; to turn up,** *etc.*

up to, *preposition*
(*a*) as many as; **the bus will hold up to 60 passengers.**
(*b*) **what are you up to?** = what are you doing?

up-to-date, *adjective & adverb*
very modern/using very recent information; **is this train timetable up-to-date? I keep myself up-to-date by reading the newspaper every day.**

up·per ['ʌpər] *adjective*
at the top/higher; **the upper part of the house was destroyed by fire.**

up·set [ʌp'set] 1. *verb*
(*a*) to make angry or worried; **he upset his mother by staying out late.**
(*b*) to turn over; **the bad weather upset our vacation plans.**
upsets—upsetting—upset—has upset
2. *adjective*
(*a*) angry or worried; **he's upset about his test scores.**
(*b*) ['ʌpset] slightly sick; **she has an upset stomach.**

up·side down ['ʌpsaɪd'daʊn] *adverb*
with the top turned to the bottom; **don't hold the box upside down—everything will fall out; the car ran off the road and ended up upside down in a field; the boys were hanging upside down from a tree; he's not reading that book—he's holding it upside down.**

up·stairs [ʌp'steərz] *adverb & noun*
on or to an upper floor of a house; **my father is upstairs—I'll ask him to come down; can you go upstairs and get my coat from the bedroom? the upstairs of the house is smaller than the downstairs.**

up·ward *or* **up·wards** ['ʌpwərd, ʌpwɜrdz] *adverb*
toward the top; **the path slopes upward.**

us [ʌs] *object pronoun used by the person who is speaking to talk about himself and other people with him*
he gave us $2 to buy ourselves some ice cream; who is it?—it's us! our class is

very happy—the teacher has given us a vacation from homework.

U.S. [ju:'es], **U.S.A.** [ju:es'eɪ] *see* **unite**

use¹ [ju:s] *noun*
(*a*) way in which something can be used; being used; **can you find a use for this piece of wood? the stove has been in daily use for ten years; our apartment has no kitchen, but we have the use of the kitchen in the apartment downstairs; to make use of something** = to use; **you should make more use of your dictionary** = you should use it more.
(*b*) value/being useful; **what's the use of telling her what to do, when she never does what you want? it's no use sitting here and saying the car needs to be washed, let's go out and wash it.**

use² [ju:z] *verb*
(*a*) to take a tool, etc., and do something with it; **someone used my knife to open a can of fruit; he used the money to buy a car; did you use a sewing machine to make your dress? can I use these scissors for cutting flowers? he was using the electric saw when it slipped.**
(*b*) to take something and burn it, etc., to make an engine work or to produce heat, light, etc.; **this car uses a lot of gasoline; we're using too much gas and electricity.**
uses—using—used [ju:zd]—**has used**

used [ju:zd] *adjective*
which is not new; **a used car; this typewriter is worth a lot of money—it has hardly been used.**

used to ['ju:sttʊ]
(*a*) **to be used to something/to doing something** = not to object to something, because you do it often; **he's used to getting up early; she's used to hard work; we're not used to eating so much.**
(*b*) **to get used to something/to doing something** = to do something often or for a period of time, so that it becomes a habit; **you'll soon get used to your new job; he never got used to getting up early.**
(*c*) (*showing that something happened*

often or regularly in the past) **there used to be a bakery on Main Street; when I was a boy, we used to go to the seaside every year for our vacation; she used to teach history at our school; didn't he use to go to work on his bike?**
Note the forms used in the negative and questions: **he used to go by bike; he didn't use to go by bike/ he used not to go by bike; didn't he use to go by bike?**

use·ful, *adjective*
who/which can help you to do something; **I find this knife very useful when I'm camping; he's a very useful man in the office.**

use·less, *adjective*
which does not help; **this knife is useless—it isn't sharp; he's useless when it**

comes to repairing cars = he can't repair cars.

use up, *verb*
to finish something; **we've used up all our sugar; she used up all the matches trying to light a fire.**
Note: **we've used all the sugar up** *or* **we've used up all the sugar** *but only* **we've used it up**

u·su·al ['juːʒʊəl] *adjective*
which happens often/which you do often; **I'll take my usual train this morning; the mailman was late, as usual; let's meet at the usual time; as usual, it rained on my birthday.**

u·su·al·ly, *adverb*
very often/mostly; **he usually gets to work at 9 o'clock; she usually has an apple for lunch.**

Vv

va·ca·tion [veɪˈkeɪʃən] **1.** *noun*
time when you do not have to work or be at school; **we always spend our vacation on the coast; how many days' vacation do you get each year? teachers can rest during summer vacation; Mr. Brown isn't in the office—he's on vacation; when are you going on vacation?**
Note: usually used without **the**
2. *verb*
to take time off work, often to travel; **they're vacationing in Europe.**
vacations—vacationing— vacationed—has vacationed

val·ley ['vælɪ] *noun*
low land between hills, with a river running through it; **the valley of the Mississippi/the Mississippi valley; the town is at the bottom of the valley.**

val·ue ['væljuː] *noun*
what something is worth; **what's the value of this house? this is a very good**

value = it is well worth its price.
val·u·a·ble ['væljəbəl] *adjective*
worth a lot of money; **the burglar stole some valuable books.**

var·i·ous ['veərɪəs] *adjective*
several/of different kinds; **we've met at various parties; there are various ways of getting to Portland from here; he has written various books on birds.**

vase [veɪs] *noun*
container for flowers which have been picked or cut; **she put the roses in a vase; someone broke mother's best vase.**

veg·e·ta·ble ['vedʒtəbəl] *noun*
plant grown for food, not usually sweet; **we have potatoes, cabbages and other kinds of vegetables in the garden; what vegetables do you want with your meat?—peas and carrots, please; I'll have a bowl of vegetable soup.**

ve·hi·cle ['viːəkəl] *noun*

machine on wheels which travels on land, carrying people or goods; **motor vehicles are not allowed on this path; what type of vehicle do you drive?**

verb [vɜrb] *noun*
word showing action/being/feeling, etc.; in the sentence **"he kicked the ball,"** the word **"kicked"** is a verb.

ver·y [ˈveərɪ] **1.** *adverb*
(*used to make an adjective stronger*) **it's very hot in here—let's open the window; she's very tall; this meat isn't very good.**
2. *adjective*
exactly the right one/exactly the same; **he's the very man you want; it happens at the very beginning of the film** = right at the beginning.

ver·y man·y, *adjective*
a lot of; **there weren't very many people at the party; we went swimming very many times.**
Note: **very many** *is used with things you can count:* **very many cars**

ver·y much 1. *adverb*
greatly; **I like ice cream very much; thank you very much for your present; it's very much colder today.**
2. *adjective*
a lot of; **he doesn't do very much work; she hasn't got very much money.**
Note: **very much** *is used with things which you cannot count:* **very much money**

vice-pres·i·dent [vaɪsˈprezɪdənt] *noun*
person who is second to the president in command; **he's running for Vice-President; she's a vice-president in the company.**

vic·to·ry [ˈvɪktərɪ] *noun*
win (in a game or battle); **the victory of the Yankees over the Cubs.**
plural **victories**

view [vjuː] **1.** *noun*
(*a*) what you can see from a certain place; **from my window there's a wonderful view over San Francisco; you get a good view of the sea from the top of the hill; this photo is a side view of our house.**
(*b*) way of thinking about something; **in**

my view, the government ought to do something to help poor people; I try to see the president's point of view** = I try to understand the way he thinks.
(*c*) **in view of** = because of; **in view of the weather, we had the party indoors.**
2. *verb*
to see; to watch; **he viewed the problem in a different way.**
views—viewing—viewed— has viewed

view·er, *noun*
person who watches television; **most viewers like this program.**

vil·lage [ˈvɪlɪdʒ] *noun*
small group of houses in the country, often with a church and a few stores; **we live in a little mountain village; go to the village bakery for some bread; there aren't many children in the village school.**

vi·o·lence [ˈvaɪələns] *noun*
rough action; use of force; **the game was interrupted by violence; there is more violence in big cities than in small towns.**
no plural

vi·o·lent, *adjective*
using a lot of force; very rough; **there was a violent storm during the night; the football game was very violent— several players were hurt.**

vis·it [ˈvɪzɪt] **1.** *noun*
short stay with someone/short stay in a town or country; **he's on a visit to China; let's pay a visit to your mother; they are expecting a visit from the doctor.**
2. *verb*
to stay a short time with someone/to stay a short time in a town or country; **I must visit my brother in the hospital; we are going to visit the factory; he's visiting friends in France.**
visits—visiting—visited—has visited

vis·i·tor, *noun*
person who visits; **how many visitors are staying in the hotel this weekend? we had a visitor last night—old Uncle Charles.**

voice [vɔɪs] *noun*
sound made when you speak or sing; **I**

didn't recognize your voice over the
phone; he's got a cold and has lost his
voice = he can't speak; she spoke for
a few minutes in a low voice = very
quietly.

vote [vəʊt] 1. *noun*
making a mark on a piece of paper/lift-
ing your hand, etc. to elect someone or
to make a decision; **there were 10 votes
for Mr. Smith and only 2 for Mr. Jones,
so Mr. Smith was elected; my vote goes
to Mr. Smith's plan; if we can't**

agree, let's have/take a vote.
2. *verb*
to make a mark on a piece of paper to
elect someone/to lift your hand to make
a decision; **there were ten votes for Mr.
Smith; only people over 18 can vote in
the election; I vote that we have a picnic
in the woods** = I think we should have
a picnic.
votes—voting—voted—has voted

vot·er, *noun*
person who votes.

Ww

wage [weɪdʒ] *noun*
money which you get each week for
work which you have done; **he gets a
good wage at the factory; wages have
gone up a lot this year; I'm going to pick
up my wages.**
Note: usually used in the plural

wag·on ['wægən] *noun*
open vehicle with four wheels, used to
carry things; **the little boy pulled a
wagon full of newspapers along the sidewalk; many families traveled west in
covered wagons.**

waist [weɪst] *noun*
narrow part of your body below your
chest and above your buttocks; **he
measures 32 inches around the waist.**

wait [weɪt] *verb*
to stay somewhere until something
happens or someone arrives; **wait here
while I get a policeman; he waited for
the bus for a half hour; he gets angry if
you keep him waiting; wait a minute, I've
got a stone in my shoe; sorry to have kept
you waiting!**
**waits—waiting—waited—has
waited**

wait·er, *noun*
man who brings food to people in a

restaurant; **the waiter brought us the
soup; how much shall we give the waiter
as a tip?** *see also* **waitress**.

wait·ing room, *noun*
room where you wait at a doctor's,
dentist's or at a railroad station; **go into
the waiting room—the doctor will see
you in ten minutes.**

wait·ress ['weɪtrəs] *noun*
woman who brings food to people in a
restaurant; **the waitress brought us the
soup; shall we give the waitress a tip?** *see
also* **waiter**.
plural **waitresses**

wake [weɪk] *verb*
to interrupt someone's sleep; to stop
sleeping; **the telephone waked me/I was
waked by the telephone; can't you wake
her?—no, she's fast asleep.**
**wakes—waking—waked/woke
[wəʊk]—has waked/has woken**

wake up, *verb*
to interrupt someone's sleep; to stop
sleeping; **he woke up in the middle of the
night; he was woken up by the sound of
the telephone; wake up! it's past nine
o'clock.**
Note: **I woke my mother up** *or* **I
woke up my mother** *but only* **I
woke her up**

walk [wɔːk] 1. *noun*

(a) journey on foot; **we all went for a walk in the park; the post office is only five minutes' walk from here** = you can go there on foot in five minutes; **he's taking the dog for a walk; does anyone want to come for a walk?**

(b) paved path; **he came straight up the walk and rang the doorbell.**

2. *verb*

to go on foot; **I'll walk to the bus stop with you; she walked across the room; he was walking along the street; can you walk to school, or do you have to take the bus? they all walked up the hill.**

walks—walking—walked—has walked

walk a·round, *verb*

to walk in various directions; **they spent hours walking around town, looking for a restaurant.**

walk off with, *verb*

to go away with; to steal; **the burglar walked off with all our jewelry; she walked off with the prize** = she won the prize easily.

wall [wɔːl] *noun*

bricks/stones, etc., piled up to make one of the sides of a building/of a room or to close in a space; **he's building a wall around his yard; we have a lot of pictures on the walls of the dining room; there's a clock on the wall over his desk; the car crashed into the wall; can you climb over the brick wall?**

wal·let ['wɒlɪt] *noun*

small leather case for holding money/cards, etc., and which you keep in your pocket; **someone has stolen my wallet from my back pocket.**

want [wɒnt] *verb*

(a) to hope that you will do something/that something will happen/that you will have something; **he wants a bicycle for his birthday; they want to go to Africa next winter; she wants to be a doctor; he wants me to go to see him.**

(b) to look for someone; **he's wanted by the police.**

wants—wanting—wanted—has wanted

war [wɔːr] *noun*

fighting between countries; **in 1814 Britain was at war with France/Britain and France were at war; millions of people were killed in World War II.**

warm [wɔːrm] 1. *adjective*

fairly hot/pleasantly hot; **it's cold outside in the snow, but it's nice and warm in the house; they tried to keep warm by jumping up and down; are you warm enough, or do you want another blanket?**

warm—warmer—warmest

2. *verb*

to make hotter; **warm yourself by the fire; he was warming his hands over the fire.**

warms—warming—warmed—has warmed

warmth [wɔːrmθ] *noun*

heat; **the warmth of the fire was welcome after the cold of the outdoors.**

no plural **some warmth**

warm up, *verb*

to make hotter; **this soup will warm you up; I'll warm up some milk to make hot chocolate.**

warn [wɔːrn] *verb*

to tell that a danger is possible; **the children were warned not to go too near the fire; I warned you about that electric wire; the police warned us against playing near the railroad tracks.**

warns—warning—warned—has warned

warn·ing, *noun*

telling about a danger; **the police gave a warning about a dangerous criminal; did you read the warning sign? there's a warning on the bottle of medicine; every pack of cigarettes has a health warning printed on it.**

with·out warn·ing = very suddenly; **without warning the car ran off the road into a wall.**

was [wʌz] *see* **be**

wash [wɔːʃ] 1. *noun*

(*a*) action of cleaning using water; **she gave the car a quick wash.**

(*b*) clothes to be cleaned; **she's doing the wash** = washing clothes; **these pants should go in the wash** = need to be washed.

plural **washes;** *no plural for* (*b*)*:* **some wash**

2. *verb*

to clean using water; **wash your hands before dinner! we must wash the car before we go on vacation; they were washing the windows when it started to rain; your hair needs to be washed; can you wash this raincoat?—no, you have to take it to the cleaner's.**

washes—washing—washed—has washed

wash·cloth, *noun*

small cloth used to wash yourself; **you'll find a towel and a washcloth near the bathtub.**

wash·er, wash·ing ma·chine, *noun*

machine for washing clothes.

wash off, *verb*

to take off by washing; **I'll wash the mud off my boots.**

wash·room, *noun*

room with a toilet and a sink for washing up; **could you tell me where the washroom is, please?**

wash up, *verb*

to wash your face and hands; **I need to wash up—where's the bathroom?**

wasn't ['wʌzənt] *see* **be**

waste [weɪst] **1.** *noun*

not being any use; **it's a waste of time trying to call her—she's not in; that car is a waste of money—it keeps breaking down.**

2. *adjective*

useless/which is no use; **the company used to throw its waste products into the river.**

3. *verb*

(*a*) to use more than you need; **I've wasted three sheets of paper; they waste a lot of food.**

(*b*) not to use something in a useful way;

she wasted several hours waiting for him to come and pick her up; he wastes his pocket money on candy.

wastes—wasting—wasted—has wasted

waste·bas·ket, *noun*

metal or plastic container for garbage; **throw these old papers in the wastebasket; he's emptying the wastebasket.**

watch [wɒtʃ] **1.** *noun*

(*a*) small clock which you wear on your wrist; **he looked at his watch; what time is it by your watch?**

(*b*) looking at something; **the police are on the watch for burglars.**

plural **watches;** *no plural for* (*b*)

2. *verb*

(*a*) to look at; **did you watch TV last night? I watched a program on animals; we'll watch him play football; she was watching the children playing.**

(*b*) to look at something carefully to make sure that nothing happens; **watch the saucepan—I don't want the milk to boil over; will you watch the baby while I go shopping?**

watches—watching—watched—has watched

watch out, *verb*

to be careful; **watch out! the paint is still wet; you have to watch out for ice on the roads in winter.**

wa·ter ['wɔːtər] **1.** *noun*

common liquid which makes rain, rivers, the sea, etc., and which you drink and use in cooking; **can I have a glass of water, please? the hotel has hot and cold water in each bedroom; he dived and swam across the pool under water; boil the potatoes in a pan of water.**

no plural; **some water; a drop of water**

2. *verb*

to pour water on a plant to make it grow; **the weather is very dry—we'll have to water the garden; he was watering the flowers.**

waters—watering—watered—has watered

wa·ter·fall, *noun*
place where a stream falls down rocks;
let's have our picnic by the waterfall;
which is the biggest waterfall in the
world—is it Niagara?

wa·ter·mel·on ['wɔːtərmelən] *noun*
very large, juicy green and red fruit; he
bought a ten-pound watermelon at the
supermarket; would you like some water-
melon/a piece of watermelon?

wa·ter·proof, *adjective*
which will not let water through; is your
raincoat really waterproof? if your watch
is waterproof you can wear it when you
go swimming.

wave [weɪv] **1.** *noun*
high mass of water on the sea, which
moves forward; can you hear the sound
of the waves on the beach? the waves
were ten feet high.
2. *verb*
to move up and down and from side
to side, especially to move your hand
in this way; the children were waving
flags; she waved her handkerchief as the
train left; wave to your mother—she's
on the other side of the street; I waved
to the waiter and asked him to bring
the check.
**waves—waving—waved—has
waved**

way [weɪ] *noun*
(*a*) road/path which goes somewhere;
my friend lives across the way.
(*b*) right road/path to somewhere;
can you tell me the way to the post
office? the policeman showed us the way
to the station; he made his way through
the crowd; we lost our way and had to
ask someone; I'm just on my way to
school.
(*c*) particular direction; this is a one-way
street; which way is the wind blowing? =
is it blowing north, south, etc.? come
this way, please.
(*d*) means of doing something; grandmother showed me the way to make
bread; she spoke in a friendly way; is
there another way of doing it? he always
does it that way; I wish I knew a way of
making money quickly.

(*e*) distance/time; the post office is a long
way from here; we have a long way to go
before we finish our work; I'll walk part
of the way home with you.
(*f*) space in which someone wants to be/
which someone wants to use; get out of
the way—there's a car coming; keep out
of father's way—he thinks you broke the
window; he's always in the way.
by the way (*used to introduce
something which is not very important or
to change the subject which is being
talked about*) by the way, did you see the
TV program on cars yesterday?

way in, *noun*
entrance; is this the way in? we finally
found a way in to the museum.

way out, *noun*
exit; is this the way out? we couldn't find
our way out in the dark.

we [wiː] *pronoun*
(*used by speakers when referring to themselves*) the policeman said we could cross
the street; we came to Chicago by train;
our class went to the theater—we all
enjoyed ourselves very much; we'll go
shopping tomorrow.
Note: when it is the object **we**
becomes **us:** **we gave it to him/he
gave it to us;** *when it follows the
verb* **be,** **we** *usually becomes* **us:
who is it?—it's us!**

weak [wiːk] *adjective*
(*a*) not strong; after his illness he was
very weak; this coffee is very weak—
you've put too much water in it.
(*b*) not good at; he's very weak in math;
math is his weakest subject.
weak—weaker—weakest

wealth [welθ] *noun*
being rich; a lot of money; he's famous
for his wealth.
no plural

wealth·y, *adjective*
having a lot of money; he's a very
wealthy man.
wealthy—wealthier—wealthiest

weap·on ['wepən] *noun*
thing which you use to fight with; the
soldiers were carrying guns and other

weapons; he used a broken bottle as a weapon.

wear [weər] *verb*

(*a*) to carry on your body (especially a piece of clothing); **I'll wear my brown coat today; the police are looking for a man wearing a blue raincoat; everyone was wearing a uniform; she's wearing my watch.**

(*b*) to become damaged through being used a lot; **the car tires are worn; I've worn a hole in my pants.**

wears—wearing—wore [wɔːr]—**has worn**

wear a·way, wear off, *verb*
to disappear gradually; **the writing on the wall has worn away; the effect of the cough medicine has worn off.**

wear out, *verb*

(*a*) to use something so much that it is broken/useless; **he wore out three pairs of shoes; the engine wore out** = ran so much that it doesn't work anymore.

(*b*) **worn out** = very tired; **after that game of football I am worn out; she came home worn out after a day at the office.**

weath·er [ˈweðər] *noun*
conditions outside—that is, if it is raining/hot/cold/windy/sunny, etc.; **what's the weather like today? the TV said the weather was going to be bad; the weather is always cold in the mountains; look at the rain—is this your normal summer weather? if the weather is good, perhaps we'll have a picnic.**
no plural

weath·er·man, *noun*
person on TV or radio who tells what the weather will be like; **the weatherman said it was going to rain.**
plural **weathermen**

Wednes·day [ˈwenzdɪ] *noun*
day between Tuesday and Thursday, the fourth day of the week; **I saw her last Wednesday; we've got a day off next Wednesday; can you come to dinner on Wednesday evening?**

week [wiːk] *noun*
period of seven days; **there are 52 weeks in the year; we have two weeks' vacation at Christmas; my aunt is coming to stay with us next week; what day of the week is it today?** = is it Monday, Tuesday, etc.? **we go to the movies once a week; a week from now I'll be on vacation.**

week·day, *noun*
normal working day (not Saturday or Sunday); **the office is open on weekdays.**

week·end, *noun*
Saturday and Sunday; period from Friday evening to Sunday evening; **what are you doing over the weekend? we're going away for the weekend; come to spend the weekend with me; I went to Boston last weekend; we usually go to the lake on weekends.**

week·ly, *adjective & adverb*
which happens/appears once a week; **we have a weekly paper which tells us all the local news; we pay the milkman weekly.**

weigh [weɪ] *verb*
to measure how heavy something is; to be heavy/to have a certain weight; **can you weigh these potatoes for me? this piece of fish weighs 12 ounces; how much do you weigh? I weigh 120 pounds.**

weighs—weighing—weighed—has weighed

weight [weɪt] *noun*

(*a*) how heavy something is; **what's the weight of this bag of potatoes? what's your weight? I'm trying to lose weight** = to get thinner; **he has put on a lot of weight** = he is a lot fatter.

(*b*) something which is heavy; **if you lift heavy weights, you may hurt your back; put a weight on the pile of papers to keep them from blowing away.**

wel·come [ˈwelkəm] **1.** *noun*
action of greeting someone; **they gave us a warm welcome** = a friendly welcome.

2. *verb*

(*a*) to greet someone; **they welcomed us to the office; we were welcomed by the dogs when we got home.**

(*b*) to be glad to hear news; to accept;

he welcomed the news that he had passed
his driving test; I would welcome any
advice on how to make bread, because
I've never made it before.
**welcomes—welcoming—
welcomed—has welcomed**
3. adjective
greeted with pleasure; **the trip was a
welcome change; you're welcome** = (*said
in reply to* **thank you**) it was my
pleasure.

well [wel] **1.** *noun*
very deep hole in the ground with water
or oil at the bottom; **they pulled the
water up from a well; there are many oil
wells in the North Sea.**
2. adverb
(*a*) in a good way; **he can speak Russian
quite well; she did her homework very
well; the store is small, but it's doing well.**
(*b*) a lot; **it's well after 9 o'clock; it's well
worth trying to get a ticket; he's well over
sixty** = more than sixty years old.
as well = also; **I'm bringing my cat,
but can I bring the dogs as well? you
can't have a piece of cake and ice cream
as well.**
as well as = not only, but also; **he's
deaf as well as blind; the man sells candy
as well as newspapers.**
3. adjective
healthy; **you're looking well! he's quite
well after his cold; he's not very well, and
has had to stay in bed.**
4. interjection
(*which starts a sentence, and often has no
meaning*) **well, as I was saying; well, the
laundry is finished, so what shall we do
now?** (*showing suprise*) **well, well! here's
old Mr. Smith!**
well-done, *adjective*
(*a*) performed in a good way; **the play
was very well-done.**
(*b*) cooked completely; **he likes his steak
well-done.**
well-known, *adjective*
known by many people; **he's a well-
known actor.**

went [went] *see* **go**

were [wɜr], **weren't** [wɜrnt] *see* **be**

west [west] **1.** *noun*
direction of where the sun sets; **the sun
rises in the east and sets in the west; the
town is to the west of the river.**
2. adjective
referring to the west; **the west coast of
the United States; he lives on the west
side of town.**
3. adverb
towards the west; **the ship is sailing west;
if you go west for ten miles, you'll come
to a little village.**
west·ern [ˈwestərn] **1.** *adjective*
of the west; **Great Britain is in Western
Europe; they live in the western part of
Canada.**
2. noun
story/film about cowboys; **I like watching old westerns on TV.**

wet [wet] *adjective*
(*a*) covered with water; **I didn't have an
umbrella, so I got wet waiting for the bus
in the rain; the carpet is all wet where
you spilled your coffee.**
(*b*) rainy; **February is the wettest month
of the year.**
(*c*) not yet dry; **don't sit there—the paint
on the chair is still wet.**
wet—wetter—wettest

what [wɒt] *adjective & pronoun*
(*a*) the thing which; **I saw what was in
the box; did you see what he gave me for
my birthday? what he likes most is just
sitting in the sun.**
(*b*) (*asking a question*) **what time is it?
what's the time? what's his name? what
did you say? what's the German for
"table"? what's the matter with Mrs.
Smith? what happened to you? what kind
of car do you drive?**
(*c*) (*showing surprise*) **what a beautiful
house! what lovely weather!**
Note: after **what** *used to ask a question, the verb is put before the subject:*
what's the time? *but* **they don't
know what the time is**

what a·bout (*showing an idea*) **what
about stopping here for a picnic? what
about something to drink? we've sent
cards to everyone we know—what about
Mrs. Smith?**

what·ev·er, *adjective & pronoun*
(*a*) (*strong form of* **what**) anything; it doesn't matter what; **you can eat whatever you like; he does whatever he feels like doing; I'll buy it whatever the price is** = however much it costs.
(*b*) (*strong form of* **what** *in questions*) **whatever made you do that?**

what for
(*a*) why; **what are you painting the door for? what's she sitting on the floor for? we're going out—what for? he's calling the police—what for?**
(*b*) **what's that handle for?** = what does that handle do? **what's this little button for?**

wheat [wiːt] *noun*
grain from which most bread is made; **we drove past endless fields of wheat; would you buy a loaf of wheat bread for me?**
no plural: **some wheat**

wheel [wiːl] **1.** *noun*
(*a*) round part on which a bicycle/a car, etc., runs; **a bicycle has two wheels—a front wheel and a back wheel; the truck had very large wheels.**
(*b*) similar round thing; **in English cars, the steering wheel is on the right-hand side.**
2. *verb*
to push along something which has wheels; **he wheeled his bike into the house; she was wheeling her motorbike down the steps.**
wheels—wheeling—wheeled— has wheeled

wheeled, *adjective*
with wheels; **a three-wheeled vehicle.**

when [wen] **1.** *adverb*
(*asking a question*) at what time; **when does the last train leave? when did you see the film? when are we going to have dinner? since when has he been in your class?**
Note: after **when** *used to ask a question, the verb is put before the subject:* **when does the film start?** *but* **he doesn't know when the film starts; when is he coming?** *but* **they can't tell me when he is coming**

2. *conjunction*
(*a*) at the time that; **when I was young, we were living in New York; when you leave the house, don't forget to lock the door; do you remember when we all went to the beach in your old car? tell me when you're feeling hungry; we were all singing when he came in.**
(*b*) after; **when we had finished, we sat down; turn off the TV when the news is over; when you've had your breakfast, please wash the dishes.**

when·ev·er, *adverb*
at any time that; **come whenever you like; I go to see her whenever I can.**

where [weər] *adverb*
(*a*) (*asking a question*) in what place/to what place; **where are my glasses? where's the restaurant? where did you put the book? where are you going for your vacation? do you know where the manager is?**
(*b*) (*showing place*) **stay where you are; he still lives in the town where he was born; here's where he hides his money.**
Note: after **where** *used to ask a question, the verb is put before the subject:* **where is the bottle?** *but* **he doesn't know where the bottle is**

wher·ev·er, *adverb*
to/in any place; **wherever I go, I meet interesting people; I'd like to find her, wherever she may be.**

wheth·er [ˈweðər] *conjunction*
if; **I don't know whether it's true; do you know whether the manager is in or not? whether you're tall or short—it doesn't matter.**

which [wɪtʃ] *adjective & pronoun*
(*a*) (*asking a question*) what person/thing; **which hat should I wear? in which hand do you hold a pen? which boy is the one you saw? which of you girls wants to help with the dishes?**
(*b*) (*only used with things, not people*) the thing that; **the house which is across from the post office; here's the bread**

which we bought this morning.
Note: with an object **which** *can be left out:* **here's the bread we bought this morning**

while [waɪl] 1. *noun*
(a) length of time; **we had to wait a little while for the bus; he left a little while ago; it's nice to go to the movies once in a while** = from time to time.
(b) **to be worth while** = to be worth doing; **it's worth while having two keys to the door, in case you lose one.**
2. *conjunction*
(a) during the period that; at the same time that; **while I was making breakfast, everyone else was in bed; you can't do your homework while you're watching TV; while he was on vacation he caught a cold; I'll set the table while you take a bath.**
(b) (*showing difference*) **he earns $200 a week while I only earn $100.**

whip [wɪp] *verb*
to beat; **his mother made chocolate pie with whipped cream.**
whips—whipping—whipped—has whipped

whis·per [ˈwɪspər] 1. *noun*
very quiet words; **he spoke in a whisper.**
2. *verb*
to speak in a very quiet voice; **he was whispering to his wife during the whole film; she whispered to me that she felt sick.**
whispers—whispering—whispered—has whispered

whis·tle [ˈwɪsəl] 1. *noun*
(a) small instrument which makes a loud high sound when you blow it; **the whistle blew—it was the end of the game; the policeman blew his whistle.**
(b) loud high sound which you make by almost closing your mouth and blowing through the hole; **he gave a loud whistle.**
2. *verb*
to make a loud high sound by blowing air through your lips; **he whistled and his dog came running up; she was**

whistling as she worked.
whistles—whistling—whistled—has whistled

white [waɪt] *adjective & noun*
of a color like snow or milk; **he was wearing a white shirt; a white car always looks dirty; the snow was so white that it made my eyes hurt; you need three egg whites to make this cake** = white parts of eggs.
white—whiter—whitest

who [huː] *pronoun*
(a) (*asking a question*) which person/which people; **who's knocking at the door? who threw the stone through the window? who are all those people in uniform? who are you going home with? who was she talking to? who did you see at the party?**
(b) the person that/the people that; **the friend who came to see us yesterday works for the post office; people who didn't get tickets early can't get into the theater; there's the man who I saw at the store; do you remember the man who helped to push the car?**
Note: with an object **who** *can be left out:* **there's the man I saw at the store**
Note: when **who** *is used as an object, it sometimes is written* **whom** [huːm]: **whom was she talking to? there's the man whom I saw in the store**

who·ev·er, *pronoun*
anyone who; **whoever finds the money can keep it.**

whole [həʊl] 1. *adjective*
complete/all (of something); **he has eaten the whole cake; she stayed in bed a whole week; the whole country was covered with snow; the whole school came down with measles** = all the children.
2. *noun*
all/everything; **he stayed in bed the whole of the morning; I liked the group of paintings as a whole** = taken together/generally.

whom [huːm] *see* **who**

whose [huːz] *pronoun*
(*a*) (*asking a question*) belonging to which person; **whose car is that? whose pens are these?**
(*b*) referring to who; **the people whose car was stolen; the man whose hat you sat on.**

why [waɪ] *adverb*
(*asking a question*) for what reason; **why did you call me in the middle of the night? why isn't he at work today? why is the sky blue? she told me why she didn't go to the party; I asked him why the train was late; why go by train when the bus is cheaper? why not take the car?**
Note: after **why** *used to ask a question, the verb is put before the subject:* **why isn't he at work today?** *but* **they don't know why he wasn't at work**

wide [waɪd] *adjective & adverb*
having a certain width; which measures a lot from one side to the other; not narrow; **how wide is the Ohio River? the cupboard is three feet wide; the main road through town is wider than our street; she left the door wide open** = completely open; **he was wide awake** = completely awake.
wide—wider—widest
width [wɪdθ] *noun*
measurement from side to side; **what's the width of the river? the carpet is 3 yards in width.**

wife [waɪf] *noun*
woman who is married to a man; **she's the manager's wife; I know Mr. Jones but I've never met his wife.**
plural **wives** [waɪvz]

wild [waɪld] *adjective*
(*a*) living freely in nature; **he was attacked by a wild animal; you can find many types of wild flowers in the mountains.**
(*b*) **wild about** = liking very much; **she's wild about horses** = she likes horses very much.

(*c*) careless; rough; **he leads a wild life; it was a wild party.**
wild—wilder—wildest
wild·life, *noun*
wild animals; **you can see many types of wildlife in this park.**
no plural: **some wildlife**

will [wɪl] *verb, used with other verbs*
(*a*) (*to form the future*) **they will be here soon; will you be staying long in Italy? I won't be able to come to dinner; if you ask him to sing, he'll say "no."**
(*b*) to be certain to happen; **the cat will keep eating the dog's food.**
(*c*) (*to make a polite form of asking someone to do something*) **will you all please sit down? will someone turn the light off?**
(*d*) (*showing that you are eager to do something*) **leave the dishes—I'll do them; the car won't start.**
Negative: **will not** *usually* **won't** [wəʊnt]
Past: **would, would not** *usually* **wouldn't**
Note: **will** *is often shortened to* **'ll: he'll = he will**
will·ing, *adjective*
eager to help; **is anyone willing to wash the car? I need two willing boys to move the piano.**

win [wɪn] 1. *noun*
beating someone in a game; **our team has only had two wins this year.**
2. *verb*
(*a*) to beat someone in a game; to be first in a race, etc.; **our team won their game yesterday; he won the race easily; which team is winning?**
(*b*) to get (a prize, etc.); **he won first prize in the music competition; I won a vacation in Greece in a newspaper contest.**
wins—winning—won [wʌn]**—has won**
win·ner, *noun*
person who wins; **the winner of the 100 meters race; he was the winner in the music competition.**

wind¹ [wɪnd] *noun*
air which moves outdoors; **the wind blew
the leaves off the trees; don't try to put
your umbrella up in this wind; there's no
wind at all—the smoke from the fire is
going straight up; the flags were blowing
in the wind; wind instruments** = musical
instruments which you have to blow to
make a note.
wind·shield *noun*
glass window in the front of a car or
truck.
wind·y, *adjective*
with a lot of wind; **a windy day; what
windy weather!**
windy—windier—windiest

wind² [waɪnd] *verb*
(*a*) to turn (a key, etc. to make a
machine work); **do you need to wind
your watch? my watch needs to be wound
every day.**
(*b*) to twist round and round; **he wound
the string into a ball; she wound the towel
around her head.**
**winds—winding—wound
[waʊnd]—has wound**
wind up, *verb*
(*a*) to twist round and round; **he was
winding the string up into a ball; the road
winds up the mountain.**
(*b*) to turn (a key to make a machine
work); **have you wound up the clock/
wound the clock up?**
(*c*) to finish; **he wound up his speech with
a story about his father; let's try to wind
up this meeting now; she wound up with
someone else's coat** = she ended up with
it.
Note: **wind the clock up** *or* **wind
up the clock** *but only* **wind it up**

win·dow [ˈwɪndəʊ] *noun*
opening in a wall/door, etc., which is
filled with glass; **look out the window—
you can see the garden; it's dangerous to
lean out of the train window; he threw a
stone through the car window; the burglar climbed in through the window; I
saw a camera in the store window.**
win·dow·sill [ˈwɪndəʊsɪl] *noun*
flat piece of wood at the bottom of a

window; **she kept a lot of plants on the
windowsill.**
wine [waɪn] *noun*
alcoholic drink made from the juice of
grapes; **let's have a bottle of red wine;
pour the wine into the glasses; three
glasses of red wine, please.**
Note: usually singular: **some wine; a
glass of wine;** *plural* **wines** *means
different kinds of wine*
wing [wɪŋ] *noun*
one of two parts of a bird, butterfly or
airplane which it uses to fly with; **the
butterfly has white spots on its wings; the
plane has V-shaped wings.**
win·ner [ˈwɪnər] *see* **win**
win·ter [ˈwɪntər] *noun*
coldest season of the year, the season
between autumn and spring; **we can't
play outside in the winter because it's too
cold; last winter there wasn't any snow;
if we go on vacation in the winter we try
to go to a warm place.**
wipe [waɪp] *verb*
to clean/to dry something with a cloth;
**I've washed the plates—can someone
wipe them? you need a handkerchief to
wipe your nose; wipe off the table before
you set it; please wipe the mud off your
shoes before you come in.**
**wipes—wiping—wiped—has
wiped**
wipe out, *verb*
to kill; **the whole army was wiped out
in the war.**
wire [waɪr] *noun*
thin metal thread; **tie the basket to your
bike with a piece of wire; electric wire** =
wire along which electricity goes; **you
have to be careful with this iron—the
wire's loose.**
wise [waɪz] *adjective*
very smart and careful; **he's a wise old
man; it was wise of you to take some
business courses in college.**
wise—wiser—wisest
wis·dom [ˈwɪzdəm] *noun*
knowledge and good sense; **the wisdom
of the very old.**
no plural

wise·ly, *adverb*
in a wise way; he wisely avoided getting
wet; she smiled wisely.

wish [wɪʃ] 1. *noun*
what you want to happen; best wishes
for a Happy New Year; please give my
best wishes to your mother; she made a
wish before she blew out the candles on
her birthday cake; he has no wish to go
to prison = he does not want to go.
plural **wishes**
2. *verb*
(*a*) to want something to happen; I wish
it didn't always rain on my birthday; I
wish I could live on an island; I wish you
spent more time on your homework; I
wish you wouldn't talk so loudly; I wish I
hadn't eaten so much.
(*b*) to show that you hope something
good will happen; he wished me good
luck; she wished me a Merry Christmas.
**wishes—wishing—wished—has
wished**

with [wɪθ] *preposition*
(*a*) (*showing things/people that are together*) he came here with his sister;
they're staying with us for the weekend;
I like ice cream with my apple pie.
(*b*) (*showing something which you have*)
he came in with his hat on; she's the
girl with blue eyes; the house with the
red door.
(*c*) (*showing something which is used*) he
cut the bread with a knife; he has to walk
with a stick; she was eating her dessert
with a spoon; they were attacking the
enemy with bombs.
(*d*) because of; my hands were blue with
cold; he was sick with measles.
(*e*) I'm with you = I agree with you.
Note: **with** *is used with many adjectives and verbs:* **to agree with; to be
pleased with,** *etc.*

with·out [wɪˈðaʊt] *preposition*
(*a*) not having; not with; I'll come without my sister; they lived for days without
any food; he was stuck in Italy without
any money; how can you do your shopping without a car? he was arrested for
traveling without a ticket.

(*b*) not doing something; she sang for
two hours without stopping; they lived in
the mountains for months without seeing
anybody.

wives [waɪvz] *see* **wife**

woke [wəʊk], **wok·en** [wəʊkən] *see*
wake

wom·an [ˈwʊmən] *noun*
female adult person; there were three
women at the next table; an old woman
asked me the way to the post office; a
woman doctor came to see me; are there
any women airline pilots?
plural **women** [ˈwɪmɪn]

won [wʌn] *see* **win**

won·der [ˈwʌndər] *verb*
to want to know something; to think
about something; I wonder why he
always wears a green tie? I wonder where
the teacher has gone? he's wondering
what to do next; we're wondering who'll
be the next president.
**wonders—wondering—
wondered—has wondered**

won·der·ful, *adjective*
very pleasing/excellent; we had a wonderful vacation in Sweden; the weather
was wonderful; you've passed your driving test?—wonderful!

won't [wəʊnt] *see* **will not**

wood [wʊd] *noun*
(*a*) (*often* **woods**) many trees together;
the road goes straight through the woods.
(*b*) material that a tree is made of; the
chairs are made of wood; he hit him on
the head with a piece of wood; he put
some more wood on the fire.
no plural for (b): **some wood; a
piece of wood**

wood·en, *adjective*
made of wood; a wooden chair; she mixed
the soup with a wooden spoon.

wool [wʊl] *noun*
(*a*) hair from a sheep; in the summer the
wool is sent to the market.
(*b*) long threads of hair from a sheep,

twisted together; she used three balls of wool to make my sweater; are these socks made of wool?

(c) material which looks like sheep's wool; **steel wool** = thin threads of steel put together in a ball, used to clean pans.

no plural: **some wool; a piece of wool**

wool·en, *adjective*
made of wool; **a woolen pullover; a woolen carpet.**

word [wɜrd] *noun*
separate piece of language, in writing and speech not joined to other separate pieces; **there are seven words in this sentence; he saw me but didn't say a word; you spelled the word "through" with two g's—that's a mistake; to have a word with** = to speak to; **I'd like to have a word with the teacher; in other words** = to explain something in a different way; **the manager is sick, in other words I have to do twice as much work.**

wore [wɔːr] *see* **wear**

work [wɜrk] 1. *noun*
(a) something which you do using your strength or your brain; **digging holes in the ground is hard work; don't ask me to go out—I've got too much work to do; he doesn't do much work—he just sits and watches TV; when you've finished that piece of work, I've got something more for you to do.**

(b) job/something which you do regularly to earn money; **I go to work by train every day; we start work at 9 o'clock in the morning; he doesn't come back from work until 7 o'clock at night; he's out of work** = he has no job.

(c) something which has been made/painted/written, etc., by someone; **a work of art; here are the complete works of Shakespeare** = everything which Shakespeare wrote.

no plural for (a) and (b): **some work; a piece of work**

2. *verb*
(a) to use your strength or brain to do

something; **if you work hard you'll pass your exams; he doesn't work very hard so he doesn't earn much money.**

(b) (*of a machine*) to run; to make a machine run; **the clock isn't working; the bell works by electricity; the typewriter didn't work very well; he works the biggest machine in the factory.**

(c) to have a job; **he works in a car factory; she used to work in a butcher's shop; he had to stop working because he was so ill; I don't like working in New York.**

(d) to succeed; **do you think your plan will work? if it doesn't work, try again.**
works—working—worked—has worked

work·er, *noun*
(a) person who works; **he's a good worker; she's a slow worker.**

(b) person who works with his hands; **the workers left the factory.**

work·man, *noun*
man who works with his hands; **three workmen came to fix the pipe.**

plural **workmen**

work out, *verb*
(a) to calculate; **I'm trying to work out how much gas the car uses; she can't work this sum out.**

(b) to succeed; **everything worked out all right in the end.**

(c) to exercise; **he works out four times a week.**

work·shop, *noun*
very small factory; place where things are made; **he's making a table in the workshop behind the house.**

world [wɜrld] *noun*
the earth on which we live; **you can fly right around the world; he travels all over the world on business.**

worn [wɔːrn] *see* **wear**

worn out [ˈwɔːrnˈaʊt] *see* **wear out**

wor·ry [ˈwʌrɪ] *verb*
to be afraid and not sure because of something; **she's worrying about her final exams; I worry when my daughter stays out late; are you worried by the**

high cost of food? they're worried that they won't have enough gas.

worries—worrying—worried— has worried

worse [wɜrs] 1. *adjective*
(*a*) less good (as compared to something else); **the weather is even worse than last week; this TV film is worse than the one I watched last night; I'm worse at English than at geography; that boy is very naughty—but his sister is worse.**
(*b*) more ill (than someone else/than at another time); **he was feeling all right yesterday, but is much worse today; she has gotten worse since she started taking the medicine.**
2. *adverb*
less well (as compared to something else); **he drives worse than his sister.**

worse *is the comparative of* **bad, badly** *and* **ill**

worst [wɜrst] 1. *adjective*
worse than anything else; **this is the worst film I've seen this year; she has the worst grades in her class; he's the worst swimmer on our team; her worst subject is history.**
2. *adverb*
less well than anything/anyone else; less well than at any other time; **which team played worst? he sings worst when he's tired.**

worst *is the superlative of* **bad** *and* **badly**

worth [wɜrθ] 1. *adjective*
(*a*) with a certain value; **this house is worth $60,000; that car isn't worth $6,000! what's your car worth?**
(*b*) useful to do; **that film is worth seeing; it's worth knowing something about car engines.**
2. *noun*
value; **I want $5 worth of gas; he bought several dollars' worth of fruit.**

would [wʊd] *verb used with other verbs*
(*a*) (*to make the polite form of asking someone to do something*) **would someone please turn off the light? would you please sit down? I asked him if he would help us.**

(*b*) (*past of* **will,** *showing that you are eager to do something*) **he wouldn't come with us, even though we asked him twice; of course the car wouldn't start when we wanted it to; he forgot my birthday again this year—he would!** = it is something which he always does.
(*c*) (*showing something which often used to happen in the past*) **she would get up at eight o'clock every morning; he would always be standing outside the station selling newspapers, until one day he died; my uncle would often bring me candy.**
(*d*) (*used as a past of* **will**) **they said they would be here by nine o'clock; she hoped she would be able to come.**
(*e*) (*following a condition*) **if he could come he would; if she were still alive, she would/she'd be a hundred years old today; if you invited him, he would/he'd come; if it rained we would/we'd stay at home.**

Negative: **would not** *usually* **wouldn't**
Note: **would** *is the past of* **will; would** *is often shortened to* **'d: she'd be a hundred; he'd stay at home; would** *does not have* **to** *and is only used with other verbs*

would rath·er, *verb*
to prefer; **I'd rather stay at home than go to the party; are you going to pay for everybody?—I'd rather not; they'd rather not go.**

wound¹ [waʊnd] *see* **wind²**

wound² [wuːnd] 1. *noun*
bad cut made on the body, usually in fighting; **the nurses were bandaging the soldiers' wounds.**
2. *verb*
to hurt someone badly in a fight; **he was wounded in the war; the police wounded the burglar as he was trying to escape.**

wounds—wounding— wounded—has wounded

wrap [ræp] *verb* (*often* **wrap up**)
to cover something all around with paper/cloth, etc.; **he's wrapping the Christmas presents; look at this package**

wrapped in blue paper; wrap yourself up in your blanket if you're cold; you'd better wrap up before you go outside = dress warmly.

wraps—wrapping—wrapped— has wrapped

wrap·per, *noun*
piece of paper used to cover something; look at all these chewing gum wrappers on the floor.

wreck [rek] 1. *noun*
something which has been badly damaged; her car was a wreck after the accident; the house is a wreck! = it's very messy; she's a nervous wreck just before Christmas = she's extremely nervous and worried.
2. *verb*
to damage something badly; he wrecked the car; you wrecked my guitar!

wrecks—wrecking—wrecked— has wrecked

wrin·kle [ˈrɪŋkəl] 1. *noun*
deep line; his face is full of wrinkles; there are lots of wrinkles in the back of your shirt.
2. *verb*
to make deep lines; try not to wrinkle your dress.

wrinkles—wrinkling—wrinkled— has wrinkled

wrist [rɪst] *noun*
place where your hand is connected to your arm; wrist watch = watch which you wear attached to your wrist.

write [raɪt] *verb*
(*a*) to put words or numbers on paper, etc.; she wrote a few words on the back of an envelope; who wrote "Teacher go home" on the blackboard? I'll write my name and address for you on a piece of paper; can you write your telephone number on the top of the letter? he has written a book about the local police.
(*b*) to write a letter and send it to someone; have you written to your mother yet? she writes to me every week;

don't forget to write as soon as you get to Hong Kong.

writes—writing—wrote [rəʊt]— **has written** [ˈrɪtən]

write back, *verb*
to answer by letter; he got my letter, and wrote back immediately.

write down, *verb*
to write on paper, etc.; he wrote down the number of the bus; she wrote down all the information on the back of an envelope.

write out, *verb*
to write something long; I'll write out a list of the things I need.
Note: **write the list out** *or* **write out the list** *but only* **write it out**

writ·er, *noun*
person who writes; do you know who is the writer of this letter? he's the writer of six books.

writ·ing, *noun*
something which is written; don't call, please answer in writing; can't you type your letters?—your writing is so bad I can't read it; *see also* **handwriting**.

wrong [rɔːŋ] 1. *adjective*
not correct; what's the time?—I don't know, my watch is wrong; I'm sorry, I was wrong—he does live across from the post office; there's no one called Smith living here—you've come to the wrong house; I think we're on the wrong road—we should be going to Toronto, not away from it; can I speak to Mr. Smith please—sorry, you've got the wrong number; what's wrong with the soup?— there's nothing wrong with it, I'm just not hungry.
2. *adverb*
badly; everything has gone wrong today; you've spelled my name wrong; I think you've added up the check wrong.

wrong·ly, *adverb*
not correctly; the waiter added up the check wrongly; she spelled my name wrongly.

wrote [rəʊt] *see* **write**

Yy

yard [jɑːrd] *noun*

(*a*) measurement of length (equal to three feet); **the post office is only a hundred yards away; the piece of string is ten yards long; can you move the chairs a couple of yards to the left?**

(*b*) area at the front or back of a house often with a lawn and garden; **your father is working in the yard; they have a vegetable garden in their front yard.**

yarn [jɑːrn] *noun*

long thread of wool or other material used in knitting; **she used six balls of yarn to make my sweater.**

year [jɪr] *noun*

(*a*) period of time, lasting twelve months, from January 1 to December 31; **in the year 1492 Columbus discovered America; last year we went to Quebec on vacation; next year I'm going to work in Africa; the weather has been very bad this year; the New Year = the first few days of the year; I start my new job in the New Year; New Year's Day = January 1.**

(*b*) any period of twelve months; **he was born two hundred years ago; she's ten years old tomorrow; the school year starts in September; how many years have you been living in this village?**

year·ly, *adjective & adverb*

every year.

yell [jel] *verb*

to shout; **they were yelling at each other; yell when you're ready.**

yells—yelling—yelled—has yelled

yel·low [ˈjeloʊ] *adjective & noun*

of a color like that of the sun or of gold; **he painted his car bright yellow; she's wearing a yellow hat; look at the**

field of yellow flowers; do you have any paint of a lighter yellow than this?

yellow—yellower—yellowest

yel·low pag·es, *noun*

telephone book which lists stores and businesses; **look up "Restaurants" in the yellow pages.**

yes [jes] *adverb*

(*showing the opposite of* **no**) we asked him if he wanted to come and he said "yes"; do you want any more coffee?—yes, please; does she like horses?—yes, she does; didn't he go to school in New Hampshire?—yes, he did.

yes·ter·day [ˈjestərdeɪ] *adverb & noun*

the day before today; **yesterday was November 13, so today must be the fourteenth; we went to Spokane yesterday morning; he came for lunch yesterday afternoon; the day before yesterday.**

yet [jet] **1.** *adverb*

until now; **has the mailman come yet? I haven't seen him yet; he hasn't read the newspaper yet; have you done your homework yet? have you cleaned your room? not yet = I haven't cleaned it, but I will clean it later.**

2. *conjunction*

but/still; **she's fat and yet she can run very fast; it was pouring rain yet the children went out for their picnic.**

you [juː] *pronoun*

(*a*) (*referring to someone we are speaking to*) **you're taller than me/than I am; I'll give you my phone number and you'll give me yours; you go first; Hello, how are you? are you both comfortable?**

(*b*) (*referring to anybody*) **you never know what will happen; you need to be a very good student to go to college; you'd** think he would know better than to call at this time of night.

Note: you is both singular and plural

young [jʌŋ] *adjective*
not old; he's a young man—he's only twenty-one; my sister is younger than me/than I am; he's the youngest boy in the class; this is a TV program for young children.

young—younger—youngest

young·ster [ˈjʌŋstər] *noun*
child/young person; the youngsters would rather go to the zoo; her youngsters are all in high school.

your [jʊr] *adjective*
belonging to you; have you brought your toothbrush with you? this is a present for your sister; your pants are dirty.

yours, *pronoun*
belonging to you; this book is yours, not mine; you said he was a friend of yours = one of your friends.

your·self, *pronoun*
(*referring to* **you** *as a subject*) you were washing the car yourself; did you cut yourself on the knife? are you all by yourself? = all alone; did you build the house all by yourself? = with no one to help you; did you both hurt yourselves? look at yourselves in the mirror! I hope you all enjoy yourselves.

plural **yourselves** *refers to* **you** *as a plural subject*

Zz

ze·bra [ˈziːbrə] *noun*
animal like a horse with black and white lines on it; her favorite animal at the zoo is the zebra.

ze·ro [ˈziːrəʊ] number 0
the answer is zero; the temperature fell to zero (0°); it's very cold—it's below zero.

zip [zɪp] *verb*
to zip (up) = to do up a zipper; to be fastened with a zipper; this dress zips up at the back; can you zip up this dress for me/zip me up?

zips—zipping—zipped—has zipped

Note: zip the dress up or zip up the dress but only zip it up

zip·per, *noun*
thing for fastening clothes, made of two lines of small teeth which join together; her dress has a zipper in the back; can you do up this zipper for me?

zoo [zuː] *noun*
place where wild animals are kept, and which people can go to visit; we went to the zoo on Sunday afternoon; I had a ride on an elephant at the zoo.